THE DIARIES OF NELLA

PATRICIA AND ROBERT MALCOLMSON are social historians with a special interest in diaries, Mass Observation and everyday life. Patricia is also author of *Me and My Hair: A Social History* (Chaplin Books, 2012). They live in Nelson, British Columbia.

THE MASS OBSERVATION ARCHIVE at the University of Sussex holds the papers of the British social research organisation Mass Observation. The papers from the original phase cover the years 1937 until the early 1950s and provide an especially rich historical resource on civilian life during the Second World War. New collections relating to everyday life in the UK in the twentieth and twenty-first century have been added to the original collection since the Archive was established at Sussex in 1970.

THE DIARIES OF NELLA LAST

Writing in war and peace

Edited by
PATRICIA AND ROBERT MALCOLMSON

PROFILE BOOKS

Published in Great Britain in 2012 by
PROFILE BOOKS LTD
3A Exmouth House
Pine Street
Exmouth Market
London EC1R 0JH
www.profilebooks.com

10 9 8 7 6 5 4 3 2 1

Typeset in Garamond by MacGuru Ltd
info@macguru.org.uk
Printed and bound in Great Britain by
Clays, Bungay, Suffolk

The moral right of the authors has been asserted.

A CIP catalogue record for this book is available from the British Library.

ISBN 978 1 84668 546 0
eISBN 978 1 84765 846 3

The paper this book is printed on is certified by the © 1996 Forest Stewardship Council A.C. (FSC). It is ancient-forest friendly. The printer holds FSC chain of custody SGS-COC-2061

CONTENTS

'I like to feel near to the "beat" of life'
(Nella Last, 20 September 1941)

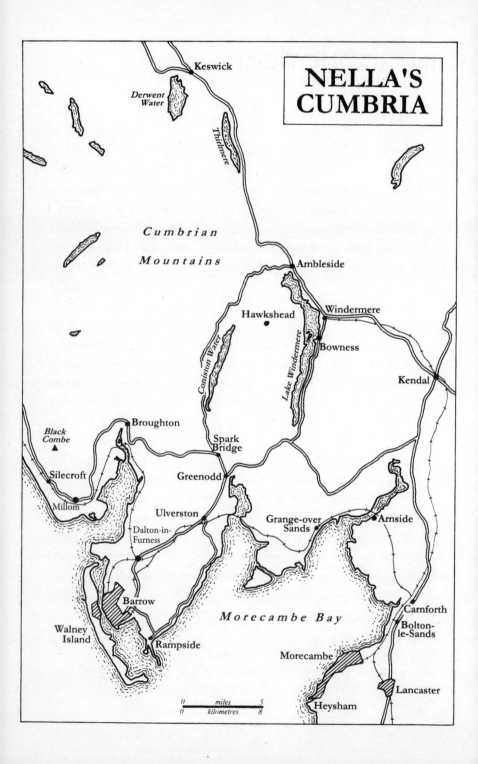

NELLA'S CUMBRIA

Keswick
Derwent Water
Thirlmere

Cumbrian
Mountains

Ambleside
Hawkshead
Windermere
Bowness
Coniston Water
Lake Windermere
Kendal

Broughton
Black Combe
Spark Bridge
Silecroft
Greenodd
Millom
Ulverston
Grange-over-Sands
Arnside
Dalton-in-Furness

Barrow
Morecambe Bay
Carnforth
Walney Island
Bolton-le-Sands
Rampside
Morecambe
Lancaster
Heysham

0   miles   5
0   kilometres   8

INTRODUCTION

'Words have always fascinated me.' (Nella Last, 24 March 1945)*

'If I'd been clever or had a less sketchy education, or perhaps more time
on my hands, I'd have loved to write. Funny how things work out. I
often think of the many books my letters and my diary would make!'
Nella Last wrote these words in early 1942 in a letter to her elder son,
Arthur. Clearly she thought of herself as a writer ('When I was a girl I
always craved to be a writer', she declared on 20 October 1940) – at least
she did in her more confident moments – though hardly anyone else did
until the 1980s, well after her death in 1968. Now, decades later, Nella
Last is the author of three books. *Nella Last's War* was first published in
1981 and reissued in 2006 with some new ancillary material, including
photographs and a few words by her younger son, Cliff, written shortly
before his death in 1991. (This volume was the inspiration for the television film *Housewife, 49*, starring Victoria Wood.) Her more recent two
books, also published by Profile Books, are *Nella Last's Peace* (2008)
and *Nella Last in the 1950s* (2010). She is now a writer whose work has
been enjoyed – and admired – by tens of thousands.

While selections from Nella Last's diary have been published in these
three volumes, most of what she wrote between 1939 and the time she
ceased writing, in February 1966, actually remains unpublished. This is
mainly because the quantity of her writing is vast. Nobody, to the best of
our knowledge, has read the diary from beginning to end; a rough estimate is that it may be around ten million words in total. In many years
she was writing at least a third of a million words – perhaps more like

---

* This was written in response to Mass-Observation's questionnaire – known as a
'Directive' (DR) – for February–March 1945. Details on M-O, the social research
organisation established in 1937 for which Nella wrote, are provided below, pp. 435–37.
Since 2006 the hyphen has been dropped from its name.

half a million in some years. Her discipline and commitment to writing are extraordinary; she wrote regularly even when little was happening in her life, which she deemed to be for the most part 'uneventful' (19 September 1939), and this meant that when something out of the ordinary did occur, she had her pencil or pen at the ready and was primed to record her thoughts. In one diary entry in November 1941 she wrote that she was feeling ill all day – and yet she could still produce in the evening (this is when she did most of her writing) some 2,000 words. And she did this almost every day, year after year, except when she was really sick or travelling. Of course, it is virtually inconceivable that all these words can be published – or indeed *should* be published.

The three volumes mentioned above present perhaps 10 to 15 per cent of Nella Last's handwritten diary, although some periods of her writing are more fully represented than this. Thus, most of her diary has never reached a wider audience. A major reason for producing this new volume is to bring more of her writing to public attention, especially what she wrote in the early 1940s, much of which can only be read in the Mass Observation Archive or at Mass Observation online. The editors of *Nella Last's War*, Richard Broad and Suzie Fleming, were pioneers. They, in a sense, discovered Nella Last in the Mass Observation Archive, digested what she wrote during the upheavals of the Second World War and produced an immensely appealing book of a manageable size that embraced the entire period of the war. Inevitably, given publishing constraints, they could not include a great deal. Consequently, much writing remains unpublished that is vivid, sensitive, engaging and astute. This previously unseen material comprises almost all of Part One of *The Diaries of Nella Last*, which concerns the years 1939–43 and in many ways builds on Broad and Fleming's wartime edition. There is minimal overlap between the two books; less than 5 per cent of the material in this volume is also found in *Nella Last's War*. Part Two, 'Peace', is different. It presents highlights from *Nella Last's Peace* and *Nella Last in the 1950s*, along with a few previously unpublished selections from her post-war diary, mainly from May and July 1945 and 1955. Part Two, then, presents a retrospective of Nella Last's experiences of post-war living, writing and social change.

In this book the Nella Last who features most prominently is the disciplined and skilled writer who was a keen observer – an observer of herself, her family, her neighbours, the natural world and the larger society in which she was living. In one passage (24 February 1941) she wrote of how it would be nice to have the gift to compose music, but, she went on: 'Best of all, though, I would like to write books and travel to far places to see and hear things to write about.' She imagined herself discovering and writing about 'wayside treasures'. Nella never did travel very far (although her son Cliff emigrated to Australia after the war); in fact, she did not travel much at all outside her rather isolated home town, Barrow-in-Furness, its adjacent countryside and the nearby Lake District. But within her limited geographical world she was always on the look-out for wayside treasures that could be remarked on and described in her diary at the end of the day – remarks overheard, interesting conversations in which she participated, unusual incidents, stories of comedy or tragedy, changing attitudes and customs, noteworthy public events, current history, the peccadilloes of family and friends, gossip and rumour, feelings and emotions (hers and others'), individual actions that in her view warranted praise or criticism.

Diaries are documents of everyday life, and they are often packed with mundane, unremarkable details. But along with Nella Last's accounts of preparing food, house-cleaning, gardening, shopping, bodily complaints and the vagaries of the weather are hundreds of pages of her writing that contain passages of narrative richness, psychological insight and colourful observations of people forging lives for themselves in often challenging times. Nella had an excellent eye for captivating moments; and when she saw or heard them, she possessed a skill with words that allowed her – perhaps almost compelled her – to write about them. While it might be said that words came naturally to her – 'I get a pencil and gallop away' (30 July 1940) – this knack was certainly learned and cultivated, for it was to a large extent a consequence of her immersion as a child in books and the thousands of hours in which she absorbed herself in reading. Because of a childhood accident, she was lame, often forced to be sedentary and solitary, and pushed towards private pleasures, notably engaging her mind in literature and the world of the imagination. 'I was a queer, intense child', she wrote in her reply to M-O's questionnaire of February/March 1939, 'who at a very early age learned to escape from pain and loneliness into books – any books.' The novels of Charles Dickens had been central texts for her in these formative years of self-education.

Editing Nella Last's diary might be likened to mining for ore. The valuable ore is there, in those millions of words, but it needs to be extracted and separated from writing of less value. And judgement is exercised and has to be exercised in deciding what is good enough to publish, or even what *must be* published, tasks about which editors, past, present and probably future, are bound to differ. A passage that strikes one editor as highly appealing might strike another as unremarkable. Moreover, whatever is selected needs to be given shape. This shaping includes the creation of chapters (they, of course, are not in the original diary) and paragraphs (which she rarely constructed), the composing of passages that summarise and characterise weeks or even months for which no diary selections are presented, and the shifting of certain pithy observations from the diary entries in which they appear either to these connecting passages or to occasional footnotes. At all times our principal objective is to show Nella Last at her best as a writer and as a sharp-eyed witness to her life and times in the middle decades of the twentieth century.

* * * * * *

The various characters that appear in Nella's diary are identified on the following pages. The appendix 'Editing Nella Last's Diary' (pp. 432–34) outlines our criteria for selecting passages to publish and summarises the more technical aspects of our editorial practice. A few quotations in this book are drawn from her responses to M-O's regular (usually monthly) questionnaires, called 'Directives'; these are identified below as 'DR'. The symbol † in the diary indicates a word defined or a proper name identified in the Glossary (pp. 427–29).

NELLA LAST'S FAMILY, FRIENDS, NEIGHBOURS AND ASSOCIATES

Agnes (Schofield)	*Former girlfriend of her elder son, Arthur*
Arthur	*Elder son*
Atkinson, Mr and Mrs	*Next-door neighbours*
Boorman, Mrs	*Women's Voluntary Services (WVS) worker*
Burnett, Mrs	*Head of Barrow's WVS (up to 1941)*
Cliff	*Younger son*
Cooper, Mrs	*Cleaning helper (1945–47)*
Cumming, Mrs	*WVS member*
Dearie	*Nella herself (as she was known by family)*
Dick (Redhead)	*Norah's husband (post-war)*
Dickinson, Mr	*Port Missionary in Barrow*
Diss, Mrs	*Head of Barrow's WVS (from 1941)*
Doug (Hines)	*Friend of Cliff*
Edith (Picken)	*Arthur's fiancée, later (from 1944) wife*
Eliza, Aunt	*Sister of her late mother*
Ena	*Cleaning helper (1941–43)*
Fletcher, Mrs	*WVS worker*
Fred (Lord)	*Brother*
Garry	*Dog (from 1952)*
George (Holme)	*Neighbour; husband of Jessie*
Gorst, Jack	*Friend of Cliff*
Gran	*Deceased maternal grandmother; a Rawlinson*
Harry	*Brother of Will*
Heath, Miss	*WVS worker*
Helm, Mr and Mrs	*Neighbours in the house attached*
Higham, Mrs	*WVS worker; later a good friend*
Howson, Mrs	*WVS worker, neighbour and friend*
Hunt, Mrs	*WVS worker*
Isa (Hunter)	*Neighbour, wife of Jack, a prominent grocer; disliked by Nella*

Jessie (Holme)	*Neighbour, wife of George*
Joe	*Cousin of Aunt Sarah; lives with her*
Ledgerwood, Miss	*WVS worker*
Lord, Mrs	*WVS worker*
Mac, Miss	*WVS worker*
Machin, Mrs	*WVS worker*
Margaret	*The Atkinsons' younger daughter*
Mary	*Cousin (a generation younger than Nella)*
McGregor, Mrs	*WVS worker*
Miller, Dr	*Family physician*
Mother	*Will's mother*
Murphy	*Cat*
Nelson, Mrs	*WVS worker*
Norah	*The Atkinsons' elder daughter*
Parkinson, Mrs	*WVS worker*
Pattison, Mrs	*Cleaning helper*
Peter	*First grandchild (born 1948)*
Ruth	*Cleaning helper (up to 1941)*
Salisbury, Mrs	*Cleaning helper (1943 and post-war)*
Sarah, Aunt	*Sister of her late mother*
Shan We	*Cat*
Sol	*Dog*
Steve	*Husband of Mrs Howson*
Thompson, Mrs	*Head of WVS canteen*
Wadsworth, Dr	*Psychiatrist*
Waite, Mrs	*Head of Hospital Supply*
Walpole, Hugh	*Author of the* Herries Chronicle *(4 vols, 1930–33)*
Whittam, Mrs	*Friend; farms in Walney*
Wilkins, Mrs	*WVS worker*
Will	*Husband*
Willan, Miss	*WVS worker*
Woods, Mrs	*WVS worker*

PART ONE: WAR
1939–1943

CHAPTER ONE

POINTS OF VIEW

August 1939–September 1940

Barrow-in-Furness, once in Lancashire, now in Cumbria, and largely surrounded by the sea, had a population of a little over 70,000 at the beginning of the Second World War and was overwhelmingly a one-industry town. Its giant shipyard – Nella commonly wrote of it as 'the Yard' – dominated the seafront and employed in 1942 around 18,000 people. Almost all the women known to Nella had husbands, or uncles, or brothers, or fathers, or boyfriends/fiancés who worked at the Vickers-Armstrongs shipyard, some as 'bosses', others as skilled or unskilled labourers. Since September 1936 Nella had been living in a new semi-detached house – 9 Ilkley Road – on a pleasant estate a mile north of the centre of town, just off Abbey Road, Barrow's longest and most important artery. Her husband, Will – she almost never refers to him by name – had his own joinery business in partnership with a brother on an older street where they had previously lived. Nella situated herself socially as one of the 'ordinary middle class people' (12 November 1940). The Lasts were prosperous enough to own a car but in the early 1940s did not have a telephone; Nella portrayed herself – almost certainly accurately – as less well-off than many of the women she worked with in the Women's Voluntary Services (WVS), some of whom presided over large houses. Both her unmarried sons had, as boys, won scholarships to the grammar school. Arthur (born 1913) was a trainee tax inspector living in Manchester; Cliff (born 1918) was still in Barrow at the start of the war and about to be conscripted into the Army.

In late August 1939, when the international crisis seemed very likely to lead to another terrible war, Nella and other volunteer 'Observers' had been invited by Mass-Observation (M-O) to start keeping a diary, and she responded enthusiastically, although she had doubts about her writing skills. Her self-doubts, we now know, were unwarranted.

Thursday, 31 August. The weather is still so oppressive – real crisis weather – and makes people jumpy. Downtown this morning no one seemed to be talking of anything but food and I saw as many prams parked outside Woolworths, Liptons and Marks and Spencers as on a busy Friday afternoon. Inside it was the food counters in Woolworths and M & S that were the busiest. I heard the news at 1 o'clock and felt as if the worst had happened in spite of the assurance that evacuation was not to be considered 'inevitable'. I felt that if I stayed in I'd worry so went down earlier to the WVS meeting. I got a real surprise for the big room was filled with eager women who settled down to swab making or evacuation or evacuation supplies. Our 'Head' [*Mrs Waite*] is a darling 'young' woman of 72 who had charge of Hospital Supplies in last war. She told us a more central room had been taken and 'for the first' [*of September*] would be open two afternoons a week. Four machines were to be installed and we were to make in addition to swabs etc. pyjamas and all Hospital Supplies. It was odd to me that there was so little talk of the big issues – just a planning of how household affairs could be arranged to enable as much time as was needed to be given. When coming home I encountered the usual 'Hitler beaten, and we are doing this to bluff him' and I wondered if it was faith – with a capital F – or stubbornness which made those of us who thought 'something will happen at the last minute' cling to their disbelief in the worst happening. When I was a small child I remember a prophecy my dad heard – that little Prince Edward would never be crowned king and that in 1940 a world war would start that would end things. I'm no more 'scared cat' than the average but I have a cold feeling in my tummy when I think the first came true. Feel so tired I cannot keep awake but my eyes won't stay shut. Wonder how the people who live on the 'edge of things' keep their sanity. Know I'll have to work hard to keep from thinking. Wish I liked meat and stout and had a good appetite to keep up. Will try and drink more milk. Wonder if I should give my faithful old dog and my funny little comedian cat 'the gift of sleep'. Perhaps it's as well my husband insists on the light out for the night.

Friday, 1 September. I feel tonight like a person who, walking safely on the sea sands, suddenly finds his feet sinking in a quicksand. Odd how I should have believed so firmly in my astrological friend when he assured me that there would be NO WAR. Today the town was full of women carrying huge rolls of brown paper from the printers to black out. I knew my younger boy had to go in a fortnight but now when it looks as if he will have to go any time and at such a time I realise his going. He is such a cocky bright eyed lad, so full of jokes and such a 'know all', I know he would be offended if he knew I kept seeing the little funny boy who was so difficult to rear. I feel I'd rather go and serve six months in the Army than let him go!!!!

I'm so tired I can hardly see for I've been shopping – had to do tomorrow's shopping as the bus service is going to be seriously curtailed as the buses are to go to help take evacuated children into the more remote Lake villages. Then I've been machining dozens of tailors' samples of about 2 x 4 inches into evacuation blankets and then tonight there has been the problem of the blackout. Ours is a modern house with huge windows rounded at one end. We took the usual weekly groceries for an aunt living about 12 miles away and found her busy getting things ready in case they brought her any children whom no one could put up. She would 'really not like more than four as winter is coming on and washing and drying is such a problem' – and she is 75!! When I got undressed and into bed I thought the process should have been reversed for all today I've had the feeling that it was a dream that would pass.

Saturday, 2 September. I decided after today's rush and work I am not the crock I thought! I'm sure the thoughts of the housewives struggling with paper, drawing pins, dark blankets etc. would be quite sufficient to cook Hitler brown on both sides! Paper jumped from 3d or 4d a sheet to 9d. My next door neighbour, who had been most careful to lay in an extra supply of bottled beer and whiskey, left getting dark out materials too late and then could not get any. Frantic SOS all round got enough bits and pieces to manage but she naturally had to wait till we had all finished. An Air Warden friend called and told me of what might easily have developed into an ugly situation. The market, library and all shops not blacked out closed at sundown. The others drew down blinds and tied paper on light they could not do without. An Italian chocolate and ice cream shop had all lights as usual and a crowd gathered muttering. The proprietor took no notice and police were sent for who dispersed the crowd *and* the light. I could not understand his attitude at all for he and his brothers were from here and have always talked 'British'. It seems though that he has lately had his wireless tuned in continually to Italy and quotes Mussolini freely. My elder boy who is home from Manchester for the weekend says he has noticed a growing feeling against Jews, particularly foreign Jews. I hate the shut in feeling of closed windows or paper curtained over ones, wonder what it must feel like down a coal mine or in a submarine. The Air Wardens seemed to think we might hear of something 'big' tonight but now it is tomorrow as my boys used to call after 12 o'clock and we are still wondering. My cat seems to feel the tension for he is a real nuisance and follows me round so closely I have tripped over him several times. Last night he hid until I'd settled off and then jumped quietly on the bed and settled on my feet – not a trick of his at all!

Sunday, 3 September. A violent thunderstorm has cleared the air and it's cool now. It's been so close and heavy for over a week – just as it is before a storm breaks. I'm having a morning in bed to rest but don't feel like resting. The boys say there is an important announcement coming over at 10 o'clock so have decided to get up.

Bedtime. Well, we know the worst. Whether it was a kind of incredulous stubbornness or a faith in my old astrological friend who was right in the last crisis when he said 'no war', I *never* thought it would come. Looking back I think it was akin to a belief in a fairy's wand which was going to be waved. I'm a self-reliant kind of person but today I've longed for a close woman friend – for the first time in my life. When I heard Mr Chamberlain's voice so slow and solemn I seemed to see Southsea Prom the July before the last crisis. The Fleet came in to Portsmouth from Weymouth and there was hundreds of extra ratings walking up and down. There was all 'sameness' about them that was not due to their clothes alone and it puzzled me till I found out. It was the look on their faces – a slightly brooding, far-away look. They all had it, even the jolly looking boys, and I wanted to rush up and ask them what they could see that I could not – and now I know.

The wind got up and brought rain but on the Walney shore men and boys worked filling sand bags. I could tell by the dazed looks on many faces that 'something' would have turned up to prevent war. The boys brought a friend in and insisted on me joining in a game but I could not keep it up. I've tried deep breathing, relaxing, knitting and more aspirins than I can remember but all I can see are those boys with their looks of 'beyond'. My younger boy will go in just over a week. His friend, who has no mother and is like another son, will go soon – he is 26 – and my elder boy is at Sunlight House in Manchester, a landmark. As Tax Inspector he is at present in a reserved occupation.

Tuesday, 5 September. Tonight I had my first glimpse of a blackout and the strangeness appalled me. A tag I've heard somewhere, 'The city of Dreadful Night', came into my mind and I wondered however the bus and lorry drivers would manage. I don't think there is much need for the wireless to advise people to stay indoors – I'd need a dog to lead me. Heard today that a big new Handicraft Centre is commandeered for a hospital. I wondered why we were not starting making shells etc. as in last war. It's a good thing that my husband likes his bed and insists I go up when he does. I feel so over strung tonight I 'could fly' and know if left alone would have gone on sewing – silly to knock oneself up so early. Best get into the jog trot that stays the course.

Thursday, 7 September. Today Ruth, my 'morning girl', and I were a bit dumpish. We can generally find a bright side to talk or laugh over but this morning all was quiet. Suddenly I heard laughter and she said 'Well, God love it!' I went to where she was in the clothes closet in hall and found Murphy my cat sitting snug on a rug under the dinner wagon. 'He has found his air raid shelter like a Christian', Ruth declared. Bless my little cat and his funny ways. He seems to 'work for his laughs' like a seasoned trouper and he scores a point in his cat-mind if he makes me laugh, I'm sure!

We took a large room for WVS and find we could do with one twice as big! No one was actually turned away. Tailors' pieces or wool for blankets were given to those who could not sit down but those of us who were sitting down worked under such cramped conditions that our output of swabs and pneumonia jackets was lessened and we all had bad heads. I've often felt ashamed of my sex but never so proud as the way the 'right' women have rolled in. No 'butterflies' who want particular jobs, no catty or what is worse bitchy women, and when an old woman who it seems had had some authority in the last war got peevish at being 'one of the crowd', she hushed and blushed at the way her complaints were received. I get the oddments any tradesmen give us to look over and advise best things to make for I have clever fingers.

Saturday, 9 September. I went into the Maypole and jokingly said to the girls 'What – got stuff on the shelves yet? Seems to me you girls are not trying!' It was a feeble kind of joke and I was startled at the way they laughed and gathered round for a 'crack' – there was no other customer. They asked 'How long the war would last' and I said 'Just a day at a time and the first seven years were the worst'. The manager and counter man joined up to join in the laugh and he said 'Well, it's a treat to find someone who can find something to joke about these days'. With two sons and a brother and the knowledge that my husband's men (four for a start and two later) [*might be conscripted*], which will mean there will be little they can do as shopfitters etc, I don't know I've got much [*to laugh about*] but it gave me an idea. I've always been able to joke and see the funny side up till now and I'll keep on if I crack my face doing it. If my nonsense can raise a smile I'll think it worth the effort and perhaps it will take the picture of those naval boys out of my mind. It's all right when I'm working and have to keep my mind on my work but if I relax they pass before me. Gave myself a treat today. I hate stitching pieces of cloth together for hospital blankets – am not a good routine worker. I like to design or plan and see others do the drudgery!!

Sunday, 17 September. Decided as petrol was still unrationed to go and take a last look at Morecambe – a favourite Sunday run. It was a lovely day and many were like ourselves – only there for a short time. Coming back we were hailed by a girl of about 22 and a boy of 8 or 9. Barrow people, they had missed a connection. With them a little way off was another woman, a cripple well known to us. A Jewish family reared in the town, she had something to do with her when small and her bones never hardened. She walks with the greatest difficulty and is in a metal frame from the waist down. Our car is a Morris 8 and she about filled the back – she is very broad and fat. We could have sent the boy on a friendly motor cyclist's pillion but the look of wild terror on the boy's face made us pack the two in the tiny space left, the boy sitting on the girl's knee. He smiled but said little and we women talked about WVS and ARP[†] and got very interested in each other's talk. I turned round once to ask the little boy to come and sit on my knee for a change but he only smiled and said he was 'quite alright'. His English was a little broken and I said 'Is Eric a foreigner?' for he was a fair, blue-eyed, pink and white type. I learned he was a German Jew from Barrow who had made a long journey across Germany and to England in the company of other refugee children, and his parents and brother had come later on last train and boat allowed to leave Germany. After over an hour's drive we got to Barrow and when the car stopped no one offered to get out! Miss Wolf the cripple could not without help and Eric, white-faced, was trying to get to his feet. We found that the iron of Miss Wolf's 'frame' had pressed to the bone in Eric's little thin thigh and calf and he had stuck it with a smile, said it was 'quite alright' – a phrase he uses a lot. Miss Wolf said he must have gone through terrible things on his journey for he never complained of any inconvenience and was puzzled at the way people 'dared' to protest at things. One of the oddest things was his hero worship of policemen – went out of his way to walk past them and if they looked at him pleasantly or *smiled*! – well, Eric was happy. When Jews were spoken to by 'Nordia' and came into the shop and talked in the ordinary way he behaved so oddly that the Wolfs feared they had taken a mental child. He has been six months or so with them now and

settled to our ways but somehow that nice ordinary little boy brought
home to me what cruelty and oppression really meant in Germany.

During the rest of 1939 and through the winter of 1940 Nella wrote of all sorts of
matters, including her volunteer work at the WVS centre, which involved various
activities, notably organising raffles to raise money, working for Central Hospital
Supply Service and providing 'comforts' and other goods for the Sailors' Home.
(Nella was keen on seamen: 'my heart', she wrote on 2 November 1940, 'is and
always will be with the men who sail the little ships and go for dangerous voyages
to sweep mines'.) She got much satisfaction from this volunteering – 'I felt such a
thrill to think I too belonged to WVS', she remarked on 30 October 1940, after
hearing on the radio of the organisation's work. The WVS in Barrow had around
100 members in 1940, and Nella normally worked at its centre, which was actually rooms attached to Christ Church, two days a week. She also wrote during
these months about the beginning of Cliff's military service; she commented
on the blackout (householders who allowed any light to show might be fined),
the arrival of evacuees in the countryside from south Lancashire and the severe
weather of January–February 1940; she described day trips to the nearby Lake
District, many of which included visits to her much-admired Aunt Sarah in Spark
Bridge; and she touched on matters related to the nearby sea. From time to
time she reminisced, usually about family – her beloved maternal grandmother,
a farmer near Greenodd and a Quaker, was always remembered fondly – and
she sometimes reflected on the horrors of warfare, which were still, for most
Britons, more anticipated than actual. This was not, though, a time when she
produced her most vivid writing.

    These months included what came to be known as the 'phoney war' of
October 1939 through early April 1940. Most of Britain's military conflicts during
these months were on the seas. Otherwise, there was little loss of life. Civilians –
and most soldiers – faced no real threat. Most consumer goods were still readily
available. Rationing was minimal, and it only began at the start of 1940. As early
as 30 September 1939 Nella was noticing how little interest there was in war
news – 'Perhaps it's because all is so "quiet on the Western Front".' 'War seems
to be so far away', she wrote on 24 February 1940. It certainly lacked a sense of
day-to-day immediacy, at least in a seriously negative way – Barrow's economy,

after all, was booming. One entry in her diary that was war-related comes from early spring, with the launch of the aircraft carrier *Indomitable*.

Tuesday, 26 March, 1940. When Ruth came she said launch was at 11.30 so I had to hurry and do my few odds and ends of washing I'd put in the water and prepared and left lunch and Arthur [*who was visiting from Manchester*] and I went off. It was only ten minutes run to Walney and we got last bit of parking place between a big chara[†] and a Rolls, and I know we only got it because our car, being small, could just squeeze in. There were crowds already there but I knew by yesterday's turn of the tide that we had a while to wait. Planes droned or roared overhead in the thick clouds which had gathered and air wardens pacing about made me have a sick feeling at the effects a German bomber would have on the dense packed crowd. There were thousands by 1.30 and the last of the ten tugs had been manoeuvred into place. Across Walney Channel the open end of aircraft carrier poked rather cautiously from stocks and we noticed men beginning to run about as if in answer to orders. A faint cheer which strengthened into a roar, and she began to slide down to the hoot of the tugs. Arthur and I were standing on car seats and our heads through the sunshine roof so we had a grandstand view. She gathered speed and smoothly slipped into waiting tide without a splash – like a smooth drawer being pushed out of table or chest. I'll never forget the cheers and 'God blesses' from all round, where greasy oily shipyard workers had stood crushed in between fur-clad women, soldiers, sailors and 'high ups' in Yard.* When the aircraft carrier had got right into the water she turned with the pull of the tide and it was as if she turned in answer to cheers to show her full length – a wonderful piece of work – and the look of exaltation on some of the work-grimed faces of the men around as ship took water so proudly, and so sure, was a sight to see.

I became conscious I was leaning over car gripping a cloth-sleeved arm firmly and then remembered, as ship started off stocks, a man rushing up and down trying to see over the dense rows of people's heads. I beckoned him and helped him up backward onto car step and for the few minutes taken for launch had held him by one arm! – funny what excitement can do!! By his broad Glasgow accent and by his queer pitted skin – and also by his breath! – I think he was a ship's engineer. He pulled off his cap and said to Arthur 'Lad, it was grand. And thanks to your leddy I saw it "aw"'. Arthur sometimes gets cross with me for being impulsive but he only laughed today and said 'You *do* do some odd things, my pet!'

Arthur shares my love of ships and sea and when he was small I used to take him to see all the launches. We – the townspeople – had full run of the Yard in those days and we always used to stand close to stocks. I recalled a launch I'd heard my Gran talk about – the first steamship to be launched at Barrow, the *City of Rome*. They did not know much of steamships those days and had put boilers in and launched her with her own steam. My mother, who was married twice, had delayed her honeymoon so that she and her husband could accept invitation to launch lunch, a much coveted honour even today. An explosion took place and one man was flung high into air and killed. Most of his blood fell on my poor little mother, a bride of twenty. Her silver grey dress was splashed and the bunch of ostrich plumes in her bonnet were dyed crimson. Exactly a year later her husband died and her unborn child only lived a few weeks. In after years she married my father but I never remember her happy and smiling. It was as if she was frozen somewhere.

When the *Mikasa* was launched – our first Japanese warship – I was a little girl and was taken by some friends to see it – mother never went to a launch. I can see high platform now, crowded with twittering kimono-clad Japanese ladies. Instead of breaking a bottle of champagne to launch her a huge wicker cage of the most beautiful white pigeons was opened on all sides by a pulled ribbon. It was a lovely sight, and a novel one, to see the clouds of lovely flashing wings circling over slowly moving hulk, but suddenly a curious hissing chatter and shaken heads above on platform made us realise that something on platform was wrong and then we saw pigeons had only flown over ship once and then had gone back to their wicker cage. I believe it was the gloomiest lunch that had ever taken place in Yard after launch – and in Russo-Japanese war she sank as untrained gunners let off all guns on one side and tide caught her and keeled her over!

Winston Churchill [*First Lord of the Admiralty*] would get a pleasant impression of our northern town for sun came out again and it was a glorious day. Arthur says if Germany could miss such an opportunity of wiping out our two aircraft carriers – the new one [Illustrious, *soon to be commissioned*] was held back, it seems, for big War Office party to see – Winston Churchill and a few thousand skilled workers conveniently collected together to make an easy target, she will never bomb anywhere in England!

Wednesday, 27 March. The chief topic of talk everywhere was Winston Churchill – he seems to have made a very good impression by his 'ordinariness', and his free and easy manner and knowledge of things in general. He, together with his son and a big party of big-wigs, made a tour of the machine shops. I asked if he had a new hat for occasion and learned that he had walked round with his hat on end of his stick!

I baked bread and spiced gingerbread to send to Cliff and called it a day for Ruth said she would do anything else so that I could take time off with Arthur. We decided to go to Coniston by way of Woodland Valley. It was lovely and clear but the hard winter has bitten deep at moors round Woodland and as yet there is no sign of greenery on their bare rocky slopes. We ran into a real blizzard of snow and it was odd to be so surrounded by big snowflakes and to look a little way ahead and see the sun. We got out of car several times to catch, and put back over fence, little frisky lambs which had squeezed through tiny gaps and could not get back to their mothers.

Coming home by Coast Road we found we had half an hour to spare so I told Arthur I'd like to go and look at aircraft carrier again in Channel. We were just in time, however, to see her being towed round through swing bridge to her place under the crane. It was nearly as interesting as seeing her launched. Two tiny tugs drew her like Pekinese drawing an orange crate while two in reverse pulled nearly as hard to keep her on her course. Two fussy little tugs each side kept pace with the helpless hulk and a fire boat stood by. She reached her position – but in centre of dock. Then the two near side tugs scuttled quickly and joined two off side ones and the four turned as one and like clever little elephants headed her to her berth. All the time from open ports on carrier the clang of hammers and the glow of electricians' and riveters' braziers told of ceaseless work that would go on night and day for months.

On the first Sunday of May 1940 Nella and Will were enjoying the sunshine in the seaside town of Morecambe, and in walking about listening to people's conversations she heard 'not one remark of any kind about the war!!' This, however, was about to change. From the second week of May 1940 there were many startling developments on various battlefronts, including the German assault on Western Europe, the rescue of most of the British Expeditionary Force (BEF) from Dunkirk, the fall of France, the exposure of Britain to German aerial attack and the intensified commitment almost everywhere in the country to civil defence.

Mood swings during these tense weeks were to be expected. In late May women at the WVS centre were worried about their sons in the BEF – and then were much relieved a few days later when news arrived of their safe return. Nella's own feelings were often mixed. On 6 June, a lovely evening, she was at the seaside at Walney and 'We parked near a big crowd and I noticed they were Jewish. Our Jews are decent respected tradesmen who have been here for at least one and sometimes two generations and grown a part of growing town and I looked at the pretty girls and babies and thought how each family had at least one son in Forces and I contrasted their happiness and quiet content with their relations and friends on the Continent.' Nella felt that the Nazis had tapped into and were driven by a profound Evil – and while they seemed to be in the ascendant, she thought they were stoppable. 'If I thought I were in the right', she wrote on 12 July, 'I'd kill – or be killed. That's why I know we will win for our soldiers know they are in the right and that knowledge will be a spur.' Sometimes the war to her seemed near, sometimes far away. Her confidence in the future ebbed and flowed. 'I think war nerves come and go like waves', she wrote on 30 June. An encouraging military event or Churchill's bracing words on the radio might buoy her up (he became Prime Minister on 10 May). The expectation of German air attacks, perhaps even invasion, forced Nella and her fellow WVS members to ponder their personal resources of courage and fortitude, which had not yet been seriously challenged but which soon, they thought, would be. Some feared that Barrow would be in peril 'once' the Germans took over Ireland.

During ten days in the first half of August, Nella wrote about a wide range of matters.

Sunday, 4 August. It's been such a lovely day and after a soup, cold meat and apple pie lunch we went up to Coniston Lake. Arthur and I climbed a steep path through the woods, looking for sloes.† We were unlucky for the blossom had not set and only a brown crumble was where purple sloes should be. The early promise of a good nut crop has vanished as has also the holly berries, partly through caterpillars and also the too dry spring. It's a delight to see the fat contented lambs munching the new sweet grass where only a week or two ago they searched the brown scorched ground so vainly. It's such a puzzle to me how cars from Glasgow, Ipswich, Southampton, Northampton, York, Cardiff etc. can come all the way to the Lakes, as well as scores of Blackpool and South Lancs cars. There must be a lot of petrol about somewhere. There was crowds of people about, hiking and cycling as well as motoring, and it looked as if there were people staying in the villages. Evacuees too were about in numbers and altogether the peaceful Lake road was unlike its normal quiet. Arthur loves Coniston Lake as I do and found no fault today in the 'tripper' atmosphere and when we got above in the woods and looked over the water it seemed impossible that War and the upsets of today existed. All was so still and the hills looked so ageless, so unchanging that even Hitler and the threatened invasion fixed for today seemed futile.

Arthur says the Board has called for Inspectors to go to East and South coast to relieve the Tax Inspectors who are losing so much sleep they cannot work. He volunteered but Cliff said there was no use sending his name through till after he had got his Commission [*after writing final exams*]. Only another two months for him to go now and then he will be off again and he says he will volunteer again so he will be in the danger line somewhere. He is right and I cannot take the attitude his father takes – that he is a fool. We must all take our share and help each other and I've noticed that 'wisdom' does not always bring the happiness that 'foolishness' does. 'Whoso saveth his life must lose it', and I wonder if the hidden meaning is that we must not grow to think of ourselves too much and that in helping others we help ourselves more. I look at my two aunts of 73 and 75. The deaf one [*Sarah*] of 75, who has had a life of hardship, has the sweetness and calm that radiates confidence while the other [*Eliza*], who had a family to care for and plenty to manage with but who always seemed to expect things of life and people, is a real worry both to herself and others. She says no one wants or loves her, but she does not want them really and although she clings to me so, it's only because she likes to be comfortable and likes what she calls the 'peace and quiet' of our house. She does not care really whether I'm there or not. The swallows are dipping very low and my lavender bush smells overpoweringly sweet and in spite of lovely day and evening I feel rain not far away.

Monday, 5 August. My husband came in and asked if we would like to go to Morecambe as his brother had given him an extra petrol coupon. I'm always ready for a festa[†] of any kind and it did not take me long to pack a picnic tea and we were off at 1.30. It was lovely after the rain and all looked clean washed ... I saw few changes in Morcambe from peace time except of course the air raid shelters and the uniforms. It was full of visitors and I thought of Scarborough and the East Coast ports and seaside resorts. It's so queer everywhere now – nothing is 'fair' or equal or 'right' anywhere or for anyone. It *does* look as if we were under an evil star or some kind of influence.

We always go on Heysham Head and we met some teachers who were staying from Barrow and I sold them some of my Sweep tickets. They had heard about them and teased me and said I'd have the police on my trails – the last Chief Constable was very down on Sweeps of all kinds. I said I'm not at all worried for the late Chief's wife has two tickets and the new Chief's wife has taken a book to sell for me!

There was such an odd collection of people on the Head and it was quite a while till I could place the difference to the usual crowd. It was an intense interest – a happy interest – that gave me the clue and I said to Arthur 'Do you know I believe many of the people here are seeing Morecambe for the first time, or a very rare time', and we had a kind of game as we did when the boys were small – an 'I spy' game. Arthur said I did not play fair for I went into the ladies' toilet and on the pretence of getting two half pennies changed into a penny got talking to quite a crowd and found that quite half were unused to a day trip which 'cost such a lot of money'. Two were agricultural workers' wives and they were staying over the weekend – one had a son in the Air Force stationed at Morecambe. I said 'It's lovely here, isn't it? Did you never think of paying Morecambe a visit before this?' She smiled and said 'Aye, thought on it, but it's first time I'd had cash eno'. Happen next year we will aw come for a week, if t'money's as good.' There was an old happy looking woman who smiled and nodded to all and told how her grandson – a *grand* lad – had said for her 'to come and he'd pay her fare and give her a good time' and went on to say that grandson was working on new chemical works going up. Poor old lamb, she could have been a danger if spies had been about for she seemed to know far too much about construction of new works. A severe looking little girl with pigtails said rather smugly 'Careless talk costs lives, MY TEACHER says' and the old woman said 'I'd never dream of telling a SPY anything. I'm sure there are none here.' As there were four at wash bowls and several combing hair, not to speak of waiting queue, and all strangers, it might have been a question.

Tuesday, 6 August. I'd a busy morning for I'd a wire from Cliff [*in Chester*] to say he would be home by lunch time. In the middle of the morning two little girls came and solemnly presented me with a cardboard box with 1s 3½d in – ALL for the soldiers! They had made a 'bran tub' and charged ½d a dip and judging from a handkerchief that I saw that had come out of 'tub', their mothers would be far from pleased when the handkerchief drawer was visited. They said their mothers had told them to ask me what they could do and as I was busy and wanted them to go I said 'What about collecting silver paper for soldiers and papers and magazines for the sailors and I'll take you down to Sailors Home and you can give them to Mr Dickinson yourself?' I thought I'd got rid of them but they were soon back with a pile of a woman's paper called *Mother* and when Arthur opened it at random it was at a page on 'What to do the last week before the little stranger's arrival'. We had a good laugh at imagined remarks of a minesweeper or submarine crew!

I dashed down to Centre to meet my sister-in-law and arrange about Savings Group and raffled a lovely flower jug and got 16s and arranged for someone to take a bunch of flowers round for a 1d raffle and help Mrs McGregor make tea and then told Mrs Waite I was coming home AND that as I'd arranged all for Thursday I was taking day off! She was so cross and when I said 'There will not be *one* thing neglected and it's only one day' she said 'I don't see need for you to be off *all* day. I think you could come in for half a day.' I just laughed and said 'Now don't be stuffy. You will have a whole day's peace with no one to tease you.' I've got two new knitters and there were four sold books of tickets handed in and others taken and now nearly all books are out.

Wednesday, 7 August. We went to Spark Bridge this afternoon and Aunt Sarah was so delighted to see the boys. [*Cliff was now visiting Barrow, as well as Arthur.*] Cliff wants to go up Friday night and we will pick him up on Saturday when we go. He has my love of liking to be alone sometimes and wants to tramp about by himself. He says it might be the last time he is able – such a silly thing to say; perhaps he means to stay with Aunt Sarah. I hope it's not one of his hunches but Aunt Sarah is 76 on Friday and seems to grow tinier every time I see her. Cliff says he sees a great change in her, but she is as bright as a robin and always gay and happy with a trust and faith in God's plan I have never seen in anyone else but her mother, who was my Gran. The boys were off dancing tonight and my husband and I went off to see James Cagney in *The Roaring Twenties*.

The following day was Arthur's 27th birthday, and Nella laid on a cake and other treats. 'I felt as gay as a bird when I saw my two darlings' faces, so bright and happy, and while no doubt a bit of their gaiety was a show for a birthday tea, I knew they, like me, had memories of many happy birthdays.' That evening 'We sat round the fire after supper and talked and wondered when we would be altogether for a festa again. Cliff insisted on his cards being read and I saw broken journeys and changes and a far off place. He seems to think he will be at Chester for duration as it's a busy training place and Physical Training Instructors are kept busy. Arthur's cards were of a strange unrest of mind and body. His passing of his exam will not be the "journey's end" of things he is anticipating and so eagerly banking on. Cliff said "You are not as good as you used to be, old thing" and I said "No, I am out of practice", but I thought of the days when there was so many gay things and happy little trivial things to see in cups and cards. Now it's as if there is only one thing to see – a muddled greyness with at the best a lighter grey. It's a silly thing anyway to tell cards or to try and see ahead. Just a day at a time and let tomorrow look after itself is best for ordinary people and leave the plans for the future – *and* the worry – with clever people who have forethought and courage in addition to being clever.'

Saturday, 10 August. The boys have gone dancing – more to meet friends who happen to be on leave or still left. It's not many who are for he had not a lot of friends who worked at Shipyard and so many of the older boys who knew Arthur were in Territorials and called up right away – it was estimated that one in four of them were lost at Dunkirk. I made some soup tonight – I have never kept my stock pot going so much in summer as this last year. My mother-in-law never uses the giblets of a fowl so sends them up and this week I'll have Cliff's favourite soup tomorrow and as he got some more mushrooms I'll add some of them in Monday's soup. I'll add sliced tomatoes and Arthur will have one of his favourites. While Arthur and Cliff have been home and I've had extra cooking and work and Arthur has needed the dining room table to papers and books – and quiet for study – I've got no sewing done so have concentrated on some knitting. I bought enough wool for vest about last Easter when I had a little surplus one week. It's been rather a bogey whenever I thought of them for I am no knitter but I've got one finished except for stitching together and quite a quarter of the other.

Sunday, 11 August. We sat and talked of beliefs and faith and Arthur said suddenly 'What *do* you believe, Dearie?* I never remember you teaching us to pray to Jesus – always God, our "Father". Don't you believe at all in Christ?' I was taken back for a few minutes and had to think, but try as I would I could not put my thoughts and beliefs in plain words. I often think my 'religion' is odd and wonder if it's because of my quiet-eyed Quaker Gran who always spoke of our 'Heavenly Father' and then again a sister of my father's always had the name of the Saviour, Christ or Jesus Christ on her tongue and yet got me so many whippings by her tale telling that I both hated and feared her! Anyway, for whatever cause I'm definitely not a Christian and I could not say I was – nor would the boys have believed me. Cliff really likes to go to church and communion and I go with him but I rarely go alone although when young we all went as a matter of course. I think my religion is a mixture of wishful thinking, nature worship and a stern belief in God that is Jewish, although as far as I know for at least four generations that I can trace on my father's side of the family and none since Elizabeth on mother's side – at least – has there been Jews in the family. I tried to tell the boys my views – a beginning again [*i.e., reincarnation*], belief in God's Plan, trying to help those who needed it, and being true to oneself rather than to any creed – but I didn't feel I did it very well. They will find their own faith and roots themselves no doubt as they grow older.

Monday, 12 August. Woolworths was a sight for German housewife's eyes with its huge stock of tinned stuff and sweet biscuits, although the

---

* In reply to a question from MO about names (DR, May 1946), Nella reported that her parents had wanted to call her Deirdre but the Canon objected to its Irish roots, so she was named Nellie, which she always hated (this is the name on her birth certificate). However, her mother called her Deirdre, 'which got shortened to Dearie and which the boys as well have always called me'. The name Nella was once used in a school concert; she was delighted, and it stuck.

way people were buying it would not last long. I see they are not a 6d store any more for prices are up to 10d – in many instances for same lines in food. This cold snap has brought out all the new fur coats and I laughed at Arthur's surprise at so many new ones. When one lives in a place like Barrow where so many people are known, if only by sight, and most people's circumstances can be guessed at by knowing their trade, it's amusing. Arthur said shrewdly 'I don't know much of fur values but some of these coats don't look as if they had come out of Barrow. They look high class even for Manchester.' I said 'Well, the best ones come from Glasgow, from the visiting furrier, but now I think our shops have a "sale or return" system'. Arthur and his father can wear the same overcoats so today we went to order a winter all-weather coat for my husband's birthday. It is costing rather a lot so I'll say it is for Xmas too. It's such a grand navy waterproof – not mackintosh rubber but a rubberised fabric and guaranteed to stand 24 hours steady rain. I've ordered a pair of leggings too and the coat is £2 12s 0d and the leggings are about 15s 6d. It's a lot of money but I'll feel more content when he has it for last winter was severe and he cycles to work.

Tuesday, 13 August. I seem to have bought popularity pretty cheap today! A few jokes at Centre, some paper bags to greengrocer and the remark that the bacon was delicious to grocer and I was surprised at pleasant smiles in return. As one of the jokes was what Mrs Waite calls a 'rude one', it was a yell rather than a smile but it was good to be back among them all and I missed them. We were very busy for Millom are forming a Hospital Supply and had sent for samples of bandages etc. I had my work set for me, getting all the women together who had said they were joining the Group Saving for my sister-in-law was shy. She will not be again for everyone tried to be friendly and put her at ease and we collected £2 5s 6d, and I feel sure it will increase …

My husband had planned a business trip to Ulverston so that we could have a run out on business petrol and it was not raining so I decided to take some aspirins and go. [*She had a cold.*] We came home over the moor and I never remember seeing the heather such a lovely carpet of soft colour. There was the coolth[†] and sadness of autumn over all and the golden patches of bracken made us think winter would soon be here. It's so terrible to think that when I am so quiet and safe in my bed that the raiders may be over Southampton and Portsmouth and little children will be cold and scared in shelters. We often grumble in Barrow over living in a 'dead end' but so far we have only had warnings to Shipyard and no general air raid alarms.

I was so sorry tonight to hear from Arthur that he had been down to see Dorothy [*whose soldier husband had been killed a few weeks before*] and she had told him she 'just *lived*' at the Spiritualists' meeting house. She doesn't come to see me now and I wondered how I'd offended her but she told Arthur that she would never forgive me for refusing to 'tell her cards and see what had happened to Bill'. She said I'd 'seen her meeting Bill and also marrying in a hurry and parting from Bill' and that she could not understand my meanness. Poor Dorothy – I could not make her see that things done to amuse at a party could not be applied to serious things.

There is a lot of fortune telling and Spiritualists visiting going on here, in back streets and quiet houses where the police will not be likely to hear of it. Last war I knew women who bought their houses with the 6d and 1s they got from credulous munition girls. I said to one I knew well 'How do you do it, Mrs Adams? Do you really believe in what you tell people?' She said 'Yes and no. I'm psychic but even more observant and I think I get the drift of their hopes by their remarks. Anyway, what do you expect for a bob!' It was not the money, for the girls made a lot, but I remember a friend of mine who used to haunt the fortune tellers to ask after a boy who had 'kissed and rode away'. We all knew that it was just a flirtation on his part and that he had never been serious but Sis went from one to another asking 'if he would come back' and dropping out of all the little festas that she had been used to sharing. All her friends paired off and married and she lived in a dream and after her wartime job in an office went she had nothing and now is an unpaid nurse housekeeper to a crabbed old aunt.

Friday, 30 August. Today I wondered whatever the reactions of the women – the housewives – in areas that are bombed so often. It was not only that I felt tired but I felt it impossible to settle to ordinary routine. I wanted to talk to people and see what they thought of last night's air raid, how they felt, and had they heard anything about it? My next door neighbour's butcher boy told us the simple facts – there had been bombs dropped, six of them and not nine as was first reported. By nothing short of a miracle they had done no damage and only one had fallen on Biggar Bank on Walney Island and made a hole and the blast broke windows in tram shelter. The others fell on what are called the 'gullys', a marsh which is flooded every tide and is a squelchy place without any bottom. A split second [*probably 'earlier'*] in releasing bomb and they would have fallen on Shipyard, only a few hundred yards across the narrow Walney Channel that separates Island from mainland …

After tea we went to a social evening got up by some school teachers in aid of Motor Ambulance Fund. It was 1s 6d and tea and biscuits were handed round. There was music and a sketch and I knew most of the people and we talked of how we felt. I was quite grateful to find out that many had felt like I did – not really frightened but queerly shocked and ill and when I said I hoped next time I could 'master' the feeling of dread a lady said 'Oh, you will do. I stayed at Bolton and got used to it and could snatch a nap in the day.' I planned a comfortable little 'hidey hole' under stairs and put two stools in with woven tops and thought my husband and I would be best in there. We could put my ironing board that stands in there across our knees and play two-handed bridge or try and read for there is good light. I think I'll get a few sweets and put a tin with some biscuits in and if things got bad I'd make a hot drink in flask at supper time and leave it there. We might as well be comfortable if we can!

Saturday, 31 August. It looks as if the peace and quiet of Furness has gone for good. We had an air raid warning for two hours last night and it must have been a serious one for the furnaces were damped down at the Steel and Iron works [*the second leading industry in Barrow*]. With us standing high and the wind being from the west, it was like a gas attack and the queer acrid smell lingers about today ... I wonder how long it takes to get used to air raids. Everyone I've met or talked to complains of tiredness but I've not spoken to a single person who is jittery at the thought of the air raids we will be sure to have in the near future now that we have been 'discovered'. I hear plans of turning downstairs rooms into bedrooms, and today everyone in our road was turning out under the stairs and asking advice on the subject but there seemed no surprise or shock of the last two nights, just a general plan of readjustment. Most people of my age seem to have felt as I did – really ill physically but not mentally. One thing I'm very thankful for and that is that I know my nerves will not take the form of panic.

Sunday, 1 September. We had such a nice afternoon. It was sunny and my husband said 'If you had not got enough blackberries we would have gone blackberrying'. I said 'Come on then. Mrs Boorman would like some, I know, and she gave me all those lovely apples' – for myself to store. It was so lovely on the tops behind Greenodd. The wind blew gently off the Bay and the Coniston hills looked dwarfed with us being so high. Perhaps it was the peace of the old days when I was a happy child and ran the roads and fields of Gran's farm but I felt the glow of content soak into my tired head and when we sat eating our picnic tea I wondered if there was another spot more peaceful in the whole world. A wild, eerie call of 'yoich, 'oich, 'oich' came floating over fields and soon the soft 'moo-oooo' of the homeward cows and their hooves knap-knapping on stony road. They were mildly curious about car and us and their soft warm breath gusted and blew as they turned their heads to look at us. They went and the peace descended again. Not even a bird called and I felt I wanted to sit quiet and still and be part of the living peace. My husband said suddenly 'I think your Gran owed her poise and peace a lot to always living here – always looking at the hills and never hearing discord'. I looked across at the little old farm and remembered that now the farmer's son runs a butchering business and I said 'Yes, but times have changed even there' ...

Tonight as I listened to J. B. Priestley I too went back to the outbreak of war.* It was a long journey although my days are so short. Cliff was at home and Jack was always in and out and Cliff brought other friends and there always seemed talk and laughter. Now all is quiet except on the rare weekends Cliff or Arthur gets home. Life changed altogether – widened in most ways for me if narrower in others. I turned to war work and service to fill the 'blank spaces' and made Centre an interest that has grown. I've found companionship and unexpected laughter and gaiety, understanding and sympathy. They have brought out unsuspected little gifts of money making ideas and organising. No one thinks my ideas are 'crazy' or 'fine ladyish' or 'so different from other people's ways' – or if they do they only laugh and never make me feel like a freak. My work has brought me strength in a surprising degree and I don't care tuppence for *anybody* – not even Mrs Burnett [*then head of Barrow's WVS, and anathema to Nella*] – not one scrap. I've found a serenity of mind and purpose that this time last year was, or seemed to be, impossible and I thank God and pray I may keep it and that it will increase as need arises.

Sunday, 15 September. I've always loved the sea, in all its moods, and it was a pleasure to me to stand on shore and face the crash and roar of the big waves – but not now. I see too many pictures [*of destruction*] when the sea rides high and I hear the wind tear round the chimneys. My husband said one day 'You are changing your mind about the sea and the Lakes. You always have liked to go to Walney and watch a heavy sea and now you prefer sitting by Coniston Lake. Why is that?' I thought for a few minutes and I said 'They make different pictures for me – one of violence and death and suffering and the other of steadfastness, quiet and calm'. I thought to myself 'You are altering your outlook too when you don't cut me off when I talk of "mind pictures" or listen to me when I

---

* Priestley spoke this week about the first anniversary of the outbreak of war, and of how 'The true heroes and heroines of this war, whose courage, patience and good humour stand like a rock above the dark morass of treachery, cowardice and panic, are the ordinary British folk': *Postscripts* (London: Heinemann, 1940), pp. 60–65.

talk "fancifully". I often look round and see how people are changing and
sometimes when I have not seen friends for awhile the change is more
apparent. It's a kinder, friendlier kind of change, a more tolerant feeling.
I was surprised at Miss Ledgerwood on Thursday. Mrs Waite and Mrs
Machin congratulated me on success of my little 'brain wave' [*a party to
raise money*] and hoped I had another winner 'up my sleeve' when Miss
Ledgerwood interrupted and said 'Brain wave nothing. Mrs Last wants
a rest and it's time she got back to helping in the bandage cutting. Mrs
Boorman and I miss her.' As I know Miss Ledgerwood disapproves of my
lipstick, high 'tapping' heels, silly habit of humming when I'm washing
up, my slang AND 'rude' jokes, I wondered what she missed, and thought
perhaps she only meant to be kind – a rare gesture from her anyway.

I hope my brother writes a letter to me this week.* I got one last week
but it was posted before the horror descended on London. Today I've
walked in 'fancy' along the Embankment and watched the sun fade –
our sunset tonight was a bit Turneresque and only needed smoke over
the 'hard' pink of dying sun. I'm glad I knew the old London. I went
the first time about 43 years ago and saw it change vastly up to my last
visit 10 years ago. Perhaps it was because my father's people came from
Woolwich and spoke of it as home but I'd always a feeling I belonged
– more than to the quiet of the hills and Lakes of my mother's people.

Nella by this time was writing more often of matters military and of sights in
Furness that reminded her of the realities of war. On 19 September she concluded her writing on that miserable, stormy day by saying that 'I feel so sorry
for the soldiers in the tents on Walney and the Coast Road, and at the "listening
posts". They look so cold and last night when we were over Walney we gave two
of them a lift back to town. They looked smart and trim but the heavy odour of
stale sweat and damp khaki was overpowering in the little car and made me think
of all the discomfort our Servicemen had to undergo – dismal discomfort that can
be deadlier than danger itself and more hard at times to bear.'

---

* Fred Lord, Nella's only sibling, was eleven years younger and a bachelor. He lived in
London and was a photographer with the London, Midland and Scottish Railway.

CHAPTER TWO

WATCHING, WORKING, WAITING

September 1940–April 1941

As the summer of 1940 was ending and autumn beginning, the realities of warfare had yet to bite deeply in Nella's corner of England. Rationing, although it had started, was not yet really troublesome. 'I cannot see a shortage of anything at all unless it's sugar, butter and condensed milk', Nella wrote on 14 September. Belt-tightening was minimal, although some people expected that it would soon be more severe (and they were right). On 21 September 1940 Nella was around Spark Bridge in the Lake District and recorded that 'The countryside was a painted glory of crimson and gold and green – so heartbreakingly lovely – and it was so impossible to believe that in the South – *our* South – there was death and destruction.' (The London Blitz began on 7 September.) She felt a queer 'unbelief' about her nation's crisis, but wondered 'Will I keep it until bombs come and work havoc in Barrow and I've seen destruction and death for myself? I feel as if between me and the poor London people there is a thick fog and it's only at intervals that I *can* believe it is our own people, not Spaniards or French or Dutch etc.' During the several weeks from later September there was a creeping sense in Barrow of alarm and imminent threat: price increases, scarcities of some everyday items, postal delays, newspapers arriving very late, reports of carnage in London, barrage balloons going up over the city, sirens sounding, public discussion of such mundane matters as what bus drivers and passengers should do in case of an alert, talk of the need for shelters – Nella was a keen exponent of 'deep shelters'. The prospect that the town would soon be blitzed was a common topic of discussion. 'Barrow is really getting shelter minded', she remarked on 12 November; for the first time she wrote this month of Anderson shelters, and Will had just devised a shelter at 9 Ilkley Road under their stairs.

By November, then, war and its perils seemed much more real to Nella and most of her fellow citizens than they had done a year earlier.

Saturday, 16 November. Barrow is plunged in gloom over the terrible Coventry bombings for it's a town where many Barrow people have moved to in times of bad trade. I have many friends and old neighbours there and also a cousin and his wife and no word as to their safety or otherwise has as yet come through. At Spark Bridge there was the same feeling of unease for several people had sons and daughters who had gone to work in Coventry. One woman was very upset for she had refused to let her daughter come home to have her second baby. There was some trouble when she came home to have her first baby and the mother said she was tired of being 'put on' and daughter had plenty of money to pay for attention. The poor woman was distraught as she remembered her daughter's words about the flat she occupied 'in the shadow of the Cathedral'. One farmer had kept his son down so much that he jumped at offer of a visitor from Coventry to get him a job there. Such a feeling of 'If we had only known'.* Aunt Sarah looked so sad and unhappy over her friend's troubles as she repeated her slogan – we must all be very kind to each other; 'it's *always* best to be kind, my dear, always remember that and act on it'. She is as poor as Job's turkey in money or anything that counts in the world's eyes but so rich in courage and hope and in friends. I'll never live to 76, I know, but if I do I pray I keep my ideals and courage undimmed as my little deaf aunt has done.

Saturday, 23 November. My cousin Mary had a huge pile of gramophone

---

* The devastation of Coventry is well recounted in Juliet Gardiner, *The Blitz: The British under Attack* (London: Harper Press, 2010), chapter 7. Unusually, the Government allowed details of this catastrophe to be published. In the words of Gardiner, the Ministry of Information 'decided there was more morale-boosting potential in revealing the extent of the damage, thus giving the impression of the enemy as a brutal bully ... and also that London was not the only city in the front line' (p. 164). Chapter 4 of Gavin Mortimer, *The Blitz: An Illustrated History* (Oxford: Osprey Publishing, 2010), includes some excellent photographs of the damaged city.

records for me. They had been collected for salvage but she begged them for my sailors. On the little mine-sweepers a gramophone is a treasure and the Sailors' Home is always eager for records. These were such a nice lot of homey old-time songs and tunes – no jazzy or out-of-date swing numbers. There was Xmas carols and good hymn tunes – altogether they were about the best mixture I've seen. I had two parcels, each as much as I could lift into car. I found rejoicing at Spark Bridge for Auntie told me that her neighbour's girl was safe and will come home from Coventry to have her second baby after all. She is trying to salvage a few bits of her home and then will come home for a few months. I looked at the few townspeople who were on the country roads. They look unhappy and unsettled, only the children seem to be able to adapt themselves to a country life in winter. I'd hate it myself if I had to go and live in most of the country cottages around with no proper sanitation or water and the door opening directly into the living room and letting out all the warmth as soon as it was opened. I saw two new whitening writing signs today in Ulverston – NO SMALL BATTERIES and NO DRAWING PINS – must save a lot of time both to dealers and customers. We were surprised to see that Woolworths had so much Xmas stock left in Ulverston. In Barrow if a stock is put out in the morning by afternoon it looks as if a swarm of locusts had been over! I got a thick writing pad at Ulverston – they saved it for me when re-doing window. I thanked the girl and said 'I wish you had saved me two', and after a little hesitation she said "I believe there *is* another one upstairs' and she brought me another one ...

I've a nasty feeling that Birmingham is as badly hit as Coventry. I got a feeling of seriousness this morning [Sunday, 24 November] when the clergyman in the morning service prayed so earnestly for 'sufferers through air raids and those who had been killed'. I have a curious reaction to war news – I like to know the worst and find my own 'bright side', or feel pity and mourning for hardly hit people and places. If I don't know and only fear the worst I feel a nagging worry that is worse than actually knowing that things are bad. I don't know whether my cold is making me a bit pessimistic but I cannot 'maffick'*† over Greece. I remember Finland and the outcry of delight at her 'splendid resistance', and soon she was beaten flat by Russia. I cannot think Hitler will let Mussolini lose face too much and will soon help them and Greece will not have it all her own way for long.*

Monday, 25 November. I had a visit from a very old friend I'd not seen for years – quite three years. She was up our way and called for a cup of tea and told me she had had to give her work up – Spirella Corsetiere – and take an Insurance Book to collect. I was very surprised for I remembered the last war when anyone with anything either different or expensive made their fortunes. Miss Jones said 'This is a different war altogether and we are getting down to it early and all steel will go into aeroplanes' etc. She told me that the big Spirella works had only a third for corsets and would soon have less to do when steel and rayon were further restricted. She lives in Hindpool, a suburb where the Iron and Steel works are situated and her brother has a good position there although in slump he was like the rest and without work at all.

She tells me that although money is good it's not the same as last war and we discussed it. We wondered if people with a different standard of living spent their money differently. She recalled the time when all the pawnbrokers' shops were full of unredeemed pledges – rings, brooches and watches – and fat red hands had rings on every finger and sometimes two – costing from £20 to £60 each! – when every boy had a gold watch, the height of his ambition those days, when as much as £40 and £50 was going into a tiny house, where father and several sons were working at Iron works. Those days rent was paid and no one moved and furniture was 'good enough' and granny's patchwork quilt was thought quite the thing! Now, Miss Jones said, the houses on a new adjacent estate have been sold, and just before the war the jerry built 'outside fanciness' of them deceived no one and seemed a white elephant to builder. Her 'book' is partly in the new estate and she said she had known most of the families for 40 or 50 years – she will be about 58 or 59. Among

---

* Her prediction was sound; German forces attacked Greece and occupied it in April 1941.

the things they have bought, beside the pretty big deposit on new house, are grandfather clocks, eiderdowns, wireless sets, bicycles for all the family, fur coats, perms for mother, dancing classes for children etc. I said 'What about pianos?' and she said 'I did not see one – funny now I come to think of it for that was the old "standard" of prosperity in many homes, wasn't it?' I said 'Well anyway, it's better to buy things to give pleasure and give warmth than the old days of the riotous drinking of the Ironworkers, when only liquor brandy and even champagne was the weekend drink and beer was *swilled* like tea or water.'

A woman came in to pay a bill while Miss Jones was in and as it was so cold I said 'Come into my "workshop" and have a drink of tea'. She might be classed as a 'new rich' for war has trebled – at least – her income. She looked at my row of smiling dollies† and said in a grand tone, after asking me how much I charged, 'I'll take the lot. They will do for Xmas presents and I can send what is left to Hospital'! I said 'I'm sorry but these are all ordered – by friends – and if I'd time to make another dozen I'd send them to Hospital myself'. She sat and ate all the chocolate biscuits in my little glass dish and as Miss Jones pointed out put three lumps of sugar in each of her two cups of tea. Miss Jones said 'Greedy pig. They have so much money they are losing their manners.' I said 'Well, Mrs Milne never was greedy in the old days. I think it's thoughtlessness and forgetfulness on their part and they don't realise there is any shortage yet. So far their money has been able to buy anything.' It was really a gesture to put out my whole quarter pound of chocolate biscuits. I hate stint and myself could never in any circumstances 'polish off' a whole lot, either from a diet or manners standpoint, so I did not think anyone else would do so! Added to that she said 'Try and get me some of these *delightful* little biscuits at your grocer's, and a few tins of sardines if you can. My grocer will only let me have one tin a week.' I said 'I cannot get any more chocolate biscuits – they are finished – and as for sardines, well, we like them ourselves and I can only get an odd tin'.

I seemed to sew and sew but make little impressions on dolls' clothes – fiddling things to do – and the wireless was impossible on all stations and my head and face ached so I came to bed early and wrote to Cliff. He is a lot better and hopes to have a few days leave soon.

Wednesday, 27 November. My husband said 'You look so quiet and sad as you sit there sewing those everlasting dolls. Why don't you talk instead of thinking?' I felt really startled but I said 'Well, if I think aloud you will only say "Oh, don't rave about things you cannot alter and bother your head so about shelters and ships and loneliness and fear" – for my mind is only a jumble tonight'. He said 'I'll never say such to you again as long as I live. I cannot argue with you as the boys do but all the same, tell me.' After years of 'What *odd* things you say', 'I don't hear any other woman talking of things like that', 'Why do you bother so about such things?', 'Don't be silly', 'Oh, stop thinking about it', it's hard to begin new habits and with my husband not liking people in at nights when he was home I've got into the habit of 'stitching my thoughts' into my words – he does not like me to get immersed in a book and 'too far away'. Now I believe he would let me bring anyone in and talk to them and I'd not have the guilty feeling I'd driven him from his own chair by the fireside or the reproach of preferring someone else's company. War *is* changing people but it worries me when my husband is so different – I fear he is ill.

I had such a queer dream the other night – no sense in it at all to put into words but a feeling of such aloneness that might fall on the 'last man left in the world'. It set me off thinking how lonely really most people were, if they were stripped of all the little rags of custom and usage and habits of everyday life. There must be a lot more soul sadness than we know among the bombed cities. If everyone bombs everyone else and cities and towns are bombed flat in England and Germany, when will they be ever built? Not in our lifetime – if ever. Miss Ledger-wood talked of a book written by the women of Poland to the women of America and touched on the contents. She said 'I'd like to read it, wouldn't you?' I said 'Dear God, NO. My heart would break in pieces. I'm not very strong minded and what I cannot help I shun.' It's good for the people of America to read no doubt for they are far away and are not having their own people bombed. It seems so odd to think of our own people suffering, and so near for Liverpool gun flashes can be seen across the Bay.

Thursday, 28 November. One woman came in to Centre to ballyhoo that we had not acknowledged her daughter's previous gift for £5 raised by making felt posies. Mrs Machin is very methodical and clever and turned up her book for last month and said 'Oh Mrs Dodds, I wrote a letter myself'. Mrs Dodds said 'That's not it. I think it's as little as you can do to publish it in the paper'! They are *rolling* in money at usual normal times and now, as I said, *wallow* in it and could afford to give £50 and never think of it again. Mrs Dodds puffed and wheezed and waved her arms about and I said suddenly 'What lovely perfume you have. I never smelled anything like it quite.' She said 'Mr D brought me a case from London with four £7 10s 0d bottles in and 'Djew know Mrs Last, the lot was not as big as a double whiskey.' She should know: they made their money in pubs and, report says, switching brands of whiskey after a man had had a few and his palate was dulled! When she went out of Committee room it was just a cattery for awhile and among things I heard were that Mrs D had had a German mother, never had kept a maid as all food was locked up and doled out, kept a bottle of whiskey in her bedroom etc. etc. Suddenly Mrs Waite laughed loudly and said 'Look at our pussy sitting there and listening to us all and never saying a word'. I said 'Oh I was waiting to say the worst thing. She pays £7 10s 0d for a teaspoon of perfume when little children have to wait for fresh warm clothes after an air raid, when so much could be done with 7s 6d, never mind £7 10s 0d. After all her morals and her disposition are her own concern but for the sin of wasting so much money I would have her *whipped*.' When I thought of how we planned and worked and collected our raffles, and begged, I felt *no* punishment could fit the crime of not only Mrs Dodds but of many more, not the big people but the 'new rich', and suddenly I saw greed and ugliness in what we have gaily laughed at and told each other little odd jokes about.

The war does make me intense about things. I never realised that I could get so carried away. It's perhaps a good thing I'm so busy or else I'd be off carrying a banner for something or other. I feel I want to DO THINGS – help in a *real* way, for there is such a lot to do everywhere.

During the next couple of months Nella wrote a great deal about domestic matters and the management of the household economy: shopping, shortages, food prices and provisioning, preparations for Christmas, house-cleaning, gardening, preparing meals, household efficiencies, sewing and mending, making dollies, sitting by the fire, listening to the wireless, her dog and cat, nursing herself through a cold or the flu, receiving visitors (some were welcome, some were not) and looking forward to seeing her sons – Arthur came for a Christmas visit, Cliff was home on leave for a fortnight from 1 January. Nella was a proud and fastidious homemaker, and her husband often lauded her skills. Just before Christmas, on 22 December, she wrote of how the men in her family 'always tease me about getting the best out of things, but I could have purred like a happy cat when I saw my tea table. It was *loaded* with goodies and there was not one thing I'd acted meanly to get – that was the happy making part of it. I'd hoarded out of my rations to make paste for jellied apple pie. My lavish "butter" was a beaten mixture of butter, margarine, and milk done in my cute little jar churn. My lovely cake, which tasted just as good as it looked, was the result of forethought last Spring as was my mince meat and rum butter. I've plenty to share with whoever comes in.' Nella, an enemy of waste and extravagance, was a great proponent of planning, thrift and prudential practices. 'My recipes are all so very economical', she wrote on 7 January 1941, 'and I've a real gift for making a tasty meal cheaply, but even the most economical of them I ponder over and wonder how I could make cheaper without taking from food value or too much from taste and appearance.' Will had good reason to see her as the model housewife.

Nella's diary also included details on her unpaid work outside the home – WVS, Hospital Supply, Sailors Home – and occasionally during these weeks she remarked on larger public matters. On 6 December 'I Listened to the *Postscript* 'In Poland Now' and I felt sick to my soul case[†] as I realised that if such dreadful horrors are broadcast, *what* were the hidden ones?' A week later (13 December) she wrote of the frustrations of people who had been evacuated to the Lake District. 'Round Greenodd, where mothers came with children, it did not make for happiness for they found fault and criticised and the children took the cue from them and were bad to manage. Where children were by themselves they seemed to adapt themselves and soon be part of the family. I cannot see evacuation ever being happy unless it's done on a base where families *can* be families in their own place, if it's only one room.' She also thought that many evacuated women from towns and cities missed 'the pulse of life felt where people *do* things and *think* things'. 'All the talking and talking by men cannot know the real torture that a lonely uprooted woman can feel, both for herself and her children' (15 December). Then there were the personal tragedies that forced themselves upon her. On 30 December 'The face of a little boy I saw the other day came to me. He is here from Liverpool. He saw his mother and two sisters killed, spent seven nights in a shelter before and after his home was shattered at Liverpool and finally was trapped with an elder sister and lay on her dead arm for hours before rescue – and he is *seven*. His eyes are frenzied and he talks in stutters and if he fall asleep wakes in a lather of fright and shaking and screaming. He is lucky – he has come to a kind understanding aunt – but what of the others?'

Wednesday, 22 January, 1941. I had a caller this afternoon – she comes to Centre to sew – a nice gay little woman whose daughter married her soldier sweetheart and who has spent her brief married life living near wherever he was stationed, and now he has gone overseas for two years. She is a tall handsome 'brooding' kind of girl – only 22 – and today [*when she and her mother called*] her beauty was clouded and dimmed and the gay amusing hat she normally looks so chic and smart in looked like a carnival hat stuck on anyway. My heart ached so for her, and for all the unhappy girls like her, and when she was going I felt my tongue – *my* tongue that can generally find something inconsequential to say to bridge any gap – stick to the roof of my mouth and not one word of comfort could I utter. I felt so full of pity for her I was speechless – like meeting a friend after she has lost her husband or child by death. She seemed to understand that I felt what I could not say and as I showed them to the door she turned to me in hall and said 'Isn't life odd, Mrs Last? Bob and I adored each other and longed passionately for a child, and no signs, and we were married nearly a year. If I'd been a soldier's pick-up I'd have had a baby in my arms by now.' Mrs Holt, her mother, flushed scarlet and said 'Laura, you shock me when you talk like that' and I felt sorrier still for the girl. If she cannot talk and say whatever she likes to her own mother and find understanding and sympathy, where can she do so? ...

I find I've prepared over 30 dollies, cut their bodies out and fixed waxed faces on ready to embroider. I've stuffed over a dozen of them and finished two Gretchens and got well on two gollywogs and two cowboys (ordered) so in spite of a wretched backbone that aches in every joint and makes turning my head a pain – just nerves, I expect, and after effects of my wretched cold – it's been a good day. I like to feel my days are worthwhile – it keeps away black thoughts like howling wolves in the night – and if I know I've done 'something to help' it's better than aspirins to make me sleep. Ruth said 'I never remember you having so little for Sailors Home' and I said 'I've only got two waistcoats and those books and papers are no use for them – they are *Women's Weeklys* and will go to Hospital. I think everyone is busy collecting for Rest Centres for town.'* Mrs Waite said yesterday 'Would you like me to buy some children's clothes – coats and suits etc. – from Mr Bell (a tradesman from whom we get part of our wool and blankets and sheets for sick bays for the soldiers at Fort)? She says he has got a job lot[†] of things and for £5 would let me have a good consignment. I think they will be salvaged. I said 'Let's look at them first and if they look good value we will buy two lots for soon I'll be making more money [*from raffles etc.*] and you could spend half of whist drive money that way'. Bless her, she knows my love of spending money and always tries to let me spend and shop for as she says 'If you see the *value* of money, pussy, you will have fresh encouragement to make some more'!

Thursday, 23 January. As I listened to *These Men Were Free*, to my way of thinking the most marvellous and thrilling feature the BBC have ever

---

* Rest Centres were set up as temporary shelters for people who might be made homeless as a result of air raids (Barrow had as yet been hit by only a few bombs).

had, I could not help thinking how lucky England – Britain – had been for as long as history records. Our Civil War and small uprisings were either local or quite gentlemanly affairs compared with the massacres and overruling of other countries and I wondered if in the eternal ebb and flow we were to have our turn as have all the countries on Continent. Everywhere I hear talk of invasion, but not defeatist frightened talk. It's either a 'Better get it done with' attitude or else a joke made about it – like when a date is fixed a gay remark is added like 'invasion permitting' etc. ... Today at Centre there was lots of remarks I overheard that still seemed about invasion, but in a light vein. It even overshadows the small meat ration as a basis of women's conversation and the wail of 'What can we make for dinner and what can we make soup of'. Many take so badly to having money and not being able to 'live *really well*' – chops, roasts, fowls and lots of expensive fish like plaice, hake and halibut.

Saturday, 25 January. Ruth called in on her way to another 'day place' and her first words were 'Did you hear Mr Brown's account of what Germans would do if they conquered and won?' I said 'Yes – we have no need of thrillers to chill and curdle our blood nowadays, have we?' She said 'Well, Lil' – her friend – 'and I talked it over carefully, Mrs Last, and if invasion takes place and there is any chance of falling into Germans' hands we will carry a safety blade always. We went to ambulance classes and "know our veins" and would never hesitate to open one if the worst came to the worst.' She stood there so calmly, such a sweet, strong young thing with steady kind grey eyes, and a shadow seemed to fall on my heart as fresh problems rose in my mind and a pity for mothers of girls crowded out the feeling I always have for mothers of boys.

Wednesday, 29 January. What with buses, post offices and Shipyard, girls are leaving positions as maids to flock for good wages and I know several women who are trying to run huge inconvenient houses with a char[†] where four servants were needed. One huge, central heated and really marvellously equipped house owned by a retired corn merchant has none at all except the 'lady' housekeeper, a naval man's widow who is wearing herself to a shadow in effort to keep the old man warm and fed in reasonable comfort in huge bleak house, for she cannot manage central heating that needs *one ton* of coal a *week* for house, big green houses etc. She was told at Labour Exchange that no maid would consider 'Arnolene' in ordinary times unless there was four or five of a staff and then it was hard work, and dark hints were thrown out that it may be commandeered soon! It would be ridiculous to pass by such a wonderful hospital of a house.

Wednesday, 5 February. Poor Ruth is so distressed for her fiancé has calmly told her he does not know whether he prefers his former girl or her – after two years happy friendship and three years since he saw his other girl friend. When they parted it was because she 'wanted to have a good time for a year or two before settling down'. Presumably she has now had her good time, or as Gerald's mother shrewdly said 'found no one else and heard of Gerald's high wages here in Barrow'! She lives in Leeds and Gerald has never heard of her until this Xmas when she sent an expensive scarf, recalled old times and begged him to write and 'make it up'. There seems unhappiness for everyone in some way or another and I felt so grieved to see happy little Ruth so sad. She is such a kind sweet girl and deserves nothing but love and happiness. Young things all seem to get hurt nowadays – partings and sadness and break-ups of marriages and engagements when the lovers and husbands have to go. Makes older people so baffled and helpless to see their eyes and not be able to do one thing – except pray that some day soon the shadows will pass and the sun shine for them again.

Friday, 7 February. I had been up early enough to tidy round and dust and vac so walked from hairdresser's into town and I noticed another sweet shop was closed and my husband said when I told him at lunch time 'There are 13 shops vacant now in Dalton Road', our main shopping street which only takes ten minutes or so to walk from one end to the other. Several windows – my grocer's were one – had bold lettered placards prominently displayed, 'Young Lady Assistants Wanted' – such a rare thing for Barrow where there is normally nothing for girls except the Shipyard offices and the few vacancies for shop assistants etc. In our slump years there was a big outcry at Woolworths demanding a Higher School Certificate! I felt very sceptical and plucked up courage to ask manager once when I was in shop. He said it was perfectly true and gave his reason. He said that over thirty girls answered advert for three girls and, to use his own words, 'all peaches', fit for good class trade and every one with a matric.[†] Obviously it was impossible to choose and he said 'Any of you girls got your "Higher"?' and three stepped forward and were engaged! That was about seven or eight years ago and there's plums of jobs now for every girl. I've a tatty looking little thing to bring my papers – she never looks as if she was properly washed, or fed – and newsagent has to pay 16s for her morning and evening delivery of papers. She confided in me that riding a bike was 'stretching her out fine' and as soon as she was 'big and strong enough' looking she would go on the buses and ride into Yard. I suggested meal porridge and potatoes and she flashed a cheeky grin at me as she said before she dashed away 'Don't *you* start. Mom says it's the only way to fill us all for she is a widow and there is five of us not yet working.' ...

A man in our road who keeps hens and knows all about them says I should not keep these hens I've got another winter but as each finishes laying I should kill it and then replace with pullets.[†] They are such nice kind hens it's a pity. I wonder if I could keep several of my six good layers and get just a few new ones, or would they fight and hurt each other in small space. I wish my garden was bigger and I could get a piglet. There's something very appealing in a pig – so clever of it to eat such trash and give such good bacon and ham.[*] My husband said 'Why not rabbits?' but I'm so fond of furry things it would be useless to rear them and

---

[*] Household pig-keeping, where it was feasible, was actively encouraged in wartime as a way of offsetting consumers' demands for commercial meat production. Moreover, Denmark, a traditional supplier of bacon, was occupied by the enemy. Pigs could be and were fattened on all sorts of kitchen waste.

think of killing and eating them. I'm not so sure I'll enjoy my little hens when they go into the pot!

Saturday, 8 February. When I listened to news I said to my husband 'Does the war news seem real to you? Do you worry or rejoice much?' And he said after some consideration 'Not really. War seems to have receded since we had few air raids over England.' It's really astounding to me sometimes how little I *do* think of war! I'm terribly single minded and know and think of what I'm doing to the exclusion of most things, but when I consider how much of my life now is centred on 'war things' – bandages, comforts and money raising for same – and yet how little I think of big things, I'm often amazed at my limited vision and wonder if others have it. They came today to ask about billeting people in case of a blitz and I said I'd made my own arrangements. The Group Warden was amused and said 'A bit early, weren't you?' but as I told him, if I have to do a thing or think I'll have to do a thing I like to make a plan, think things well out, arrange it – and then forget it until need arises, for I find it's less worrying. If I have to have a soldier and Ruth and her aunt have to come to live with me I'll be full up, unless of course it's a case of tiny ones we could push in anywhere. I hope whatever comes it does not tie me for I must keep on at Centre. I've that fact drilled into me constantly by Mrs Waite and Mrs Lord and I can really see it's the best work I can do for I've a real gift of 'being bright' and of tactfulness however I feel inside me. Think next time I come [*on earth through reincarnation*] I'll be qualified for a stage career for I've done quite a bit of 'laugh, clown, laugh' [*clowning despite being sad*] here. Then I can coax pennies, and pennies soon make pounds, and after nearly two years of working and understanding I've got a really good raffling and begging psychology worked out. There's nobody but can be done without, but I realise we must all do our best and my best is at Centre and not just in the house working after evacuees as billets.

Nella had already written warmly of some of the friendships fostered by work at the Centre, her admiration for some of her fellow volunteers and the importance she attached to this volunteering. 'I like to be busy', she wrote on 29 December 1940, 'and I like the company too at Centre. I like to be with people when I'm working. This week has made me realise even more what a blessing to me my work is, and what a lot I owe to it.' She had resolved to be a soldier in service to others – just as 'my Cliff' was a soldier. 'It's a great privilege … to work down at Centre', she wrote a few weeks later (6 February). 'I am never sufficiently grateful however I try.' She liked being among women who did not think her odd, and who valued her talents. And in one entry the following month (23 March), after regretting that, with her boys grown up and away from home, 'There's nothing "growing" now in the house – only older and downhill', her next sentence recorded that 'I'm always so grateful for Centre when I get a little fit of the miseries and I wonder what my life would have been without its organised service.'

Sunday, 9 February. One thing I cannot do as they advise on BBC – eat raw vegetables at this time of the year. I think it's because cabbage and carrot are rather too woody and coarse but neither my husband or I can digest them although when they are young I use a lot of carrots raw. I scrambled eggs on brown toast and we had a piece of mince pastry that I warmed slightly. My husband said 'I think I get fonder of nice meals and dread the thought of being so short of food that they are impossible'. When I looked at my so simple lunch and bowl of snowdrops on embroidered cloth I said 'Don't worry my dear. It will be a bit yet before we reach the bread line standard.' And he laughed and said 'Yes, and when we do I bet you toast it crisp and cut it in fingers and serve it on a gay plate to make it look nice'. I'm so finicky myself I think other people are as well and I know that if food *looks* good to me, well it *tastes* good.

We went out for a little run in the car and the damp sweet air coming in through open top was like perfume. All the trees are greening along branches as if good new blood is starting to stir again and they lift their bare branches eagerly as if waiting a signal before they start to throw out buds. Moss and lichen and polypodies[†] glow emerald bright and we got a big armful of catkins – enough for us and for Margaret and some to give to Ruth tomorrow for we all share a love of 'live' things about. Suddenly I said to my husband 'Have you noticed anything about country people walking today?' and after awhile he said 'No, except they all seem to be carrying a bunch of sticks as if they were flowers'. I said 'That is what I meant. Do you remember we always took in "enough twigs to boil the kettle" when we stayed in the country when the boys were small?' It used to be a feature of the boys' stay to gather sticks and fir cones out of the wood and put them in Aunt's wood shed. In later years the firewood cart took bundles of firewood and firelighters to the remotest country shop but now even in towns there is an acute shortage and people are always begging wood when they see my shelf in garage. My husband said 'You will have to stop giving so many sticks away for there is so little wood in workshop there will be none to follow and you will have to be careful of what you have'.

We had a little adventure today and it kept us laughing all the evening. Cutting down a quiet country road, we saw an obviously 'town's man' standing. I've the country woman's understanding of giving a lift and always remember Gran giving all and sundry a lift in the old gig, so we drew up and said 'Going Barrow way?' and as man got in with thanks my husband said 'You're Murray the painter, aren't you?' and mentioned a place they had been to see about a contract. It seems he had been to see his fiancée and had to return early as he had a service in Dalton at 6, and also that he was a Gospel Haller. They are a very strict denomination – I've known several – and think it a sin to go to a party or pictures or even a football match, and find their amusement, recreation, pleasure and what not 'studying God's holy word'. Perhaps if he had not breathed so heavily down the back of my neck, or mentioned that he had appealed against [national] service in any form, I'd have listened and said nothing, but I felt really belligerent. I said 'Excuse me, Mr Murray. Do you realise that each book of the Bible was written by a different writer? What makes you call it "God's word" altogether and interpret it to mean a narrow joyless creed? And another thing – if invasion comes would you stand and see your wife attacked without raising your hand to defend her?' He said 'Yes, if it meant attack, but I *would* attempt to stand my body between my wife and an assailant'. I said 'Well, that's something anyway, but a well bred collie will stand between the fire and a small child. I think Christ who drove the money lenders out of the temple would have done better than "stand between". I must have got a bit eloquent for he said 'Ow, Mrs Last, you talk like the gentlemen at the tribunal where I went to appeal' and offered to let me read all he had said and had said to him, all typed out 'plain and proper like'. I thanked him sweetly and said I would not *dream* of putting him to so much trouble. '*No* trouble, Mrs Last. A pleasure, I'm sure. We like to talk to people who do not understand us. We are really very misunderstood, Mrs Last. A Gospel Haller has to be a mixture of patience and courage – to stand up for the teaching of Christ, you know.' I'd had all I could stand of Mr Murray and felt slightly sick. Luckily we had just reached where he got out so I added 'Yes, I'm sure no "everyday" man could possibly be the mixture you describe and I should imagine you would need a good streak of exhibitionism too in your makeup'. When we drove off I saw my husband was laughing and I said 'Ugh – that one reminded me of Uriah Heep' [*an unctuous, hypocritical, ingratiating character in Dickens's* David Copperfield] and my husband said 'I know' and laughed harder than I've seen him for some time. I joined in when he told me I'd addressed the poor man as Uriah when speaking! My tongue did not wait to be told by my mind. So odd!

Friday, 14 February. Such alarming news in the papers today – looks as if all the world will be aflame soon and no sanity or peaceful corner left anywhere. Arthur says 'The sooner the better, it will hasten things'. How hasten, though, when it's death and destruction. I've laughed at Cliff's Australian friend for his 'Japanese bogey' but it looks as if he had grounds for his fears and talk of 'yellow peril', and Australia is so huge and defenceless a place with its thousands of miles of flat unprotected coast line. With everybody killing and fighting each other and sinking each others' ships and crops not getting planted and labour shortage everywhere due to men being soldiers instead of growing food, how soon will there be famine over the world? Whole countrysides, it is said, are lying waste in China through the war there and there is the wasted farms and land in Europe. Men cannot fish in the plentifully stocked

sea because of mines and U-boats – such senseless useless waste. Food
and beauty for all in this world and yet soon none will have the first or
care about the second – so wrong and twisted. I know I will never see
the end of this tangle for it will take too long for men to think sanely
and straightly again for my length of days. I used to wish we had all gone
to Australia when we had the chance but there soon will be no spot to
long to fly to and feel 'far from turmoil and strife'. If people were fighting for something it would be understandable – some big gain – but it's
so dreadful to have to fight and kill and destroy just to let live peaceful
ordinary lives. It's odd to call the Force of evil that is loose today by a
name but Hitler is as good, or bad, a name as Satan, or the 'anti-Christ'
an old friend of my Dad's was so fond of talking about. Poor old lamb,
we thought he was crazy when he talked of 'Armageddon' – looks now
as if he was extra wise! Nowadays when my husband and I hear bad news
on the wireless we just look at each other and don't talk much about
it. In his eyes I read a puzzled wonder, as if he cannot believe what the
announcer says. I wonder what he reads in mine?

Wednesday, 19 February. Among our visitors today was the first gypsy
of the season. I think there must be a kind of secret intelligence among
gypsy people for they always call about lunch and without asking for
tea I know somehow they expect a warm drink. Today it was an old
crone I've known since I was a child – and she looked very different
then! Gypsies are always sensibly shod and warmly clad and I have never
found rudeness or ill breeding among them. She was selling cheap oddments that looked as if they were from Woolworths and asking 1s 6d
and 2s – and she would 'read your hand'. She was grateful for cup of hot
soup Ruth took into garage and said 'There is a parting between you
two women folk, but no harsh words and you will always come back
with a feeling of welcome' [*Ruth was soon to be called up for national
service*] and went on 'You have not been very lucky in love, my dear.
You will need a lot of patience with your man.' Ruth and I laughed and
I said 'Black, white or yellow, my dear, take it from me, any and *every*
man needs that!'

Thursday, 20 February. Ruth says it's not this week but next month she registers so we are going to try and do our spring cleaning early and have all cleaning done by time she has to go. We will start on Monday and turn one room out. I boiled an extra pan of vegetable scraps today and threw it out of dining room window onto garden for I could not bear to see the flock of famished gulls, crows, rooks, starlings and all the lovely little finches, tits, robins, etc. Strange today there were no blackbirds or thrushes. I lay and watched the beating wings till I went to sleep and woke feeling rested and sewed a little. Miss Mac came in and nearly drove me frantic by her nail chewing – they are down nearly to half moons. She looks so ill and says her nerves get worse and is getting to sleep so badly again. She said 'It's dreadful to wait and wait and wonder if invasion will come in a day or a week or a month'. I said 'I try and not think of it, but think of how much worse it is for South and South-East England' and got the answer 'I seem to only be able to think of them landing on our Coast Road, or on Walney Island, and I wake up at night wondering and wondering if I can hear a strange noise or it's only the wind, and if it's very quiet I wonder if the siren has gone and I've not heard it'.

Sunday, 2 March. Bowness was full of strangers and the waterfront was as thronged as on a summer day. There were a few big 'offcome'[†] charas parked at different villages as if parents were visiting evacuees. All the Home Guard were out at manoeuvres at crossroads and strategic points – gentry, farmers, farm labourers, retired townsmen – all alike and working together as one. We will be more socialist after this war and barriers that started slipping in the last war will go for good. I am old enough to have seen many changes in the countryside. Wide gulfs and barriers between class that were like the bars at a zoo. My own Gran was a snob – bless her – and she was as poor as Job's turkey! Of a family who were 'free men' and yeomen farmers of standing in [*Queen*] Elizabeth's time and with Rawlinson's[†] name on hundreds-year old tombs and church walls, she had an intense pride of race, and her standards were high. She had the ideals and the dignity of a duchess and although rather comical in a farmer's wife she taught her family to be true to the best in themselves, to help others, to be clean in mind as well as in body, and to speak the truth and keep their word when given. Her scorn of what we now call 'new rich' was cutting and I can remember the look on a woman's face who had loftily offered to buy an old little tea pot that stood on the dresser. Although all words are forgotten, I said 'It's an old teapot, Gran – why did you get cross?' and faintly recall 'upstart', 'money not always "talking" wisely' etc.

Whatever indications there had been that the people of Barrow gave the war little thought, by March 1941 this feeling of distance had clearly eroded. The signs of combat were more and more manifest; reminders of potential death and destruction were edging closer to the relatively remote Furness peninsula. These signs included bombing alerts (and the consequent loss of sleep), increased aerial activity, anti-aircraft gunfire, and actual though small raids. Nella took notice of soldiers in nearby camps, the lack of shellfish in the market because of gun practices on Morecambe Bay that restricted fishing (22 March) and kerfuffles concerning the first steps in the call-up of women for national service (18 and 19 March), which initially was to apply to those born in 1919 and 1920. The conscription of women in wartime was without precedent and set tongues wagging, and Nella thought that 'it seems in some odd way to have finally "brought war home" to some people' (19 March). There were reports of heavy raids on other port cities, including Plymouth, which was well known to the naval families then in Barrow, for Plymouth was where some had friends and houses (25 March). A thirst for revenge was almost certainly intensifying. 'I felt a real thrill of satisfaction tonight', Nella wrote on 24 March, 'to hear of our latest "fortress" airplanes. NOW we will start in earnest. I'd like to see Berlin flat – and *what* a smash it would be if all the pictures of huge glass houses of flats are typical of their buildings. I've no real animosity toward the German people as a whole, but I'd like to know they were frightened and homeless as our poor ones were in London, Bristol, Coventry and Liverpool, and be *happy* to know they had to sleep in tubes – if Germany has tubes – and stand for hours in damp shelters. They have not the resistance and courage of free people who can choose and think things out and no reserves to strengthen their backbone.' As for Barrovians' sense of security, some people feared imminent attack, others felt that the war would be over by the end of the year. 'I often wonder whatever *would* happen if we got a blitz', Nella wrote on 31 March. 'I think we have stayed *too* safe and secure and a general feeling that we are "too out of the way" prevails.'

Monday, 7 April. I heard my next door neighbour talking rather excitedly to her milkman and then she called over and told me 'Bombs had been dropped in the Shipyard'. I thought it some kind of catch and did not take her seriously but when my husband came in he told me it was true. I went to whist drive and everyone was full of it. Many of them had had their husbands return home as it was two time bombs that had been dropped. The amazing – and to us the really terrible – thing about it was that airplane came with our lights shining and was let pass and we had no Alert, and it was over so quickly none of us heard anything. The amazing thing is that a gypsy woman has been going about telling fortunes and saying that we would have a blitz on the 6th of April! Cards were a very secondary feature and everyone talked of shelter and I was surprised to hear of so many being ordered, to be put up in dining rooms and sitting rooms ... We have lived in a fool's paradise like Glasgow did, a 'they-cannot-find-us-for-we-are-hidden-by-the-mist-that-always-lies-over-us'!!

Friday, 11 April, Good Friday. We had intended making an all day outing today and going to Morecambe but with all being so dull we felt undecided and were trying to make up our mind whether to turn back when we saw a very dejected couple by the road side. The man was a tired unhappy looking airman and the woman about ten years older, dressed cheaply smart and with black hat, scarf and gloves. They looked so lost I said 'I wonder if they would like a lift' so we stopped and asked them. They were so grateful for they were in deep trouble. A wire had brought them at daybreak from Blackpool to Meathop, a TB sanatorium where the airman's wife and woman's young sister was dying. They stayed until she died and the taxi could not be kept as it cost £2 10s od to travel straight there and back. Today there were hundreds of Army lorries on

Great North Road and all kinds of trade lorries but few private cars and no service buses, and they were trying to get to a station. We decided to take them as far as Lancaster and then they could get a bus straight to Blackpool. She was of that beady black-eyed type who thought it 'only manners' to describe her sister's illness and death, but the poor lad looked as if he could stand nothing more. Luckily I saw 'Harry Korris' splashed across a playbill and said 'I'd like to see him again. He has got on since the days he was at Central Pier at Blackpool.' The next thing we were talking of BBC shows and I took good care to keep the conversation up and chattered on without a break and the sister-in-law joined in and stopped talking of the horrors of her poor little sister's illness and death.

My husband said bitterly after we had dropped them near bus stand at Lancaster 'I suppose there *are* bright, amusing nice people who want lifts but my God, if there's a depressing, smelly or aggravating wretch on the road, *you* will pick them up'. There was the making of a real row but somehow suddenly all the sorrow of the world seemed to wrap me round and I could have keened† like an Irish biddy at a wake, and tears poured out of my eyes. I so rarely cry – when awake – that it always gave my husband and the boys concern. To save my soul I could not have told why I cried. The futility and suffering, the fear and terror that is about everywhere, the cold and misery, the partings and heartaches, the 'never to be' of so many young things nowadays seemed all about me. Perhaps it was the heavy day and the memory of other Easters. Perhaps I'm not very well just now. I never am when my back and head ache so much. It passed and my husband said 'Is there anything you would like at all?' and without thinking I said 'Yes, an orange'. So silly a thing to say – it made us both laugh ...

I felt a bit dim and came to bed early. All is so quiet and still and a mist is over all. I wish it was a mile thick over England and nowhere did the moon shine brightly this full moon weekend.

CHAPTER THREE

AFTER THE BOMBS

May–June 1941

Barrow had so far largely escaped the ravages of German bombs. This was to change over the Easter weekend of 1941, when, on the night of 13–14 April, Barrow endured the first of two consecutive nights of German air raids. These terrifying experiences, for those under attack, were vividly captured by Nella: the penetrating noise, 'an inferno of sound' (15 April), close at hand, from guns, aeroplanes and explosions; the smashed and collapsing buildings; shrapnel pouring down on roofs; fires breaking out around the town; and, of course, the almost universal fear of personal injury or annihilation. Still, the damage sustained was (by the standards of other raids on Britain) modest, and by the end of April, Nella was writing of these incidents as 'our little blitz' (26 April). The month of May brought much more destruction; there were three nights of heavy bombing between the early hours of the 4th and the 8th. She and Will were uninjured, though their nerves were seriously frayed – a year later she recalled that 'when the raids were on I had nerves so bad in my throat I felt choking if I tried to swallow and was sick if I ate much' (1 May 1942); but by contrast with the crippling fears of others she knew, she later felt that 'my nerves wobbled a bit and then steadied and I could go on' (28 December 1942). The Lasts' house was damaged, several people they knew were killed and a walk about Barrow revealed to its residents what seemed to be a devastated landscape.* Before Barrow's raids Nella and Will had been discussing the purchase of an indoor

---

* Much of Nella's writing about the bombing of Barrow and its immediate consequences up to 10 May has been published in *Nella Last's War* (2006 edn), pp. 117–44. She understood that in the April raids 'there are only 30 killed, although many in hospital' (17 April). Officially, 79 civilians in Barrow were killed by German bombing in 1941, all or almost all of them in April–May; there were only four further deaths from raids in Barrow during the remaining four years of the war (National Archives, HO 198/245).

shelter (cost, £12) but did not get around to ordering one until the evening of 14 April, after the first attack. Five days later this welcome protective device arrived, and they put it in the dining room. 'It does not look too bad and I'm schooling myself not to be too fussy' (19 April).

Friday, 9 May. Another night of it – and this time the Yard has got it. Thank God the men are not in a night shift under the areas of glass roof. Cliff [*home on leave for a few days*] and I had a really serious talk. He says 'It's all right you taking this "The coward dies a thousand deaths, the brave but one" line like Fred does, but you are not strong and your nerves will only stand so much and you must make arrangements for getting a good night's rest sometimes. Let's see what we can do.' So off we went to Spark Bridge and on our way called in Mary's, my cousin at Greenodd. After a chat we decided to take a small mattress and a rubber bed up and my three best blankets and we could be sure of a bed for she has only two and if we took one it would mean either Uncle or her sleeping in a makeshift one. The trek out of Barrow was unbelievable. They went on everything, from a big outgoing lorry that had brought half finished machinery parts to the Yard to a push bike and a baby pram. A lot are homeless now and try and get their things where they will be safe. Six grown-ups pile into Aunt Sarah's tiny cottage and it's more than a bit galling to have the two Londoners smugly lock their door and go to bed early – and only living there through Ruth Tomlinson's 'gesture of grandness' when she 'lent them a cottage for a little rest from the London blitz' and she only paying to have her furniture stored in Aunt's cottage! Aunt was too kind and too tired to make a fuss and did not like to point out that only storage was being paid and it's gone on since a month before Xmas. Now with Aunt having so many to worry about in Barrow I don't know what the outcome will be. The Miss Harts are quite nice women but the type who give up all and scuttle for good – the elder was a Town Councillor at Epping and has resigned from everything.

I never thought I'd be so thankful to see either of the boys go as I was to see Cliff go, and the trains ran from the Central station in spite of the wreckage. Hundreds of people jostled and milled to get into the train and the London and south travellers had to fight to get into it. The poor things with bundles and bedding were only going one or two stations out and there should have been a 'local', and a *free* one, even if only made up of wagons. It was so pitiful to see the look of terror at being left for so many lived round the steel works and the Yard. In all that crowd I heard no whimpers, no complaining. A few 'Aye, we got a direct hit in our street' or 'Blast made all our houses unfit to live in'. I've always been fascinated by words all my life – had a real Rosa Dartle complex [*an enquiring, discontentedly sceptical character in Dickens's* David Copper-field] and 'wanted to know you know' not only the meaning of a thing but 'meaning behind the meaning' in dictionary. The word 'morale' has had a fascination for me lately and I've sought and sought its hidden meaning. It seemed a mixture of 'moral' and 'rally' and now I'm quite convinced it is – all the 'moral' bits and bobs we have in our make up being 'rallied' and made into something new and splendid, like a new metal from materials that have been there and used for years.

The damage to station was bad but order was coming out of chaos and tidy piles of planks and pieces of iron were about everywhere on platform. All the railway people have known me for years – my Dad was an accountant at the old Furness Railway. I stopped to chat to one old man who remembered him. I said 'Do you remember the red geranium in the signal box window in the old days?' He said 'Aye – and when a tip of tuppence got you a drink of beer if you wanted it, and now 2s is no use at times for a drink or a smoke!' Cliff surprised me by telling me that this week most of the hotel bars in Barrow have been closed after 10 – no draught beer and little bottled and little or no spirits or wine. He said 'One double or two halves' for the evening was the ration for all the customers and 'chance' drinkers only got one – or none!

When we came home I learned with pleasure that the service buses were all running free after a certain hour to take anyone out to nearby districts. They have been sleeping in hedges and fields all round outside town. No one has any faith in shelters for after first small attacks when people died in bed and amid their ruined homes and the shelters stood up unharmed practically all deaths have been in shelters when houses crashed on them. In the centre of town last night it was dreadful for after the bombs started to fall and crash the poor things rushed from the little box-like back streets shelters into their houses and then out into street, frantic with fear and not knowing where to go. We have no really decent shelters. I don't think our Council ever really thought we would 'get it'. I don't really think many people did.

Sunday, 11 May. A night without an alert – perhaps for the devil murderers to make a mass attack on London [*where there was a particularly deadly blitz*]. We were keyed up and waken at the usual time, about 1 o'clock, and puzzled when we heard aircraft circling and yet no barrage – the first time fighters had done sentry go! I have packed all I can in parcels and bundles for ease of removal in case of need. There are hundreds of houses untenanted with no roof tiles or doors and we may too have to seek somewhere for our goods and chattels in a hurry and I'll plan for a swift handling. Meanwhile I've pushed all under stairs and will make small strong sacks tomorrow and put all my tinned goods in them tied up strongly – wooden boxes are quite unobtainable now. If we get a direct hit nothing will matter but if it's only messy blast that makes a house unfit to live in I'll want no delay to pick up separate things for I'll have to work fast. All I can jam under stairs I do so in the hope of salvage and all our decent clothes hang there – several things on each hanger and all suits of my husband's and Cliff's have either a nightdress of mine slipped over and pinned or a dust sheet to protect from dust.

Monday, 12 May. There is no shortage of meat, fish, biscuits, milk – even cigs seem more plentiful this week and it looks as if bombed towns had preference. The streets are littered with heaps of debris put on kerb and people push hand carts or follow carts with their bits of household treasures on. There must be hundreds of houses unfit to live in. Snatches of conversation as I passed were of 'bombs in parlours', 'a tree right on roof and 'im only planted it the day before and it cost him 5s 6d'. 'I only noticed I'd odd shoes on when I stopped to pick my dropped glove off ground'. 'There's martial law in Liverpool – the people have all rebelled.' 'They are Polish airmen in the patrol over Barrow. They put them on when there's extra guarding to be done for they hate the Germans so much and stick at nothing.' I made some small sacks and my husband has got a few small boxes to pack any stored goods in for easy lifting in case we have to get out in a hurry, but dear knows where we would go. Half the town seems to have taken in someone else and no street or few houses have escaped damage of some kind. I heard talks of Barrow women who *still* go shopping and grabbing to Kendal and Morecambe and the traders say they are helpless to stop it. Rot! If I was a trader and someone asked for a scarce article I'd politely ask to see identity card – and then *not* so politely refuse the greedy grabbers. I often feel that we all need a bit more aggressive spirit – the grab alls seem to have wakened to the idea. Why not people who try and do the decent thing and want to help and not hinder? My husband says 'Always some bee in your bonnet. If it's not one thing it's another.' He is such a pacifist and half the times my 'bees' are indirectly buzzing in his direction! He was really furious when I'd not go out of town every night, but just because someone said I had 'guts and was the type to stick it' he goes about as if he has grown a tail and talks of 'It takes more than a few bombs to chase MY wife out of town!' Men *are* so odd. I often feel I give up trying to understand them at all. Perhaps they feel like that about us!!

Tuesday, 13 May. A busy morning and a rush to get washed before lunch and ready for out and down at Canteen for 2 o'clock. I called in the bank and had to wait, with one eye anxiously on clock, until bank clerk had explained in detail the land mine that wrecked his home – same one as Mrs Waite's – and his reactions and his wife's and his wife's mother's and the Wardens at Post and so on! And I called in a shop and the girls had their heads together swopping bomb stories. Perhaps it's a good sign really for people up to now seem to have had a sick dumb horror and if they talk of their battered homes and losses they will not fret. It's really unbelievable on looking round that in the whole week there has only been 50 or so deaths up to now, although there are a lot of casualties. Ruth told me that in big Shop where her boyfriend works at Yard there was a call for fire-watchers last Saturday night, after considerable damage was done in early hours. Out of the hundreds of men and in spite of 30s. a night being offered only five volunteered. They had the laugh on their companions for nothing happened and they picked up £3 easily, for it was for Saturday and Sunday. All the men out of work are put on demolition and tidying up and feeling a bit 'green about the gills' over it with it being the first time. There is a Bristol foreman on one shift and he delights in telling real horror yarns and 'setting their teeth on edge'!

Wednesday, 14 May. There's always odd yarns knocking about but it's not often one hears of a true *and* funny one at first hand. A tradesman here living in a big house had his two sons and their wives and babies staying – bombed out of their homes. They had no shelter in spite of all their money and plenty of room for one – he was one of the 'They'll never come here' line of thought. Last Sunday when so many high explosives dropped a huge bomb fell opposite their house on Mrs Burnett's house and wrecked the front. Then there was a lull of noise and they became conscious of a tick tock, tick tock. TIME BOMB someone whispered and they all tore madly out of house and rushed over the hill. They were picked up and taken to Rest Centre and on investigation it was found that vibrations had set metronome on piano off that was used by the children when practising! ...

I've been the most popular woman in street today – easily! A shopkeeper has lost his nerve and is selling all and clearing out. He is a nasty piece of work and ran a cut price store and reports said that at times when he went buying to Manchester 'asked no questions' where stuff came from. My husband boarded his windows up and said 'If my wife had known you had been selling tinned milk she would have been down'. Today a huge box of milk syrup, tongue, stewed steak, glassed prawns and chicken – and jam – over £3 worth! I did not want it – I've got what will do me in an emergency and it only cost me ordinary prices as I slowly collected it, but other people I asked jumped at chance! The

jam and boxed cheese that Allan stored will be a liability. Women with
a rather dazed look have carried heaped baskets from his store – there is
no 'one only for each' – they have got *all* they asked for. He must have
had many thousands of pounds of stock saved for a rising market. He
paid excess profit on his turnover in the last war.

Friday, 16 May. We [*on the WVS mobile canteen*] went round demolition squads and bomb disposal squads, grave diggers and repair gangs
and the cry of 'The Jolly Roger' made me chuckle when they saw our
van – it's called that. When I looked at Mrs Cumming wrestling with
an engine that needed attention and when I'd nearly taken a header
out of a door that catch was faulty, I could only add amen to her lurid
description of the ultimate end of the sonofabitch who was responsible
for maintenance but who 'went out to sleep each night' and had 'absolutely *no* time'! I hope that Barrow is not representative of many other
towns – I do indeed. With the second-in-command of Home Guard, a
quarter of the special police and more than half ordinary Home Guard,
uncounted AFS† and Wardens and about *all* the voluntary fire watchers
flying into surrounding districts at about 8 o'clock at night, I wonder
what we *would* do if incendiaries fell in the numbers they seem to do in
other towns. Mrs Cumming is 'Naval', with all the Navy's 'gift of expression', and I thought her description of wooden-headed, fat-bottomed,
cigarette-grabbing, fur-coated louse for one woman who refused her
SOS was pretty good. I reflected that it was rather a pity I'd answered
the M-O question and posted it – I felt I could have really let myself go
on the question of conscription of women – for men too for that matter,
the Home Guard and AFS. Perhaps I am old fashioned but it seems so
dishonourable to go back on a 'plighted word' and so many rushed in
to avoid calling up into the Services. I thought they were a sorry lot at
the time and when I looked at Isa's husband [*Jack Hunter, a prominent
grocer*] I felt a better man than he was in spite of my 51 years and not too
good health as against his 34 years and thick set sturdy body.

I said to Mrs Cumming 'Let me get you a rota if you want one. I
know of quite a few eager ones – the "lower decks" of WVS are sound

enough. A lot of us waited for a call and there was so much muddle and confusion.' And she said savagely 'Pity the blasted bomb did not wipe out that inefficient creature of a Burnett [*head of Barrow's WVS*] and let someone take over who knew their own mind – AND had one to know.' I said 'She is really well meaning – she has no actual spite, you know', in a feeble effort to stick up for a fellow townswoman. Mrs C. said 'Bah – give me a real bad hat† if they are strong minded rather than a flapdoodle† with an elastic mind that anyone can pull in any direction'.

The destruction saddened me as we went from one group of demolition workers to another and to bomb disposal groups and grave diggers with our welcome hot tea and sandwiches. So many have been brought into town from districts outside town – Cumberland and Westmorland mostly, and many over age miners – and things are a bit at sixes and sevens yet. Others, coming into town by bus each day and returning to sleep, have no hot drinks but bring food and it's so bitterly cold. The barrage balloon boys try and wangle tea but we have to be hard hearted for they are well looked after by their own Army and Service vans that *never* give tea to any civilians and our tea has to go round so many. Looking round Barrow it's amazing to see the wasted bombs – the huge craters and shell holes in fields and sands and mud flats. A plane dropped bombs and land mines early this morning – stuff that could have wrecked half the Yard. It fell on mud flats with the exception of one in the docks that did little damage. Every street seems to be damaged, more or less, and few houses have escaped, but services have not been much damaged or disorganised and only about 50 deaths so far ...

I lay down each night with a prayer that if the raiders come they drop bombs in the sea and on the fields instead of on the poor people's homes and rise with a prayer of thankfulness if we have had a quiet night and that I can tackle all that comes my way in the day and take things as they come. Not very inspiring but very simple and not a bad rule of life – at least for ordinary people like myself.

Saturday, 17 May. When I got to Control I found no one had thought of a driver for mobile canteen and a mad hunt by phone began. *Such* a muddle all seems in – no rota of anything at all. At last we thought of applying to Mr Newman, the head of ARP – or seemed head – and he growled over phone that he 'would see what he could do' and hang on. After another wait he phoned that a fireman was on the way. I kept looking out and when I saw Mr Newman I walked to meet him. He is hilariously like Alfred Drayton, the stage and screen star, just his slightly jaundiced expression and hoarse hoot of laughter. He said 'Hallo Mrs Last, I did not know you were on control' and before I could answer went on about one thing and another and after a few minutes said 'I'll have to pop off. I've a darn fool WVS woman waiting to see me somewhere about!' I frowned and threw me coat back *à la* 'sheriff of Red Gulch' and showed my badge and he said 'God Lord! What are you doing in that bunch of saps?' I said 'Oh, I'm not in the Canteen really. I'm Hospital Supply really and only a Jolly Roger pro tem.' He said 'Well, take care it is only "pro tem" or they will drive you crazy for they work without system or sense!' I suppose all towns have the need of settling in, but oh dear, there does seem muddle and inefficiency, childish fear and cowardice and a dropping of all responsibility here.

Monday, 19 May. We went out in the car and sat by the sea. I read the papers. There were hundreds queued up to sleep out of town and the appalling muddle extends there for the Shipyard buses are filled at beginning of journey and then pass waiting men at places where they have always been picked up and brought in, and are now often an hour late for work! Why on earth the railway do not run a 'jitterbug' local and take them out and bring them back in again in the morning is a mystery; something like that will have to be done before long. Really the irritating little muddles everywhere is astounding. It's as if Barrow people, and especially the powers that be, have up to now lived in a beautiful dream and, waking suddenly, have the dazed 'Where am I?' of a person wakened up roughly. One good thing though – our War Weapons Week was a triumph and we made well over twice the amount we aimed at, £350,000 [*in savings stamps, certificates and bonds*], the price of a super sub' like the *Thetis.*

Talking over fence as we gardened, Mrs Atkinson said she felt tired. I said 'We have had peaceful nights – don't you sleep well?' and she said 'No, I take all up ready to fly up the street to shelter and feel as if I only sleep with one eye shut all the time'. I know there will be nearly £10 a week going into the house for her husband has a good position in the *Barrow News* printing works and the elder daughter is a typist and has a good post, and I said 'Why not get an indoor shelter like us and go to bed and feel safe? It's no use worrying about upset of a well kept home now. We have so much to think of.' A rather odd look crossed her face and she said 'Upset indeed. It's not that at all that keeps me from getting a shelter. I just cannot afford it. We put all spare money on the house and I have paid more than half – my husband thought it best. A year ago when we got the new furniture I got carpets, lino etc. that we could have done without, and you would stare if you knew how big a slice went out of my weekly allowance for "instalments". I'd buy a shelter tomorrow if I could get one by weekly payments.' I felt so sorry for her. She is such a nice neighbour and I reflected that a small allowance and no prospect of 'big money' is not always to be despised for it never allows for urges that would be tiresome to keep up and not leave a tiny margin for vital things.

The gardens are so dry and the big clouds pass over and it looks as if we are going to have a drought like last year. Green fly and 'maggots' are everywhere. The lonely beech I brought in was so ragged and 'eaten' this morning that I threw it out. Two of my three little apple trees look promising with blossoms, and the third is not too bad. It's curious, though, how different I feel about storage of food since our bombing. Perhaps it's seeing the smashed-flat look of houses getting a direct hit. Perhaps it's the knowledge of difficulty of getting furniture and goods not only salvaged but removed and stored; but a curious and hitherto unknown feeling wraps me round and seems to change my outlook entirely. I've not had it long enough to see it clearly but it's an odd *mañana* feeling, a 'live for today' I've never known in all my well ordered, well planned life. I've always *had* to dodge and contrive, save and plan, to do the things for my boys I set out to do, always to try and prepare for eventualities, to be able to meet setbacks, to 'have a cake in the tin' so to speak; to always face *anything* that could crop up, and that's saying a lot with those two boys. Cliff especially had a positive flair for the unexpected and to keep pace with that one's 'gift of friendship' and prepare for the oddments he picked up and brought home, from a stray cat or dog to a lonely Australian, homesick and ill in a London hotel, took careful budgeting, in time as well as money.

Now my little loved home is cracked and battered, my household goods packed for safety, my nice little dining room a bed sitting, and we don't undress properly. Perhaps it's the shock of it all; perhaps really I've been so shaken that all the veneer has pealed off, but I've a queer impatience with things – things I possess. I feel that 'one off and one on' would be the ideal, not cluttered up with things that don't matter at all. I reach to my well stocked shelf and get a tin of fruit etc. in a manner that before bombing would have been impossible – it was 'for the lean times' I feel sure will come. So far it's not spread to my garden and hens, perhaps because my chicks are so helpless and wee and need all my care. I've schooled myself never to look back. It took effort I did not think I possessed – iron control and a shutting down and a refusal to look back that for a time only found outlet in bitter sobbing in my sleep. That passed, and I found forgetting in work at the Centre, but I think it unknowingly strengthened my 'thought for tomorrow'. That's gone and very odd. My husband used to get so cross when I picked many flowers out of the garden. Now when I have a vase of big yellow daisies on the sideboard and my little table garden is gay with pieces of rock plants he just says 'It makes a place look gay to have flowers. We seem to have been a long time without many about.'

Thursday, 22 May. A bitter wind and threat of rain this morning but I got up early and got my chicks attended to, Miss Ledgerwood's breakfast made, and we were down early to Centre, and only six turned up, and five of Committee. I made a cup of tea as usual for it was so cold and draughty; it was dreadful in the whole building – puddles on the floor through holes in roof, no doors and wind sweeping through the church and down passages. Perhaps it was the dismal day but I'd a shadow on my heart, such a queer 'never more' feeling. We have lost so many members, and five of original Committee. Several more are 'staying out of town indefinitely'. Mrs Waite seems to be *so* different. Her brisk assertiveness has gone altogether and she turns to me with a queer loving smile and says 'Mrs Last will see to it, won't you dear?' and she said 'You are a good friend, my dear. You know you are faithful, not just to me but to Hospital Supply. Mr Waite said you were a kind little thing.' She sits quietly and looks her age and never seems to get cross with Mrs Lord's 'feather' outlook – and dear knows she is worse than usual lately. She should not be in any authority where she should be in a position to lead. She has no idea of giving a warm garment – and letting it go at that; she insists on rigging people out fully if she takes a fancy to them, and she really made me cross today. Old Mrs Nelson, one of our original members, is slightly doting and I should imagine has always had a somewhat clutching hand and if she sells raffle tickets for me begs both won articles and odd tickets off people. Mrs Waite and I don't like it but it's no use so we try and keep her in the background a little ...

I've only seen the farthest edge of things but, dear me, I've heard some things – graft and wangling to get a few extra pounds – and from people who would not steal a pin but as it's the Government seems to think it's perfectly right! It was good to hear of so many cases where our people had been so kind to each other and only getting to know each other by sitting sewing at same table, when homes went, offered beds and sanctuary, or storage for a few salvaged treasures. There are over 3,800 houses in Barrow damaged, not counting shops and business premises.

Our laugh today was hearty, even if the subject was macabre! I've grown from a child alongside two of our members, sisters, from a queer exhibitionist family who dramatised everything. They lost their mother of 85 in the air raid and someone was getting a bit weepy over the 'poor old dear – to live to that age'. I said 'Nonsense, it was a lovely end. Look at the poor things we know of dying with cancer and other terrible things. I hope my end comes like that.' Betty turned and said gushingly 'Yes, I feel like that and I saw that everything was beautiful at her funeral.' I said 'That was nice of you Bets. Flowers are more plentiful now and you would be able to have a lot.' Betty drew herself up and said 'I meant *behaviour*, Nell, not flowers. Mother brought us up proper and to know how to take our cue and my husband said when I was going to the funeral "Betty my dear, don't forget you are the leading lady today and your sisters are not here – you must PLAY YOUR PART"', and she struck a real Sarah Siddons [*a famous late eighteenth-century actress*] pose! She went on 'So I did. I knew Mother would have liked me to look nice and I look horrid in a black hat so I got this blue one and had my hair waved freshly and I stood at church door on steps and shook hands with everyone and said a few pleasant words and everyone seemed impressed!' – or dazed as the case may be!! Mrs Waite went out to a funeral – surprising the deaths there have been since the blitz that can be traced to those two terrible nights. This one was a man of only 47 whose house collapsed on him and although he seemed fit and well he collapsed and died the other day.

I looked at scanty and altered Committee as we sat and drank our afternoon cup of tea – so different altogether. Mrs Wilkins is a grand worker but was born and raised in Coniston and has the village woman's narrow outlook and rather tattling tongue and repeats little things she hears and I can already tell it will not make for smooth going. Mrs Higham is a thoroughly nice woman but thinks Mrs Waite is 'too autocratic altogether' and as she has not worked so long with her does not understand her as we do. Mrs Woods has a weathercock mind and veers round to opinions of the last one she spoke to, and Mrs Lord is charming but really maddening in her feather headed way – reminds me more and more of 'Mrs Feather' [*a character in the 1941 film* The Fine Feathers] in her way of dealing with things – and if things go wrong can with wishful thinking make them appear alright.

I'd such a sadness, such a feeling of 'Thanks for the memory – – –, We did have fun, and no harm done' of the song, but would have altered it to 'We did have fun and much good done'. We worked so splendidly together and our boxes of Red Cross work and comforts were really amazing. Surely all cannot be crumbling as I feel it; surely when things get a little more normal we can pull up and go on as we did. It was so good, so vital, the way we all pulled together and worked and laughed together. It is as if a bundle of sticks were untied. I've so realised the truth of the old adage 'United we stand, divided we fall'. I don't know whether it was the stolid partnership of Mrs Waite and Mrs Machin or the steady balance of a well tried Committee that kept Mrs Lord from getting too much say and pursuing such an erratic course – I cannot put my finger on it or find a cause I could alter, or try to anyway. Mrs Murray will leave now old Mr Smith is dead so she will not take Mrs Machin's place as secretary. I'm not clever – I cannot take it. Any talents I've got are to make people laugh and to make tea or smooth things over. I cannot add up or write business letters and so it would be hopeless for me to say I'd 'try and do it'.

I see a shadow on Mrs Waite's face. I feel that the shock of her ruined home is only beginning to be felt. I see 'interest' having to be turned to battered homes and evacuated children and the shifts being altered at Yard is another blow to our Hospital Supply. When men don't go out until 1.30 for the 2 o'clock shift or return at 2.30 from it, it is impossible to leave the house or meals. The queer 'What's the use of anything, anyway?' I feel as I reach for a precious tin off shelf and my tin opener seems like the green fly in my garden, spreading to everything. I'd like to go to some badly blitzed place and go round invisibly and hear and see if they feel or felt like we do and for the first time since I've done M-O I've got an idea – only a glimmer – of the sense and value behind it. For those of us who come through this mess there will be an adjusting and a fighting that will be hard and I see the word 'reactions' as a shuttle weaving in and out of tattered threads and binding and repairing them into a pattern strong enough to 'hold' until stronger measures by younger hands are ready.

Saturday, 31 May. When an alert wakened me last night and the steady beat of waves of bombers going over and the crash of A-A[†] gunfire started, I wondered if there *was* a means of knowing in which direction to expect trouble, particularly when cousin Mary told me the Lancaster firemen had come into Ulverston. I felt really angry when I got to Spark Bridge and learned how another cousin – Aunt Eliza's daughter – and her husband had crammed all their hoards into Aunt Sarah's cottage and taken oddments of Aunt Eliza's furniture, including a feather bed. That meant Aunt Sarah having to give up her bedroom – she has only two and her old cousin Joe has the other one – and move up into an attic which is only an 'apple loft' really and not meant for beds for it's only a very small space for standing up in and the rest slopes so much. It's stifling hot or freezing cold and I looked at Aunt Sarah and thought what a shame she should be so put on after a hard life and at 76. I really did fly off the handle and I said 'Hell roast the lot of the selfish, greedy pigs, Auntie. They never looked near you till now. WHY do you be so spineless and let them walk over you?' She said 'Come, come my dear, such language. Swearing never got anyone anywhere! It will pass and they had nowhere else to go to!' I could feel better if the Londoners had not the whole cottage next door, or if they would be nicer about things for they know Ruth [*Tomlinson*] only pays to have her furniture stored and it was a gesture on her part to seem big in 'lending a cottage in the peaceful Lakes, my dear' ...

All is so hushed and still and the rising moon so bright. The balloons only look like floating silver toys in the soft light and the scent from my lilac bush is overpoweringly sweet. I've a great bunch in the dining room and a bowl of lily of the valley – on top of air raid shelter! So quickly have I got adapted to that steel monster I don't think anything at all about it now and get ready for bed and turn in comfortably and securely. The planes and guns 'terrify' me and yet don't 'frighten' me – a queer subtle difference. The recurrent noise makes me feel very sick and ill but not that I'd run away and hide. Rather does a hot wild feeling creep over me, a mixture of rage and stubbornness and a passionate desire to strike back. In my way of thinking Hospital Supply and its continuance, the tea made and served by the Jolly Roger, even my dollies and little chicks are a part of my weapon – a feeling of 'I'll *not* give in; they are MINE and I'll fight for them'. If I'm beaten that's that, but I'll not give anything

I've got up without a struggle, *and* I find hidden strength and hardness in my nature that I never suspected. I've always been so weak minded and loved peace that I'd give way often when I'd rather have done other things, but that's gone and I know I'm really fanatical if I thought a thing was right and nothing would make me turn aside. I wonder if this feeling is the English way that makes people say we are good fighters. It's a new and remarkably strange feeling for an up-to-now gentle woman who liked peace above all things and to whom stubbornness and pig-headedness was a fault if not a downright sin!

Thursday, 5 June. We heard last night that our smokescreen lamps were to be lit and were warned that food had to be covered and any silk materials in the way of curtains etc. taken down. Mrs Atkinson and I were both tired and we decided to close windows, and open them if there was an alert. I hate closed windows even though I tried to get plenty of fresh air in house earlier in evening and then left the dining room open and work ended with a heavy sickly headache and it was a big effort to get ready to go to Centre. I felt thankful I'd mixed my chicks' food last night and I left extra bowls of water about for them and scattered a lot of coarse crumbs. Mrs Higham called and ran me down and after opening up I went shopping and to see if wool shops had had any instructions about further wool supplies for us. There were queues for chocolates at one shop – they allowed 1s worth for each person – for tomatoes at 6s 6d a pound! – cigarettes, sausage, biscuits, silk stockings and meat pies!! I said to my grocer 'I wonder what some of them will do when war is over. I don't think they can bear to see anything in a shop window or on shelves.' He said 'That's a fact, and there's a greedier spirit growing daily. If I get anything in I keep it in the back now. I don't keep it on show.' We share a real prejudice against queues and the feeling behind them and we often talk over ways and means to do away with them – there is really no need. If people would be content with a little share, as grocer decided his stock would divide, and all took it when and how it was best, it could be managed and marked off a card issued privately. The Co-ops here have a good non-queue system, except in the chemists who carry cigarette stocks. It's a list of things like tinned salmon, tinned fruit, milk and dried fruits and before they were rationed syrup, honey, jam and cheese. A card did not guarantee a supply exactly – women had still to go once or twice a day on the days the stocks arrived – but if the man who put up order saw the 'green ticket', as list was called, had few stars to cross off any dainty bit, he had a small stock to draw on, and it makes for a much fairer distribution and stops the real hunting instinct possessed, or generally said to be so, by all small boys and many men – 'What a funny thing, let's kill it', or 'collect it', as the case might be. We laughed at ourselves over lunch. We had all seemingly passed through the stage I had when, after the blitz and we saw many people's furniture carted off, I wondered if my store cupboard and shelves were a debit rather than an asset and started to use things rather freely; and anyone who was short I let buy with less thought of the future. I soon settled down but talking today I got a glimpse of a difference in thought – an acceptance that life was changing and would change in increasing tempo ...

The odd and really bewildering thing is how little people – myself included – talk of war. When I can recall the really bitter arguments of my Dad and his friends over the Boer War when I was a child and the endless conjectures and 'Now *I* would have done this, or that' of Great War, and now when it looks as if it *is* the Armageddon of *Revelations* that was foretold, well, people just don't seem to bother nearly so much. When I see people I know who lost their homes and shops and businesses in our blitz, I see their 'sayonara' acceptance and I cannot quite understand what it can be. It's not bravery or morale – or is it the latter, I wonder, a hybrid word for a hybrid state of mind? We used to say 'Poor Mrs So & So, she never got over the loss of her husband, or son etc.', and when I saw Noel Coward's *Cavalcade* and Diana Wynard's moving acceptance of the loss of her loved boys I'd a feeling of '*beautiful*, but not quite true to life'. Now every day I hear of something as beautiful – loved boys who will never come back, quite young wives whose husbands are going overseas and who turn to work and not to 'dance little lady' ways of thought and living, and a general feeling of 'we cannot alter things – why worry – if it happens it happens'.

Tonight we went to sit by the sea and met a local Home Guard. I teased him about the second in command, Chislett, our Town Clerk, who was such a valiant soldier until the guns went off and now goes off at 6 o'clock and returns at 8 in the morning, and the worst of it is that where he sleeps is quite three miles even from a phone. I mentioned a few more 'gingerbread' soldiers, in a teasing mood, but he was not to be drawn. He just smiled and said 'There's going to be a bit of a shock all round this next fortnight – you will see', but would say nothing more. By the hooky, though, I'd like to see a few of them made to remember that they *were* Home Guards and ARP Wardens and AFS. The latter *have* tightened up and Isa complains bitterly that 'poor Jack cannot get out to Ulverston every night but has to sleep in the nasty old AFS station every night'. A really vindictive spirit possesses me about some of our Home Guard. I looked at them when they joined and *knew* it was only a save-my-skin policy rather than a desire to do their duty to their country, and the ones who have stood fast are in most cases men who would be liable to crack through health or age in a big struggle.

Sunday, 8 June. At Ulverston yesterday I watched the plainly dressed country folk buying eagerly – 'real' country folk whose grandams and grandys had to rear big families on such tiny wages. Everything alters so quickly nowadays as if things change and go faster and faster. There were few farm hands about in spite of the Whit week – Martinmas [11 *November*]. There used to be big fairs at our country towns and big hiring days when likely lads and lasses who did not 'want to stop on' lined up for inspection down the main street. The strongest looking were snapped up first and in a bad year – and looking back the farmers had so many of them – few but the best got hired and one met disconsolate farm hands with a knot of straw in their buttonholes – a sign they sought service – wandering round the cheap jack stalls and merry-go-rounds and freak shows. How I loved the fair days when I stayed with Gran for school holidays and when nothing would have stopped me going for Whit. People on farms divided into shifts – two generally – and the older ones got up and went off and left the young ones to milk and do morning chores and returned early to do evening milking and feeding – why worry when the fun, including the dancing, started at 9 o'clock in the morning (!!) and went on till midnight on at least four days of Whit week? Gran never hired from the Fair – not in my memory for her servants 'stopped on' and when they left there always seemed younger additions of the family who were eager to follow older brothers and sisters, so our visits to Fair were for fun and to meet friends not likely to be seen for another year. Every corner of Ulverston seemed changed yesterday – memories of 'that's where the Circus always stood' and 'that corner always had a fat man with a trumpet who played a few ear splitting notes and then yelled WALK UP, WALK UP'. I was always so curious about it all, until I heard my Uncle and his friends roaring with laughter and plotting something in which an Ambleside 'wrastler' were mixed up and I think it must have been a boxing booth and one of the Lakeland lads I think got the better of the professional.

It's odd to lie scribbling for a thing like M-O under an indoor iron shelter and think of peace filled leisurely days like those – only 'over my shoulder' and yet as far away as the days of ancient Rome! ...

Today at Morecambe Bay two carfuls of happy people sat within earshot and I caught scraps of conversation, and there was so little of war and war worries. Even the clothes coupons were dismissed with jokes about 'having to go into pants to save stocking' and an energetic little boy was begged to 'remember his pants' as he scuffled happily on concrete edge of grass edging, but the rest of the talk seemed to be of 'whether our Margaret should stand so much of Bill's nonsense – girls were daft nowadays to bother about things like that'. I was so curious about Margaret's particular daftness! Priestley was discussed and dissected and argued over. Opinions were divided whether BBC had given him a 'raw deal' and whether he was 'touchy' and wanted a fuss made over him. One man 'believed that Priestley and Churchill were not too friendly' and one said JBP was a Communist really and was 'agin the Government' all the time. Odd how I've never read anything like that in his kindly human talks.*

I could not help seeing their picnic and spread from where I sat and wonder if they had the curious little feeling I had about stored things – a wonder if it was worth going on saving them so closely. There was tinned fruit and cream and chocolate biscuits to help out the marg and bread and they were so happy and gay. At one time I would have envied their gaiety and longed to have the boys or friends of my own, and it would have made me chafe at my husband's dislike of company, or what was worse at times his spasms of liking it and then if I invited people I had the agony of wondering if he would offend, or amuse, which was so hatefully worse, by his attitude. Now nothing ruffles me, and I seem in some odd way to have reached a feeling or state of 'being' rather than 'wanting to be', a queer acceptance of all that comes along. I wonder if it's the war or the fact I'm getting older and the fires of youth are dying. So hard to define really. It's not that I'm getting resigned. I find myself 'going up in the air' and sticking to the point of things as never before. Rather is it a 'tomorrow and tomorrow and tomorrow' feeling and that each day as it dawns has to be threaded on to a chain smoothly and fairly, not ground by worrying, not chipped by regrets or attempts to alter it by futile attempts that only fray the chains and don't alter the 'bead' – not really. It sounds like a cheap Eastern philosophy when defined – best not to think of it at all.

Tuesday, 10 June. There was a tendency to blame Chamberlain for his way of 'giving in', but we have been at war 18 months and muddle and overlapping and wishful thinking rule. Will we never wake up, or fight with tooth and nail and with every scrap of energy and force? Sometimes I see us dragging on for years and years and years, killing, destroying, maiming, starving in those countries where fighting is fierce and there

---

* J. B. Priestley's famous radio talks started on 30 May 1940 and ended on 24 September that year. They were vastly popular (his popularity rivalled that of Churchill), although many Conservatives objected to his socialist leanings, and it was widely thought that his BBC appearances were terminated as a result of political pressure.

is no chance of a harvest. Fighting and muddling on and coaxing work-people not to take holidays or buy luxuries and save their money and their paper and old iron – coax, coax, coax. When the boys were small I ruled supreme – as wisely and kindly as I knew how – but supremely because I knew best what was good for the future for them and because I was wiser than they were. Why don't clever wise people rise and take a lead? Aren't they asked? Don't they want to bother? I've always main-tained that a small select body of men, strong and ruthless as Churchill is, clear seeing and experienced as he, should be in full charge. Parlia-ment as we know it should go – and for good. Talk about the 'will of the people'. I've met more silly boring flannel-brained people who were in Westminster, or wanted to get there, than seems possible. I've listened to such silly, childish, one-sided arguments, such fiery windbags with views and opinions that made me either annoyed or smile indulgently as I listened. To even *think* of them making broth for those running the country would be bad enough, never mind about them having power to shilly shally. Those poor lads on the beaches, the broken hearts and lives of the women who loved them – is there no magic or power in their agony? Must all be in vain and go on repeating itself until everything is gone? I look at barricades of coiled wire netting, smokescreen lamps, A-A guns and balloons floating up in the air. Men *must* pull together to think and carry out schemes like that, but in big things there always seems such a muddle.

CHAPTER FOUR

FACTS OF LIFE

June–September 1941

Wednesday, 11 June. We have had papers round from billeting officers to fill in giving in all particulars as to space etc. in houses. I'm curious as to what happens. I feel I should be let keep the boys' bedroom for them and I've got some of my sister-in-law's things here until they get their house mended fit to live in and I've two days at Centre and half a day on mobile canteen. In our short road there are 12 houses empty at nights and for best part of day, for owners do not get in until 10 and leave again at 4 or so. Five are empty altogether and owners are staying out of town for duration. I feel I cannot possibly undertake to work and look after billeted men, not without giving up Centre, and I feel that there are so many who should be made to do their bit, and may well never do it until they are compelled, and after all it's over two years since I joined with WVS and kept on steadily and sometimes I feel as if it's less and not more work I want and especially of late.

We had a big round – two big rounds of tea. I had a woman driver – Mrs Cumming was engaged – and we could not pass the smoke blackened soldiers toiling in the hot sun clearing the smoke screen lamps. We are only supposed to look after demolition gangs but the YMCA does not get round much. We were pestered to death to do something about getting cigarettes and tobacco in van; we only have tea now and when we had anything else it was only sandwiches. The bulk of men – some hundreds – come into town each day, some having a two hour coach journey and they have neither time to queue up at home in Cumberland or in Barrow. I said 'Sorry, but we cannot help you. You must get your wives to queue at home for you. Women have to do it here for their husbands.' One man said 'What I want to know is – where is all the tobacco and cigs going, for by all accounts there's a shortage everywhere, even in army canteens?' When we drove off, Mrs Ricketts, my driver, said musingly 'I believe everyone is smoking more. I rarely smoked or bought sweets and chocolates until recently and now I always feel I want a "cig or a choc" handy.' I said 'It's a pity that Wrigley's chewing gum seems to have vanished – and "sucky" sweets', and she heartily agreed. We wondered if rather restricted diet had anything to do with 'craves' for cigs or chocs, and for the way women queued for them ...

Tonight we went and sat by the sea on Walney Island. All was so peaceful and still – and happy. Far out in the low tide soldiers bathed and frolicked on the sands and happy children – and dogs – played. Strangers laugh at the Walney dogs for, like those of Scarborough, they know when the tide is coming in and gravely trot off alone, if no one takes them, for a swim in the hope of meeting someone to throw a stick in water for them. They swim, play awhile and then make for home. More and more rolls of barbed wire are being put round Walney and Irish Sea and Morecambe Bay, and I wondered if the 'big ones' – some of them – had got bees in their bonnets about Ireland. My husband and the boys have always been amused at my insistence on Eire being such a danger spot but when I read in papers odd bits lately I fear I am not alone in my dread of that divided land – not that unity in a land is much good against the terrible might of Germany. They seem to have tapped a source of force and evil that never before had been tuned into by man – some dreadful 'natural' force.

Sunday, 15 June. I packed tea after all and we went and sat by Lake Windermere, and to our surprise found it a lot warmer – must be a sea wind. All was so lovely after the rain and I'm astounded at promised crops on new ploughed land – green sheets of grain blades without a weed and huge fields of potatoes neat in their banked rows. The haysel[†] is well up – quite a foot – and will soon be ready for first cutting. What really puzzles me is how all the crops round here will be gathered, and especially when I think of all the extra crops sown in the rest of the country. More than school boys or 'proffered labour' will be needed. My husband reminded me of last war and German prisoners helping but I cannot see, in the view of invasion, that it would be feasible now. The peace and quiet was like a blessing and at Bowness hundreds of people had come from mill towns in motor coaches – I counted 49 big ones on one parking place alone and there were many more. When I look at car registrations from so far away I'm always amazed at the amount of petrol they must have – people I can tell are on holiday or on a short school day trip.

As I sat so quiet and still a question in M-O that I had done this morning came back into my mind – the war's effect on sex. Speaking personally, I could only say that at 51 sex questions answered themselves, war or no war.* But I began to think, perhaps it was the scantily clad girls with shorts rolled back to show thighs – so many unfortunately would have been better covered. It's so rarely a girl with really shapely limbs bothers to display them, and also the too thick or thin, the bandy, spotty red or knock kneed girl who delights in exhibiting them! It came as a real surprise to go back in thought to when I was a girl, and after all that's not such a very great while since. I remembered an incident that a parish nurse once told me. Before Health Insurance most churches had a nurse to look after the sick poor of parish and this one was so good and kind – did that little more always. She was attending a woman who was far on her journey with TB and who had at times to stop in bed. Hearing she was not so well nurse went round early to get the children washed and ready for school. Not expecting nurse so early the woman called wearily over the stair rail and thinking it was her husband off night shift, 'Is that you John? Do you "want me" before I get dressed?' The husband came in just then and not quite catching what was said shouted 'What's that?' and on the question being repeated said 'Aye' simply. That seemed the whole keynote of married life. To greater and lesser degree, a woman was expected – and brought up – to obey. We had not got far from the days of Victorian repression. Men expected to

---

* It is likely that by the early 1940s, at the latest, Nella and Will had ceased to have sexual relations. (The Directive Responses for 1941, including hers, have not survived.)

be masters in, widely, sex questions. No woman was ever expected to be out, for instance, when her husband came in for a meal. Gosh, how I've nearly broken my neck to race home in time to brew tea and pour it, although rest of meal was laid ready! No woman was let go on a holiday alone – that is in Barrow. I think perhaps Barrow was extra provincial by its geographical position, shut off as it were on an island.

Last war was the start of a difference in sex life in a general way with men having to go to France but women did not always behave too well. There were some gay goings on and one heard whispers of 'women in the know' that the munitions girls and women said 'got one out of trouble and kept one out of trouble'. I had been married four – nearly five – years before I knew of such a thing as birth control as a 'decent' thing and not as a 'horrible French practice'! I went down to live in Southampton when my husband went into RNVR.[†] He was a C3 man[†] and got a shore billet which meant he could get home weekends and I went and lived in the New Forest to make a home nearby. I remember the crowds of disreputable and diseased looking girls and women who infested camps on roads where soldiers went, the way that the soldiers seemed to shout after you if you were out alone and the bold glances you were always conscious of. I worked in a canteen after my Cliff was born [*in December 1918*] – just odd times for I was always ailing. Girls were either unwilling or not let [*to go out*] by their mothers for the soldiers were regarded as 'wild beasts seeking whom they may devour' kind of thing! Now I sense a different spirit. One never sees the pub doors disgorge groups of fuddled soldiers and harpies either hanging on to their arms or waiting outside. Lads and men with set faces walk in groups, bathe in big batches off the shore at Walney and kick a bundle of tied up paper about if they have no football. Everything in the sex respect is altering. When I think of naughty old men I knew engaging front seats at a music hall we had then 'because they could see the girls' knees when they danced', and when I think of what they could see of the 'female form divine' (?) on a country walk – well, I chuckle. As to actual intercourse, what sweeping changes *must* have taken place with everyone being parted, civilians through evacuation as well as soldiers.

At one time it was taken as a foregone conclusion that if a man left his wife alone or vice versa they 'asked for all they got' if the one left behind 'went off the rails'. Yet here in Barrow I've not noticed anything much different and when I tried once to explain my views to Cliff – about Army then – he said 'Ah, they *dope* the Army lads – give 'em bromide or something'. I laughed and said 'I see. You all line up and take it like good boys – like Mrs Squeers [*the abusive and sadistic wife of the master of a brutally run boarding school in Dickens's* Nicholas Nickleby] and her brimstone and treacle.' He said 'No, they put it in our tea', which seems a bit tough on the two and three cup men!!

Monday, 16 June. I smiled at the tickets on dresses etc. Instead of 'Smart, Chic, Up-to-date, Fashion Latest' etc., already tickets boasting 'Solid Value, Good Wearing, Good Value, Will Wear Well' are appearing. Just another straw in the wind that is changing all and everything we have known! I heard of a girl going to be married to a man in RAF whose people are 'frightfully posh', as she put it, and whose home she will stay near if not actually in after her marriage. She has worked on our local paper, in the office, but still it's grubby enough there and she has worked a lot of overtime and like the rest of us 'let herself go' in stockings etc. but announced that she had plenty saved up and the week after she left work and the one before she married was to be a 'shopping orgy' and she would never wear a single thing of her old things after her marriage. She is distracted now. Gone are her plans for a fine wedding and trousseau and she is wondering how she will even 'look decent' on 22 coupons. Several friends have given odd pieces of dainty underwear as wedding presents but as she wails 'My stockings alone'. Although it's laughable at sight, I hate to think of the way she has worked so long and such trying hours, denying herself, and then contrast her to some women with such a lot of time and money and who *can* brag and *do* of huge stocks of now rationed things, particularly stockings.

My husband was working in a jeweller's shop today – our best shop where 'presentation' things like silver tea sets and gold watches etc. are made a big feature and where people go when they subscribe for a really good canteen of cutlery for a workmate. He said he was staggered by the money passed over counter and he said 'You would not believe me if I tried to tell you of the gold wristlet watches, the expensive rings etc. – and the requests for *solid* silver articles. They were not plated or pewter tea sets and trays asked for and any cut glass had to be "the very best".' I said 'Ah, I'd believe anything, *however* fantastic in the spending line, and I know a woman whose hands fascinate me – work worn hands now wearing rings that a duchess would not turn her nose up at – and not just one! I think it is a kind of investment in some cases to avoid income tax – or compulsory saving.' I've heard the remarks 'Goods are better than money' so often and I sometimes think it's a bit muddled thinking, as regards expensive jewellery at any rate, for if the war goes on we shall all be so beggared that a covering will be all that will be expected and we will have grown very simple in our tastes. It looks somehow as if a new society is growing nowadays. Instead of the old order – the aristocrat and the 'lesser orders' – there will be those who have 'given and striven' and who are left with nothing – health, home, breadwinner, in some cases hope itself – and the other will have leisure and comfort and scrounged rations from black markets, money saved, hoards of everything – and devil a bit of 'sacrifice'. Perhaps Hitler and his airmen will level up things a bit but it's going to be a very oddly different world when the pot ceases to boil and the world settles again, and it *will* be a new order in all conscience.

My next door neighbour called over and said 'Would you like to go to a whist drive tonight up at St Mathews? Only a little affair in aid of the organ fund.' I was eager to go. I like doing things rather than watching them and get more pleasure out of a whist drive than out of the pictures, unless it's a really good show. It was 1s, and the organiser had announced it in the paper as it was so short notice and she 'did so want to raise £5 or £6 and then about £2 off a raffle'. It started at 7, or was supposed to, but the way people rolled in was amazing till we remembered that things are so at a standstill in Barrow. It's not Hospital Supply alone that has gone down but all little whist drives and dances too, many through the halls where they were held being damaged and many taken over for the soldiers and one – the largest – for a Commu-nal Feeding Centre [*soon to be known as a British Restaurant*], but when I saw the different kinds of people so eager for 'a bit of forgetfulness', as I heard one woman say, I thought it such a pity more efforts had not been made to keep on. I recalled my husband's words as to jewellery buying very forcibly for by the time the game started there were 84 tables – and they prepared for 30! Some cards ran out and people played using pieces of paper and cards were used that looked positively mouldy – dug up from any old corner or borrowed from anywhere! One woman I played with had a brooch buckle on. It was the loveliest thing of its kind I'd seen, a simple ring of diamonds about the circle of a penny piece. I did not know her but listened eagerly to scraps of talk of it. I gathered that she had always wanted a ring – a diamond ring that would 'knock' all her friends – but when her husband got enough money her hands had knotted with work and rheumatism, and as she good humouredly chuckled 'Nothing would do my hands justice except gloves'. Business had taken her husband to London and she had gone to see this brooch at Gooches (?) and immediately wanted it, and it had cost over £100!!! On a woman who always did her own work – or up to now anyway – it was a queer adornment.

Wednesday, 18 June. Ruth was busy working about and I said suddenly 'I'd a question in M-O about sex, Ruth. It was really a personal ques-tion but I've wondered, really, what was others' opinions. Do *you* think thoughts, or actions, differ about sex since the war?' She wrinkled her brow seriously and rubbed energetically for a moment or two and then said 'Well, it's hard to put what I think into words, but once all the boys and girls round us seemed to tell dirty stories and jokes and kiss and cuddle in every corner as soon as it was dusk, but now it's as if they *do* things and don't talk about them. I cannot tell you exactly – I don't mean they are "bad". It's as if people don't think it's wrong any more, or giggle about so and so and her being "as good as married"'. She said earnestly 'Life *is* different, Mrs Last. It seems now there is so little but work. There is no dancing or hiking and only about fortnightly can we go to the pictures in the evening or go off to see our pals on Gerald's (her boyfriend) motor bike, and there is less petrol and we never go to see Gerald's aunt in Leeds as we did.' As I looked at Ruth I suddenly saw how altered she was from the plump rosy girl she was four years ago when she first came to me. I recalled how she now scolded the dog and cat so for their paw marks or grumbled when it rained on her clean windows! ...

We finish with the mobile canteen this week – for the present. There are no demolition sites now without means of water, or gas etc. to heat it, and many of the men are being billeted. There has been heated controversy about supplying tea by ARP, and I had such an interesting talk with a 'ganger', as he called himself. I jokingly said 'I know you don't like us coming and stopping work but it's only for an odd few minutes and I'm sure the men work better'. He is a big scowling brute of a man with hands like hams and he struck his fist on canteen counter and said 'It's charity – just charity – and waste of your time as well as mine to give this pack of swine tea. They are the worst bunch of slackers and wasters I've ever struck!' I said as I looked over group of men sitting on debris drinking tea, 'Pooh, you should see *some* of the gangs. These are all strong men – and many look as if they draw Old Age Pensions.' He snorted angrily 'Mine are mostly *Irish*' and the way he said it I felt startled at real venom! I said 'Well, if my memory serves, the Irish – and the Italians – have always supplied the ganger with most of his labourers', and got the answer 'Lady, do you know what's the curse of the boss's life today?' Rather haughtily I said 'shortage of cigs' but the ferocious look on his face showed real frenzy of feeling as he went on. 'Do know how much he – and he – and he gets a week?' pointing to different men. 'Well, I'll tell you. This one got £6 4s od last week, one £6 14s od and one £9 8s od for he drives and loads the trucks!' I must have looked unbelieving for he called them over and they admitted it but said – the £9 8s od man – 'Sure what's the use of big money these days with the Government ready to claw the half of it off you?' The ganger said something else very surprising for he said, in front of men who could have contradicted him, 'Thank goodness for one thing, though. They don't

get off home as often as they did. They could work for six months, stay
in Ireland ten days and get their fares paid over and 24s 6d "subsistence"
allowance and *pay no income tax.*' I must ask Arthur [*a tax inspector*]
about that – sounds fantastic!

Thursday, 19 June. Everyone at Centre today seemed edgy and touchy
and there was a queer 'What do you think of things now? Do you *really*
think Turkey is our friend, or is she edging and will join Germany?'
Miss Ledgerwood and Mrs Waite have had a queer optimism that they
seemed to derive comfort from to a degree – that this month would see
'the beginning of the end'. From laughing or disagreeing with them I've
passed into a consoling 'Well, perhaps you are right' and today I said
'You know, you *may* be right; this radio location may be that beginning'
and as we have – or are supposed to have – the largest experiment in it
here in Barrow, they looked a bit cheered. Then there seemed dismal
remarks about the strike among some thousands in Yard and I heard
of a meeting today with a Government man who had come down from
London to settle things. There is a more bitter feeling about our 'new
rich' springing up than I've yet known. It's caused by them being able
to go out each night either in their own cars or clubbing together in
a friend's car. They go out and stay at an outlying farm and have bed
and breakfast – home cured ham or bacon and eggs – and bring in
butter and fresh eggs and in some cases cream and home made jams and
chutney bought at fancy prices from farmers' wives. I said 'Why don't
you let the Food Control know if you have proof? Why grumble and
growl and say and do nothing? If eggs are being had 1s a dozen more as
you say they are, well, *someone* ought to suffer for it!'

Wednesday, 25 June. Ruth had to wait a long time at the Labour Exchange
and did not get up till nearly 10 o'clock ... I am to lose Ruth in a month
and the head of Labour Exchange said if Ruth would take advice from
her she would try and get post as nurse, even if for only two hours a day
to relieve a nurse. There is no chance of a post woman's job for they had
such a stampede that a fresh rule was made and only wives and sisters of

postmen were taken. They asked Ruth if she would go into industry or Services, particularly Land Army. Ruth is very like myself in some ways and has both a horror of noise and hatred of smells of oil and machinery and seems to rather shrink from 'launching out' in ATS.[†] All her talents are in the home and with personal circle. She took all the little awards in St John's Ambulance and passed all examinations and then took her 100 hours to make her eligible for Civil Nursing. She is such a dear girl. I would not like her to be unhappy. She would work so much better if she could be in her own niche. I've written to Matron at the Hospital to see if she can help in any way. I think she will for I've always tried to help her all I could.

During the next two months Nella wrote a lot about housewifery and shopping. There are many references in her diary to rationing, prices and the scarcity of many goods – and queues, queues, queues. Perhaps Barrow really was worse off than other places. 'Food really does seem short in Barrow', she wrote, 'if we are to believe what people from other towns, or visitors to there, tell us. Queues are killing pastimes – beside time-wasting. Then again, so much house-keeping money is about among the Shipyard and Steel and Iron works men's wives, who feel quite rightly that their men *must* be fed.' (Overtime pay was swelling household coffers.) Some people grumbled a lot, others took pleasure in their successes in acquiring provisions off ration. As Nella observed, those who produced some of their own food, 'in a small way perhaps, have the same housekeeping problems [as industrial workers] and a little extra is welcome … It must be a temptation to supply "privately"… I'm not referring to the "big" black market – just the farmers and higglers and those who grow fruit and vegetables' (16 August).

The daily grind loomed large this summer. Nella recorded (sometimes in great detail) the prices in shops and at stalls, as well as people's search for cigarettes and other valued commodities; she wrote a lot about her chickens and her satisfaction in minding and feeding them; and she gave details of her cooking, baking, sewing, mending, alterations of old clothes and making dollies. Her volunteer work took her to the Centre two or three times a week, where there was much gossip, irritability and back-biting, though Nella was hopeful of improvements when it was learned at the end of July that the capable Mrs Diss was to become the new WVS Organiser. The Lasts refreshed themselves with drives to Walney, Morecambe Bay and various places in the Lake District, and they saw the occasional film. During August they received visitors from out of town – their younger son, Cliff, on leave from his base in Woolwich for a few days (the Lasts were taking two weeks' holiday), and Jim Picken, the brother of the young woman in Portadown, Northern Ireland, to whom Arthur had just get engaged. Now and again a celebrity visited town to boost morale. 'Gracie Fields came today and got a good reception in an ENSA† concert at the Yard and more stood to see her pass than did to see the Duke of Kent last week – so they tell me' (16 July).

A rare instance of a discussion of international issues took place at the WVS Centre on 3 July. 'Over lunch we talked of the terrible fact that we had to have Russia as an ally and "glad to do it". [Britain and the Soviet Union became military allies after the German invasion of the USSR on 22 June.] We recalled the horror the very word "Bolshevism" caused. We wondered if good could possibly come out of evil – the evil of associating ourselves in any degree with people whose thoughts and aims differed so widely from ours and felt a fear at the desperate plight of things when we did it.' Still, there was an acknowledgement, even in these passionately anti-Communist circles, that a Russian defeat would be disastrous for Britain.

Saturday, 30 August. We picked a soldier up on Coast Road who was going to Ulverston. He was a very superior type of soldier and in conversation told us he was a Londoner, an accountant and married to a Leicester girl. We talked of war and its drawbacks as regards ordinary life. He has had a hard time – last winter up in Scapa Flow – but it was not ordinary hardships of cold and discomfort that he so bitterly resented but the frustration, the wastage, the sinking of every scrap of individuality – our Cliff's complaint. He looked so 'fine drawn' and nervy as he talked of how a year ago he was recommended for an officer. It always seems so cruel to me when recommendations are given and men just *live* on hope – and then when nothing more is heard get such a bitterness. I asked him to come whenever he felt like it but don't suppose he will be able as his camp is a long way from our house and there are less and less buses and the last one leaves the centre of town at 9.10 and it would mean leaving our house at 8.40 or so to catch it.

All the harvest is being quietly and swiftly cut and gathered and it astonishes me how they do it with so little labour. Aunt Sarah looks fretty and ill – I bet Aunt Eliza worries her. And things are so bad to get in the country where all hawkers and door to door canvassers for orders have stopped beyond the fortnightly delivery of rationed goods. That means that oddments are missed from village shop and from town grocer for obviously the village shop keeps its few scarce things for what few rationed customers they have and from the town delivery of a fortnight 'bits' are missed. I said 'You should have registered at village shop' but knew that sentiment was responsible, for Dorothy Parker, the grocer of Ulverston, was a childhood Quaker friend of Gran's, and a strong friendship existed and we always dealt with the Parkers, and country people resent change and keep faithful with old ways. Eager would-be blackberry pickers were on roads and fields but I saw no ripe ones for there has been so little sun lately. We called at Mrs Thompson's, our part-time secretary from the Centre, to take the Gretchen dollie for her poor little girl and she was in bed and Mrs Thompson said 'Come upstairs and give her the dollie and have a little chat'. It's such a lovely home and the big primrose nursery was a delight. Walls and ceiling and finishing all in soft golden yellow and carpet, curtains and bed cover of soft leaf green. No expense spared, money for every comfort possible – and only a poor dreadful little idiot girl in the lovely bed. She lifted her queer little face with its soft thatch of dark hair and made noises at me and I said 'I was sorry her tummy was bad and I'd brought her a dollie to keep her company' and she managed to say 'Truda' and her mother was delighted. More than ever did I realise the fact that it is not money that makes for happiness. She is 15 and her mother adores her but she *must* feel unhappy about her, and she is such a sweet woman. Such a burden.

Tuesday, 2 September. Someone [*at the Centre*] started a queer line of talk – a kind of 'Turn the clock back, if but for an hour'. It started about 'peace again' and led on to whether we would like the world to step back to old ways and days. I said, speaking personally, I'd not live a year of my life over or go back to anything, that I'd rather 'march on' to better days than go back to any I'd lived. Mrs Waite said 'You would rather have the "shadow" than the "bone", I can see', and that started a discussion as to whether the old days *were* the delight the sentimentalists would have us believe, of beer so cheap that Saturday night was a horror, of wages and standards of life so low that children went barefoot. Mrs Woods, who was a teacher, recalled the swollen faces of poor kiddies with bad teeth that ached with every cold wind, of faces that were scabbed and raw with impetigo. One talked of heavy woollen stockings and underwear, boned bodices, dresses that trailed in the dust that were so 'sweetly feminine'! Then off we went along another track – men's attraction to their wives and visa versa. There were two women in the discussion whose husbands have always to my knowledge had big salaries but their lips had a bitter twist as they spoke of 'having to account for every damned penny'! We wondered if this dreadful mess of war would release people from taboos and inhibitions as the rest had undoubtedly done, if, when it was over, much bad, wrong or raw would have gone.

Then we thoroughly picked two of the morning women to pieces, one for wearing four bracelets, *two* of them wristlet watches. I said 'She always reminds me of a Xmas tree' and Mrs Higham said 'Have you seen her newest watch?' and I had to confess I'd not looked closely but it seems that it's the loveliest and silliest watch they had seen, a tiny gold face with big diamonds round! Captain Corbyn's wife shocked us all by keeping her car and sailor chauffeur while she did some *very* bad sewing and had a good gossip – for over 1½ hours. Talk about wasted manpower. What with one thing and another there seems as much in the Services as anywhere! He is such a strong virile looking young man too and lackeys round Mrs Corbyn like a poodle. He looks resentful and Mrs Wilkins, whose two boys are in the Navy, said 'I'd hate to think my boys had to do a thing like that' ...

I've had rather a surprise lately at the savage sentences – for our courts – that have been passed on looters from blitzed houses. Several quite respectable people have been sent to prison for two and four months. Today Mrs Burnett came in from the country – odd, but she is *lots* more human when she is not head of WVS; she seems one of those people who cannot stand 'authority'. Her house was so badly damaged and walls and ceilings so bad they were warned they had not to move about in it until the worst had been demolished. Her store of tinned goods and three crocks of eggs were in a deep cellar and she felt quite happy about them being 'so safe'. Her house stood in its own grounds so perhaps the thieves could work slowly and unobserved, but when the Burnetts finally got into their house to remove anything of value they found all gone that could be carried, and the cellar's stock of food, wine, eggs – even coal and wood – gone. It started an 'I heard about' kind of conversation and made us wonder what the police had been doing since our bombings, for what with looted houses and gardens a really shocking picture of theft and utter lawlessness was revealed. It made us wonder what it was like in big cities. We had seen a remark of magistrate's somewhere in London where he said he wondered if there was 'one honest demolition man' in the whole of London, and there were several who told of demolition men going home from Barrow to outlying districts with bundles of curtains, bedding etc. rolled up and carried quite openly under their arm!

Thursday, 4 September. This week there has seemed such a lot happier spirit at the Centre. Perhaps it's the glass in the windows, or the roof getting mended and the dirt and discomfort lessened. We are all excited to hear of a boy of 17 who has been awarded a medal [*by the Boy Scouts*] for his bravery in our blitz when as a messenger he went from one post to another while the raid was at its highest and worst. It seemed so splendid to find someone who had stood fast, for so many who should have done fled. I suppose it was the dreadful shock of 'first time' that shook people, although hundreds still go out to sleep yet. They make the excuse that 'no glass in the windows' and only the shutters of felt depress them, and women who should conquer their fears for the sake of toiling husbands or sons laze in apartments in the countryside while their men folk struggle backward and forward on too full buses or if it is near enough their bicycles. I was shocked at appearance of a workman of my husband's. He is about 58–60 and always looked so fit and well and was such a grand worker. His wife would not live in Barrow, 'would sleep under a hedge rather than do so', and they found a very old labourer's cottage on a farm a few miles out. It was in terrible condition and he worked like a slave at nights and weekends to make it habitable and now they live there and he is still working and then has the daily journey and the 'sketchy' midday meal. The homeward journey has to be made up a very steep hill when he has to walk and push his bike. I look at his fat complacent wife when she comes in to shop and go to a matinee. I think it will be a bitter regret someday and by the look of her husband not very long, for he daily grows more bent and grey and loses flesh.

Friday, 5 September. Perhaps it is the time of year but restlessness is laying hold of me – a feeling of change, of saying 'today I will do so and so' but never that I will do it 'tomorrow'. I had the same feeling but to a greater degree before Easter. I felt I could never admire or love my little house enough, put clean curtains up to my wide windows, alter my bits of brass to catch the sun, change my rugs and chairs round. Now with my indoor shelter in the big bay in dining room, my cracked ceilings, the packed up china and pictures, I have more the feeling one has for a sick child – no real joy. I packed my things up when we had a week of raids and when so many homes went of friends, and when I want to straighten things my husband keeps saying 'Wait, you don't know what will happen any time', but I am getting tired of living in a state of siege and if this and next month passes [*without raids*] I shall insist on his moving things back to their places. If I ask him to do a thing he goes on and on. I did not want wardrobes bringing downstairs but he insisted and says they are best there.

Sunday, 14 September. My husband had his books to get ready for auditors so Arthur [*who was visiting from Northern Ireland*] and I went for a little run. Arthur shares my deep love for all the Lakeland and today

all looked at its best. For the first time for a long time we were not sig-
naled for a lift by any service man. A girl with a heavy bag was standing
waiting for a bus at a lonely road end and we asked her if she would
like a lift and she was quite glad for she doubted if there would be a
bus pass for hours. After tea – rather late – we sat talking. Arthur has
such different ways of looking at things than we in England. He thinks
there is no danger of invasion as long as Germany is busy with Russia
and without exactly saying 'the back of the war is broken' really thinks
the worst is over. He seems so out of things somehow – rationing even.
Northern Ireland has up to now been 'off the map' except for the raid on
Belfast [*on 15/16 April and 4/5 May*]. He went down to meet Cliff but
came back without him and we wondered if he had missed the train but
there was a later one not in timetable and in strolled Cliff an hour and a
quarter after. He looks well and is growing a mustache again and looks
older. He went into pantry and came back into dining room laughing
and said 'Gosh, Mum, have you gone crazy and forgot the war? There's a
fowl and mince pastry and apples and a Xmas cake, gingerbread, shortbread biscuits and some walnut bread. I'll drop a line to Lord Woolton
[*Minister of Food*] about you!' I said 'Ah, he would not worry, duck.
I've saved it for a long time. My cake and mincemeat were made last
March and after all my darling "time is measured by heartbeats and not
by figures on a dial" and we will have our Xmas and our festa now when
we are all together again.' I saw his face change a little and when I took
his fresh towels upstairs before he had his bath he told me that he will
be going abroad soon. I felt a chill. In spite of brave words that mothers
speak, down in their hearts there is a protest against fate that *their* boys,
their babies should go. It was not the half dressed figure in khaki I saw in
the steam of the hot tap. It was my little boy. We had no time to talk. My
husband will have to know sooner or later and I will just let Cliff break it
to him himself. We cannot keep worries from people nowadays, and try
as we may they have got to know things. The noise, the cigarette smoke,
the old dog calmly trotting upstairs to sleep by their bedside, rolled the
years away. Dear God, mothers don't ask much for heart's-ease.

CHAPTER FIVE

PAST AND PRESENT

September–October 1941

Wednesday, 24 September. After tea I was very surprised when a cousin called whom I rarely see and she sat for awhile and I kept wondering what had brought her and then it came out. She wanted to see if I could get her a job in the Civic Restaurant! I gasped, not believing my ears. She is the daintiest, most aloof thing imaginable, has always been pampered at home – that aunt married very well – and has always had everything. I said 'My dear, the only jobs at the Civic Restaurant are both hard and dirty – dishwashing and cooking'. She said 'Well, Mother is dead against the Services. I would not be able to stand up to heavy farm work. I've not had office training and am scared of machinery – so I'll just have to make the best of it and not grumble.' I explained that I could do nothing – she would have to get any job through the Labour Exchange – but that if I saw the Head of restaurant I would see what I could do. The thought of Jean washing piles and piles of dirty crocks made me want to giggle – *or* of keeping regular hours. As she was going out she said 'We live not far from you, you know – got a furnished house since ours was blitzed. May I bring Mother round when I come to see if you have been able to do anything in the matter? She will be lonely when we are both out – and you were always her favourite niece. She says you were always gay.' I said 'Well, no one can be that nowadays, Jean, but you may certainly both come'.

Friday, 26 September. Often I think of the drastic changes going on all round and when the announcer said 'All shop assistants between 18 and 25 except food shop girls would be called up', I realised his words had wiped one racket away, at least here in Barrow. There is practically nothing for girls in Barrow, except the Shipyard offices and teaching, and many clever girls have had to waste their talents, or else leave home and go to the cities. When permanent waving came in fairly cheap – say 10–12 years ago – big premiums were paid to learn it at the two or three hairdressers who went away to learn the art of perming and setting, tinting and bleaching. They in turn were set up by parents who were only too glad to start their daughters in a decent career and they in turn took premium apprentices, charging about £20 to £25, and then paying it back in a few shillings a week learning the trade – two/three years. It was like a snowball and the more that started the less the premiums grew until to get girls latterly the advert has stated 'No premium to really smart girl'. I know a number of girls who learned the trade, got a little money and their drying and perm machine on hire purchase and two assistants – and themselves not be over 20. Prices dropped all round until a 'full head' would be done for 7s 6d, or if it was the first one done and the person liked to chance it, for 5s! Now all these little half trained things will go and the day of 'curl rags in the morning' return.

Saturday, 27 September. However I appear and whatever people think of my 'gayness and cheerfulness', personally I realise that under it I feel thinner skinned and know that I could not be as patient as I was. I often speak sharply to my husband when he gets beyond a certain point. My end of patience is reached quicker now – such a pity, really, for more forbearance will be needed ...

We went to pick blackberries for a sister-in-law who has no car and we got quite a lot although everywhere people are out picking them. I had put Cliff's slipper on and not tried to force my shoe on [*she had a swollen foot*], so after awhile I got tired of limping round and sat down on a little raised bank. Gran's old farm is just off the road from where we were and I started on a train of thought – as the airplanes zoomed low over the hill. I'm not very old – say it's 40 or 44 years since I used to sit on the same bank covered in the summer with bright yellow 'ladies fingers', where Gran said the fairies played. The hours I've particularly sat waiting in the sunshine with the hot sweet incense of the whin† bushes round and the only sound the bumble of bees. I wonder if everything *was* so heavenly peaceful, so gay and bright, so generous, so bountiful, so kindly as my memory insists; or had my Gran's 'gift for living', as I once heard it described, a lot to do with the mellow rhythm of those days, I wonder? She belonged to her day. Her serenity would have been shaken by the bombers as they passed over and it would have hurt and bewildered her not to be able to give and share all the good food of a farm and she would not have been happy in these days of cheese-paring. The fields are all getting ploughed and set again and from where I sat the clouds of birds in the distance betrayed more freshly dry land where I could not see it. A blessing seemed to lie on the quiet countryside, so still with the long shadows of the hills. I am so lucky when I can go and share it – it always does me good to sit quiet and still amongst it all ...

My husband has put the 70th shop window in this week – not bad when he has lost three apprentices and one of the men lives out of town and is getting old. Every master joiner and builder has had to 'take up the tools again' however old he is and work hard to get all shipshape after blitz, and there are a lot of shops heavily shuttered yet and waiting for a little window to be let in and for all to be made light and weather proofed for winter.

Sunday, 28 September. My husband said 'What about making an inventory of each room in case there is a fire?' I've been at him for weeks so we sat down, he to write and I to prompt him. He has a very peculiar aversion to insurance and beyond an endowment policy due next year, we carry *no* insurance for either of us. It's no use at all saying anything for he has all the stubbornness of a weak minded person and no amount of advice from my parents did any good. The house is insured, but that is mine, and I bought a lot of the furniture when we came back from Southampton after the last war and my Dad died. I insured it and it has been increased through war risk to £300, and that includes the £70 or so for the car. I've kept on and on about it not being enough to cover all the furniture but today even I got a shock. We took each room and made an inventory. All my good rugs, eiderdowns and bedspreads I made, and for much less than I could have bought. My lovely cushions were all home made when I went to handicraft classes and they were cheap, and the two bedroom suites my husband made, so there was no 'high prices'. We only put £20 down for the piano and much of the furniture was discount price, and yet when added up came to nearly £700 worth. My husband said 'I'll see about increasing the insurance tomorrow', but I've a nasty feeling we have left it too late. I seem to remember a time limit – I hope I'm mistaken ...

I think it was catching a glimpse of the rising moon through the ragged black clouds that set me thinking of raids. Terrible as it sounds, I wish there *were* a few odd ones. Sometimes I feel that each day adds an imperceptible layer of dust on me. Dust of apathy? No, not quite. Indifference? Hardly that either. It's as if I am getting too complacent about things. While no doubt it's best to take life as it comes, adjusting myself to all changes, I feel I am getting rusty instead of razor keen. I try to keep on my toes, never leaving anything till done and working as hard as I can, but there is that 'got used to things' I don't feel right about. I wonder if other people feel like it. I feel many do for I hear remarks like 'Hitler will have his hands full all winter. WE have no need to worry.' Many of my friends have put all their household treasures out that were packed away and many have stopped clamouring for indoor steel shelters – 'they are ugly things to have about anyway'. I see either burst useless sandbags in porch corners or none at all. Gone are the buckets from many gardens or else falling leaves float on the half filled ones that are there. One good thing of the strange 'it will not happen' feeling is that many people are coming back to their houses now they are roofed and weather proof. Our school children are evacuated to places where there has been little or none before, and whatever the children experience in the way of billets, the masters of one school who are at Tebay [*north-east of Kendal*] are having a grim time as 'unwanted guests'. One very nice master asked if his wife could spend her holiday – ten days or a fortnight – at Tebay, in Cumberland. When she went the landlady said sourly 'You can share your husband's bed – if that's what you've come for – but I cannot do with you about the house in the day and I won't cook for you. They cannot *compel* me to do *that*.'

All this compulsion must make for unhappiness. I looked at the dirty unhealthy looking people who came to our lumber sales† – not really poor people for they had well filled purses – both Friday nights, pay nights at Yard. We said 'Just imagine having that one – or that – billeted on anyone, anyone clean'. Mrs Higham, who comes from Liverpool, said 'I never realised you had the real slummy people in Barrow. There is little excuse here in a so modern town.' We passed the remarks among ourselves about the dirty white 'cushioning' hands of some of the dirtiest women – no sign of work worn fingers. People like that should *never* be billeted on anyone. They should be in camps or some place where they could be shamed into some semblance of cleanliness. The people who only need a chance should be helped in every way but to see women with unwashed faces and straggling hair after tea – and purses full of money – showed a lack of decency rather than anything else.

Nella was now volunteering part-time at a stationary WVS canteen that served refreshments to the Forces, and her work there had a prominent role in her life. She also continued her work with Hospital Supply on Tuesdays and Thursdays.

Friday, 3 October. Isa called and I was glad of her help to carry my dish and pile of begged plates and saucers and the two big basins of potted meat and beef and ham roll. The cakes and bread did not come [*to the canteen*] till 3 o'clock but we cut beetroot and tomatoes and the beef roll and washed and dried lettuce and got kettles boiling and then the rush started and we got a real surprise. There were six of us, one to make tea, one to take money, one to wash up, two to serve, and I cooked, and whenever we could do we went on sandwich making. We were going to be really smart and make the evening shift a pile of all kinds of sandwiches but we used them as quick as we made them and there was beans on toast, sausage and potato cakes, and waffles or pancakes as some called them. I made them as quickly as I could but try as I would I could not get them out quickly enough, and then the flour gave out for the order from the wholesalers was late. One young soldier came in and said rather shyly 'A plate of waffles please' and Isa said 'Do you think the flour will be long?' I moved to counter and said 'I'm sorry, we have no more flour at present – would you like sausage and a potato cake and two slices of bread and butter for 6d?' He hesitated and said 'No thanks, I'm not a "working man" now and those waffle things were jolly good. I'll wait. They are such a "fill up".' A pity seized me. Such inequality. Some lads earn big money and stay in their homes – or good lodgings. Others leave all and have muddle and frustration and maybe lose their lives. Surely there must be a pattern. Surely somewhere, someday all will work out right.

By 4.30 we all felt we were 'heading for the last round up' as the squeaky old gramophone blared out old cowboy tunes and the men sang or whistled them. As a rule 5 o'clock sees a falling off and they reckon on an easier time to straighten things up and leave all tidy for next shift but we worked hard till 6 and the next lot were slow in coming in and we worked on till full shift could take over.

Sunday, 5 October. My husband was sleeping upstairs with having such a heavy cold and people were all round in the quiet houses and as I turned out the light I thought of lonely women in isolated places. People's nerves are too taut and strained for sadistic horrors to hurt and terrify their bruised mind and people who like those sort of plays* should go work at a canteen and see the real horrors in some of the soldiers' eyes. Perhaps because I like and understand young boys – as much, that is, that one person can understand another's inner hopes and fears – I see such quiet desolation, and my Cliff's letters often sadden me with their outcry of frustration. For one really happy looking boy there are twenty who only 'laugh with their lips' and if one sees a 'jolly good fellow' he is generally a very young soldier or the 'club man' type. A merry eyed

---

* She had woken up in fear from a bad dream that she attributed to a 'horror play' that had been broadcast a few days earlier on the BBC.

laughing boy with sparkling eyes and wide mouth showing perfect and marvellously white teeth laughed and joked at the counter and won Mrs Walker's heart completely. 'Such a *nice* boy. So *gay*. I *like* people like that, Mrs Last.' Me, I like them without that 'touch of the tarbrush'[†] that his dusky nails and kinky hair showed. It was racial inheritance rather than a happy heart that made his happy smile.[*]

Mrs Walker would delight a clever person who wrote books. She is the present day Mrs Kenwigs [*a character eager to please in Dickens's* Nicholas Nickleby] and coming from Durham County has either a whine or a gush in her sing song voice. She is a good worker and brings me roses and onions to raffle and is just the kind of person I attract always! As soon as she heard at Centre that I was on [*at the canteen*] Friday afternoons, she rushed off to Mrs Thompson, the head of Canteen, and asked to be put on my shift as I was 'such a good sport'. I said '*What* a pal, Mrs Thompson. Would *you* like her on your shift?' It's no use worrying, and she is a good worker, that's one thing, and we all have our funny ways. She will be about 45–50 and calls everyone 'love' and promises 'a nice kiss' as a reward. The other day I went to the store cupboard and left the door so that I could see to find the switch. There was a draught and a soldier got up and shut the door and Mrs Walker said 'Thank you, luv, you deserve a nice big kiss for that' and his pal said 'He would have to have an athletic missus', and Mrs Thompson said they did not know where to look for they all wanted to laugh. I wondered what the joke was when I came back grumbling about having to find my way back in the dark and with my hands full of tins ...

On this approach to winter I have none of the wild uncertainty of these last two winters – rather the feeling that I can 'put my hand into the hand of God and go out into the Great Unknown'. It's a blessed feeling for a scatty nervy woman to attain – one who sits and thinks too much. I've no wild regrets and longing for the dear past when the boys were at home and they and their friends filled the house with laughter and noise, and no bright golden hope for the future; just take each day

---

[*] Nella's conflicted views on race are revealed later, pp. 381–84.

as it comes and at night lay it aside like a brick on the wall that stands
between me and the terror of brooding and worry. I try to make it a
good sound brick and my wall stout and true. When I know I have done
something for the fighting men, even if only a rag dollie for the funds at
Centre, I am content. More do I get a thankfulness for Centre and the
Canteen, and to know if a blitz came I've my place without having to
'wonder what I can do'.

Monday, 6 October. I got my curtains mended and put away and a
cowboy dollie finished tonight and I could have done more but an aunt
and cousin came in. She is a nice aunt, a sister of my father, and I rarely
see her, but she is lonely and has taken a furnished house near where her
own was blitzed. She is only about eight or ten years older than myself
and she said when she half apologised for wanting to start, 'You know
Dearie, I must be getting old. I have such a longing for my "own folks"
and lately I've had a positive craving to go down to Woolwich, which
was always home to mother and where we spent all our childhood holidays.' My husband likes her and she is gay amusing company so it will be
very nice if she comes round sometimes this winter.

It is so heavy and close tonight. No air seems to circulate anywhere
and the moon looks unreal as it hangs against the misty sky like a plaque
on a wall. Cliff's letter today from Newcastle [*where he was now based*]
did not mention the raids again. It's nice but quite silly of him to think
he is sparing me worry. News travels fast these days and people travelling
between one shipyard and another take news and it filters into town.
There are still 7,000 people homeless in Barrow although everyone connected with repairs have worked marvellously and roofs and doors have
gone on houses and plasterers work all the hours God sends.

Wednesday, 8 October. Unkindness and frustration, cruelty and suffering [*for servicemen*] – and it seems to grow worse. To so hurt a sick man,
to let him think he was going HOME [*on leave*], to love and care, and
then to act like that [*cancel leave*]. The tears I've shed, when an imagi-
native little crippled girl and when books were my life, over Harrison

Ainsworth's *Tower of London* and *Windsor Castle*, and the sick horror
of the Spanish Inquisition in *Westward Ho!* [*by Charles Kingsley, 1855*].
I remember my Dad saying soothingly 'But that is all past, my little love.
No one acts like that now. They did not know any better then.' All our
progress, our civilization, our cleverness – and yet sick and pitiful men
can be so used. There will be sad hearts in lots of homes tonight – poor
mothers and wives …

Mrs Diss, the head of the WVS, came in this afternoon and she
looked fagged and unhappy. I wonder if there is another so hateful a
Council as ours in the Kingdom? Every obstacle they can put in her
way they do. One would think the WVS was a Communist or Fascist
organisation bent on smashing down instead of her trying to do all that
should have been done these last two years when Mrs Burnett was in
charge. Now to make matters more complicated Mrs Burnett is going to
start a rival canteen to 'show us' and I was interested to learn that 'that
clever little Mrs Last was going to be asked to help'. Ye Gods – I wish
the old battle axe *would* ask me; it's quite a while since we have crossed
swords. She will want someone to cook, plan and manage and then she
will 'take a bow'. I do hope things pull together a bit better for Mrs Diss
is such a good worker, tactful and clever, and if she got support would
put our WVS on a footing with the rest of them who have done such
good work in different places …

The friend we have our house and furniture policy off – through –
came tonight to tell us it was alright about increasing our insurance and
I will do it for another £300 for we only have it for £400 at present. It
means too our clothes and the car will be better protected and as Cliff
has a lot of good clothes too I shall feel easier. He was telling me that his
wife and child have been in the country since our blitz and he has let his
house, sleeps at First Aid Post and gets his food at Communal Centre.
I said 'You manage fine, then, Lacy', and he stared into the fire and said
'Oh yes, I suppose so, but I've no home life you know and when we had
a quiet summer [*for raids*] I wish Maud was not so nervous'. I said 'It's
rather a long way to Broughton to go by trains each day' and he said 'Yes,
when Maud said she was going I made it quite clear that she must not

expect me to act like a lot of these daft fools who to please jittery wives get up at 4 o'clock to catch an early bus and stand waiting in the rain at night to struggle home late and tired'. He talked of various people we knew who when we had 'the first little bother' left their job for anyone to do and flew out of town not caring who carried on. He said 'Oh, you know Nell, I'm perfectly convinced that quite 65% or 75% of British people *yet* do not realise war. It's only in the big badly hit places and other people are going along in a dream of rosy hope.'

Friday, 10 October. The Canteen was full all afternoon and it was so nice to see the two old but good settees full all afternoon – lads sprawled out reading – and in the reading and writing rooms I could see them quite at home. I said to one boy 'I thought you might have deserted us now there is one at the Methodist church in the centre of town, so much nearer to your camp'. He was a twinkling eyed lad of about 22 and he said 'Not for me. I dislike the 'earty 'andshake they insist on giving all of us "dear boys".' One of our lot this afternoon brought in an armful of decent records and I was surprised to find we have quite a good gramophone – must have been the scratchy old records that made such an awful noise. The wife of one of my husband's cousins came and I could have groaned when I saw her for she is a rackety† cocktail drinking girl who lives with a cigarette always in her mouth and I wondered how she would fit in with my busy efficient gang. Cigarette ash was dropping into the coffee and beans she was preparing and she said in a would-be clever way, 'I *always* smoke when I make our own meals and I'm not going to stop now for Mrs Thompson or anyone else. It will do for pepper in the beans. Don't you ever smoke?' I know the little cat – never had anything in her life till she got working in an office and married a man who could seize opportunities. I said 'Oh, there is a time and place, Dora, and what can be jolly good fun in one place is merely bad form in another'. I knew that would shake her. People like her have a horror of the word 'bad form'.

Saturday, 11 October. The lashing cold rain has marked a definite step into autumn and this morning all was crystal clear in the cold sunrise. Gone was the heavy close feeling of the last few days and all looked new in the hard sunlight. Lately when we have been so short of pans I could do with another gas stove at Canteen I've felt like doing a bit of looting from the ruined houses near to us! In one house there is a good gas stove going red rust and a lovely dining table, couch and chairs – just do for Canteen. Last night I found a cousin's husband was the solicitor and I've got the address off him and written to the owner and asked if we can take the things and use them. It looks a bit hard faced, my husband says, and it was not an easy letter to write, but it's done, and posted. The real owner died through shock and the sister who now owns it lives in a hotel at Grange and she is old …

We called in at cousin Mary's at Greenodd and picked up the good blankets we left last spring when we thought we might be glad to have some place to go and sleep when bombing was 'on'. My husband said 'Why not leave them at Mary's? We might need them yet.' But I pointed out that small country cottages were damp and my good new blankets might mildew; besides I like to look after my own things and see that they are cared for. Mary is a part-time post woman for she has to look after her widower father and she looks tired. I said 'Will they make you take a full-time job, Mary?' and she said 'Don't talk to me of full-time jobs and the Government's "cry for women"' and said at Labour Exchange they say there are no jobs for women 'just now' at Ulverston and at the Armstrong Siddeley works they are 'laying them off'! I said Ruth was given a quick choice between the Services and the Yard and Mary said 'We were asked in a "don't say yes" tone of voice if we would like to be an ATS girl and when I said "What about the Yard at Barrow?" was told "They have more than they want down there at Labour Exchange"'. When I think of all the households where the maid was taken and women left to struggle with a big house and a small family – I mean small children – and then girls not wanted, when I hear the clarion call for women to work in factories, sheds and Yards, I wonder how much longer there will be overlapping and muddle. I used to feel unwanted myself and had to look for jobs and have always felt so grateful for Hospital Supply but I often hear people say 'Oh, why worry? I've offered my help. Let them come for me if they want me' – and they cannot really be blamed.

Monday, 13 October. We got a surprise last night when the siren went and when I put the light on to see the time found it only just after 11 o'clock. The guns roared and spat from A-A camp not far away and shrapnel fell like hail on the roof. It's very funny how brave you feel when the guns are not going off and how they give you palpitations and make your skin tight as soon as they do. Noise of any kind, from 'hot' music [*jazz*] to a mechanical pick, are all distasteful to me. Luckily the sticks of bombs fell across playing fields and did no damage to anything worthwhile. I got up feeling tired and very sick. My tummy is a weak spot and last blitz made me sick for weeks ...

After tea cousin Jean popped in for a while. She hopes that I can hear of a small house so that she can get married. She has a good position at the Yard in the tracing office and will have to go on working. A few girls and young marrieds will get a shock when they heard tonight that women were to be called up quicker. My hairdresser will be about 27–28 and said 'Oh, I'll not be called up till November. A lot can happen before then.' Now it looks as if the 31s will be up in a few weeks time. Isa cannot see that *she* will be affected, and anyway she 'does voluntary work', one half day at Centre and one at Canteen! There was a picture of her sister Dolly Fell in the paper tonight and it was a lovely one of both Isa and Dolly in the latter's wedding group. They are the most astonishingly ageless women I know – or have ever known; frail looking but can work, play, eat – and drink like strong men. Dolly looked a little shrinking girl, and is 37 and marrying a man 27 or 28. He looks that much older in the photo. Dolly has racketed round and been a weekend girl and had more fun and experience in her life than any three women I know, and if I know [*her*], that one will go on doing so in the WAAFs[†] where she will be called up this week, and her Captain husband goes East. Isa said smugly 'We are the Liliths [*female demons*] of the world' – someone had been telling them so!

Tuesday, 14 October. Mrs Burnett came out in the open with the scheme we had heard was to be in opposition to WVS. She has never had any sense – and I've known her all my life – but this 'beats Brannigan† and since he beat the Devil', as the Irish say! It seems she has taken a large house, £100 or so for the year's rent and rates, and in which there is little or no furniture, crockery etc. There are three equally impractical women in the scheme which is to turn into a kind of hostel for WAAFs or girls in the Yard, of which there are only 40 from out of town. She has got a licence for tea, buns and biscuits 'for the girls will only want breakfast and supper'. I got hilarious – I *felt* like it – and got all dense and pretended I thought she was 'expecting bears or sumpin' and expressed surprise that she had not included nuts 'just in case', and she lost her temper and said I was a fool. I said 'Of course I am – but I score by knowing it. You don't seem to see what a mad scheme you are lightly undertaking. What about cooking? You *cannot* give a girl a bun and your blessing to start the day, and a cup of tea and a biscuit for supper may be alright for you but not for a girl working hard.' I went on to ask about carpets, chairs, bedding, towels. Who would keep the place clean, make the fires etc? And I could see by her blank look that there was a lot she had not taken into consideration. I asked her if the Government was subsidising the scheme and how she expected to pay £100 for rent and rates, coal, light, gas for cooking on. Forty girls who were only in to sleep – and buns and biscuits! Mrs Waite sat and let me do all the talking and when I asked her crossly afterwards why she did not speak up she laughed and said 'Oh, I liked to hear your cross talk and you seemed to think of everything' …

Mrs Lord was in distress – a huge shell cap had dropped through her roof and broken her bathroom curtain on Sunday night. I raffled a little basket of groceries – I got 14s 6d – and sold some sloppy looking blackberries and some cooking apples and helped make tea and at 4 o'clock I had done all my own work and didn't feel Pollyannaish to stay and help clear the big room and said 'My back is pretty bad. I think I'll go home.'

Coming home in the bus I'd such a strange experience and I feel undecided what to do – whether to report it to police. I had to stand for awhile and then there was a vacant place on seat that goes the same way as wheels and I took it. As I sat down the other occupant gave a loud yawn and half smiled and I said 'You are tired' and she said 'Yes, I think it's the weather'. Then there started one of those hard to remember little conversations – about Sunday's raid and how the first night made one the tiredest and she mentioned she had been in London all last winter through the raids and we discussed our raid of last May. She asked me if I was frightened and I said 'Oh, *horribly*, but not frightened enough to run out of town'. She had such greenish grey rather prominent eyes and she stared at me and said 'Well, it's best to get out of town if you possibly can. In a little while from now there will be no buildings standing in *any* town'. I said 'Oh, I think our defences are better than that. We are better prepared, you know, and the Jerrys won't have it all their own way again.' Just then we stopped and she got up and glared fiercely at me again and said really malevolently 'Well, I *know*' and got out. She was such an odd looking woman with big greenish grey eyes and the oddest looking fur cap seen in Barrow for some time – if ever!

Wednesday, 15 October. I kept waking up and thinking of the words of that woman in bus – not in any frightened sense for myself but rather the effect on others, and I wondered if she was Fifth Column, amateur or professional. This morning, in spite of my extremely busy and well filled day ahead, I went down to police station and told a sergeant in charge. He did not laugh – listened carefully and said quite frankly that 'Little could be done in circumstances', but after taking a statement he asked me to go through and have a word with a detective. He was looking at a paper in his hand and at my statement on desk and he asked a curious question. He said 'Tell me, Mrs Last, what were your reactions?' I did not quite see what he meant and said 'Well, I thought she was foolish and might frighten people' but could see that was not what he meant and he said 'Did she strike you as showing off or threatening?' and after reflection I said 'Rather the former, I think', and when I had spoken I wondered if the woman was really one of our 'back street seers'! I wasted 1¼ precious hours and was rather tired to start the day but my mind felt easier ...

I often feel worried when I look at my husband. He does not worry about the war as he did and I am always careful to not let him see me down and I always try and be gay and chattering about little amusing things that happen at Centre and I keep all worrying things away and always try and make home the one peaceful place where worry and trouble can be shut out. When the boys were young and got to quarrelling I used to run them out in the big yard in the other house and say 'Go and scrap outside. Home is no place to quarrel. It's a place to rest quietly and safe – and to lick your wounds for a fresh fight, like a dog over-fond of a fight.' They often laugh at me for things I said and did when they were boys but they love and turn to their home as a place where 'all comes right'. My husband sometimes looks so all-in when he gets home* but when he has had his tea and is sitting by the fire with his feet outstretched he often says 'It's good to be home' and I always correct him and say 'It's good to *have* a home, my dear'. It makes me feel so grateful for my 'own fireside' and I try so hard to work and work to help even in little ways that come along. I have not the slightest 'communal' spirit, and would view with horror the thought of communal feeding or always being with people. Although I like to work and play with others I like to be alone as well and I like *all* my own way in cooking and serving food. Of course if I was working 'properly' I'd be glad of meals made for me, no doubt, but I don't see myself being happy in a 'crowd living' state of existence. Perhaps I'm old fashioned and the next generation will like that way and changing conditions will make for changes in general living, but I would rather have my own corner to live and work than share in a palace. I'm not at all consistent, though, for I'd like to plan cooking etc. for others living in a communal way and really enjoy planning and helping for Canteen.

---

* Nella had observed earlier in this entry that 'he works harder now than he ever has done since a young man and has so much outside work in draughts'. Repairing damaged buildings was keeping men in the building trades exceptionally busy. Nella thought of both Will and herself as people of delicate health, probably with reason.

Thursday, 16 October. I had to rush round rather when a note from Mrs Higham came to say she would not get down to Centre before lunch. I got all the teacups and saucers out and then went out into the main street on an errand. I'd told Mrs Waite about the strange incident of the woman in the bus and strange to say I saw her again, a queer sluttish figure with untidy hair and down-at-heel shoes. I'd a very busy day with the usual tea making and raffling and I sold pears and apples and some lovely crysanths I'd rather have raffled but someone wanted them for a sick friend so I sold them. When I got in there was a ring at the door and to my surprise it was a young policeman with the police car and a request that I would go to head office, and he would run me back again. I said 'No, I cannot come now for I have my husband's tea to make'. He said 'Inspector Thompson wants badly to see you. Should he come up or can we possibly arrange for you to come down? It's important.' I decided to go down and was rather surprised by cordial reception and was shown into a small room where Inspector Thompson was. He said 'We want your help and I cannot tell you much but we want to link up and identify this' – and he tapped some papers on desk – 'with your tale of the other day. We know where the woman lives – with a foreigner – and we want you to positively identify her with the woman of the bus'! I said 'Well, I cannot go and knock at the door and ask her, can I?' and he said 'Well, her name is Mrs Guise – or the name she is living under with the Norwegian – but it is an Intelligence case and I can tell you this much. She has lived in Canada – hence her "coon cap"! – with an enemy of England, has lived in London in comfort if not real luxury, has been the mistress of a member of the household of a European royal family, and we *know* she is not the slut she pretends to be and we want you to be sure it is the same woman who was so venomous in her remarks as to 'no building standing in any city or town in Britain in a short time'. He said 'The Chief says she must not be frightened in any way but we *do want* that identification'.

We sat and pondered and then I said half seriously 'She had very curious eyes – like a fortune teller. How about me going and asking her if she told fortunes?' To my real dismay he jumped up and said 'Talk about woman's wit. You *will* do it, won't you?' I felt really awful and as if I wished I'd not come and told them but he went on 'If I dare tell you more I would and you know your [*WVS*] badge carries all kind of responsibilities – it's a Service badge'. I just could not promise anything. I felt all jumbled up – spies in my quiet well ordered life – and I felt sick. I had palpitations. I stood waiting for the bus and feeling dreadful and I asked God if it mattered to please give me courage to go and knock at the door, and not think of silly stories I'd read where spies shot people dead. I had a walk up a street when I got off bus and if I'd been going to a dentist's to have a mouth full of teeth pulled out without gas I could not have felt worse. I lost my taste for detective yarns and spy stories for good but the courage I'd asked for took me to door and I knocked.

It was a terrible looking house. All the windows shuttered helped and it had had a few knocks when the blitz came and was very dirty. When the door was opened I could have gasped at the change in the rather vacant faced sluttish woman of the bus. Beautifully made up, good tailored costume, but still the fur cap, she faced me imperiously as I faltered something about how she had frightened me by talking of coming air raids, and she said 'Little fool, don't you read the papers for yourself?' and said 'Why come to ME?' I shook with sheer terror but managed to say that I thought perhaps she could read the crystal or something. She glared at me and said 'Certainly not. And I don't like strange women coming to my door and making requests like that. Go away.' It was no acting on my part when I tottered down the path with the awful remembrance of 'shots in the back'!!

I got to a public call box and I felt I'd better call the Inspector – I had said I'd contact him if I had news and he said he would come up anytime. I'd never used a call box and felt woolly headed but there was such a nice RAF boy standing by the box and I said 'Can you phone from a public box?' and he said 'Yes' so I said 'Well, come and help me for I have rather an important call'. He was such a nice boy for he showed me how and as soon as I mentioned 'police station' he went out quickly. Looking back I've a gigglesome feeling that I've given that lad a tale to tell! When I got in my husband had read my message and had his tea and cleared away and he said 'Good gracious, what's to do?' and when I looked in the glass I was pale green rather than white! I told him but was a bit incoherent for he looked at me as if he thought I was lightheaded but when Inspector Thompson came and was so emphatic on the 'splendid turn I had done them and how gratified they were' and how 'word would go to Intelligence in London who had been rather insistent of more detail' and how 'all would be told as soon as they could safely tell me', I could see by his face that his head was spinning like mine was.

CHAPTER SIX

STEADY ON

October–December 1941

Sunday, 19 October. I got my M-O done and a pile of letters and had my Sunday morning rest for I'd made my very good soup yesterday and boiled a piece of meat to eat cold. I had mutton bones in stock pot and two lots of chicken giblets that my mother-in-law sent up and I put celery, onion, carrots, barley and small beans and the soup alone was a meal. We had brown bread and meat to follow and as I had a headache with writing so much I made a cup of tea after and we had a biscuit. My husband is always saying how good a manager I am and I think sometimes that if I had been less agreeable to make do on little I might have got more in the past! If I had nagged for more perhaps he would have run his somewhat inefficient business better. Such a lot of good work done and yet we don't seem to get the results in a good living. It used to puzzle Arthur when he did income tax returns – he used to say 'More than twice or three times should be made from this business'. It's too late to worry now and anyway the thrift and economy that is my second nature now is more valuable than if I'd had plenty to 'go at'.

Friday, 24 October. I had my fortnightly visit to hairdresser's and as I sat I wondered how much longer I would go for she will have to register soon and things are rising in price so rapidly and getting so scarce that the older woman whose business it is feels worried. Candidly speaking I think the 3s a fortnight I spend could be saved but it's my only luxury or extravagance for I rarely eat sweets or go to the cinema. When I hear girls say 'Hairdressing is a *necessity* – we could *not* do without well dressed hair', I recall my shining mane of dark brown hair that I religiously gave the '100 strokes with a stiff brush' that girls of my day were

brought up to do, washed it every week with soft soap taken from the
tin used for household purposes, plaited it overnight when we wanted
a wave – I never heard of perms or tints or 'sets'. Yet we had a good time
and more 'romance' than most girls of today. The boys seemed to like
us as we were – 'in the raw' as one pert little thing called the girls of our
day!

Saturday, 25 October. An old friend at Spark Bridge [*talking of the war*]
said 'I feel we will be up against the wall – not, mind you, that we will
lose the war; we have too many recourses – but that the winning will
be a hollow thing and only be worthwhile for those who come after'.
My Aunt's cousin [*Joe*], an old man of nearly 70, used to get annoyed
with me when either I would not discuss the war or failed to share his
enthusiastic conviction that the whole of Germany would crack in a
year, the railways would not stand large movements of troops or guns
for the rolling stock had been so neglected as to be *done*, that Germany
knew it had to be a quick, sharp war. He sat over the fire today and when
I went through and sat down he started talking of Russia, of scorched
earth and the desperate courage that would make Russia destroy as they
left their home – to live where? He looked sadly up at me and said 'It
looks as if you are right, my lass. It's going to be a hell of a long war
and the "end of the world" all right.' My husband took up discussion as
we travelled through the gold and brown and green glory that was the
countryside we love – so peaceful, so content to sink into sleep, with
no rebellion, just an acceptance of 'God's plan'. He said 'I wonder what
will have happened before the trees leaf again? It's a queer feeling isn't
it – like waiting for something? I feel in a way as I did when I waited
for the boys to be born and you were so dreadfully ill and I'd the uncertain feeling of wondering what the next hour would bring.' He said a
very curious thing for he said 'I'm thankful for your calm acceptance of
things and for the peace you radiate. You give me courage, my love.' At
one time I would have been terrified, thought he was going to be ill to
talk like that, but now he says things that surprise but don't alarm me.
I said 'It's odd, you know, my dear. I am not strong, nor do I feel very

well *ever*, but I am so conscious of the peace and serenity you speak of –
and the strength – although it's not mine at all. I feel as if in some way
I have "tuned in" to something and that however afraid I am of bombs
and raids there is something I can hold onto and say "this will pass, be
not afraid", and we will find comfort and support.'

When we came in Mr Atkinson, our next door neighbour – such a
nice wee man – was tying up his crysanths in the garden. I said 'What
a lovely day, Mr Atkinson. It makes us forget the war, doesn't it?' And a
shadow fell across his face as he said 'Aye, for awhile, but for how long
now will our feeling of security last'. It was odd that so many different
people should have the same feeling so uppermost in their minds, and
I never remember on one day meeting so many people who shared the
same thought, or talked of it so freely.

Friday, 31 October. When I set off for Canteen I felt I carried a chip on
my shoulder and the feeling was not improved when only three turned
up to help me. With it being a cold frosty day there was a great demand
for hot waffles, potato cakes and bacon – there was no sausage to be had
from butchers this week. Meat must be scarce and what is made will
be 'wanted for customers'. I felt irritable at lack of oddments – the tin
opener broken last week had not been replaced, there was only beetroot
for sandwiches, and a little cheese. There was no flour for baking either
but luckily enough bread and tea cakes left over from last night to enable
us to carry on till baker brought our supplies.

The conchies[†] working on cement unloading on dock came in and
I thought of an old music hall joke when I looked at them – 'What
were you before you joined the Army?' Reply, 'Happy' – they looked
so sullen and apart from the rest. One leaned over counter and said in a
surly tone 'Bacon and waffle and potato cakes'. Off flew my 'chip' and I
said 'Will you please choose something from counter and I'll get you a
cup of tea'. There is one who looks like a school teacher and they seemed
to have a little debate and he walked back to counter and looked down
at me – he is very tall – and he said 'May I *awsk* why we are refused a
cooked meal? Is it because we are non-combatants?' I smiled sweetly – I

hope! – and said 'Supplies are limited and we try to keep cooked meals for soldiers and sailors who for some reason or other have not had a hot meal in the middle of the day. You, I understand, have regular meals and hours.' The rest stood round and glowered at me as he stood round and glowered at me as he drawled 'Oh! If *that* is the case – I thought perhaps you were taking it on yourself to draw a line, madam'. I could have smacked him in the face with a meat pie as I said 'and if that *was* the case, would you deny to others the right you claim yourself – free thought and action and a right to your own way? This is a *voluntary* canteen and we work hard – too hard – with short staff, and I will be obliged if you will make your choice off counter, eat your meal and leave room for others who are waiting their turn.'

I turned to cook a good hot meal for three sailors – real Cockneys. One had a curious jerk to his hand and when he saw I noticed it – he nearly knocked a plate of cakes off – said 'I was in an open boat for four days and must have got cold, or knocked it as we were torpedoed, for I was not wounded at all'. I was busy but I could have taken the floor mop and charged those conchies who sat over their empty plates and left my sailors to eat at counter. I said 'There will be a seat in a few minutes' but when there was a vacant table they stayed at counter and one told me he had been blown up and in life boats on three occasions, and the other two, including the boy with the jerk, had been in the evacuation of Dunkirk. Such 'beardless boys' – the oldest would not be as old as my Cliff.

Sunday, 2 November. We had an alert again last night and I thought we would have a raid, so bright and clear the night. It did not last long and we settled off again, so thankful for the bed under the indoor steel shelter. I shudder at the thought of some of the damp – even wet – outdoor shelters and wonder how ever people can stand the damp and cold ...

At my own grocer's there was one girl assistant who was a very heavy smoker and who once hinted to me she would like the packet of cigs I get by being a member of the Co-op and having a cigarette ticket which entitled us to 20 a week. I've seen several women hand over a packet to her and have a shrewd suspicion that they got more than their share of extras. One woman in particular never went without slab cake each week. I don't buy it and in my innocence thought that she got it through people like myself not taking it but on reflection the large piece she got and the packet of cigs she handed over so secretively seemed connected.

Tuesday, 4 November. Mrs Lord has got such a good char and says she can spare me half a day – rather more for she will come on Wednesdays from 9 to 2.30. Things have got a bit on top of me lately for scrubbing or reaching soon knocks me out and in spite of the spirit being willing the flesh cannot be driven past a certain point. She will do outside work – windows and paths, the scrubbing and polishing. In spite of war and a certain slackening of standards I find I cannot go below a certain 'set line' and for happiness sake as well as comfort I find my standards fixed. Lately I've felt tired to begin the day and when Wednesday has to be a hard work day and Tuesday and Thursday a hard Centre day with Canteen Friday, it has rather got me down.

Friday, 7 November. The 'working party', as the conchies are called, all clumped in [*to the canteen*] and the place was empty as they called in on their way to docks and we had not even had time to take our outdoor things off. I was nearest ready so moved to counter to be greeted with 'Cup of tea and a kind look'. I heard Isa giggle in the cupboard where we hang our things but her face was straight as she brewed tea and put it on counter. The one who had asked counted the 22 cups in a row and then said with a leery kind of smile 'And the kind look?'* There was a sound

---

* A few weeks later, on 12 December, there was a follow-up to these canteen encounters with conscientious objectors. 'I was taken aback by one big dirty soldier whose leather jerkin showed he was on labour duty. He said "Cup a tea, lady, and I ain't a conchie". I said "I beg your pardon" and he said with a jerk of his thumb "My mate said 'If you want a smile and a joke with 'em at the counter, tell 'em you're not a conchie in spite of being in the Labour Battalion. They never joke with conchies – just pass their tea and grub over and say thank you.'"! We must have shown it plainly.'

of laughter and feet jigging in the passage and two young sailors came in stepping to the tango on the wireless. The way the counter cleared and the conchies drifted to one end all together and sat quietly talking was really funny – the sailors were such boys and several of the conchies had greying hair. We had to laugh at antics of the sailors – and that egged them on and they danced a dance of their own that was a cross between a Salome dance, a hornpipe and an Apache dance and was clever enough for the halls!

When Mrs Thompson came in she brought a friend and they were busy talking of the Russian crisis and the bills that have sprung up overnight on all the hoardings, 'Russia's Crisis is Britain's Peril', in vivid scarlet on a white background. [*German forces were encircling Leningrad and threatening Moscow.*] The friend was emphatic about it – we should and *must* take part of the strain off Russia and attack Germany while we had the chance. Mrs Thompson and one of our squad said 'Oh, I don't know. Germany is definitely cracking – 4½ million of her soldiers gone. She cannot hold out at that rate.' Another one said to me in a quiet voice 'It's so easy to rile and govern from a safe place' and I said 'Well, I cannot see how we could get all our soldiers and supplies across. I feel Hitler would like us to start something and then he would smash his way into Britain from his scattered points of invasion vantage, and the Navy could not be everywhere.'

I looked at Miss Butler as I spoke and remembered her life story. She had two brothers in the last war, handsome fair-haired lads of 19 and 22, and both were killed and later the man she was to have married. Her dress was made and guests invited, even the wedding lunch cooked, and he was killed. She took up the broken threads and learned to manage – they are well-to-do people and she had no fixed job of any kind – and her life has been given to the poor. She goes managing little bed-ridden children, often in poor and not clean homes, and has made her life full of thought for others. She said something that set me thinking for she asked 'Don't you think all this waiting and waiting will have a rather bad effect on our soldiers? I mean it will give them too much time to think of what is in front of them – to realise how very little they can look forward to. You know I'm not in sympathy with flag waving and shouting but somehow it must be extra nerve wracking for the soldiers of today. My brother went out in a flame of enthusiasm that carried them along and did not let them think of tomorrow while these boys have so much time to think of tomorrow and tomorrow and tomorrow.' I looked over counter and at the group of talking men and the quiet ones who were writing or reading long letters of many pages. Perhaps it was Miss Butler's words but the 'shadowed' look seemed so plain. It's a dreadful thought – so many hells, so many heartaches.

Tuesday, 11 November. Somehow I cannot feel that religion as we know it will outlast this war. It got a shaking last war and I feel that after this one is over people will turn more from priests who offer things that mean so little – not turn from God and a feeling of goodness and order some-where but from old fashioned and out-of-date creeds and shibboleths and of beatitudes that Oxford Group curates [*preaching moral rearma-ment and spiritual renewal*] twist into defeatist utterances that lose their value either as a comfort or guide. John McLintock came the other day and I was glad I was out. Why that man ever looks at me I don't know or bothers about asking for Cliff's address. Cliff collects the oddest friends but that lonely curate is one of the oddest and I will *not* have him round me. He annoys me and raises a devil of contention in me that could quickly be turned into an abusive manner. His Oxford-Group-cum-Conchie attitude is like a red rag to a bull to me and I know it's only in a spirit of mischief that Cliff bothers with him now. I did not mention his note to Cliff [*who was at home on leave, with a friend, George*].

Wednesday, 12 November. After tea Cliff and George insisted on their Tarots being read and George thinks it is uncanny. I don't think he has ever had them spread and read for him before and what to me sounded an odd jumble of events and people to him were understandable. I told him they were 'not sailors' cards', and there is a job at the Admiralty [*George was in the Fleet Air Arm*] in the offing that he feels keen about as it would allow him to go on with his chemistry. A girl either slightly older or taller would re-enter his life and unless he cared enough to marry her would cause him to feel a 'fool or a cad', and a quarrel with a man who limped, and a surprise in the way of a little money from an old woman – grandmother probably. The two latter were laughable for George's father gets gout and is very cross and they get at variance and his grandmother died a fortnight ago and there is a suspicion in the family she has a little hoarded away somewhere in her effects and it is being searched for! Cliff has changes soon – and the 'island plainer' – but no immediate going overseas. What looks like another course of training and a queer 'calamity' round him – might be a bad raid wherever he is. To see their interested faces was amusing. I am always tickled at the boys' attitude to my 'parlour trick' of card or tea cup reading. I never mention it or offer to 'read' and they hint and hint and then rather sheepishly pass their cup over, or I find my cards on top of my work basket or on table by me! My husband won't ever have his read – just because I once 'saw' a 'blank' in his cards and a strange bed for him – and he had six months illness of sciatica and was unable to work and was at Buxton [*in rehabilitation*] for nine weeks.

Thursday, 13 November. When I think of the slap happy way ugly little houses were strewn for miles along roads, with no thought of a centre or plan of living, my husband says 'ribbon building' was cheaper for the builder who had no street planning – I do so hope there are definite plans for the future and not vague hopes. When I recall Greenodd in my childish days it was a centre and magnet for all the countryside. Church on Sunday. Band of Hope. Sports and hound trails on Bank Holidays, always followed by a dance. Field day for the Sunday school scholars – a glorified garden party – Harvest Homes etc. We seemed to be all friends together and when people were sick or in trouble it was *known* and helped. I don't care what George says – it's that indifference to little things that has got us into the mess we *are* in. If we don't stop to pick up a kiddie that has fallen or ask after a sick neighbour and do her shopping or mind her baby we will not worry about Poland or Russia's feelings and hurts or try and understand big things.

George said 'You are rather a funny person, you know – you have some odd viewpoints', but isn't everyone funny and odd somewhere? My Gran was 'funny', and so is Aunt Sarah, but they are kind and their odd ways of looking at things hurt no one. George thinks if we batter and kill and kill and break up the Germans our troubles will be over, but you cannot kill *all* of them, and anyway there must be quite a lot of Germans who are good and sensible and 'ordinary'. By Gad, I'd not like to stand or fall by lots of own townspeople never mind countrymen – you cannot judge in masses. George says 'It will be over in nine months' but pressed for a reason does not seem very coherent. Short of Europe being sunk under the sea for 24 hours, I cannot see his very decided opinion being worth much.

Friday, 14 November. It gives you a feeling hard to describe when you have seen a ship launched and built and sailed away. It's a person, splendid and powerful, and I can understand the white faces and tearful eyes in the Yard when one that has been there has gone down. [*It had just been learned that the aircraft carrier the* Ark Royal *had been sunk.*] ... When I got in to make tea at 5.45 I found the boys already in – two very changed ones too. Gone was the gay irresponsible Fleet Arm lad and a quiet eyed man who said little after he had said *'1600 people* on the *Ark Royal.* I wonder how many got off?' Cliff had a withdrawn look and tea was a very quiet meal and soon after Isa came in to say goodbye to them and we then went to the station. I think wartime stations the nearest place to the old-time idea of Hell there is. Darkness and confusion and bitter cold. I feel as if I have a nasty cold coming on and got a bit of a throat, and standing round waiting for a train that was late chilled and depressed me and I kept thinking of the *Ark Royal* and all the valuable lives that might be lost.

Nella's new home help, Ena, had come for the first time the previous Wednesday, 12 November. According to Nella that day, 'she is a scrap of a woman with a very troubled lined face although she is only 30, so perhaps I'll not have her long'. Her husband worked in the shipyard.

Wednesday, 19 November. When Ena came this morning she could hardly croak with a cold and said 'Half Barrow seems sniffing and coughing'. I said 'Are you fit to work, Ena? It's good of you to come, really.' She said 'Well, I'd not have gone anywhere else but I said to my husband, I'm good at sizing folks up and Mrs Last will not insist on windows and outside work today and will find me a job indoors'! She is an odd scrap with that stunted look of malnutrition in childhood and the quick fierce pride of one who has had to fight a battle to keep up appearances in the face of odds. Her shoes were dreadfully broken and squashy and I decided I'd give her my house shoes that I use for lighter housework. I said carelessly 'If your shoes are damp, Ena, you had better change them. See – I'm sure mine would fit you.' She thanked me and put them on and I said 'If you find them comfortable you could keep them'. She just said 'Thank you' but after awhile she said 'I've never been lucky enough to work for anyone with small feet before', and she looked down at her feet contentedly and then said quickly 'But I'll stop a bit longer this afternoon for you'. I smiled and said 'That's nice of you, Ena', and nobody's pride was hurt. She is worried rather at having to register on Saturday – so afraid of having to go into the Yard now her children are evacuated for she is not really strong and she says, if she had to work day in and day out, could not stand up to it.

Thursday, 20 November. In walked my cousin Jean and her fiancé and started jabbering. I am not in tune with them one bit and their silly plans for their wedding. I felt rather sorry for Jean as I looked at her tonight somehow – and for all the girls of today who marry. They just 'go on' and there is not the thrill of a new life and house, just their job, 'the only difference being you sleep with your husband instead of your sister', as Jean put it. They will have two large rooms from Tom's father and have really nice bedroom and dining furniture and will share the service of the housekeeper and maid and Jean will not be alone when Tom is fire-watching or on Auxiliary Fire Service duty and as Jean said brightly 'If I get tired I can always have a baby and rest from work, can't I?' It's like a union between a suet pudding – a cold one – and a feather plume. Odd how they have an attraction for each other. I hope it turns out better than I feel about it.

Wednesday, 26 November. A wet cold day and Ena came half an hour late and looked so tired and fagged with her cold I felt sorry to see her working about, but she said she felt 'not so bad'. She was railing about the rivetters – her husband is a labourer in the rivet store. She says they are selfish and make so much money the ordinary working days that they won't work overtime 'for the income tax' and says boys who are barely out of their time can earn from £10 to £15 a week. Her husband can only earn £3 7s od for an ordinary week and, as she says, when 18s has to be sent for the five children who are evacuated – or them kept at home – it's not much at all ...

There was a ring at the bell and my husband showed in two over-dressed women and I smelled new rich at once. The conversation started 'Are you Mrs Last – the one who makes such wonderful dollies?' 'I'm Mrs Last' (I felt 'short'). 'Oh, then perhaps Mrs Wilkins has told you about my order for them. I'll buy *any* quantity but if you have a dozen now I'll take them. I HAVE THE CAR.' And I knew jolly well she had not had one long, or her lovely fur coat, or her earrings like chandeliers sparkling in the light, or her rings on her fat hands, or her really lovely perfume that spoke of matched cream and powder as well as perfume. My husband was in the kitchenette and he said afterwards 'My dear, I never heard anything funnier. I was glad I was out of room and could laugh in peace.' *I* was not amused. Flu and irritation at people like that cracked my manners badly and I said 'I think there is some mistake. I have a *hobby* and I make dollies for my *friends*, or kiddies at the Hospital. Till last Xmas I had never taken money and if I average one a week all year it answers my purpose – to pay for tea, biscuits and sugar to "turn over" at Centre. There is six hours work in each dollie – pretty hard going. Where and how do you imagine I can mass produce them? Or do you realise that 5s is even yet a charity price – and I only as I said make for friends.' She said 'You are not at all obliging' ... She went on – and this is what made my husband laugh although like me he really felt angry – 'Well, I'll HAVE to have a doll from somewhere for my little girl, and I'll pay extra if you will make it. I've just paid £5 9s 0d for a train set for the boy and all the girl wants is a doll. Look here, if you make me a really NICE cowboy I'll give you SIX shillings! There now!' If she had said £1 I would not have made it – not for anything at all.

I felt mulish. My husband said 'Well, you have often talked of the new rich and what mean streaks they had, but now I know'. I said 'Ah, if I'd put a doll in a shop window and marked it at 2 guineas – "exclusive" – she would have rushed to buy it and bragged of big price.' My husband knew the family and she lives with her father and brother who ran a good tobacco shop. They have both gone into Yard and are either boiler makers or rivetters like her husband. Although the shop does little now she runs it and has a maid to do the housework – a rather mental although hard working woman who will not be taken off them – and they live entirely free, all of them, for the slight services she renders her father and brother in keeping the shop going. I looked at my little smiling cowboys – the four out of the six I *must* make for Hospital, for I cannot let Matron down altogether – and I thought 'I'll *not* let you go there, not if I cancelled all my Xmas orders and sent you all to the Hospital'. I like to think of them going to a good home or else to a child with no toys or a sick child. I felt so cross it made me sick.

Saturday, 29 November. Yesterday when I was in the car with Mrs Diss she said 'You really should have a WVS coat and hat for if there was bad trouble I count on you to take over a district or else the mobiles and be recognised as an official. Hospital Supply might cease to function, you know, and although I would never take you from there in ordinary circumstances, for I really do appreciate your work there, I have a job and place waiting if there was a blitz or invasion.' Me – I don't like to be rushed into things so said I'd think it over. I talked it over with my husband and asked for my Xmas present to be money and he said he would give me £1 which will buy my hat and scarf. The coat is £4 10s 0d and I've got £1 which I would use and as my coat will not come till after Xmas I could scrounge and save the other, for I've not much of my own wee income this year. My old tweed coat is now four year old and showing signs of giving out soon and anyway would not last much longer and if I've to go on 'being a soldier' I'll need a heavy 'good' coat. Mrs Waite will be *furious*. She set herself so on being 'on her own' in Hospital Supply and not a part of WVS. She ran Hospital Supply last war and, poor old lamb, she hates either cooperation or being part of WVS. I'll be tactful and not wear it to Centre. She is old and must not be upset for she is really a grand old trouper.

Monday, 1 December. I went to the hairdresser's today and will go in future on Mondays for I'm rearranging things generally and with Friday afternoon at Canteen, it's too hard to go out in the morning as well. On a wall where I pass on my way there are always town announcements and I noticed today a big poster issued by Communist Society and calling on the Youth, who will have to rule the world in the future. It's puzzling and rather upsetting to many people to read on the Communist posters that they are held in the Town Hall itself, where *no* meetings were held before the war and now are only held because there are so few halls available. The fact that our Director of Education is a big Communist, and in last war was a conchie who spent six months in jail for insulting remarks and behaviour toward soldiers, puzzles people who come to Barrow even more. It's a startling thought that more people are being encouraged to be Communists now and it will no doubt be one of many problems after the war.

Tuesday, 2 December. It was a dreadful morning and I felt a bit nervy going down in the bus through the thick fog for visibility was so bad that we kept stopping with jerks that nearly shook our heads off! ... I went into a stationer's for a 1s 3d calendar called the Churchill Calendar, with twelve large 'alive' and vital pictures of Mr Churchill. Someone had bought one and we thought we would like one for Centre. Mr Spencer, the shopkeeper, said 'When I bought that lot the traveller stared and said "Are you buying one for everyone in Barrow?" but I bet I am refusing them before Xmas, never mind New Year, for they are selling at the rate of six or seven to every other kind' ... I had a sadness as I walked the foggy street, a regret for the spirit that craved so for 'life' and 'expression'. Is this what Arthur calls sublimation? I wonder – this 'straight ahead and don't falter or look back' – or is it age? I don't look old – my hairdresser said yesterday that my skin and hair were ten years younger than my age. I don't bulge and my step is quick, but I feel so old, so aged, since war broke out. I wonder if this feeling of the inevitability of *having* to keep on is what brings that sadness to many soldiers' and airmen's faces – ground staff airmen? I never saw it on a naval man's face. I am often startled at Canteen at the types which seem to sort them-selves out. The khaki battle dress helps but it's often as if individuals are being merged into types. It's the folded lips that make for the likeness I think, the lips that pressed tightly to keep back the cry that would have 'keened' out into the silent night those words of protest, refusal, protestation.

Wednesday, 3 December. I felt glad when Ena was coming this morning to help with the heavier work and not even the deep trouble the poor thing was in stopped her from scrubbing and polishing. I've always been struck by the trustful credulity of the extreme poor – and their dis-trust of banks or savings accounts. Poor Ena has paid 2s 6d a week for 24 weeks and had only another two to pay to draw £3 5s 0d. When a money club is started they have 26 members if it runs for 26 weeks and each week one of them gets 'the draw', which is decided by drawing numbers out of a hat and each member knows the date of her draw and works accordingly. Ena changed with one woman who wanted an early draw for, as she said, 'With five kids one wants a bit of money at Xmas'. The woman who ran the club draw was sent to prison last week, for six months, for inciting a lad to steal. I said soothingly 'She will have "books", Ena, and those who pay in their half crowns will take them and you will get yours whether the woman who runs it is in goal or not', but Ena says that she 'never bothered with books or accounts – just trailed round collecting it' ... Ena is a great talker and today entertained me by details of her first husband's neurasthenia and rather horrible suicide

– he cut his throat at an open window and fell into the street. I was thankful when she hurried over her work to finish early – 2.30 – to go an errand for a neighbour.

She lives in one of the oldest streets in town and it was condemned before blitz and if we had not had so much Council property destroyed and damaged it would have been cleared away. The people living in the houses are all very poor people who up to the war seemed 'on the dole' or Public Assistance. Ena's neighbour has a husband, son, and brother in the Yard and, as she puts it, 'doesn't know what to buy with all her money'. Ena [*says she*] knows a farmer well and was going to see if she could order a goose for Xmas and a turkey for New Year – price NO object at all! Ena said 'You should see what she has bought for Xmas. She has spent all the coupons in the house and the girl has a dance dress that must have cost points[†] and will be done with once on – and gold slippers too.' She has paid 30s for a box of [*Christmas*] crackers with lovely velvet flowers on each and got a full dinner set and paid £7... I felt tired out and my back ached so badly and I said 'I think I'll go to bed although it's only 8 o'clock and I'll get my writing done and then lie and read', but Isa came and stayed till after 10 o'clock and I'd supper to make. She looks so peevish and it wipes the look of youth off her face like a sponge. She so resents having to go into her husband's shop – even to escape the Yard ...

Such a lot has gone from life – repose and serenity, leisure and enjoyment in little things like reading or a gay piece of embroidery growing under fingers that are smooth and well kept. It's wicked to grizzle over such trifles. Perhaps it's my back aching again that makes me give a slight backward look over my shoulder ... I count my blessings, as Gran used to sternly tell us to do, and I've so many, fire and warmth and a soft bed and a door to shut out all that troubles and work at Centre and not too bad health. At least I can keep on. Sometimes I wonder if it would be better to have a wailing place like the Jews at Jerusalem and go there and think of all the misery and anguish, the pain and loss that is in the world, and wail to the heavens above. Not keep shying away from thoughts of things, of refusing to think of Rostov, of starving Greece, of our boys in Libya. Thinking can be such a curse. I can well understand why mind tortured people take to drink *or* drugs, for a little nirvana.

Thursday, 4 December. I felt glad when no one called – I like the *Please Begin With Us* and J. B. Priestley programmes [Listen to My Notebook, *at 20.30, written by Priestley*] on Thursday night. J. B. always seems to start one on a train of thought, and tonight my husband said in a startled tone 'Was it *really* like that 100 years ago?' and we talked and wondered if the same startling changes would occur in the next 100 years and if our descendants would shudder at life as lived today, or whether the mad spin the world has got into would have thrown us back even further. My husband gazed reflectively into the fire and then said 'What a long time it seems since Arthur and that pale lad in glasses – I forget his name – used to sit and talk so calmly about this "inevitable war" – and do you remember how Ted and you used to nearly fight over your arguments as to whether germs would be used?' ... I felt the warm tears on my cheeks and as I turned for a handkerchief to wipe them away I was surprised to see my husband's eyes wet. He said 'What a slice went out of our lives, at one stroke. I've only realised lately, my dear, how you must have missed them all [*the young men of her sons' generation*]. You seemed to mother them all, didn't you?' I just nodded.

CHAPTER SEVEN

WINTER'S TALES

December 1941–February 1942

Saturday, 6 December. We went on to Spark Bridge and went into Woolworths at Ulverston for I thought I would like some little oddment about 6d to put in four gay bags I've made for Hospital Xmas tree. I thought they would do for older children. I was unsuccessful – there was nothing suitable under 1s 3d. I thought of a tablet of toilet soap – there was not one piece on the toilet stall, and lately there has been hundreds, of every make. I went back to look at the household stall and there was very little of any kind of soap powder and only a small 'tray compartment' of ordinary soap. It's puzzled me that soap should have been continued making in such amounts, with fat shortage.

Aunt Sarah looks failing and each winter has looked frailer and this fall downstairs has shaken her more than she will admit. She refuses to discuss it – says it's past and 'not worth thinking about' – but at 76 even a strong mind is not enough to override bad attacks of flu and falls down stairs. Aunt Eliza was not in – she is down in Barrow looking for a 'bed sit'. She is tired of the country. Such a difference from Aunt Sarah. One gives to life and the other demands as 'a right', and the one who has given and given although having so little to give has the serenity and balance and the conviction of 'all coming right somewhere'. Aunt Eliza, who has had plenty of money all her life, spent it as she got it, and had a way of seeing the worst in people – *and* telling them! – has no one who really cares for her and her three children don't like her very much – I don't myself. There is no foundation for a liking at all.

People are talking of a pawnbroker's advert – see Thompson's advert in December 6 *Barrow News*. In his three shops there has been an astonishing number of rings, round about £80 and £100, and they have all disappeared from view and a lot of women have got rings who never had them before the war. Today is the first time such an open advert has appeared in our papers. A diamond necklace priced at £700 and a 'bargain' ring at £110 advertised as an 'investment' seems so shocking these days, and in a place like Barrow where there is *no* unearned income unless it's a retired income, and they are never very much. Mrs Atkinson said 'It's a bit odd to have adverts to "save and lend" and those to invest in £700 diamond necklaces in the same paper'. We talked and laughed at another odd advert – she notices them even more than I do with her husband working at the *News* and *Mail*† office. It was worded 'Domestic help may be a reserved occupation and exempt. You will receive good remuneration at ___ Abbey Road', and a number in the 100s told us that it was likely enough a boarding house and one that advertised 30s a week for a maid the other week.

With getting at least four eggs a day I have rather too many and today let Mrs Atkinson have half a dozen – greatly to her delight. I'm keeping accounts and putting any egg money away in my Post Office box in case I decide to buy day-old chicks again in spring. As my bill for mash comes to only 5s 8d I find it's a cheap price to pay for all the eggs I want for table and cooking. It's a bit embarrassing to receive so many enquiries for eggs and to be told that 'I'll be glad to buy any eggs you have left' by so many friends. I decided to keep hens, though, for our own use and because my husband is not a strong man and I feared food shortage would be greater before this and he would go down through me not being able to get enough of the little extras I've always got for him, and I feel quite callous to pleadings for 'only one egg for John's tea'. I think '*No* – you skitted† at my "messed up" lawn and only reluctantly put a few cabbages in the borders'. Mrs Atkinson heard me refuse the last mentioned neighbour and say I 'needed all my eggs either for myself or friends' and she said 'Well, of all the perishing nerve. I'm glad you refused to let her have even one. She had enough to say about you starting to keep hens and would not even let her husband put a beehive in the garden as it made it untidy!'

Such a good programme tonight. I love the full Saturday night programmes with *In Town Tonight*, *Week in Westminster* and *They Also Serve*, and the new *Circus* serial sounds good – such marvellous 'effects'. Of all the things I'd like to do would be to potter round Broadcasting House 'seeing the wheels go round', not as a visitor to be rushed from one thing to another but to wander for days round it and meet all the interesting people and watch some of the programmes for myself. I like to see the 'effects' best of all. It often intrigues me where some of our family get their love – and ability – in acting or producing. It's on my mother's sober farming side too for my cousin's girls are such experts in dancing or teaching dancing – rink skating or designing really wonderful dresses for stage work in local amateur shows. My two boys always 'played stage' and when Arthur was a tiny tot he arranged his toys puppet fashion and talked for them, weaving conversations for them in a sequence that lasted for days. Arthur is a good producer, can write in extra scenes, act and make up like an old hand who has been taught or used to it and no one seems to know where it comes from! Gran used to vaguely hint that it came from 'the Spanish hussy' in the family tree!

Monday, 8 December. Oddly enough I found her [*Nella's hairdresser*] jubilant over the war spreading to America and Japan. She said 'It's time the Japs were put in their place and it will make America realise there *is* a war on and they will have to wire in and forget their strikes'. I said 'There is another angle. What about help to Russia and Turkey as well as the munitions, food, tanks and planes for us, and the ships she sends petrol in? I cannot see your view. I am appalled myself.' She said 'I had never looked at it from that angle' and we began to talk of what it would probably mean. Since it has been 'passed' that no married woman has to go into Services, she tells me there is a big rush to get married by women who dread going into ATS and who hope to get into the Shipyard here. She is thinking herself of getting married and going into her fiancé's butcher's shop – he is exempt through what the doctors call varicose arteries …

When I went for a bus to come home after leaving hairdresser's there was a long queue and most of the buses were nearly full of women who had been to matinees and only two or three could get on. Two boys in Air Force uniform rushed from the bottom of the queue and elbowed their way on to the platform past waiting women and children but one big old man calmly 'hooked them off' by coat collar and said 'Now then lads, none of this "Lords of the Air" stuff – wait thy turn' and it made a good laugh. A woman said 'I've noticed in a certain type of youngster of 20 that a uniform seems to develop a swagger and makes them think they have gained importance!'

I was in in time to dash round drawing blackouts – after feeding the hens. Four lovely eggs today. They are always such a thrill to me and seem much more wonderful than they really are. I'd the fire poked into a blaze from its banked† up smoulder and my husband's slippers warm and tea ready to pour out when he got in tired out. We had stewed prunes, cheese, jam, whole meal bread and butter and cake cut into thin slices, and my husband said 'I wish everyone was as lucky as I was. I never seem to know there is a war on. You *do* seem to manage well, my dear.' It's odd to hear him talk like that for he never used to notice how I managed and contrived and took everything for granted. Now he looks at my baking on baking day and says 'All that out of rations! I *do* think you are clever'!

Wednesday, 10 December. With Ena being here I managed to get settled to my Hospital sewing at 1.30 and had a real good afternoon and evening, from 1.30 to 9 o'clock, with only getting up for tea making and serving and feeding the hens – three lovely eggs today – I *am* a lucky woman. I asked Ena if she had got her 'draw' money she was worried about and she said 'Aye, all but 15s, and I'll maybe get that this week', so I felt very glad for her. One of the little girls insists on coming home – I can hear of many evacuees coming home for Xmas. The news of the *Prince of Wales* and *Repulse* [*sunk by the Japanese*] was a sad blow and what about the men? My husband came in looking vexed and he said 'The Bruccianias' – a local Italian family with several shops – 'tuned into Italian and German news and they say our ships were sunk by masses of explosives rained from planes and they had no chance as wave after wave of planes poured down on them and they sunk immediately'. He went on, 'I always say they are no friends of ours for they repeat the foreign news with such glee'. The boys were all born and reared in Barrow but they had big business interests just outside Florence and one brother or the father were always over there and children born were christened Bruno and Edda. *Always* they reminded me of greedy little boys of 10–12, uncouth and bad mannered and grabbing and with all the unlovable traits that most boys pass through and grow out of – they kept theirs and added to them.

If I had been sewing anything else but the dollies for the Hospital tree I could not have kept on tonight. My husband sat so troubled and white and he has got another bad head cold and that depressed him more. [*Sidney*] Strube's dreadful cartoon in the *Express*, so stark and simple with Hitler taking the call for 'Author' against a back cloth of the world in flames, was the only way of thinking of things today. I've always felt that things would be worse before better so cannot say that I've had a shock over the turn of events but I've a sick fear growing as to what will be the next move. Will Hitler start here again? I can never think as so many do that 'he has his hands too full in Russia' to think of us. I feel he is building and creeping and planning and, like a watching patient cat who to onlookers seems unobservant, will pounce and tear, and Britain is so small and where could we hide and keep safe all the helpless ones, I wonder? Any little triumphs that we hear on the wireless sound so small in comparison to the *Ark Royal*, the *Prince of Wales* and *Resolve*. Common sense says that we *must* inflict punishment when our armies go over to Germany but we don't *know*.

A dread of Xmas seems to hang over me. I wish the sun would shine and chase a few of my 'mulligrubs'† away. I feel as if the effort to be bright and cheerful will get me down.

Saturday, 13 December. We went to Spark Bridge and I took a nice pierrot dollie for a cousin's baby girl whose father is in the RAF. I don't know her very well but she is a very nice girl and when I saw her delight at 'being thought of' I was glad I'd taken the dollie. She will save it for Jeanette's stocking. She is such a lovely blonde curly-headed baby of three with the manners of a grown-up. She said gravely 'My daddy cannot come home for Xmas – he has to smack a few Germans out of the sky' and her mother said 'I don't know where that child picks up some of her expressions!'

Monday, 15 December. I saw a funny sight and chuckled whenever I recalled it as I went round town. There is an electric light standard with a waste paper basket at our bus stop and a well dressed woman was standing at that end of the queue. Suddenly she pounced on the waste paper basket and drew out a newspaper saying 'There now, that's lucky. I've a lot of shopping and no paper to wrap things up in. Does anyone else want a bit?' And she dispensed pieces of newspaper with the grace and aplomb of a duchess! I always take paper and a bag or two and a few rubber bands to hold small purchases together. I find them useful.

Wednesday, 17 December. There is a big house across the street from Mrs Lord's taken by RAF for billeting purposes. A little incident I saw at the door this morning made me think BBC 'knew best' and made me more tolerant of Tommy Handley and Jack Train's programme, and perhaps *Band Wagon* and *Garrison Theatre*. A huge covered lorry stopped and through the open back I could see tired, worn-out, unshaven lads who looked as if they had travelled all night and were too stiff to climb out. They started to make a move and one shouted 'After you Claude' and the reply was roared '*No*, after you Cecil' and laughter broke out.* There was a smallish lad who was last and he shouted plaintively 'Don't forget the driver' and everyone laughed and lurched about to limber up and numb feet were stamped. I felt a 'God bless' in my heart as I saw them – and it included Tommy Handley and Jack Train. It's no use getting irritable over things one doesn't like. If they can cheer and bring laughs they are invaluable.

---

* These were staple lines from *ITMA – It's That Man Again* – a comedy show starring Tommy Handley that was on its way to becoming one of the most popular and celebrated radio programmes of the 1940s.

Ena got her final 15s of her money draw and I talked seriously to her and begged her to go into Co-op mutual or the club they run, or else save up in the Post Office. She said 'I believe I will and all. I got a proper fright over this money club and it's been a job to get my own.' She is such a clever little thing and makes and mends and struggles to keep all respectable and she cooks and follows 'that nice Freddie Grisewood' and 'that there comic Mrs Buggins' [*on the radio*] in a way that would flatter them if they knew!

Friday, 19 December. I've decided to give poor Mrs Cumming the chocolate biscuits for her two little ones' stocking. Poor soul – she will be desperately unhappy this Xmas for her thoughts will go back. Commander Cumming's mind *must* have broken for he was such a kind man and would never hurt anyone let alone his wife. Death can be more terrible when it's suicide. She said plaintively that 'There was not even a sweet or chocolate to be had', and now I remember she gave me a huge box of chocolates either last Xmas or the Xmas before, to raffle at Centre, and I made about £1. I got out all my Xmas treasures for my little artificial tree for centre of table and I'll put a bunch of holly in the corner and put all Jack's 'Mickey Mouse' lights on. To other people the glittering balls and ornaments would look like rubbish but I'd not change them for gold and jewels. They are *alive* – with 'memories that bless and burn'. The saying that 'God gave us our memories that we could have roses in December' is truer to me every year – memories that grow stronger and are more real to me than the ugliness of today.

I'm a lucky woman to have such a memory garden where even the weeds were only little ones and had flowers on them. Always the boys had such nice friends and they always kept the two rules I made – no quarrelling and no dirty dishes left for me to wash the next day; *then* they could do as they liked. Ted was such a quiet thoughtful boy. He was older than Arthur. The year before war broke out I bought some tiny crackers – only finger length – for my little table tree. When it came to take them off Ted said 'Don't spoil the look of the tree. We have had so much and rather wrecked the look of the table and the big tree.

Let's keep the wee fellows till New Year's Day.' I think they all went to a dance. Anyway, the 'wee fellows' were never pulled but went away in the box for another year. Ted had no mother. He always said with a wry smile that he 'never had one – only a granny' and I never asked questions. He said once he was 'never a kid till he met the two Last boys' and had never hung his stocking up till he was 26 and slept at our house and shared the Xmas fun. Dunkirk took Ted. There are only my two boys and Jack Gorst left now from that last party – that party when the shadows cast on their faces by the candles that Cliff loved for party teas upset me so that I waked my husband and the two boys by wild sobbings that I could not explain and where I felt a strain to keep all going as usual and felt glad when they went home. I was glad it was Canteen day. I'd have wept all afternoon – and that's no use to anyone and I'd only have had a headache.

Saturday, 20 December. We took a parcel of shirts and socks to the Sailors' Home and some books and I got one of the biggest shocks I've had since the war – and that includes our blitz! I went in as usual and in the little cubby hole of a canteen, which leads to Mr Dickinson's office and which I always just walk through, there was a woman in a white apron very much at home. She came forward to speak – and it was the 'woman in the bus' and whom Inspector Thompson said was 'under observation by Intelligence Office and who was a suspicious character all round'. I feel sure she recognised me and when Mr Dickinson came out of the office and took me through I had a good opportunity of making sure it was the same woman, and also seeing how at home she was. When I went out my husband said 'What ever is to do?' so I must have looked upset and when I told him he said 'We had better go round to the Police Station. The Sailors' Home is one of the last places in Barrow where a suspected spy should be.' I asked for Inspector Thompson but he is off ill so saw another Inspector who is taking his place, called Cotton, and the sergeant who took my statement and he said 'My God' and they looked at each other and then said 'Thank you very much. We will get in touch with Inspector Thompson immediately.' I felt so upset. I thought of that bad woman like a spider in a corner, listening to the sailors talking and, who knows, perhaps hearing vital scraps of news about ships coming and going. I was not frightened this time – not like last time. I felt I'd have helped take her away from that kind peaceful place where the Port Missionary tries so hard to make a home for sailors and seamen and where shipwrecked men are cared for.

Wednesday, 24 December, Christmas Eve. Ena was telling me of her Xmas shopping and the presents she had bought her three little girls and her husband's two little boys. She had bought house slippers and said she had to pay a little extra on each pair and the postage too for the four pair and it meant she had had to 'strike herself off the list for anything new'. She had talked so much about a new blouse and she is such a brave little thing. I could not bear her to be disappointed so I gave her my shell pink ninon† blouse. It's a nice blouse and nearly new but it's more for Ena's age – it was a bit too young for me, anyway. I gave her a little pot of homemade jam and a jelly to make for her eldest girl who had insisted on coming home for Xmas and had helped the farmer's wife with whom she is evacuated pluck chickens and ducks and had saved up for her bus fare and to buy a little present for her mother and father. She is a nice little thing – only ten and while 'being sure there is no Santa Claus' has a wistfully sneaking hope there is! She looked longingly at my little table tree and there was little to give her for it only had glittering glass ornaments and some tiny finger length crackers on it. I said 'Would you like one?' and she nodded and I passed her one and said 'I don't know if there is anything in, dear – open it and see' but she did not and later said confidentially 'I'm putting this in my stocking for a little surprise just in case Santa Claus does not come to our house'. I'd given Ena a lovely rosy apple, a bar of chocolate, two chocolate biscuits and a shortbread one and some Xmas paper and ribbon to tie them up in, and Ena had the slippers and the stepfather had got a writing pad and envelopes and some pencils ...

A neighbour has lost her son – a lieutenant in the Army and only 22. It must have been an accident for they brought him home and he was buried today, Xmas Eve. This is their second son to go and their third and last boy is an air pilot. He went to school with Cliff. It looked so sad to see the military escort standing there, mostly lads themselves, and think of all the boys going – going with all their bright hopes and ambitions unfinished.

Nella sometimes encountered the reality of personal loss. On Boxing Day this year, when she was at the canteen, she noticed 'one lad' who 'seemed so dreadfully ill and dazed and his two pals had a "protecting" air toward him. One of them came back to the counter for more tea and told me he had just got in from Hull where he had been to the "funeral of his family". To my look of surprise he whispered hurriedly "His father, mother, and brother and sister were all killed when a bomb fell at 11.30 in the morning on their house – and it was his father's first week on nights for over a year and he was asleep."' She again encountered this sailor at the canteen on 20 February 1942 and he was not in good shape. 'Now there is a "big eyed" look about his thinner face and he has really maddening fidgety tricks, like tapping with his spoon on his cup all the time or lightly kicking the counter front. He never sits down and drinks cup after cup of tea – one girl asked him if he had a hollow leg! … I suggested he had a tonic. He said "I'm not going near that Medical Officer again if I can help it. I'm not ill, you know – and I know it as well – so why should he say what he did?" Pressed for an explanation, we gathered the doctor had implied he was "doing a bit of lead swinging".'

Thursday, 1 January 1942, New Year's Day. I don't know what I said or how I looked but last night but my husband gave me a bit of a shock this morning for when he came down he said 'A Happy New Year! What would you like to do today for a real change? I think it's time you had one!' I said 'Lunch out and go to Morecambe' – in joke, really, but he said 'Right, we will' and we went. I got up and ready – and all ready – and the hens fed and the fire banked to be ready to poke into a blaze when we came in and we set off at 10.30. It was such a nice soft day and the sun shone at times and I felt so thrilled to have a day out. We had lunch at Carnforth – roast pork, sprouts, carrots, potatoes, kidney soup – and

I had custard apple and my husband had custard and plum pudding. It was beautifully cooked and served at a hotel and was 3s 6d a head. I *do* love a meal out and it's such a long time since I had one so I enjoyed it more than ever. All was quiet on the roads and the shops shut in Morecambe but we went round Lancaster and the shops there surprised and delighted me. I love shop windows and there was not one shuttered or 'masked' – all as usual. Lovely furs and clothes, cakes, fancy goods, silver and curios, although no display of sweets, chocs, or cigarettes. In Morecambe, instead of hundreds of airmen getting grounded in 'foot work' there were WAAFs wherever one looked – girls and women of every shape and size and few looking better for uniform or trying to all 'move together'. Men generally look better for drill and discipline but women rarely do.

We called round at my in-laws to wish them a Happy New Year and I nearly started the year by quarrelling! One of the two of my husband's sisters was in and the talk turned on eggs. Her husband earns at least £9 a week for he is a very good electrician in the Yard. She said 'I'm lucky for I can buy all the eggs I want and get for our Flo as well from Millom from a chap Stan knows. I pay full price of course, 3s 6d a dozen.' I said 'The price is 2s 6d, Elsie – that woman could get into trouble'. She said 'Don't be so damned daft. She would not let me have them for 2s 6d when she could take them to a packing station and get 3s 6d.' When I explained she got vexed and I could see she thought it 'another of Will's wife's odd ways' so I turned the subject. She is one of many I hear of and who cannot see they are 'doing anything wrong' or being a little black market on their own.

Friday, 2 January. The conchies all clumped in to Canteen bringing a dreadful smell of oil for they were unloading it at the docks. They gulped their hot tea and asked for a sandwich to eat on their way back to the docks. I despise conchies and won't cook for them for they get regular meals and no 'double guards' but somehow this lot has grown to be 'my' conchies and as such I have a grudging feeling that they will have to be looked after – and there is not much comfort in a beet sandwich.

I took a thick slice of bread and butter, spread it with beans, squashed a potato cake on and another slice of bread on and wrapped it up and said 'How's that?' and a chorus of 'Same for me, please' went down the line. I said 'You must hold it by the paper and not touch it with your oily hands. It would not be good to get that oil in your mouth.' Men *are* children. They all talked at once and wanted to tell of worse things they had handled and talked noisily and praised the tea and thanked me for their 'okey-dokey' sandwiches! One of the helpers said 'Fancy *you* making a fuss over that bunch. I thought you hated conchies.' I said 'I dislike a quitter of any kind but "hate" is too strong a word to use to that lot. I feel like a school marm toward them. Although their "principles" are not mine, they are doing a job and a very dirty one at that, today. Thinking things over, Mrs Hunt, I believe I dislike them less than many in the Yard who flew there and dug themselves into good jobs at the first hint of war.' There is a cousin's wife of my husband's at Canteen and she kicked my shins till I could have yelled and afterwards said 'When you drop bricks, Nella, *do* look where they land. Mrs Hunt's husband, son and [*daughter's*] husband are all among the "fliers" you talked about.'

Saturday, 3 January. It's high time some system of pooling tradesmen's vans and lorries was made compulsory. It's really shocking how some tradesmen waste petrol, and here in Barrow there is no check or stint of petrol. If a painter or plumber has a trailer on his car for business purposes he just asks for and gets all the petrol he wants. That means all his friends can get odd coupons for joy riding. Those trades people who went out of town during the blitz and who bought or rented cottages and go backward and forward must use transport petrol and when I see the overlapping of milk alone in our district I always think of the petrol waste. There is one delivery that makes a detour of over a quarter of a mile to deliver milk to one neighbour who recently moved here and who 'always has got her milk at Crow farm and couldn't change now'. The thing that has always shocked me ever since the war has been the joy riding of cars and buses to Lakes – by the registration plates, coming from a good distance. By the papers Canada is cutting out all private

motoring and South Africa and Australia making drastic cuts in petrol
but we have gone on and on wasting petrol. Although our little Morris
is the joy of my life and about the only pleasure I have, I still say that
more drastic cuts could and should be made. We don't seem to have that
ruthless cooperation yet. It's as if our leaders are afraid of the people and
their reactions to war changes. Celery was very dear today – 1s 2d and 1s
3d a stick – and I felt very glad ours was big enough to dig up ...

We got the decorations down. There is no Twelfth night party now
to keep them up for. All my tawdry but dear glass balls and Jack's Mickey
Mouse electric lights are packed carefully away and I rolled up the best
streamers of crinkled paper in case I cannot get any next year. I had a
'wonder what will have happened before these come out again' but a
feeling of relief that Xmas was over and behind me. I've felt somehow as
if I'd been 'playing a part' these two weeks for I've been gay on top but
underneath I've felt a sadness rather hard to explain. Perhaps the boys
not being here, and my husband is not at all well and needing all the
vitality I have to spare to keep him going – all my care and thought as
to food and that 'giving in' to keep him happy, or at least not miserable.

As 1942 began, Nella's mood was, indeed, sometimes low. On 6 January she
was ruminating on her sense of unimportance. 'I can do nothing for any of the
boys – not even make them a cup of tea. Nothing at all. They have all gone, all of
them, and if they come back into my life will be so different as to be strangers.'
She was – at least temporarily – overtaken by a sense of loss, and anxiety for a
precarious future. These, of course, were tumultuous, uncertain and, for many
people, deadly times. The following evening, 7 January, as she heard Big Ben
tolling the hour before the nine o'clock news, 'I could not form sentences in my
mind. I felt a sadness and futility and a feeling that we were all part of a whirling chaos, each whirl taking us further away from stability, security and all we
know – or did know. To "pray for peace" is to ask a miracle – like the prophet
of old asking the sun to stand still. And if "peace" was granted it would leave a
tiger that had tasted blood rampant – in the Nazis and Japanese.' There was, she
acknowledged, no way out of war and all its miseries. And she was critical of the
'wishful thinking' of those who had persuaded themselves – unrealistically, she

thought – that the tide of the war was turning in Britain's favour, and that the conflict would soon be over (8 January).

Friday, 9 January. When I got down to Canteen there were two lorry loads of reproachful soldiers who told me it was 'a minute to two and no kettle boiling, Mum'! I sent one flying for the milk and one for the key and when we all went in they took blackouts down, lit gas radiators and helped get out cups and saucers and joked and laughed as I counted out biscuits for they had no time to wait for toast. I often get laughed at for my fussing over plates being hot and knives and forks matching and not a huge knife and a little fork. Our cutlery is terrible and ranges from three-pronged country forks to tea knives with coloured handles bought from Woolworths. Today one of the lads got a plate and said 'Give us 1d of those beans'. They were only plain boiled and I'd not added the tomato soup square that colours and flavours them and I said 'Alright, they won't take a minute to heat'. He said 'Don't bother, I'll have them cold' and as I very doubtfully spooned them on a plate I said 'I'm sure these won't be good for you' and a laugh went up and one said 'What about kidnapping such a jewel and taking her off to our camp? It would be a change to get a *hot* hot dinner.' And turning to me he said 'Have you ever eaten cold hash or hot pot?' and I said I had not and they said 'Wait till you are in the Army'. Such a dear crowd of gay boys. I felt a 'God bless' in my heart as they stamped out so laughing and gay ...

Thousands of bright stars tumbled out of the frosty sky, and in spite of my parcel of scraps for the hens I walked home. I like to walk alone sometimes and clear my head of all trying thoughts. I've often thought as I looked at the stars that it was presumptuous to think that in all that number there were no other worlds with people on and I wondered tonight if there were indeed other worlds, all with their problems and worries – even wars. The searchlights all round the town swept in pencils of light, like feathers dusting the bright stars, for their beams seemed to stretch so far into the quiet sky.

Monday, 12 January. A woman I'd not seen for a long time overtook

me on my way to the bus and we got on the same one. She was really
beautifully dressed in spite of the bad morning and stumped along in a
pair of sheepskin Glastonburys† that fascinated me by their girth. Her
fur parka matched her lovely coat – but her gloves wanted mending.
She moaned and moaned about 'nothing to buy' and spoke of 'unnecessary cuts' by Lord Woolton – and 'What was he anyway? A dirty Jew.'*
And she at any rate would take badly with it (toss of the head) – she
had 'never been used to such pinching'. I'd had quite enough and I hate
conversations in buses that are loud enough to entertain others *and* I've
a long memory and remember that Mary Hagan was 'shanty' Irish. I said
'Don't worry, Mary. You will get used to *all* our English ways, like you
did to wearing shoes and stockings when you first came over'. I hope
she got her silly mouth closed again before lunch. She gaped like a fish
as I smiled and said 'Gooood morning' and stepped off the bus. 'Dirty
Jew' indeed – and only the fact that her father died and her mother
came over to live with a sister and work in a jute and sails mill saved her
from crying fish round Dublin as her mother and elder sister had done.
That's the worst – and the best may be – of a small isolated provincial
town: if anyone starts to 'put on dog'† there are people who remember
earlier days!

Wednesday, 14 January. I was glad to see Ena go. She talks and talks
all about nothing, like a person who is nervous and not sure of themselves. Her time – half day – is up at 2 o'clock or 2.30 and it's 3s 6d and
insurance which will be another 4d or so and although I'm thankful
to have her it seems a lot for what is done, and the way I have to keep
working with her. Then there is the lunch problem, and the poor little
thing hangs on till I have to make a cup of tea before she goes. She gets
her outdoor clothes on and if I have got washed and changed to sew she
stands talking and talking.

I get such odd glimpses of the mind of the very poor. She was talking

---

* The Minister of Food was in fact a Unitarian. Anti-Semitism was rife in Britain at this
time, and Nella occasionally gave voice to it herself.

of a man in the Yard who won £50 the other week in some football 'points'. She said 'George and me sat and talked of how we would spend it if he was ever lucky'. I thought of their five children, their badly blitzed house – they can only occupy the downstairs rooms – their battered and inadequate furniture. She went on, however. 'Yes, we have got it all planned – a month in Ireland with George's people and no work for George this side of Easter.' I felt rather shocked and said 'But Ena, you would not be let go off to Ireland without some business reason, and George would be fined for staying off work you know. Besides, look at the nice things you could buy with £50 – even yet – for a house.' She nodded but said 'Aye, that's right, but as we say, it would come right out of the blue and be no trouble to save so we would get all the joy out of it we could.' While my prudent thrifty side was shocked, the 'Over the hill to the other side' said 'Why not?' and [I had] a feeling of envy for the courage of mind that could shout its plans so gaily.

Friday, 16 January. I always used to say to the boys 'If you are in doubt as to which course of action to take, take the one that is kindest, or at any rate will cause least hurt or pain to anyone', and it looks as if I'll have to follow it closer myself in future. When the non-combatant lot came in [*to the canteen*] the conchie group among them seemed quieter. They only shouted and stamped because no one took notice of them. One impudent grinning lad was absent – he had the wide turned back lips and glossy kinky hair of a Negro although his skin was white. Last week when he looked so cold I relented and gave him a hot sandwich that I keep for A-A boys – I won't cook for the well-fed conchies as a rule. Before I could ask where he was they told me he had been killed by a lorry that either slipped its brake or skidded after they left the Canteen last week. It didn't matter but I felt so glad he had had his hot sandwich and I seemed to see his pleased grin as he took it. Mrs Fletcher said 'Wasn't it odd we should have joked with him last week?' for we none of us like conchies. We all have someone in the Services and look on them as quitters.

Sunday, 25 January. I was determined to have what the boys called 'a real banquet' of a dinner – *and* I did. [*Cliff was home on embarkation leave.*] My little shank was only fit for boiling so I boiled it till it was nearly tender and then popped it to brown among the potatoes that were nearly done. I opened a small tin of grapefruit and served it first and then the roast lamb, baked potatoes and brown gravy and lots of lovely sweet sprouts from the garden. Then jellied apple pie, warm and fragrant, with custard sauce. Coffee with a pinch of salt as we make it for the Canadian boys at Canteen and a cream cracker each with a wafer of cheese. Everything was perfection and I could have purred like a happy cat. Cliff said to his father 'You don't realise, you know, what a wonder meal this is. You should see and taste the food in hotels now. George paid 12s 6d a head for three of us at his farewell dinner and quality and quantity were far below this meal, and instead of grapefruit we had veg-etable hors-d'oeuvres.' I was very tired after I'd tidied round although my husband helped me, and I sat and rested and listened to *Hobson's Choice* – I love the Sunday afternoon plays.

The Atkinsons came in at 5 o'clock, except Norah who was working till 5, and we waited tea till 5.30 and all sat down together. It was a real Xmas day tea for I'd kept goodies for Cliff, and most of the Xmas cake. We had tongue and chutney, fruit set in jelly with a wee dab of tinned cream, mince pies, chocolate biscuits, whole meal bread and butter and warm split tea buns – and no skimpy helpings. I could have sang aloud with happiness to see them all. They had such a good tea and Mrs Atkinson said quite seriously 'Let's split our things in future, Mrs Last. I never thought of having a gorgeous tea like this when Xmas had gone. In future don't let's both "spread a feast" – I'll do it one day and you another and next Xmas the boys may all be home and we could have grand "double" parties.' I'd a queer fancy that their faces changed in the firelight – that it was an old-time party and not just four next door neighbours come in to tea ... We played Newmarket[†] and laughed and 'cheated' and pinched each others' stakes and Cliff teased and tormented the two girls and we laughed and laughed at the wit and fun that flew. I'd a big carton of 'Honeycomb' sweets I had saved from Xmas when my husband got it from a shop where he was working – such lovely 'sucky', coloured glucose blocks. The carton was gay and seemed Xmassy and Cliff said 'Let's sing carols' but instead got out his portable gramophone and records and insisted on dancing. With seven people in our dining room plus an air raid shelter in the bay window I thought it impossible, but not that one. He showed the girls some new steps – Norah insisted they were so new he had made some up tonight! He was a mixture of a silly school boy and 'travelled man' who had seen different things and from the noise and laughter there might have been twenty happy young things. We were sorry when Mr Atkinson had to go early – fire-watching at the printing works where he works – but as Norah had to be at work early in the morning and Margaret is hard at it at her commercial school, we split up at 11.30. Such a happy day, a 'memory' day.

Wednesday, 28 January. Cliff [*who had just been suddenly recalled from his leave*] said 'It's queer somehow to feel a new road is ahead and all you know is held behind. I hope you are not bombed out or anything, Mom, mostly of course for your own sake, but also because I always want to feel I've something to hold onto. I'm a queer devil I know but I do appreciate your love and care – don't forget that.' I said 'No, I won't, my love, and always remember we will think of you and if you don't get your mail never doubt that it has not been sent. I'll never fail you and whatever happens, if I am alive, there will be a home somewhere – if I have to build it myself', and I laughed a little and tried to make him laugh too. His reply surprised me. He said 'I've got my plans for after the war. I'm going to have a country pub and you shall help me. So keep young and lovely' – and he ruffled my hair. I'm not the one and have never been the other but the love that made him say such a thing warmed me and the kind look in his eyes made me feel a very lucky woman. He said 'Now don't laugh so. You know you are a born hostess and your tact and gift of peace would be a wonderful asset. Can't you see us making a fortune? Let's make a promise.' I said 'You want more than "tact or a love of peace". You want money and experience and a good

business head, you know, and neither of us have that. Beside, it's a wife
you will want and not your Mom.'

Saturday, 31 January. There was a ring and to my surprise it was Mrs
Hunt, one of my helpers at Canteen. She is such a nice sad little thing
and I knew she had divorced her husband early this year and she
had told me she was going down to London – Slough – 'on business' and would not be at Canteen this week or two. I knew her husband's people. Her mother-in-law had the morals of an ally cat and her
husband knew it when he married her so it was not surprising when
the two children were rotters, albeit charming ones, and both were
divorced. I could not tell what Mrs Hunt came for so I made a cup of
tea and we sat up to the fire. She sipped her tea and gazed into the fire
and said with averted eyes 'Would *you* take a man back after he had
lived with another woman for six months, a common factory girl with
nothing but a mop of blonde curls – and those bleached – to redeem
her from looking what she was?' Me, I don't like butting into people's
affairs, or interfering at all, so I said gently 'Would *you* forgive him,
my dear? That is the question.' And she said '*I always have*' and I felt
a great pity for her. She said 'Mother is so very bitter, Mrs Last, but
you know your generation cannot grasp the jungle law that is growing
on us today and it's women that are the worst. Among the set I was in
at Slough "morality" as I'd always known it didn't exist at all and my
husband seemed to fall into the same slack ways.' She said 'Why once
when a girl of twenty was being discussed someone said of her "I really
believe she is a virgin still" in the same tone that one might have discussed a spotty face or a slight disfigurement'. She said 'What *should* I
do? What *should* I do?' and big tears poured down her poor little face.
I'd the queer pitying detachment that thought how very little any personal problems mattered and I gathered her in my arms and as I wiped
her face I whispered 'Do as you think, my dear. It's your life. You must
do the best you can.' And she sobbed as she burrowed her face in my
neck, 'Oh Mrs Last, if he would only *want* to be forgiven, if he would
only come back'. Poor lamb, she looked a wreck in spite of bathing her

eyes and heavier makeup and I packed her some sandwiches so that she could go straight to the station.

Sunday, 1 February. When people talk so lightly of 'after the war' and as if it was only a short time now before all would 'be the same', I wonder what it will really be like. No one was ever quite the same after the last war and there was more sweeping changes than we realise, but what with so many people being killed and moved to other lands and the wholesale destruction of so much we know, there is bound to be a revolutionary change and 'passing'. How many years before production – even simple farming and husbandry – will get back to normal? How will the millions of young men – and women – react to peace conditions and above all what will all the half-trained youths do? I often wonder what Cliff will do, going as he did into the Army before he had finished serving his time and now being made an instrument mechanic. He will not know enough of his father's business to take over if, as I very much doubt, he would want to do. Then there will be no A-A instruments to attend to, and he will be too old to retrace his steps and start afresh. I tell myself that he is only one of thousands – tens of thousands – but that is no comfort. I talk sometimes to the boys at Canteen, only snatched conversations it's true, but enough to realise that a *mañana* dust and rust is creeping over most of them, a day-to-day kind of existence in which letters from home, being lucky enough to get a packet of fags, and the chances of leave space out the days and make conversation. There is one earnest corporal who, if he is let live, will go far. He persists in putting 'brains trust' questions to the other occupants of a table – questions about 'Was the sergeant right?' or points of etiquette in procedure or Army rules. He is far from popular! He insisted once on showing a woman how to cook waffles! He is I fear too small a leaven to work much good but he is one of the few 'thinkers' in the Army I've met – *and* that includes my Cliff. Cliff says 'When this mess is over I'll go roving for awhile' and he saves every penny he can and buys Savings Certificates. When I was surprised to find he had nearly £50 saved he said 'I've never spent any of my 21st birthday money and you send my cigs. If I've to do *anything* I want I'll have to have money to start off. I'll go wandering and when I come back I'd like an old country pub and we will turn it into a peaceful spot where people who are tired or hurt will come and stay and find peace and healing.' Such an odd mixture of sense and nonsense that one is – so young one minute and so old the next.

CHAPTER EIGHT

TIME PASSES

February–June 1942

'Time passes so swiftly', Nella wrote on 26 February 1942, 'that I often have to pause and think whether the date I've written on a letter is really correct.' She felt it wasn't a matter of just being busy. 'It's as if we have got into a mad whirling kaleidoscope of happenings that form and re-form, pass and re-pass, till nothing seems real and firm any more.' 'Only some great "hidden" force could account for the changes in the world of today,' she observed on 12 April 1942, 'the changes of all we know or knew before.'

Thursday, 12 February. All was so peaceful [*at the Centre*] as we sat for a little rest – and then the storm broke! A real ding dong ROW!! We were idly gossiping about salvage when Mrs Woods said 'Why don't they take those three bronze statues out of the squares? They are no use.' Mrs Waite said 'WHAT – would you destroy history like that?' Then there was a laugh all round for 100 yeas ago Barrow was a village. The docks were made and a German called Schneider started or helped to start the Iron and Steel works and was our first Mayor. A carpenter protégé of the Duke of Devonshire got on well by doing all the Duke wanted whether it was for the good of the future of the town or not, got knighted and was Sir James Ramsden. They got a huge bronze statue as did one of the Cavendishs, the eldest son of the Duke. We were all ribald at first but Mrs Waite was furious. She said 'Would you destroy a tomb-stone in a churchyard?' and Mrs Wilkins said 'I certainly would – ugly, pretentious things, doing no good to anyone'. When Mrs Waite got her breath back she said '*You* don't agree with that *do* you Mrs Last?' I said 'Yes, with all my heart. Why have ugly rows of cold marble. Why not have a "Garden of Remembrance" where trees and shrubs were planted by a gardener with a knowledge of landscape gardening and our ashes only planted? I'd like mine scattered on Coniston Lake, I think.' Mrs Woods acted the clown and said she would like a nice pond over her ashes – one with gold fish in. Mrs Higham thought she would like to lie under a piece of the crazy paving.

It was all very silly and childish but Mrs Waite got so very angry. She called me an infidel – I expect she meant vandal! – and said 'It was what was the trouble with the world today – no respect and veneration for things'. I said 'You are right in one thing – that there *is* something wrong with us all, but don't you think it's because "new skins have been patched on to old bottles" and we try to live in two worlds. Look at the Russian and the Jap. They jumped into a new world and threw aside all outworn ideas, and look at them. Would they hesitate about ugly modern (or Victorian at the best) statues or railings? Would they dither and dither and dither about things?' It was a good thing that we had to get up and get ready for the afternoon lot coming. We would have been at it for hours ...

Later we talked of black markets and ridiculous punishment meted out to offenders. Mrs Wilkins said 'They should be shot'. I said 'I know what I'd do. I'd put them in prison, give them a very stiff fine and then draft them into the Army – into the Non-Combatant lot who see to smokescreen lamps and unloading oil etc., and the first six months I'd put them on latrines.' But the worst part of this black market business is that people make it themselves. I've often been asked by neighbours and friends if I'd let them have a few eggs and of course they would pay the 'proper price of 3s 8d a dozen'. When I say I have none for sale as I let two friends have the few spare I have, and at 2s 6d, the same as they pay in the shop, they think it crazy. I've always held the rather fantastic idea that peace will never come with guns and planes but will be from 'within' – by a change of thought and purpose. What chance is there of peace or a brave new world if it's to be marred by people who have grown more twisted and warped by grabbing and greed, by only think-ing of what they can get extra?

Saturday, 14 February. Valentine's day – the day the birds mate, according to the old country saying! For a day or two lately I've noticed a lot of bird activity and they have practised notes of song. Today a blackbird sat on the fence and he had three clear notes and the thrushes had two good ones and a little warble. It's such a nice place to live in Ilkley Road for it's only a quarter of an hour's walk to town and the bus is handy and yet the wild birds are all about and the Abbey Rooks and the sea birds visit when hungry ...

I quite recklessly spent all my points today for there were few tins of ham about and I liked them so well. I got two small tins of American chopped ham and a pound tin of sausage meat – 12 points each so I'd only 4 points left and I got half a pound of prunes. Although I hardly dare hope that circumstances will bring Arthur and Edith from Northern Ireland for their holiday in June [*their planned marriage did not in fact take place until 1 June 1944*], I shall prepare and hoard up anything extra nice for that fortnight. I already have tinned fruit in my store and if they come I'll use the cake I made for next Xmas. I'm beginning to rather worry about a wedding present. I would so love to give them something worthwhile but if things go on as they have done lately I'll have no money at all of my own – I lost over £200 more that was invested in Shanghai. Poor Dad had his money [*some of which she inherited*] all over the place wherever he thought was a good investment. I've eleven Savings Certificates I've bought with my 2s 6d a week at Centre. If I go on I ought to have quite a lot more and I could give him those and help him in other ways as much as I can. Round town there were more queues than I'd seen lately on a Saturday. Long queues for sweets and confectionery, meat pies and pork sausage. On one window was a notice 'No oranges, no potatoes'! – surely they are going to be scarce.

All was stark and bleak in the countryside as we went to Spark Bridge. The near hills and moors were only sprinkled with snow but further hills and mountains were gleaming white all over. Farmers carting and spreading dung were the only signs of activity – and the wheeling screaming gulls. Aunt Sarah and her cousin Joe looked pinched and wan. It's been a terrible fortnight up at Spark Bridge for it lies rather low and the snow had drifted as high as the top of the windows on several mornings. The warm smell of baking and the good smell of the stock pot on the wood fire was like the very breath of home. They had got their first meat for over a fortnight but a farmer had brought them a rabbit on one day and some wood pigeons another so as my little Auntie said 'They had managed fine'. She said 'We must never grumble, Dearie. If we have a fire and shelter and bread we have enough to thank God for. It would be ungrateful and wicked to complain of a bit of snow when we think of all the poor ones in the world today'. She looks so frail but at 76 has the courage and faith that 'All will come right in God's good time'. Her niece Mary is going to Preston to train for some kind of engineering. I was rather surprised for I thought all unmarried girls had to go into the Services or munitions. [*Mary was in fact shortly to be employed by an aircraft manufacturer.*] She is a lovely restless girl of 24 who has never had just that courage – or selfishness – to break away from a cantankerous father and she has not had a very pleasant life.

Wednesday, 25 February. I listened to the 9 o'clock news with new hope – Sir Stafford Cripps' speech in the House. Churchill is a *grand* man and I would not belittle him or hear him belittled but there was a positive ring about Cripps' speech somehow, a getting down to bedrock. I pray he is given a free hand and that he can cut through the stifling bonds that seem everywhere. Instead of life today having one goal and aim – Peace – we seem to be going on a queer overlapping 'one step forward, two back'. Gosh I wish I could make the laws for a day – I'd be ruthless. Black marketers would not be fined – I'd keep the fines for the buyers; the sellers would go straight into the Army, old and young. I'd find them a job that would jolt them too when they got there! I'd shake up the matinee-whist-drives-in-the-afternoon, Where-can-I-get chocolates? I-must-have-flowers-*whatever*-they-cost, My-dear-it's-my-artistic-temperament-you-know. They would get a job to do, married or single. I'd find some way to make the new rich save beside buying diamond rings 'as an investment, you know' and stop the silly women carrying round rolls of notes in doll-eyed[†] handbags. I often marvel there are not more 'grab' – no 'matched' – handbags ...

My husband says I've a dictator's mind, but I haven't really – I know I haven't. But there is so much to do, for everyone, and I get so frightened sometimes. I feel we are getting close to a weir and that I can hear the seethe and turmoil of the whirlpool and those of us who work and try are only straws that do little good. For one woman who knits or helps at Canteen, or even buys my raffle tickets for my endless efforts at Centre, there are at least 50 who think we are 'so serious minded' – as if *that's* a crime! – or else plain daft to worry – England *always* wins in the end. I want to cry aloud – I don't want us to win 'in the end'. I want us to win soon. I'm 52 and a tired woman and I want my boys – to see them building their lives, not fretting at the futility as my Cliff does. I don't like hens on my lawn and air raid shelters in my dining room. I want to bring peace nearer when *everyone* can be happy. Do you never think of anyone but your over-dressed, over-fed black-marketed selves? I feel myself getting really hysterical inside me – but to what purpose?

February/March 1942 was decidedly a low point in British morale, for much was going wrong and little was going right. Although the United States was now a military ally, it had yet had time to make its weight felt. Some two weeks later, on 9 March, Nella reported her husband saying that '"I feel more depressed than I can remember about the war". I asked in what way and he said "Well, I cannot see us being strong enough to attack and yet if we don't we will soon be invaded – and then what? How long will it take to drive them out, and will England be over-run like other countries?" He spoke so sadly he seemed to set me off on a dismal train of thought and my head and back ached so badly I came to bed early.' Two days later she remarked on her neighbour, Mrs Atkinson's, uncharacteristic moroseness. 'I notice such a change in her nowadays. She has lost her pleasant "optimistic, war will be over soon" attitude and her face is taking on discontented and really feverish lines' (11 March).

Thursday, 26 February. We nearly had a row at lunch time [*at the Centre*]. Such an argument – and an unfriendly one at that! We were sitting over

the remains of our lunch when someone mentioned Cripps' speech –
and up in the air went Mrs Waite! She thought that he was 'trying to
get Churchill's place', and the nasty Bolshie! Two of us thought it a *fine*
speech – and the worst of me, if I really believe in a thing I cannot com-
promise – and I said it was 'time we all went a bit more Bolshie, if it
meant getting down to things and cutting out waste and muddle and
pulled *everyone* up with a jerk to face the realities of today'. [*Nella, a Conservative, would not have been expected to be so sympathetic to the Labour
radical Cripps.*] We all talked at once and Mrs Wilkins slammed on the
table to emphasise *her* point of view but it was difficult to hear anyone
clearly. Mrs Waite did not like either my views – or to hear me scolded
for them! – so in a soothing way she said grandly 'I can *plainly* see what
Mrs Last means, and don't worry Mrs Wilkins, after this war there will
be no Bolshies and Communists. They will have learned their lesson!!'
I could have hooted with laughter but keeping a perfectly straight face
I said 'Yes indeedy. They will all be good little Conservatives and go to
church twice on Sunday and leave their country that they have fought
and suffered so much for to all the old maids of both sexes, the dreamers
and wishful thinkers, and party politics to cook up another war in the
years to come.' That nearly started a war for me but I felt like it – 'real
nowty'[†] as Mrs Higham said. I've felt lately as if I'd like to get up in a big
roomful of people and speak all that was on my mind, to see if I could
awake a lot of people I know. I must be in a militant humour.

Tuesday, 10 March. I listened to the news and the report of Eden's terrible disclosure of Jap atrocities with a cold sick feeling. Two thousand years of martyrs and missionaries, of lives given to 'teaching the
heathen', of unceasing effort and money spent – and this can happen.
I thought of a number of Barrow and the district families who would
be feeling upset over the fate of daughters and sisters who had gone out
to Hong Kong to settle, and that 'there but for the Grace of God go
I', and the helpless women of England. I thought of little bright faced
Ruth who once so shocked me by saying that she and her friend would
always carry a razor blade in their handbags if invasion came – that no

German would get them, they would die first. Sometimes I feel I could shriek aloud for action – to do *something* – and not wait like a rabbit at the zoo for the snake's next meal! I listened to Eden telling us to 'redouble our effort' and tried to think what I could possibly do to help. My little smiling dollie on which I was stitching 'long and short stitch' hair in wool seemed so futile I put it away. I feel so helpless and useless tonight, and yet so eager to do *something* constructive, something worth doing. I looked at my husband's set strained face and wondered what he was thinking about in his innermost mind, that part of ourselves we so rarely reveal. I know he worries over the future – who doesn't? – but he is a very timid nature and I always try not to show if I feel down, but he often notices now and I'm never sure whether it's because he is getting more 'noticing' or that I am less good at hiding things.

Thursday, 12 March. Mrs Wilkins had a bit of a shock today when she went shopping and it rather unnerved her. She has always had a standing order for fish twice a week. However dear or scarce, 2 lb salmon or 2 lb filleted plaice was sent, and oysters, game, poultry and eggs. This last week or two has seen a 'NO delivery – and that means *everyone*' order has come in with a lot of shops. My own grocer started it months ago. It seems Mrs Wilkins just walked in and a queue was waiting, and a very long and impatient one for the fish had been late and had to be sorted and cut up. We were a bit uncertain as to what exactly happened for Mrs Wilkins has a love of dramatics that often makes her exaggerate, but we did gather that loud cries of 'Here, you get to the back of the queue' and remarks about 'Dressed up women thinking their money better than anyone else's' and 'Shipyard bosses' wives fancying themselves' and also threats as to what 'would be done to her fish if she dared bring it out'! I offered to cook the nice filleted plaice and wish I'd insisted for she is an indifferent cook and burned one side. She said she 'would go off fish if she had to queue for it among a lot of common women', a remark that made me smile when I recalled she was a village blacksmith's daughter and until her husband got on, by his own undoubted merits and abilities coupled with very hard work be it said, she was 'only a common working man's wife'!

Friday, 13 March. A rather subdued lot came in [*to the canteen*]. They had been to the funeral of one of the two who crashed on Sunday – a Pole. He was such a gay lively fellow of 30 or so – a sergeant pilot who was taking a spell of training and had flown thousands of miles while the other lad of 23 had been married a month. I would not like to be a canteen worker on an airfield. It's bad enough to lose a few ... One lad, perhaps 26 or so, stood at the end by the stove and we got chatting and he told me he was a chef in civil life and if it had not been for the war would have got a job as second chef in a good class hotel or restaurant to prepare him for his 'chief's' post and then having a little exclusive restaurant somewhere in London. He said he had saved £500 and his father had always said if he could save that amount himself he would put up the rest. I said consolingly 'Why that is marvellous of you to have saved so much – and anyway you will be a treasure where you are, for good cooks don't grow on gooseberry bushes, do they?' He said gloomily 'I had all my papers and two diplomas, but they put me on lorry driving and had to teach me to handle it for I'd never even had a motor bike never mind a car.' He said 'The waste at our camp would make good meals for half as many more and our food is so indifferently served that if the food is cooked properly it's cold and unappetizing.'

Nella tended to be glum about post-war society and people's capacities to put their lives back together after the disruptions of wartime. 'There will be old tired people of all ages', she wrote on 2 April 1942, 'and not just those of three score and ten. There will be people marred in body or crippled in spirit by loss of all that made their world, crowds of half trained and unsettled youths of both sexes, destruction and burnt earth – scorched earth – such a lot of building up with worn out tools.'

Saturday, 14 March. I noticed with a shock today what a lot of empty shops we have in Barrow – tobacconists, little sweets and tobacco shops and fruiterers mainly, although there is also a big one-time clothier's and a paper hanging shop that had two big windows always full of beautiful wallpaper. The empty shops, the shuttered fronts with only a small glass window for display, and the queer hybrid creatures pushing prams with pants, a woman's coat and either a pixie hood or a beret seemed to make the streets so untidy in the bright sunshine. I could not help but think that many women are seizing the excuse of there 'being a war on' to give full rein to all the sloppy lazy streaks in their make-up. When the raids were on *anything* could be understood or forgiven – but WHY NOW? Surely it's best to try and keep on as usual and not let go and grow careless and untidy? Many girls and women who were pictures of make-up and hair sets and bleaches have a really unkempt look as if their use of cosmetics has made them forget soap and water and ordinary tidiness.

Wednesday, 25 March. It is such a heaven sent night. I kept going out into the garden and breathing deep. There is such a calm sweetness over the gardens – an expectancy. I never remember such a backward spring for the warm bright sun in the day now is countered by the sharp frosts at night. I wish I'd an atlas handy. I cannot just place Felixstowe, whether it's near Dover on the South coast or round on the other side. I wish Cliff could have his leave before he starts. It's nearly due now. Perhaps if he gets so far away he will not get it.

I wonder if there *will* be an invasion. I wish I could think there would not be. Nowadays it's not an asset when one's mind turns over a thing, an annoying persistent thing. Try as I do that article in the Sunday paper comes back – '50 planes over Barrow-in-Furness' – and when our raids were on it was thought there were never more than four circling over and dropping bombs. They zoomed over when they went to blitz Belfast – and Glasgow. I wonder if there were 50 then? Sometimes when I have a strained tense feeling I look at the soldiers' faces in Canteen and wonder what they are thinking of. Hitler has perhaps been cleverer than we realise for this waiting, waiting business is setting all thinking people on edge. Sometimes I marvel at the way things have 'just worked out' in our favour – and *only* just. I wonder if our luck will hold.

On 2 April, Nella wrote again of the risk of invasion and how important it was to take the offensive. 'To let the enemy into England would be worse than it sounds.

Some place must be kept sane if there *has* to be a rising, a rebuilding. Some people say "Let them come. They will be caught like rats in a trap and never get away." But the role of a bit of cheese doesn't appeal to me at all.'

Wednesday, 8 April. Ena and I worked well and I'll make do for spring cleaning. As I put my curtains up my mind went back to last year's spring cleaning. Everything was bright and unspoiled and somehow I never saw my little home so gay and attractive as I did then, or felt so proud of it. Curtains and loose covers were nearly new and no blitz had jagged holes in them or cracked my cream walls. This year I had no pride in cleaning, none at all. Rather it was the careful 'make do' care and attention one would give to a hurt or sick child, no hard rubbing that would loosen slack and damaged plaster or ceilings, and tiles in bathroom and kitchenette to be held flat while wiping over for so many are loose, a feeling that 'There, that's over' rather than lingering to admire the polish and sheen on freshly cleaned furniture and brass and floors. Something died in me that night – and perhaps something was born, perhaps a balance was struck. Cliff says that I don't worry over things as I did, and I know I often am content to clean the places that show most and not worry unduly over the rest ...

We were not too late in [*after an evening at the Atkinsons*] and my husband did an estimate he had forgotten. What with 'being dragged out to Atkinsons' and Agnes coming at the weekend he is far from being in a good humour, but when I realise he has two excuses for two moods and I remember other days, I marvel. One thing – I'd not stand them now. I know I wouldn't. I'd say 'Oh, do be your age, my dear. I've smacked the boys soundly for less displays of tantrums' – and I'd go out. We generally 'get nuts when we have no teeth to crack them'. My courage has come too late to change things or let me be like other people and not shut up like a bird – *how* I hate things in cages. The joke is on me for I realise there was never anything to fear – only my husband's fear of life in every way. How much better if I'd realised what lay behind his refusal to go into company or have friends or go places. My energy could have been used in trying to help him instead of frittered in nervous breakdowns and frustrations.

Friday, 17 April. Little Mrs Hunt who divorced her husband and looked so sad was gay as a bird [*at the canteen*] and I could not understand why her close friend was so cool and distant with her. After awhile when Mrs Hunt was collecting dirty crocks, Dorothy said to me 'Kay is riding for a fall, running round with a married RAF officer. I'm not going to go to any more dances with her.' Mrs Hunt knew she was being discussed and tossed her head and said 'I suppose now you know what a sinner I am you won't want me on your squad, Mrs Last?' but I was not going to be drawn into any argument. When we were getting our coats on to come home she said 'Do *you* think that children keep couples together?' and I said 'Oh, I don't know. People are all different, aren't they?' and I thought that nothing could have kept Roy Hunt 'on the rails'. He had the moral make-up of an alley cat – in every way. She went on 'Here I am, 35 and *nothing*, only my Dalmation to feed and that I'm wondering what I will do with if I go down South again and get a job'. She went on, 'Isn't it odd – I never thought I would have to divorce Roy. I'd forgiven him so many times but this time he insisted on saying he was "all washed up" and did not care about his boss knowing the scandal or getting the sack, and yet as soon as he was free he left the girl.' She paused a moment and then said 'The worst thing though he ever did is to give me a taste for "rotten". I don't feel any attraction to a nice fellow now.'

Tuesday, 21 April. Mrs Diss was in the WVS office and as we have not met for some time for she has been so busy getting ready the Girls Canteen and Club and now she tells me that all the bother over the one Mrs Burnett started has been settled, by the WVS taking it over unconditionally. That wipes that muddling old hen out of it for she will only be on the rota if she wants to go at all. Mrs Diss has got £125 by 'tactful suggestion' as she puts it for WVS are not allowed to 'beg for money'. This Club and Canteen will be grand – a big writing room, small sewing, ditto reading and wash and toilet rooms. There was an electric geyser over the wash bowl and new grates in the blitzed rooms and cream washed walls. All looked so very attractive and when finished and the furniture in will be a very homely nice place. The little Canteen will be handy and easily worked and Mrs Diss said 'We could do well with a "mother" to see to running it. I wish often you were not so tied up at Hospital Supply.'

We had reached Christchurch door as she finished this and when she went into our office she laughingly said 'Mrs Waite, I've been trying to coax Mrs Last away'. Never did a few joking words raise a bigger storm. Mrs Waite was *wicked* and I was accused of underhand dealing and plotting with the WVS who, after all, were a body of upstarts whose only aim in life was to strut round in silly uniforms. Things that happened in the last war between Mrs Diss's mother and Mrs Waite were raked up and then Mrs Waite said 'I'm sick of all this WVS nonsense. I ran this place for the Red Cross in the last war and for two pins I'd cut loose and do it again and *damn* the WVS!!' I stood with my coat half off and gasped at the way she went on but Mrs Diss took it all calmly and said 'a case for aspirins if not cold water' and nudged me to go out in front of her and we shut the door and went into the kitchen where Mrs Lewis had made the morning tea. We did not say anything till she left the kitchen and then Mrs Diss said 'You can tell what a sweet hell of a job it was in the last war when the old battle axe reigned supreme – *and* with a rod of iron! She has never been crossed and that is why her two out of three sons are failures and she has no friends.' I said 'Oh, she has never been like this before and she *is* a grand old trooper in many ways and her bark is lots worse than her bite, and she is old and rapidly getting older', and Mrs Diss said 'Bless your old fashioned heart. You *are* a bit of a museum piece, you know' – and I could not quite see what she meant. I'm only about seven or eight years older than she is and there is not a whole generation of thought dividing us ...

Later the others came in as soon as they heard the tinkle of crockery in the kitchen. Mrs Woods said unthinkingly 'What was all the shouting about? It sounded like quarrelling to me.' Mrs Waite started off about 'crawling snakes' and 'tricks her mother would have done' and suddenly I got angry and said 'If I wanted to leave I'd leave. Nothing would stop me. But if you want to make me grow tired of Hospital Supply, you will start bickering and nagging. What I do when I'm not at Hospital Supply is my own concern and to talk of "liking to be where men are" in that nasty insinuating way you did when I said I would rather work in the men's Canteen than change over was quite uncalled for. I *do* like men best – I'm more used to them and anyway I've never heard a man say as many stupid childish things to another man as you did to Molly Diss. You are a very peevish cantankerous old thing and I will *not* be spoken to like that.' There was dead silence and then Mrs Waite said mildly 'I cannot see us doing without a bit of fire for a week or two' and Mrs Higham got up and went out. Later she said 'I went off to have a mild attack of hysterics. Oh, if you had only been at St Paul's and seen the way Mrs Waite has ruled for my time – and it's gone on for 50 years and the Waites have bossed and ruled all and sundry and never moved with the times and suddenly thrown up everything when a new vicar came who was stronger minded than his predecessors. When I tell George [*her husband*] about the way you speak to Mrs Waite – and get away with it – he says you have been a lion tamer the last time you were on earth.' ...

I came home early. I just felt at the end of my patience and my head was starting to tick. Such a lovely evening, and now I can plainly see the buds on the old tree at the bottom of the next door garden and soon the leaves will be out. I felt shocked to find two huge piles of bread in the garage. I was so outspoken that I know I offended several neighbours who used to send their children with wicked waste of bread etc. and I could not possibly think who would have left it. With only six hens I cannot use a lot and so much of this had been kept too long and it was green mould. My husband was very angry and he said 'We cannot put it in the dust bin. What have we to do with it?' and I said 'I'll have to burn it in the morning'.

Thursday, 23 April. Mrs Waite was in the best of all good humours and Tuesday was all forgotten. Mrs Wilkins had a new pair of shoes that nearly sent us into fits when we looked at them! She takes size 8s and they were gay navy and red *wedgies*! – anything more like coronation barges it would be difficult to find. She talked and talked of how she never looked at shoes under £3, even before the war. Mrs Higham and I smirked cattily and stuck our pretty slender sized 3s in their rather shabby scuffed shoes and never said a word. Mrs Higham is such a laugher and says she has more fun over things like that than the funniest film. She said her husband wonders how we find time to work and yet laugh so much! ...

I had the afternoon tea to prepare but luckily Mrs McGregor came in and brewed tea and poured out and I hurried round and raffled two embroidered guest towels and got 14s 6d and did the rest of the rhubarb. As I went round joking and joining in all the chatter I felt the surprise I often feel at myself – there was no talk of war, there seemed no thought [*of it*] in all the busy happy room. I asked after sons and daughters away from home and heard all the bits and bobs of news, got a new recipe for a cake with yeast instead of eggs, had a request for a recipe for rhubarb and dried apricot jam and one for home-made salad cream, showed a machinist a trick she had not heard of – how to sharpen a blunt pointed needle with a piece of sandpaper off a match box – and talked over the possibility of another whist drive soon. But no talk of war, invasion, rationing, queues, etc. I said to Mrs Waite 'Isn't it amazing?' and she said 'I don't know that it is. It's an atmosphere we have created largely ourselves and I think it's why so many come regularly.'

Tuesday, 28 April. It seems the time again for people to think 'the war will be soon over now'. Even Mrs Waite 'knows that this winter will see all over, if it's not over before it starts'. Pressed for a reason she says 'Everything points to Hitler being done'. Mrs Higham says 'Well, when little children of ten have to work it's a sign of something cracking up'. Of course I had to drop a brick. I said 'Pity we could not borrow a little of the Germans' ruthless "get down to it spirit"' – I was really still thinking of Blackpool's luxury [*where Nella had visited the previous day*]. Mrs Waite was very cross. She finds a great comfort in the shabby outworn theories that 'Britain always wins the last battle' and 'fights best with her back against the wall'. She said rather crossly 'If you are as clever as all that, tell us how long the war *will* last' but I smiled and turned the subject. To have a deepening shadow on one's heart is not a thing to talk of – or even to talk much about.

Wednesday, 29 April. I was feeling cross and edgy when the garage door opened and was let swing back in the wind and one of the few pieces of glass crashed. A boy was just tipping a parcel of bread crusts on to my clean swept garage floor – a leggy neurotic lad of about ten whose parents have taken a furnished house in the street. I felt wild and I said 'Did you leave all that bread the other day?' and he said 'Yes'. I said 'You must pick all these crusts up and take them away and not bring any more. Do you realise that if I was seen giving them to my hens I could be fined?' Those were the exact words I used and I made him take them all away, swept the floor and came in to lay table. There was the sound of voices – an angry voice – and a tap at kitchenette door and when I went it was the boy with his mother. My goodness but she was in a rage. She demanded 'What I meant by threatening to put the police on her track – and who was I to dictate to her child and make him pick filthy crusts off a filthy floor', and she spluttered with rage. I said 'You say your child tells lies. I did *not* say I would report you but by Gad if you put any more waste bread in my garage I will do.' Then I learned that 'North country women were mean and cheeseparing greedy people', that I was a 'stuck up cat' and thought I was 'too good to speak to her at the gate' and so on.

She is a Londoner – a fourth rate actress or barmaid, to put it char-itably – and how a refined man, an educated man, like her husband could have even met her never mind married her has often surprised people. She lies in bed till lunch time and slops round in brightly col-oured pyjamas and mules[†] or else red velvet slacks. Her hair is multi-coloured from bleach and dye and she has the manners and voice of the pavement. I said 'Go out of my garage at once. There is no need for personalities, and talking of North country people's drawbacks, a slut would be a slut if she was born in Bethnal Green or Glasgow.' She said 'How *dare* you call me a slut. I'll tell my husband what you say.' I looked calmly at her soiled art-silk pyjamas under her equally soiled camel hair coat and let my eyes rove over her face with yesterday's make-up still on and her untidy multi-coloured hair in heaps rather than curls on top of her head and I said 'Why bother' and she knew what I meant and she turned to the poor kid and smacked his face and whirled out with him.

In May, Nella reported various events and incidents, beyond her everyday and weekly routines: a day trip to a Red Cross meeting in Preston (13 May); her 31st wedding anniversary (17 May); a fire-fighting meeting her husband attended (20 May); Cliff's return home for a week's embarkation leave on 22 May; and two days later the arrival of Arthur from Northern Ireland for a family visit. For four days in May, Nella had the rare wartime experience of both her sons being at home together. 'It's grand to have them both here', she observed on 25 May, 'the piano going from morning to night at odd times and the sound of Cliff's favourite tunes coming from down the stair as he "baths to music" from his portable gramophone.' Occasionally she wrote about the signs on the home front of a state of war. On 22 May she remarked on the soldiers at the canteen. 'Such *ordinary* looking men they looked, and some of them looked so out of place in their khaki. I felt my eyes searching for someone I could say "He looks as if he could kill", but there was not one who had anything but a peaceful ordinary face.'

The gloom of a few weeks earlier was being partly displaced by a degree of optimism. On 24 May, Nella had reported some of Arthur's outlook. 'He thinks this summer will see the end of the Russian campaign and that the Germans will have to be on the defensive after that. I hope he is right. The Germans *should* know what conquering really means – and to have their homes destroyed and their good earth scorched as in Russia.' Later, on 15 June, in the course of an angry conversation with Isa Hunter, a woman she disliked, she spoke of her recent changed opinions and declared '"I'd kill a German and never think more of it than killing a fowl"', although elsewhere she was much more restrained.

Monday, 1 June. My husband and Arthur talked of the 'magnificent' raid [*by over 1,000 bombers*] on Cologne – it *is* so – and it's right and proper that the German people should feel what war is and to see their lovely old places battered flat. But I had a sick sadness at the devil of destruction that had been unleashed on the lovely world – a devil that only seems to strengthen and grow. If only some clever man could invent some gas or something to put all the attacking Nazis and Japs to sleep till all the violence and wickedness in their make-up was either forgotten or eliminated, and all the peace loving ones could clear up the mess and try and straighten things out. Never can I feel that scorched earth, smashed cities and homes, murdered and butchered innocent people, will 'win'. Will we go killing and battering each other till everything we know lies broken? And will it end the war? ... Evil cannot be battered and terrorised out of people. They will have to *think* differently. They will never be *compelled* to act differently – it would not be real and only real things can be used to build the new world they talk about.

Tuesday, 2 June. Arthur bought me a bedside book – such an interesting one, *The Wind on the Heath* by John Sampson. It's odd bits of gypsy sayings and writings collected and I felt happy about it till I saw the inscription, 'To Dearie, who has always had more than a little of the gypsy'. Such a thing to say. I should be used to those boys' odd views on things but I went and looked at myself in the glass. I've dark eyes, it's true, but I don't look like a gypsy. I felt a bit affronted and said 'What makes you think I'm like a gypsy?' and he said 'Your passionate love of sun and wind, your interest in wild things and strange roads, the way you can sit still with your back against a tree and look as if you were part of it, and the way animals love you and you understand them so well'. I thought of the gypsies I'd seen. None of them seemed to fit that, but it's no use feeling sore about it. I know Arthur did not mean it that way.

Thursday, 4 June. Such a marvellous summer day and work seemed a pleasure. I got up early and baked raisin bread and made pastry and from it some sausage rolls, a lemon cheese open tart and some tiny blackberry jam tartlets – and have a bit left to make a pie crust tomorrow on some tinned steak. All turned out perfect and we had soup, cold salmon mould and salad, custard and prunes and a cup of tea for lunch and as Arthur had run the vac over the lounge, hall and dining room I'd only to dust. I found time to soak and wash a new blanket – so many good things have got lost at the laundry lately I feared to send it. Arthur mangled it and I hung it on Mrs Atkinson's line and it dried so lovely and fluffy in the sun and wind. We went out in the car and sat by the sea and Arthur sun bathed. The breeze and the sun was like a blessing and

I felt I forgot that Cliff was packing up to go far away. The war – and that I should have been at Centre – all seemed to blow out of my head as I sat so sun soaked with the sweet salty breeze in my face. An old man came over the sands from setting his nets and when I smiled and said 'It's a beautiful day' he stopped for a chat and we talked of tides and wild birds and fishing. Arthur joined in and we enjoyed the chat. He never thinks it is 'common' or 'country bred' to like to talk to people. He likes meeting and talking to people himself. He said 'Your greatest charm, Dearie, is that you are always so interested in things. You never are bored, are you?' And I laughed and answered 'Why, my love, I was thinking something the same about you!' ...

Such a lovely happy day. I feel so much better for my happy week. Arthur has such a pleasant disposition. You never feel a strain in any way. He never thinks I'm silly whatever I say – or odd. Edith will be a very lucky woman and I'm glad she is such a dear girl. It's odd to think that next time Arthur comes he will probably be married.

Friday, 5 June. We went out to sit by the sea on the Coast Road. Arthur stripped off to a pair of swim pants to get 'sun browned' in spite of all I could say, for the sun was terrifically hot and I felt my forearms scorching where the sun touched them as I sewed. Happy soldiers and ATS girls from nearby camps laughed and frolicked and when I felt gasping in the heat I suggested we walked over the flat sands to meet the tide. There was a tiny breeze to temper the heat and we walked over a mile and then when we got to the sea sluggishly rolling in we walked back in the edge of it. Arthur was alright with only his swim pants but I had to kirtle my skirts and was laughing gaily and a nearby soldier said 'Now then! You playing truant? What about the Canteen?' As I was dressed in a summer dress and big white hat shading my face and he could only have seen me bare headed and in a green overall, I said 'How do you know I go to Canteen?' and he said 'By your voice and laugh'! I kept telling Arthur he would suffer for his 'cooking' and there was a lily fair ATS girl in a skimpy bathing dress who will be in real agony tonight I feel sure. We picked Arthur's sandals full of cockles and I boiled them for the wee chicks and they loved them and we felt sorry we had to come home for tea.

As I unlocked the door I saw a buff telegraph form on the mat and I felt my heart nearly stop – I'm getting queerly nervous about telegrams nowadays. As I bent I saw it was addressed to 'Nella Last' and I felt puzzled. I seem to have a few names. My name is really only Nellie but it seemed such a baby name when I grew up and I used to see it on programmes when I was an elocutionist that I dropped the 'ie' and somehow it got a letter 'a' instead. Formal or grown up friends called me Nella, old friends Nell or Nellie, closest ones D.D. or Dearie, from the name Deirdre my mother wanted me christened and which was used at home, and by Arthur. I get Mrs W. Last and Mrs N. Last and can almost tell at a glance where the letter has come from, or from whom, but a wire with NELLA stumped me. Arthur looked over my shoulder and said 'Aha, be sure your sins will find you out', for Isa told him a ridiculous and much exaggerated yarn of 'an admirer' I had at Canteen – just for fun really, and to make a general laugh.

When I opened it, it was *I* who laughed – and Arthur's face was a study. It ran 'May I come? Agnes.'

Agnes Schofield, an ex-girlfriend of Arthur's who lived in Blackpool, had been trying to reconnect with him since August, clearly with marriage in mind. She had already twice visited 9 Ilkley Road when Arthur was not there (on 12–14 August 1941 and 10–12 April 1942), trying to endear herself to his mother, and had also written her letters. These meetings were a strain for Nella, who disliked being leaned on but sympathised with Agnes's loneliness and desperation to find a mate. By June her sympathy had largely vanished. 'Agnes was so different in every way' from Edith Picken, Arthur's intended, Nella had written on 2 May 1942. 'Brought up with money in a town where money talked – Blackpool – she has different values and outlooks. I can never forgive her for the look of desolation on Arthur's face as he went to Ireland, realising that Agnes "preferred friendship only".* Why should Agnes only find out her mistake when Arthur had found hap-

---

* Nella had views about male–female friendships. 'I don't believe in platonic friendships in

piness in another girl?' Nella claimed that Agnes had rejected three of her son's proposals for marriage. On this occasion, after viewing the telegram, 'I sat on the stairs and laughed myself nearly into hysterics'. 'There was a pre-paid reply and Arthur said "Stop acting the goat like that and help me word this wire in return", and we sent "Sorry Agnes, quite impossible".'

Nella also wrote that day (5 June) that 'It's been such a happy carefree week. Arthur is such a good companion and I feel myself "uncoil" and relax in his company always – no strain, no wondering if I've said the right thing, no trying to keep the peace between his father and him [*as she felt she had to do with Cliff*], just a happy feeling of good fellowship, kindliness and good humour.'

Tuesday, 9 June. When I got in to Centre I heard Mrs Waite's voice as I went down the passage. Her appearance shocked me very much. She looks so very old and ill and her face has 'blue shadows'. I bent and kissed her and said 'Well, of all the contrary naughty old things. I thought you had to rest for awhile.' She pulled me down beside her and leaned against me and said 'Oh, it's nothing, and if I was stuck up there in that blitzed house, so quiet and still, I *would* soon be ill. I'd go mad I think.' I made her a cup of Bovril and poked the sulky fire into a little blaze and made her sit by it and put her feet up on another chair and she said 'And then you scold me for coming down. Why nobody would boss me round like you if I was at home.' And she smiled over her cup and my heart sank at her looks and quiet child like manner – it's not 'our Mrs Waite' now at all, once so dominant.

Mrs Wilkins said her piece about all the clever things SHE had done while Mrs Waite had been off last week and what extra work she had done and what she had said and to whom and I could have got her by the shoulders and run her into the street. Then she started attacking Miss Ledgerwood and saying how she 'never thought of coming early

---

the least. *One* always gets hurt sooner or later has been my experience since once as a girl I hurt someone very much without meaning to, and which was a severe lesson to me, so that I would never believe that a man and a woman could possibly be the same in friendship as two of the one sex' (13 August 1941).

and doing her fair share of bandage cutting'. That sent me up into the air. I said 'Just a minute. To compare anything you must have fairly equal things. You are as strong as an ox. You have a good maid, plus a husband who helps you in the garden. Miss Ledgerwood is old and frail, has a partly invalid sister who cannot do much living with her, no maid, no help in the garden AND don't forget this – she and Mrs Boorman cut out more bandages than you have seen in the first two years of the war AND you pick and find fault and generally act the clever devil with her till I wonder the poor old lamb doesn't attack you with your own scissors.' She tossed her head and went out and I said 'I'm sorry, Mrs Waite, but Mrs Wilkins has asked for that. I'll *not* have Miss Ledgerwood baited and badgered. Would *you* like to think we compared you to what you were three years ago? Would *you* like to have us pick and find fault at every turn? Miss Ledgerwood is my friend and from now on I'll back answer Mrs Wilkins every time she says things like that.' One thing about Mrs Wilkins – she is either too thick skinned or too conceited and puffed up with her own importance to bear ill will and she did not keep offence and beyond saying I was a 'spitfire if I got going' it passed off.

Sunday, 14 June. Cousin Mary was in, home from Preston for the weekend. I looked at her as she sat, so hollow eyed and tired, for it is her month of nights and to get home to see her father meant working Friday night and, instead of going to bed, coming to Greenodd and then going back Monday and working all Monday night. She was such a lovely outdoor girl with a clear pink and white complexion and softly curling hair. Now her face is pale and her lovely wild rose skin looks sallow and her hair misses the air and sunlight. I asked her if she was happy at work and she said 'Well, to be candid, the novelty is wearing off and it gets tiring and when the sun shines I feel distracted when I think of hills and woods. But I've never known what it is to be independent in all my 24 years and to earn money of my own and not to have it doled out for housekeeping and to wheedle the price of a new dress from Dad – well, it makes up for a lot. I'll *never* go back to the old life, whatever comes.

I'm *free* and I stay like that.' She is an 'examiner' in Dick Kerr's at Preston and makes very good money.* I said 'I hope you will save something, Mary' and she laughed loudly and said '*Save*, did you say? There is little to spend it on really nowadays. That is the general complaint.'

Tuesday, 16 June. Mrs Waite did not come in till after lunch so we got every bandage and swab out of store and sent it off to the Red Cross for it was the week for the large packing case going. She likes to keep some in hand but it's not fit to keep salvage in that damp smelly store. Mrs Higham and I gave out wool for knitting to everyone who would take it – double quantities – and I phoned to the Port Missionary that if he would come before lunch he would get a better haul than after lunch. Less than fifteen minutes after he was at Centre and the two huge heaps of sea boot stockings and comforts in the back of the car gladdened us all. We expected to get into trouble and I said 'I'll take full blame for the wholesale clearance' but when Mrs Waite came in and saw the bit of fire and the kettle on in case she wanted a cup of tea she just smiled and sat down and did not grumble at anything.

There seemed such a quiet sadness over all under the bursts of chatter. Two naval women are waiting news of husbands reported missing. One had a 'presumed dead' notice from the Navy and I lost count of the women who said their boys – and in one case of a nurse – were going overseas. I sat down for a little rest when I was raffling, for the little box of groceries was a bit heavy. I chose to sit down by a woman I knew had a son on the sea somewhere and another going any time now. She has always been a great church woman since a child and been very pious in her outlooks on life in general and her remark really startled me – she said 'It makes you wonder if there *is* a God after all, doesn't it?' Facing problems like that at 56 must be dreadful. I felt thankful I'd settled all my 'ology' when a girl and, right or wrong, it's a part of me and I have no doubts, no fears, as regards God, death or the unseen. I don't believe in Heaven or Hell or choirs of angels or eternal damnation – no rewards

---

* Dick, Kerr & Co. manufactured Hampden and Halifax bombers.

and no revenges, just consequences and a beginning afresh and chance to learn and grow and grow.

Mrs Waite said crossly 'You spend *far* too much time in the big room. What on earth were Mrs Benson and you looking so serious about?' I said 'God' and she nearly fell flat! She said '*Really*, Mrs Last, I'm surprised', and her face flushed. She looked so shocked and Mrs Thompson and I got talking and then all the Committee joined. The two old ones, Mrs Waite and Mrs McGregor, were shocked at my 'levity'. Mrs Woods, who is a woman who, though 'kind and just', manages where rations or scarce food is concerned to grab twice as much and 'doesn't care *what* she pays for things as long as she gets it', thought 'Holy things should not be discussed lightly but rather thought many people had the same feeling'. Miss Heath rather surprised us by her tight lips as she said curtly 'I've my own opinions best not discussed'. Only Mrs Thompson and Mrs Higham would talk about it, and they only skirted the fringes. Suddenly I realised what I missed most in the life of today – TALK. Hearing things argued over and joining in and perhaps being squashed, perhaps listened to, but *talking*, Arthur talking in a clever way, Cliff and Jack Gorst in either an enquiring way or else a flippant one.

I got up abruptly and went into the kitchen where it was darker and where I could blink the tears back and pull myself together.

CHAPTER NINE

AT HOME AND ABROAD

June–September 1942

Wednesday, 17 June. I had got all tidy and straight before lunch and decided to go to the pictures but there was a ring and it was Mrs Howson, a neighbour. Her husband is a naval man and she has been used to him being away – three years once – and she never has a home, just goes wherever she can be near him. He is on coastal convoy now and today she said 'Do you mind if I bring my sewing across? I feel a bundle of nerves. I've not had a letter from Steve as usual. So silly of me to get so jittery. I never used to be like this. I feel I *cannot* be alone and mother has gone out.' She works so hard at the Canteen but today said she felt like a rest ...

Always like a far off dirge when I think of Cliff going is the thought 'For how long?' and pity seizes me when I think of young wives and mothers of small children left with aching hearts. Such senseless muddle, pain, misery and heartache. Only history can see the 'pattern of the carpet'. We will never see the 'purpose of the Plan'.

Friday, 19 June. It's invasion exercise on Sunday again and I don't know yet whether I'm out [*on the mobile canteen*]. Only four vans are out and I'll know later. I hope I'm not for I like my Sunday morning for writing and a rest. I had tea when I got in and then went out to a driver friend to see if she knew anything about it but she had only got her order to have the Jolly Roger clean and ready for Sunday. I sat and talked about Cliff, and she is worried about her boy who is going into the Navy any time now. I find any women who mention the war at all so like myself about this 'Second Front' – so sure it is the 'only way', so chokingly afraid when we think of Dunkirk. Mrs Henley said 'It looks as if we will lose Tobruk again.* Are we strong enough to go into Europe?' Her husband said 'Oh you make me tired, Jerry. Women cannot argue. They get too personal about things. They have no vision.' I never liked Frank Henley as a boy and I said 'That's quite true, Frank, or we would never have children to rear into men to go and fight. It's perhaps a jolly good thing we *have* no "vision".'

For a week from the end of the month both Nella and Will were on holiday, and on most days they enjoyed excursions in their car – Spark Bridge (twice), Morecambe, Coniston Lake, Kendal, and sunning themselves on the Coast Road.

Saturday, 27 June. We went to Spark Bridge and on our way picked up two of a group of people left by the bus. I knew one and knew of the other and they were glad of a lift with their heavy shopping baskets. The one with the heaviest baskets – rations for nine people and two big jars of jam were part of her load – has an old blind aunt living with her and two Salford evacuees, her husband and self, four children at home and a lad on draft leave in the RAF and one lad in the Army overseas. She was smart in a plain country way and her quiet pleasant smile was like a blessing. I said 'What a shame that townspeople fill the buses on your shopping day and you have so much to carry'. She said 'Well, I've lived on the Common above Lowick before there *was* buses and we will just have to manage and be thankful we don't live in Russia'. The contrast between Isa [*a persistent complainer – and spoiled*] and that country woman of not many years older was a sharp contrast. It certainly takes a lot of different people to make a world!

Wednesday, 1 July. My husband is very down over the war news now and he says he hears a lot of despondent talk – and of this Second Front.

I really *have* to keep out of the garden if my next door neighbour or his wife are about [*the Helms at 11 Ilkley Road*]. I've never quarrelled

---

* On 21 June British forces in Tobruk, Libya, surrendered to the Germans and Italians. The Axis powers took 30,000 prisoners and large quantities of *matériel*.

over the fence in my life but I feel I could *assault* those two. They fled
for a year after the blitz and have only got back – after fire watching
registration so he does not do it. His only daughter's husband signed
as a baker and goes into a bake house each morning for half an hour,
although he has a big furniture shop. He has no one in the Services, does
no war work of any kind and politely sneers at those who do or those
who buy Certificates, but when it comes to criticizing the Government,
howling for a Second Front, skitting at Churchill, or mouthing plans
for winning the war, he is a real big noise. I'm not as good tempered as I
once was and if I ever do start anything, by Gad I'll finish it and he will
have no illusions about himself, his ox or his ass any more! ...

All is so hushed and still, so peaceful and quiet, and yet there seems
the same breathless hush there was before war broke in that quiet
autumn – or rather late summer. My husband said today 'We have
got half the year over – and quieter than I thought we would'. I fear
the second half will make up for it. All this talk of Second Fronts – I
wonder if a plan is properly worked out, enough stores and equipment ensured, and above all adequate protection for our men.* Now
I have seen torn roads and shattered buildings, and what I've seen of
war Pathés and newsreels make me go cold at the thought of another
landing on the Continent. Men will not have the fire and enthusiasm
either of that first attempt, although they will be better trained. Every
post that comes I look for a letter from Cliff and since he said that
their 'destination had been altered since Tobruk and that fresh code
letters had been printed on kit bags and luggage', I keep wondering
if he will be in the Second Front. Yet if he goes abroad, will it be to
another Tobruk?

July was not without amusing moments. On 14 July at the Centre Nella heard of
a joke told by a doctor. 'A Polish flyer who had been in a hospital took a turn for
the better and rapidly began to "sit up and take notice". The doctor said "I'm

---

* Of course, she was right; no Allied landing in France was possible until 1944, although
southern Italy was taken in later 1943.

delighted with your recovery. You can have anything at all you fancy – or would you like anyone to come in?" The Pole said "I think I'd like a woman now, doctor. You may send one in tonight. I like plump ones." The doctor said in a shocked way "Hush – you are in England now and not on the Continent. English ways are different altogether and they would be very shocked if they heard a remark like that" and got the reply "Then why the Women's Voluntary Services?"' This story, it seems, was much enjoyed by the women present and, according to Nella, further witticisms were spoken in the same vein and 'set a few of the more ribald ones off into a louder fit of laughter than the joke did'. Later that week at the canteen, when Nella was briefly out of the building, two Canadian Sergeant Pilots invited Mrs Howson and her to the cinema. Mrs Howson 'had tactfully refused and I felt sorry for the lonely soldiers and if I'd seen them would have suggested they come to 9 Ilkley, for they were a homely type and I knew they only asked us because of that, but it was no good talking to that giddy bunch for they insisted I'd "made eyes"' (17 July).

On Sunday, 26 July Nella was surprised to have a visit from her cousin, Tena, who was 'in need of a chat' concerning her daughter Enid. This 'lovely sprightly girl of 22 has broken off her engagement to a very eligible young fellow of 25 with a good position in the Yard and one which had excellent prospects. They seemed so suited and very much in love and I've wondered what the trouble was. Tena said "You know Nell, they are all down on Enid. Her father and Gran are really vexed" – Aunt Eliza is the gran. She went on, "I feel it may turn out for the best. Enid is so lively and loves dancing, dramatics, tennis, swimming, roller skating, hiking, or any kind of gaiety and fun." Ken shunned it all and only liked going to the pictures, motoring alone with Enid or walking alone. She said if she tried to go Ken's way she was miserable and felt unreal and he made no attempt to see her viewpoint. I laughed indulgently and said she "would settle down when she was married".' Nella may well have been thinking of her own marriage and how it had unfolded. She went on to declare that 'It's no sin to like fun and gaiety and goodness knows Enid works hard enough with all the Yard overtime. I'd not like Enid to always stand aside and give up every little pursuit, never to have friends or go anywhere alone, just wait till a man came in to take her out.' Nella felt that she had learned the hard way about the perils of trying too hard to please a man.

From July of this year there were two new developments that would have significant consequences for Nella: one was the ban on the use of petrol for private motoring; the other was the decision to set up and run a Red Cross shop in Barrow. 'The tank is full of petrol yet', she wrote on Sunday, 5 July, 'and will take us to Spark Bridge at least twice more and then all will be used and finished with till after the war ... Very few cars were about and the roads looked strangely empty.' On 12 July 'We used our last drop of petrol'. So, for Nella and Will, there would be no more day trips of the sort they had taken the previous month. If Nella were to travel outside Barrow, it would have to be by public transport, with all the accompanying bother and inconveniences. On 15 July, when she took the bus to Spark Bridge, 'I had thought I could get a bus back about 4 o'clock but the girl conductor said there was not one till 6.15 after the return of the one I was on and when she said it was generally too full to pick up any Spark Bridge people I knew I'd have only an hour in Aunt Sarah's'. Country drives had been one of the Lasts' few shared pleasures, and now they were gone. On Saturday, 1 August she remarked that 'My husband seems a bit moody about the car being laid up and having to stay at home holiday week'. As for the Red Cross shop, an idea suggested by Mrs Diss and agreed to this month, it was intended to raise money for the Prisoner of War Fund – and was to figure prominently in Nella's life for the rest of the war.

With the beginning of August, the Shipyard started its annual fortnight holiday, so most of its employees were not at work, and the Centre was to be closed for the first half of the month. August began with Nella helping out with Barrow's 'Flag Day' for merchant seamen on the Saturday of the holiday weekend.

Saturday, 1 August. We went out early with our flags and did very well. I started off well for I put my gollywog 5s in and had three 6d beside from my husband and the neighbours. We walked down Abbey Road selling as we went and looking for a good 'pitch' for our permit was for anywhere in Abbey Road. When we got to the station bridge and looked over we *gasped* at the dense crowd with suitcases, prams, babies and dogs and on going down to try to sell a few flags to those who were not wearing them found the station packed as well. It was just like a pre-war Bank Holiday except that everyone seemed to have new outfits.

A porter told me they started to queue by 12 o'clock and by 2.30 a long queue formed for the trains that went out at 6.20. Many hundreds took the day off from the Yard yesterday to 'get away in comfort'. If it was not for my back – and, these few days when it feels thundery, my feet and ankles – I'd like selling flags and I thought today that a clever person would have been able to make use of the characters if they had been writing a book. The pleasant people who came up with 6d and a pleasant word and took a flag. Little untidy boys with tiddler† nets and jam jars on their way to the park, with coppers knotted in grimy handkerchiefs and an earnest enquiry – if they 'put a whole penny in could two of them have a flag please?' They got them and nearly got a kiss each as well! Shy furtive people who confessed to 'no change'. A 'means test man' in ragged coat whom I asked before I saw his poverty. He looked old and tired and I pinned one in his coat and whispered 'This one's on me, daddy – they will only worry you to buy one in the town' – and he insisted on giving me a few wilting sweet peas out of the basket he had with a few vegetables from a friend's allotment. A lordly male who 'never bought a flag "on principle"' – I smiled at him and cooed understandingly but suggested I knew he would want to put something in my box – and the dazed look in his eyes as he turned away after putting a 2s piece in! Bet that one has a copper ready another time and keeps his 'principles' dark!! ...

A big man whom I asked to buy a flag and who was picking 6d out of a handful of change gave me another 2s when I remarked on the hope we made lots of money for we could never think enough of seamen and sailors. He smiled and said 'Thank you – I'm a seaman myself' and Mrs Howson said he was a captain on an oil tanker and on leave at Barrow with his sister. I only got rid of half my flags but my box was full and I knew it was time to stop by my aching back. When I took the box in they said 'Do have another for this afternoon. You are a born flag seller.' But I said 'Oh no – if that had been the case I'd have had a back and feet to stand the strain better'! When I thought of Mrs Howson and Mrs Hunt's full box and Margaret's nearly full one I felt glad I had turned out for they would not have gone if I had not.

Tuesday, 4 August. I went down to be at the shop for 2 o'clock but the keys were not there and we waited till nearly 2.30. Talk about *dirt*. It was appalling – blitz dirt, neglect and repeated Flag days when it was used as a centre for collectors had all added dirt and dust, and then the shop next door, a plumber's, had stored glass and glass crates in the passage and yard. It's not a very good shop, really, for beyond good windows with the entrance door between, there is only one room and not a very large one either. A passage leads to the yard and a wash bowl is in the passage and the lavatory at the bottom of the yard. Not a cupboard or shelf, not even a peg to hang anything on. We will have to get electric light bulbs and some kind of electric radiator for it will soon be impossible to sit in the shop without warmth. It is on the shady side of the street, too, and that will make it worse. Still, it's a shop and big enough for a start and if we find we do well we can move into one of the shops in the main street that we thought too big for a start. I've had a lot of things promised and hope I get some of them before we open, but as we talked things over we decided we cannot do so before the 26th of August for we do not open at Centre till the 19th and we will need a week to prepare people, collect goods and arrange about the opening day with the Red Cross.

We could see people pass and re-pass, trailing about in the chilly day. The picture houses all have 'House Full' notices on a good half hour before they started. Most shops were shut and the Park was not attractive to everyone for sports don't find favour with all tastes. Bus loads went to the shore – and now the little cheerful huts and booths that supplied tea and hot water, buns, rock, buckets and spades, sweets, aspirins, deck chairs, periodicals and books, minerals, home made lemonade, toffee, ice cream – all the little happy making necessities for a day by the sea with a pack of kiddies – have gone 'for the duration' ...

After tea Mrs Atkinson came to see if I'd go to a whist drive but they are such keen swift players there and I felt more like quiet and relaxing. She said 'You never seem to have much fun out of life. You work and work and take on more as time goes on. You will be an old woman before your time.' We were standing outside and Mr Atkinson said from over the fence where he was gardening 'You are the happiest and gayest woman I know, Mrs Last. Take no notice of my Winnie. And what matters fading hair if your heart keeps young?' We all stared at Mr Atkinson for he is such a very quiet man. He is on holiday and I've asked them to come in for a game of whist tomorrow night for a little holiday change. When I told my husband he was not at all pleased and he said 'Don't you *ever* think of consulting my wishes before you ask people in? You know I like my evening to myself.' Me – I *must* be a queer shock to him, I realise it plainly. I just said calmly 'You will have a few evenings *entirely* to yourself if you talk like that, or be odd if people come in. This winter I'm going to ask two boys from Canteen every week for an evening by the fire. Cliff is far away and Arthur might be in China he seems so far away. I'm going to ask two boys who like beans on toast to eat – Cliff's beans I saved for him.' And I will too, moods or no moods. I'm growing hardened – tough, as Cliff calls it.

Life is slipping so quickly away, so much unhappiness and grief and loneliness. We must not neglect the slightest help we can give to others. I heard today that we got £300 and over on Saturday for the merchant seamen. I hope it's true although it is a lot for Barrow, especially when so many were going off out of town. I wonder where my Cliff is tonight, if he is happy. Always there is a little prayer in my heart for my boy. I look at his smiling face on the mantel so often and smile back and say God bless, and see again the little intense boy on the other corner and they go all jumbled up in my mind and I am not sure which I am grieving for, so quickly did my little baby, my odd little boy, grow up – and then go away. I often think I was designed for a large family. It would have been nice to have had more young things at home now that Cliff has gone, and yet they too might have been boys and had to go [*to war*].

Thursday, 6 August. I had to dust and vac upstairs after lunch for this week I am catching up with any housework and will have all clean to start Centre. I laid down with a book when I'd finished but dozed off and was wakened by Mrs Higham ringing. She was in very high spirits because she had got some planks that would do for shelves [*in the Red Cross shop*] and her husband had said he was sure that he had nails and hooks enough somewhere in the garage. I felt a queer dizzy shock when I knew husbands were entering into our work, a sick cold feeling. You cannot say to people 'Look here, *do* leave my husband out of anything. I'll work and work and give you anything I can but don't let's have husbands in it for it's no use at all trying to get my husband interested in *anything*. He was never interested in his babies or little school boys, his home – he has only done what was damage repairs that could not be avoided for comfort. I told him we would need a shelf and hooks and he did not speak or offer to help. He *hates* working or mixing with either your George or anyone else. No coaxing or persuading will do anything. If he said "I don't want to do" a thing, that finishes the matter as far as he is concerned. He seems incapable of reasoning or thinking things out, of effort, self sacrifice.' You cannot tell people things like that about your man.

Flashes of when I'd tried to insist on his being 'more like other people' came before my eyes – and the surprised looks on people's faces at his attitude. One remark I'd once heard was passed by a rough but kind hearted woman. 'Look at poor Mr Last sitting in that corner. God love him. He looks as if he is going to burst out crying.' Of never daring to accept an invite till I'd asked him, of when he had been 'trapped' into acceptance and he had accepted with his 'sweet pleasant' smile, the moods I'd had till I'd thought of an excuse to refuse. Mrs Higham said concernedly 'I say, you *do* look ill. I hope your cold is not going to get you down.' I don't know what I said. Cold! Yes, but in my heart I thought of my little life I'd planned and built crashing. I cannot let those women at Centre see my life. Their husbands are 'all out' for war effort and work. I cannot let them know my husband thinks it 'too much trouble' to put up a few shelves in a Red Cross shop for us when it is not going to cost him anything even.

I felt like death when he came in. I said a little jumbled up prayer – I've prayed so often for some kind of growing up in his attitude to life and people I did not know what to pray for. I felt I held up my little efforts – I've worked so hard, often with aching back, tired head, but it *is* mine and I want it. I've nothing else now. I don't want to be 'different' at all. I only want to go on working with them all and helping. I felt my wretched tummy starting to shake and tremble as if I would soon be sick but I asked him if he would go and see some wood and pick out any that would knock up rough shelves and Mr Higham and he could put them up on Sunday when it is his Sunday off from the Yard. I saw storm clouds on his face and he never spoke and the stillness got deafening and roared in my ears! Prayer can be answered in many different ways – I've never talked to that one before like I did. He knows what I think of my married life now. I pointed out I'd had three bad nervous breakdowns but the next one was his turn. I told him again of Dr Miller's straight talks when I could not walk and my feet and legs would not function and massage, violet rays, specialists who spoke of sclerosis did no use. He talked to me quite a lot – and to Arthur – and I was very shocked when I realised there was nothing wrong with me but nerves. My husband knew it all and had been scared enough at the time to 'let' me do anything I'd wanted – as long as I only went out with him. I was quite interested in what I said in my impromptu tirade. I told him in detail the many times I'd tried to build a little ordinary life – and the times he had kicked, pushed or whined it into ruins. I remembered incidents I'd quite forgotten and then I gave my ultimatum. I said 'This helping us is none of my seeking but, by the living God, if you make things so that in my pride I leave Centre, so that they don't know what a childish, stupid, mean spirited man my lads' father is, or tell them or make excuses for you I will not, you will rue it for the rest of your days. It's my last effort to build up with worn out tools. I've not my Cliff to think of any more and I'll plan my life entirely to suit myself. I can work for myself and will go away, far away, and I'll never come back if once I go.' He has not spoken since, nor have I. I'm not sulking, just giving him time to think things over.*

---

* 'He never realises,' Nella had written of her husband the previous summer, 'and never could, that the years when I had to sit quiet and always do everything he liked and never the things he did not were slavery years of mind and body ... Recently I made my vow – to be a soldier till the war ended, to play the game and never grumble and never to ask

Such a storm in a tea cup. I think they often turn into the biggest issues. I'd give a lot for Arthur's kind whimsical face to look round the door tonight, to hear him say 'What about a stroll up Abbey Road?', to feel the night air on my face, to have a talk with someone who understood. Funnily enough I'm not a bit upset now at all. I'll fight this thing out. The boys were right – I've a weak streak or I'd have done it before. My mind is made up. If he sulks and frets and 'will not be bothered' to put up that shelf, which will cost him nothing but a few hours pleasant company and companionship with Mr Higham helping, I'll not tell any lies or make excuses any more, and pretend things, or do them and make out he has done them as I've often done.

Nella's straight talking was to some avail, for the next day Will agreed – indeed, in a cheerful manner, she said – to lend a hand and meet Mr Higham on Saturday to look over the wood and get enough for the shelving for the shop. Nella was delighted. 'I felt so happy I could have sang as I splashed through puddles in the rain. Appears to me that if I got on my top note a bit oftener and spoke my mind freely instead of humouring him at all times it would be better. He was pleasanter in the house than he had been for weeks and talked quite a lot' (8 August). But she still had to endure his whims and quirks. 'Early or late,' she noted on 27 August, 'whenever he comes in he expects his meals ready to put in his mouth and makes a scene if it is not perfectly ready. I've certainly spoiled that one.' Later that day, having picked up a reel of photos that had been developed, she found that 'the three my husband had taken of me were hopeless – out of focus altogether. When I think how Cliff begged for snaps and he would not take enough care to get even one decent one to send – and I don't think I'll be able to get another [film was now hard to obtain] and certainly not to send for Xmas. If he had said he was sorry it would have not been as bad but he was so unconcerned.'

Monday, 10 August. The other day I made a bad gaff in the Canteen. A

<hr/>

anything else except that my boys could be guarded and live their life fully' (28 August 1941).

jolly, rather fat little woman bounced in and started joking and laughing and talking of 'when we were on the Mobile together'. I looked at her again and again but could not place her. She stood there in her WVS outfit rather grubby and wind blown from her journey back and forward along the Coast Road to the big cooking place to the schools with dinners for school children. Her grey hair was a bit wispy under her beret, her wide happy mouth was free of lipstick and if her face *had* been powdered when she set off it showed no trace now. She was smoking furiously and telling a long yarn about what she had said to someone who had said 'Oh, shut up Ricky', and I gasped as I remembered the very nice but most unhelpful driver I'd had several times. Dressed so very beautifully in navy tailor mades with dainty hat and matching accessories, with high spiky heeled shoes, brassy blond hair and marvellous make-up which she seemed to repair at every place we stopped – while I washed the cups and counter down! She insisted on her full name of Ross-Ricketts. Now evidently she was Ricky!

Monday, 17 August. Mrs Waite sent her granddaughter in with the keys [*for the Centre*]. Life is odd. Mrs Waite has such a lot to say about 'girls of today' and is down on every girl who is 'fast' or dresses showily and her tongue is both cruel and cutting. Her own granddaughters are 'perfect examples of girlhood' in her eyes – but in onlookers'! I looked at 12 year old Jean as she openly prattled of dates and boys and 'getting off', of back seats in cinemas, of her admission she would like to be married soon, and I thought it was enough to raise Mrs Waite's hair if she heard. I said curiously 'Aren't you afraid I'll tell your Gran of your naughty lies to your mother and the tricks you are up to?' She said 'Oh no. Gran says you talk more and tell less than anyone she has ever met and if she had a secret she would never hesitate to tell you.' My husband laughed out loud when he heard and when I asked him what the joke was he said 'Your expression – you had such a look of comic surprise. But it *is* true, you know. You are deeper than your chatter leads people to suppose.' Hmm – as others see us!!

Sunday, 23 August. Mrs Howson came in for a chat and we spoke our vague fears and suspicions of little Mrs Hunt at Canteen. She divorced her husband early in the year and for awhile acted the fool when she came back, went 'rackety' in a too gay set in which there was a South African airman with a roving eye. She once said to me 'Oh, I know he is not much – some would say he was a rotter. But Ron Hunt made me feel most at home with rotters.' Although I work with her every week at Canteen, beyond thinking she was putting on weight I never suspected anything – I'm not really very bright in that respect and I often don't notice my friends are expectant mothers for quite a while. Mrs Howson is such a kind little thing she has never voiced her suspicions, even to me, till now. I *do* so hope it's not true for Mrs Hunt is such a nice, sincere little woman, tiny and helpless in many ways but a good worker and very reliable. Whatever she will do I cannot think. It has made me feel quite ill and so very anxious. I *do* hope that she is only 'putting on weight' and nothing more. I cannot possibly think what the poor little thing would do. The South African has gone away these months past – and anyway he is a married man.

On 28 August Nella returned to the plight of Mrs Hunt. 'It is so awkward with Mrs Hunt "putting on weight" for although nothing is said at all I saw several eye her up and down and she looks the picture of misery. She wears a smock in Canteen and never comes in a costume, always a coat.' Nella expressed her concern again the following Friday, 4 September. Mrs Hunt 'looks so ill at times' but she thought that 'one cannot go to a woman of 34 or 35 – a woman who has been married – and say "Look here, Kay, what *is* the matter with you? You are not going to have a baby are you – and divorced over a year?"' Whatever her problem, Nella remarked, 'she is heart broken over it'. 'Poor little thing – she is not meant to stand alone' was Nella's verdict the following week (11 September).

From time to time the world beyond Barrow entered Nella's thoughts. On 8 August she remarked on 'all this talk of India and wondering if all will be aflame there shortly and wondering and thinking of Cliff and if he is going there for certain. Not one corner in the whole lovely world where people can think "Here is peace to live and build".' The next day 'I felt heart thankful to hear Gandhi had been arrested but have a fear it may lead to trouble although not as big as if he had been let run loose much longer. As if Japs were not enough – the country must be divided.' 'Such bad news from Russia', she wrote on 11 August – Soviet forces were still retreating. 'The Germans seem so dreadfully strong – and such worrying news about India. There has been enough talk in the past of "Armageddon" but it looks as if soon it will be an actual fact.' 'I often think of the people in occupied countries', she declared on 12 August, 'and I think "Hitler is a fool. He does not realise that banked down fires only need a poker to spring into life and heat. He may put out some fires but not others and it will be their flame which will destroy him."' And she worried about the Second Front, which was much discussed during these weeks, and actively agitated for by some. On 19 August 'My heart nearly stopped beating at 7 o'clock this morning when the news came over the wireless about the Dieppe raid for I felt *sure* it was the beginning of the Second Front. At 8 o'clock when it was a "raid" and not an invasion I felt less upset. Always do I think of Dunkirk. I'm not very brave. I feel my bones turn to water at what lies ahead in those carelessly spoken words "the Second Front".'

Most important for Nella was Cliff, his whereabouts and well-being. For several weeks she had no idea where he was. She got a letter from him on 19 August, 'written from sea' and saying little. Mrs Howson thought he was probably sailing to South Africa. 'It will be six weeks on Monday since Cliff sailed', she reported on Tuesday, 25 August. 'I wonder if he has reached his journey's end.' Only on 27 August did she get a message from him in 'Africa', probably somewhere in the Middle East she thought. 'I'm thankful the longest part of his journey is over anyway.'

Throughout the month much time and labour was invested in preparing for the opening of the Red Cross shop, which was to be run by a committee of which Nella was a very active member. The shop had to be cleaned up and fitted out, and it had to be stocked with all sort of items that were being donated by – or begged from – the citizens of Barrow. Finally, on schedule, the shop opened.

Wednesday, 26 August. Mrs Diss called and we arranged about the reporter for the shop and taking the Mayoress to the Girls Canteen for tea. I tidied up, made celery soup and a steamed gooseberry jam sponge pudding and after lunch was over and dishes washed I got changed and was down at the shop at 1.30 – to find a long queue already formed! Mrs Diss had asked for a policeman to be at hand but they were very orderly and when the Mayoress opened the door at 3 o'clock about ten were let in at a time. Talk about money being plentiful! A set of Snow White and the Seven Dwarfs could have been sold several times – at £2 10s 0d the set. A doll's bed at £2 10s 0d, a desk at £3 with the seat as well, all used toys – went in the first half hour! Dolls could have been sold in dozens, and no quibble about the price. By 4.30 the queue was served and we could open the door wide and let in the fresh air and Mrs Woods started adding up the money. We had £50, and all felt as happy as could be. Our stock is about exhausted but everyone we served we asked if they would broadcast about the shop and find us something or beg something and all said they would. We all caught the last bus before the Shipyard workers and got home in time for tea. I'd left tea ready and I don't remember a cup of tea tasting better …

Doug Hines, Cliff's friend, had sent word by Norah Atkinson that he was coming. He is rather a lamb but a description I once read somewhere *does* rather fit him – 'He looks like the last descendant of a line of maiden aunts'! In a flash it came to me tonight why the boys and I always seem to attract people like we do – 'nice' people but those of what Cliff called the 'wet lettuce' type. Doug said rather wistfully 'Do you always know your own mind?' and I thought for a little and said 'Yes, I think so, or if I don't I think things out till I've got all clear'. He sighed and said 'What a gift. Do you know Cliff was like that and he helped me decide lots of things?' – and he must be ten or twelve years older than Cliff. Poor Doug. He actually wanted me to make up his mind about leaving Vickers Shipyard and going to work someplace else where he had a job offered! He said 'Roll on the end of the war. You know quite seriously, if you and Cliff *do* take a pub and develop it, I'll come in with you and invest what I've got. I can see to all the money side for I know you two are weak on that, and Cliff and you are both marvellous organisers and like people. We will make a good two.' I said 'Don't forget, Doug, the trifling matter – a husband, with perhaps different views – and Agnes Schofield says she is "going to apply for a job". Such whoopee. If I ever come through the war it will not be to collect cranks round me, pub or no pub' ...

Such a happy worthwhile day. It makes up for all the thought and planning, all the hurry and tiredness of the last three hectic weeks. There is no sweetness like success of effort. There will be a lot of thankful hearts through today. The poor prisoners of war will get a lot of parcels out of even today's efforts. The Red Cross said a little prayer at opening and asked for a blessing on 'the willing tireless workers who had created the shop'. I felt it had been granted from the start for everyone has been so kind and helpful and no one has refused or been curt when I've asked for help.

Thursday, 27 August. Outside it was a lovely heavy sulky 'September' day, inside [*at the Centre*] just a smelly close one with a feeling of decay coming from the blitzed church. The doors were wide open to try and get a current of air through and I walked into the church. I don't go often for the welter of destruction gives me such a sick sadness – seats, stained glass, etc. where they fell among broken slates etc. It had a direct hit on the corner as a 'torpedo's shell' sped past to smash flat a big hotel on the corner but no earth was brought to the surface, just rubbish and rubble over all, but the green weeds and grass was unbelievable for it had got a foothold everywhere. The boys had such odd notions and years ago I've sat entranced as they talked of 'all passing away' and civilization perishing and some day rising again and Ted held a theory that things went upward in some kind of a slow spiral and as it turned in its upward journey 'conditions' would be repeated again and again. I used to say 'But it couldn't happen like that, Ted. What about all the buildings, so strong and indestructible?' He used to say 'Oh, *some* things will endure to puzzle posterity, like the Sphinx and the Pyramids etc., or the ruins of Ancient Greece.' Ted knows all about it now [*he was killed at Dunkirk*] and as I stood and looked at a little firm green dandelion root I wondered how soon our vaunted civilization would crumble if bombs and destruction go on and on.

Wednesday, 9 September. I stood for 15 minutes for a queue was rapidly forming for the Coniston bus and chatted to a Londoner on holiday who was going to Coniston and coming back on the 5.30 bus. She would have liked me to go with her and I was sorely tempted but I've so little time and I'd had a task to set this day aside then to see Aunt Sarah. Poor old pet. As I got out of the bus I saw her pop out of the cottage door and gaze anxiously down the road. Her cousin Joe told me she watched every Wednesday lunch time bus and had the kettle boiling in case I came and had never given up hope that some Saturday or Sunday we might venture. Ruth Tomlinson and a Canadian friend are here for the weekend and I would have liked their butter, tinned breakfast bacon and tinned Spam and sliced ham. There was a big 2 lb tin of butter that smelled like fresh cream and the Canadian girl gets a huge parcel of dainties, with which she can hold parties and picnics for her friends every month. Then they talk of 'Save every crust of bread' and 'Think of our merchant seamen' etc. It's not right if a lot of Canadians and Americans are getting such luxury parcels. Tinned goods are very heavy and would soon make a shipload.

As I listened to all the news of the girls and boys going off to the Services, of those in India, Egypt, Iceland etc., it set me off wondering what 'the new world' *will* be like. Those who live to see it will see more changes than they realise. The little 'back to the land' will soon be stopped by private individuals and farmers gaining more feudal power with workers living with them or in hutments erected. We sat and talked of old times when no bus took lonely villagers to pictures and shopping 'for things they didn't need but only wanted', as Joe put it. He is a fascinating old man to talk to, with a good memory. He spoke of villages so self contained that they deteriorated into 'mentals', and mentioned queer 'dwarfies' and a queer terrible couple I've seen in Ulverston streets, brother and sister. The first is about 7 feet if he did not droop and the sister a tiny 'Mrs Mowcher' only up to his knees.

When I got in it was only 3 o'clock and I opened all the doors to let the sun and fresh air in and started to bake. I got bread, scones, half a dozen little rock cakes, a custard and a dish of sliced apples sweetened with syrup made by tea time. My table looked so nice, so well spread. I felt so happy to see it. My husband never seems to notice my scones have so little shortening – today only a little dripping, but they were feather light – and the bran and raisin breakfast is a find. I felt very tired but it was no use [*resting*] – I had to go and see Mrs Waite for I knew I'd not have another chance this week. She is so fretty we cannot get up oftener, poor pet, and tonight she found fault and scolded because she thinks we are not making as much as we should at Centre and is *sure* we are all 'kicking over the traces'! I looked at her with a sadness – such a sadness. She is such a grand old trooper and only asks she can 'keep on'. I do so pray she can come back to Centre for her place would be so very hard to fill. I sat and talked and the sun faded and it was soon dark. She clung to me and kissed me so lovingly and she said wistfully 'I *do* wish you would come oftener. You always make me laugh. You have a perky sense of humour.'

Thursday, 10 September. Having a Red Cross shop is a full time job for someone really, for so many different things come in ... Sometimes I feel the ceaseless planning and timetable [*of activities*] threatens to choke me. I feel if I don't break loose it will do – and yet I'm lucky to be able to plan and fit in all my odd jobs, to have health to do it and strength to go on. I say firmly to myself 'It's no use at all – you are a soldier' and smile at my Cliff's and Jack Gorst's photos and feel we are all pals together. If I slacked I could not meet their confident smiles ... Always like a black shadow on my heart is the Second Front. Will there be trenches and mud and cold for all the bright faced lads I cook for and joke with at Canteen? I look at them and see my Cliff in so many of them, in a flash of white teeth, a laugh, a jesting remark. I think 'Thank God my Cliff is out of the Second Front I so dread', and then think 'But there are Japs and cruel "natives", burning heat, and thirst where he has gone'. There seems such a doom over us all. People say 'You *never* worry', 'You are a real tonic, my dear', 'Daft as a wagon horse', 'Thank goodness you have come, we were saying how dead it was till you got down' – just words about a frightened feeling woman who deep inside feels hollow and who clings desperately to little things, little ordinary things, to keep shadows from sweeping over her. I wonder if it's true that all women are born actors? I wonder what I'm *really* like. *I* know I'm often so tired, so beaten, so afraid, yet someone at Canteen said I 'radiated confidence' just because I was not afraid of the rat [*in the building*] and the little cat runs to 'talk' to me. I've a jester's license at Centre ... What would I *really* be like if all my nonsense and pretend was taken from me? I have a sneaking feeling I'd be a very scared ageing woman with so pitifully little. It's an odd thing to reflect – *no* one knows anyone else. We don't even know ourselves very well – just get a glimpse of each other, or of ourselves. One thing always stands like stone – my work. Like an anchorage, however stormy and windswept things get, there is always work – and *real* work. I'll never have to go and look for something to do if trouble comes. I've all my energies to walk the path I see ahead.

CHAPTER TEN

'END OF THE BEGINNING'

September 1942–August 1943

Friday, 18 September. We had more sailors in than usual – off the mine sweepers in Morecambe Bay – and they seem such a hungry lot and ready for a hot meal. Some A-A boys came in to sell programmes for sports tomorrow – what they call 'lucky numbers' on them. Dolly Last, wife of a relative of my husband, is rather a spiteful person and spoke so skittingly to little Mrs Hunt [*who now claimed she had fibroids*] and her 'queer figure' was the first remark I heard. She has no family but prides herself on being sharp to see signs in other women. She says 'Umph, if that's a fibroid, Kay, it will need shoes' and there seemed such a queer tension. I said 'Dolly, Kay has told me what is the matter and I'm very sorry for her. You have no need to be mean about it. It's a dreadful thing, really. A baby would be a blessing, however sad its arrival, but fibroids – the word is enough to make me shudder.' I could see Dolly did not believe a word of it but I would have no discussion. I got Kay to do the books and Dolly making sandwiches. Whatever it is is none of our business and I'll not have Kay Hunt hurt any more. Life has been cruel enough ...

    I had to stay till 7 o'clock for there had been a real mix up at the Girls Club and Canteen and no one turned up and one of our staff and Mrs Ripley had to go and do the afternoon shift. It's about time we all had another shake-up to make us realise there *is* a war on. People seem to get so used to war. I often marvel really at my own acceptance of things – rations, queues – or going without! – blackouts, doing all my own work as well as war work [*her char no longer came*], all the contriving and fitting in of odd jobs, never having time to read a book in peace. *Everything* seems to get 'bedded in' to the pattern that is my wartime life and I just go on.

Sunday, 20 September. An autumn mist lay over the town and under-
foot the leaves made the ground slippery on the damp pavements. I felt
glad to get home. We had stayed longer than I thought we would and
we stumbled about putting up blackouts that should have been put up
before we went out. Of all the things that jar me about present day difficulties, blackouts still take first place. I hate them. I hate to feel shut in.
I like to wake and glance out of the window and see bright stars or the
moonlight, to see dawn come, to feel the fresh air blowing in through
open windows and not leaking in through stuffy blackouts. Never to be
closed in again, never to worry as to whether a chink of light might be
showing. I've long got used to rationing, but blackout both in streets
and home will always be a dreadsome hateful thing to me ...

I saw tonight that they had started taking the iron railings from
gardens down in the town. The blitz and housing shortage have pushed
a lot of nice oldish houses into slums – the 'open' gardens will finish the
look of them as the careless people who live in rooms and apartments
have broken the insides. Houses that doctors and professional men lived
in now have four or five noisy untidy families and dirty curtains vie with
blitzed shutters to depress one. Everything altering and changing and
going. What *will* have gone before peace comes? And when will all be
cleared up again?

I'm tired tonight, tired through and through. I looked at my little
bright dining room when I had come from the run-down, neglected,
rather sordid home of my husband's people. I felt a funny little prayer
in my heart, a jumbled prayer, that I could always cling to little bright
things and hold them fast. My brass tray, my little welcoming cat, the
gleam of my little aluminium teapot seemed to have a life of their own,
a *bright* life. I feel that little homey things are dearer and I spend precious minutes that can be snatched from my busy hours in polishing,
washing best tea cloths, changing my gay vases about, polishing mirrors
till they gleam. To me they 'mean something' I cannot explain, a symbol,
a gesture. If I had to live in a hole in the ground I suppose I could, but
I'd not like my home to grow into one.

Wednesday, 23 September. I was so thankful to get an air graph from Cliff and know he had reached his journey's end although it is in the Middle East and not India as he hoped ... Always there is a shadow on my heart when I think I've lost my boys for good now. Arthur will bring a dear little wife and will be his kind lovable self, but different, and as for Cliff _____ [*she leaves a blank space*]. I suppose it's a part of a woman to want 'children', to feel someone depends on her, someone she has to fight for and see they get on. Red Cross shops, Centres and Canteens keep one busy but somehow lately they have felt a bit hollow. I feel a wishful longing that if I was not firm could grow into the miseries. I always feel dim when summer goes, when smudge fires† burn and their exciting smell drifts about. It's been such a short elusive summer. I feel it's gone too soon and in some way taken something from me, something I'll never recapture. Perhaps it's Cliff's going. Perhaps I'm tired, perhaps a bit run down, but I feel such a shadow on my heart. I'm thankful at times for my gift of hiding my feelings, at the self-discipline that can force a smile or a jest when I only want to sit quiet. I've missed my quiet Sundays by the peaceful Lake more than I have realised and have relied on them more than I knew.

'I tried not to think longingly of the Lake woods,' Nella wrote on Sunday, 27 September – Sunday had been her most usual day for drives to the Lakes –'their colour, their smell, the thick green carpet of moss. It's a comfort to think they are all there, all waiting quietly and patiently.' For her the sights and sounds and smells of the countryside were restorative. She was also very aware of the contrast between her inner self and how she commonly appeared to others – patient, cheerful, upbeat. The latter, she knew, was at least partly a mask, which she felt duty-bound to put on. Her actual gloomy feelings often belied her outward sunny conduct. On 2 July 1942 she had written explicitly about her two selves. 'I feel I'm dividing more and more into two people – the quiet brooding woman who when alone likes to draw the quiet round her like a healing cloak, and the gay lively woman who "keeps all going", who "never worries about anything" ... The quiet one seems to be the real me, but the gay one is the most liked.'

Friday, 25 September. Two boys came in [*to the canteen*] very flushed and wanted something hot. I said 'You two go and be quiet for awhile on the settee. Try and have a nap and then a wash in cold water.' Very sheepishly they walked pompously to the rest room and Mrs Parkinson and I were talking of boys in general when I looked up into a humorous coal black face and a gentle voice said something about 'Minding serving him'. Perhaps I was not quick on the uptake with my cold or my mind was on the silly boys but I said a bit shortly 'I don't encourage boys to sleep off a glass too much beer – you are older and should have more sense', and I realised my mistake as soon as I spoke and said 'Oh, I beg your pardon. What did you say?' He said diffidently 'Do you mind serving a coloured man?' I felt *awful* as I said 'We serve *soldiers*, my dear. What would you like? But I must warn you we make *awful* coffee – out of a bottle.' He took tea and sandwiches and stood by the counter to eat them, and asked if 'all Barrow people were like us'. Mrs Parkinson said afterwards she had a feeling he had been in some place where he had been unkindly treated because he was so black so she said 'If you mean we don't notice people's country here, yes. You see, we have built ships for every country and got used to seeing other colours, faces and peoples.' Mrs Parkinson says she stayed at Lancaster once and heard a man say 'I'd not let *my* wife serve a dirty nigger' and she said she blushed for him for the 'nigger' in question at the Canteen was a cultured Jamaican.

It was a mixed crowd today – conchies, shabby pilot sergeants – we can always tell if a lad is a flyer without looking at his wings by the shy looks that follow them from the ground staff – seamen, 'airbornes', two downy faced lads who were on their way to their first ship and whose Navy rig looked slipping off them either because of unaccustom or being too big. Mrs Hunt is more of a mystery than ever for she really is a queer figure for an unattached female, fibroids or no. Tonight she goes to the doctors again, for a thorough examination by my doctor as well as his partner, so *surely* the mystery will be solved at last!

Friday, 2 October. When I hurried back to Canteen I saw three huge lorries outside and the counter full of boys demanding tea. Perhaps

I felt tired and cranky but the noise and hurry annoyed me and as I tore off my hat and overcoat and threw them on a chair I said sharply 'Please come to this end of the counter for your plates. Put your cakes on and move down here and I'll give you tea and check your orders.' The way those noisy lads got into an orderly line and meekly obeyed and moved off to the tables made Mrs Parkinson giggle and say 'Oh Sergeant Major, you *are* a one', but it set me wandering off down one of my crazy 'thought lanes'! Where will all this discipline lead? Will it be good that all these lads have been trained to obey? Will it sap all initiative for their whole lives, or will there be a swing away from *all* order when they grow older? When my headstrong 'spoilt' lad went I said 'Umph – do you all the good in the world. You will sort out your values a bit, my lad.' It *did* but in some way for a long time it took [*away*] decision and that individualism we call initiative and left a curious *mañana* spirit and a positive delight in not doing little things. Things like not being quite to time when he got back from leave, risking going off to London if he was within a hitch hike, climbing a wall to get in at night, and so on. When one of the older soldiers came back for another pie I said 'Any sandwiches to take back? I did not mean that the boys could only have the cakes on the plates you know. I wanted them served and away from the counter to let others get their tea.' He said 'That's all right, mum. Here's the list, and you can put them all together in this cloth – I know paper is short.' And then he said a funny thing. He said 'You have been a school teacher, haven't you?' I said 'No, but I've reared boys'! It amused Mrs Parkinson – she *was* a teacher. She said 'That's a good one – he means you are bossy' but the man said 'Oh no, but there was a ring of authority in your voice and if you were in the Army you would soon get your stripes'! It amused us for the rest of the afternoon and lost nothing in the telling to the others when they came in ...

Mrs Hunt has gone and taken her secret with her, whether fibroid tumours or a coming baby. Listening to the talk I suddenly realised how different it sounded. Different views were taken and open speculations as to 'If it was a baby, who was the father?' and counting back to just *when* Kay ran round with the 'roving-eyed South African officer'. It was gossip in its freest and most 'callous' way, but not one word of censure or sitting in judgement was passed. Mrs Fletcher said 'Well, I say as Mrs Last does, I hope it *is* a baby and nothing else'. Even Dolly Last, who is a bit spiteful, had nothing cruel to say. She married a cousin of my husband's and is a curious girl. She betrays her inferiority complex by being down on anything or anybody who is above her in any way – looks, clothes, family etc. She is – or *was* till I stopped her very decisively – very rude to Miss Butler who is one of the kindest and nicest women going. She and her mother live in a huge house in its own grounds where five indoor and two outdoor servants were kept in the old days and where now they live in two rooms and shut the others up and Miss Butler cooks weird meals and quite enjoys it and struggles in these maid-less days to carry on. Her life was one long tragedy for her two idolised younger brothers were killed at 20 and 22 in the last war and also the man she wanted to marry. Her people set their faces against the match – thought he was not good enough – and she once said to me 'You know, Mrs Last, mother might have been right, but oh if I had married and had a child to love and rear, why he would have been as old as Arthur now. I might even have had grandchildren.' She is as old as I am and has and will have such a lot of money, but nothing else, and when her old mother of 80 dies will be quite alone.

The coloured soldier who came in last week must be stationed here and got one of the Canteen's 'ration card' for chocolate or cigs. He came in today and got a Mars bar and insisted on giving it to me! I thanked him and cut it small and passed it to the rest and gave him a piece. He stood by the counter and ate an astonishing lot of tomato sandwiches and told Miss Butler he was a vegetarian.

Saturday, 3 October. Lately things *do* seem to have got me down. I feel worried over Arthur ... I never feel his body is as strong as his spirit and he gives himself so utterly to whatever he undertakes, and undertakes things without counting the cost. I feel I am so cut off when I cannot go and see him for myself. I'm thankful for Edith, and she seems both sensible *and* loving. No other letter from Cliff. I tell myself that I might have to wait and wait and must be patient but today I realised how very edgy my nerves are lately. There was a ring and when I went there was a telegraph boy standing with an envelope in his hand, which if I'd reflected was a good colour as it was blue and was only a 'greeting'. I felt I turned to stone as I stood – I *couldn't* take the wire from his outstretched hand. What I looked like I don't know but his so kind voice – not like a boy's at all – said 'It's all right, mum, it's only a greeting wire you know'. I nodded thanks as he put the wire into my hand. I could not speak, but felt a God bless in my heart for the kind boy, and wondered if he had had to deliver bad news to make him so thoughtful. It was from Arthur and Edith but if they had known the sick shock their greeting wire was to me it would have surprised them.*

Friday, 9 October. I felt a blank sadness wrap round me. I thought of all the winter ahead – the winter that started on the heels of the flying summer. The hideous Second Front bogey felt so close I could not escape. I looked at the lads' faces – the average age could not have been more than 24. Mrs Parkinson touched my arm and said 'What are you thinking about?' I said 'Oh, I don't know. Always be glad your Ian is only seven.' She said simply 'I *am*' and seemed to understand what I meant. She is not much younger than I am and lost one baby after another till this little boy, who is her idol. She said 'Let's have a cup of tea before another lorry load come in' and we got a nice cup in peace. Mrs Fletcher had one of her really hideous appearances today – such a pity for she is a charming woman, kind and pleasant, but today her look would have frightened a child. It is some kind of goitre and at times her face swells and her eyes stand out from it like a gargoyle. I said 'You are not well today. How long is it since you went to the specialist?' And she said 'Nearly a month – he said to wait a month this time'.

Sunday, 11 October. My husband worked all day in the garden for there

---

* They had presumably wired to wish her well on her fifty-third birthday, which was the following day.

was a lot to tidy round. The clematis hangs like two mats of mauve and purple and like Michaelmas daisies are brave and gay. Cliff loved them so. He loved any shade of purple. He is happy in the Middle East as yet for the novelty of it all has not worn off as it has with those who have been so long. I looked at the garden with its thick stemmed and branched rose trees. Six years turned since we came here, three since the war started. How swiftly time passes. Three years of war and no issues clear, no battles won – how long when we *do* start? ... It's to think of quiet places where trouble and strife, hurt and pain, have not gone. Yet when I've been on the bus and seen women who live in quiet villages Coniston way their faces look almost as strained and harassed as any others. Perhaps the old ones *are* right. It's the peace within that matters. All other kinds are myths and shadows.

Tuesday, 20 October. I am often surprised at my attitude to beautiful things since the war. I've so often looked at lovely clothes, jewels, furs etc. and wished I could have them, particularly if they were my own special taste or colour. I look now in a detached way hard to define – unless I think I'd like an article for Edith or Arthur. In some queer way I feel I've no interest in possessions, not even my own bits and bobs of 'treasures'. I keep my house shining and clean, but then it's a debt I owe to it for the comfort it brings to me. But where I used to think 'I'll have my walls always cream' or 'If ever I can save enough for golden or russet velvet both sides curtains, I'll get them for the dining room and lounge to draw across the window recess and cut out draughts'. I never give 'tomorrow's morrow' a thought. My damaged walls have ceased to worry me – they never did very much anyway. It's as if when I said 'I'd be a soldier as long as my Cliff was' it was a vow stronger than I realised and one which grew stronger. I don't really think about the war a lot, or have grand ideas of the importance of what I'm doing in my own way to help. Rather is it as if I've stepped onto a moving platform that slowly, very slowly, moves onward, always onward. As if I cannot carry much luggage and know it's little use acquiring more. Very odd altogether ...

As I waited for the return bus, streams of tired, dirty, trousered girls and women streamed past from the steel works. Such ordinary little girls and women – no Amazons among them. I thought of the inferno that is a steel or iron works and looked at their filthy overalls which showed they were real workers. I looked at the strange assortment of clothes worn – fancy coats and hats over dirty overalls and ragged pants where heat had destroyed the fabric. They seemed so unlike some of the women I knew. One very dirty oil smelling woman stood in the queue by me. She looked so tired, so tatty. Her bare ankles looked dirtier even than one day's work would make them, her nails were broken and dirty, her hair bleached by heat and straggled over her damp face. I thought of Isa, perfumed, creamed, massaged, in her lovely clothes, of her mad obsession about silk – *real* silk – stockings. It's an odd world, even odder than it ever was in its 'unequality'. I used to think the blurb in the papers was true – that the war was levelling people. Not a bit of it. It's making people *more* unequal – the bombed and the not bombed, the free people and the enslaved, the sheltered and the lonely wives and sweethearts, ones with money to throw about and ones with not enough to go round. I felt I should not complain that my back ached. I felt mean to feel rattled with my irritating day. I stood aside to let her get on first so she could get a seat inside and not have to climb on top.

Friday, 23 October. Such a lot of our familiar faces seem to have gone from Canteen, but a nice friendly lot come in their places. If we are laughing together they try and join in and beg to share a joke. We had had such a good laugh at a remark of Miss Butler's. Mrs Fletcher brought a book out of the reading room and said 'I'd be ashamed to see such trash about. Put it in the salvage box. It's *filthy*. Reading it would do one no good.' We teased her on her knowledge of pornographic books and someone wondered who wrote them. Miss Butler looked up and said innocently 'Well, *I've* always understood it was old maids'. Coming from her it was so unexpected and when she heard our laughter she went on in a Rosa Dartle manner 'But *do* tell me – something about inhibitions or repressions, isn't it?'

Wednesday, 11 November. I said I was going for Arthur's pillows and bolster and my husband said he would come. We had such a pleasant evening for Mrs Martin's brother, Russell Stenhouse, was a wonderful man whose life in every part of the globe is reflected in little treasures in his sister's house. He had twelve medals, DSO and bar and rewards for valour from French and Russian governments as well as our own. I looked at his brave kind face, so resolute, so strong in all his photos, whether studio or snap shot, and thought of the waste when his busy useful life came to an end when a raft capsized after his ship had been sunk in the Red Sea. Arthur's pillows and bolster took my breath away – huge *down* beauties, such a marvellous gift. I said 'Really Mrs Martin, I cannot possibly thank you. I hope some way I can return your kindness and generosity.' Mr Martin looked up and said 'Nay lass, she says they are a return for your bright gay company at Centre, when she was so depressed over Russell's going. I know all your jokes – even the rude ones – and I've passed many a good crack on, you know.' I heard my Dad's quiet voice – 'Let *me* play the fool' – and his explanation of 'the world's stage'. 'No one is interested in your bother and worries, Dearie. They have enough of their own, you know. Cultivate that gift of laughter you have, my dear, whatever you may feel like inside.' I think it *is* a gift. I am often surprised to find I *have* gifts. I always longed so to be clever and do things, but never had the education, for when young I was lame through an accident and had to 'run wild' on Gran's farm because 'I thought too much', as the doctors said. Such an odd thing to say, really. Now when I can joke and be pert it smoothes many a rough place – and keeps things together at Centre.

With private motoring abolished, the Lasts' car was laid up for the duration, and Nella had hardly been out of Barrow since July (except for a couple of brief visits to Spark Bridge). On the sole occasion in late 1942 when she did venture further afield, the day's outing prompted her to write spiritedly and at length.

Saturday, 28 November. I always have the trick of opening the landing casement each morning and drawing the blackout, look out to see what

kind of a day it is, and breathing deeply the sweet morning air. This
morning was no different – till a quite mad idea of a day out seized me,
on a Saturday when all bus travel was difficult! I hurried round and as I'd
cut off odd bits of meat from my so unattractive looking half shoulder
of mutton and made a stew ready for today, I only had to slice potatoes
and cook them and then turn the lot into a basin and stand it in water
in a pan by the fire, feed the hens, and lay the table, and I just managed
to catch the 9.20 bus to Ambleside as it passed the street corner. I did
not dare think of Coniston and the change of bus at Ulverston so went
to Ambleside in a through bus. It was a packed bus as it left Barrow
but a boy gave me a seat and he sat on a box. It was grand to see all the
landmarks we had passed so often in the car and the newly painted and
erected signposts made me think of old happy times when war was only
a bogey. Freshly ploughed fields, following gulls; huddles of sheep on
stubbled fields of marygolds; gold of bracken and clinging oak leaves;
carts and 'trees' of long timber on the creek of Morecambe Bay as we
went through Greenodd; bright yellow chrysanths in sheltered gardens;
feeding cranes in the river – little odd loved things I miss so now. Two
Canadian airmen sat in the seat in front and we talked of fishing and
places of interest we passed. One came from Manitoba – must be a big
inland part for he had never seen a railway or the sea before he left to
join the RCAF.[†]

I love bus travelling and wondering about people – whether the old
man with the pheasants had shot them, if the fierce looking 'aristocrat'
I remembered driving a lovely Rolls *liked* 'going common', if the sad
white faced girl without the wedding ring was the mother of the whim-
pering baby she carried so indifferently, if the quiet faced couple – the
man with 'wings' – were newly married and if it was a snatched honeymoon – I noticed their little weekend case in the rack above their
heads. Bowness, Windermere and Ambleside, so smug and affluent with
well stocked – lavishly stocked – shops! Toys, silver fish, lovely flowers,
sweets, bunches of grapes, tomatoes, mushrooms. It's something like
over dressed tabby blondes with discontented faces and marvellous furs.
People go in and out – a man with an old fashioned wooden leg and a

thin half starved looking dog, a woman with a gorgeous fur coat with a shawl collar fringed with tiny animal paws – most peculiar – a poor half witted boy stained with blue from the blue mill, school girls, giggling and noisy after a hockey match, a clergyman with a most unclerical face, a man in shabby farming clothes with the face of a saint. Old fashioned country folk, in and out they went. I would have liked to wander round Ambleside but the bus came back in half an hour and the next did not come back till five hours later and it would have been difficult to fill in the time, besides the risk of not being able to get on the afternoon bus, so I came back by 1.30 feeling as if my glimpse of the hills and Lake had been a dream.

Late 1942 marked a major shift in the fortunes of the war. For the first time in over three years the momentum favoured the British – along with their Soviet and American allies. Nella had for months been convinced that this would be a long-lasting war, even as many of her neighbours and friends allowed themselves to imagine that the conflict would soon be over. While she continued to be determined to keep wishful thinking at bay, she did write on 7 November of 'the marvellous news from Egypt' (Rommel had been defeated), although such good news from afar might easily be tarnished by bad news close to home – on 23 November she learned that one of Cliff's school friends had been killed in the Middle East. There was little doubt that the Allies were now taking the offensive against their enemies. Talk of possible invasion receded, and most people sensed that, sooner or later, Britain would achieve victory.

Nella tried to live as much as possible in the moment. 'More and more do I try to live in "today"', she wrote on 26 December 1942 (DR†). 'Rather a paradox to say I work hard to forget the war when all my activities are connected with it, but there it is … To look ahead brings fear and terror to my mind and confuses me and I feel it best not to think for long ahead.' She returned on 9 January 1943 to reflections on her own state of mind. 'I'm often amazed – *and* amused! – how quickly life seems to adjust and adapt itself nowadays, how I take everything in my stride and find a place for it in my "design for living". Nothing seems to have power to really upset me for long, no extra work to be a burden.' She tried to have faith in a higher purpose – and spoke of 'the Hand of God'. 'If I'm very tired and the worry bogey gets through my defences it makes me glad of my "escape", makes me glad of the little wall between me and the terror and despair which is on the other side.'

* * * * * *

About a quarter of Nella's diary from 1943 has been lost, including all or almost all of May, June and September; and none of her diary survives between 31 December 1943 and 3 May 1945. Her writing from 1943 has less of the sparkle of earlier and later years. This is partly because her life was much more constricted. Lacking petrol for the car, she did not get about much and thus missed out on the sorts of experiences she had once enjoyed in Morecambe or Spark Bridge or the Lakes or even at Walney that had often inspired some of her best writing. But now her life had narrowed noticeably, and her writing reflects these limitations. Moreover, her sons were never around to boost her spirits – Cliff was abroad and Arthur in Northern Ireland – and her husband was no font of vitality. While WVS work afforded satisfactions, a lot of it was now routine. Gossip and complaints in her diary tended to overshadow observant storytelling, wit and crisp descriptions. Moreover, this fourth year of war had an air for Nella, and probably most Britons, of plodding dreariness. The following selections highlight a few of the livelier passages from her 1943 diary.

Thursday, 18 February. The other day I was glancing at the paper at the breakfast table where Mary [*her cousin, now working at the Yard and boarding with the Lasts*] and I sat and I read out an article about people being unkind to girls who had been billeted on them and wondered if it was not exaggerated. Mary's reply surprised and saddened me. She told of far worse things in Preston than printed in the paper, of women who would not allow poor chilled girls warmth of a fire or a hot drink and who left the windows open in the bitter weather till the bedrooms were cold and often the beds damp where rain had blown in; of never speaking to the girls – just laughing mockingly when they had left the room. It made me think Barrow was not quite as bad as I thought for although I've heard of places where girls have been happier than others

I've not heard quite such dreadful things. Yet if peace came tomorrow, those landladies would be the ones to cheer the loudest and carry little Union Jacks and talk of how WE won. There is so little we can do about people like that, either, until they think rightly. No force or coercion will alter them. Mary said 'You know Nell, if you wanted boarders I could get you dozens, on the strength alone of my packed lunches and teas, and no one really believes me that I've a hot bottle in my bed and dainty supper tray waiting for me. You would either "make a fortune or break your heart" if you ran a boarding house. Some people would put on you, you know.' That's life, anyway. But it must be a hard, hard heart that denies warmth and comfort to unhappy people.

Friday, 5 March. It was nearly 7 o'clock when I got home for Mrs Parkinson and I waited [*at the canteen*] till three of the next shift came before leaving. Such a lovely evening, with branches roughening with buds against the blue grey of the darkening sky. The winter has flown by and the cold of the last two seemed a dream. Soon it will be high Spring – and then what? I'm really very lucky in that I *have* to keep on with work that tires me so that I cannot think too much. I've always had a very active mind but even active minds can only think to a certain point and if tired are bemused and drugged and the big terrifying things lose their sharpness. News of a ship sinking, of men lost, used to wring my heart and make me ill with horror. Now I can serve them and laugh and chaff with them, remember their different likings – this one with a waffle with his sausage, this with chips or fried bread – see their plates are hot, that I have a little hoard of the particularly messy pastries they all seem to like. I feel in a dim way that I'm rooting for them, as my boys used to say, that I'm part of the Plan and march with them. The soldiers accept my preference for the Merchant Navy and the Navy and beyond looking at the counter and asking 'Have you got any jam puffs or cream slices hidden away?' they only laugh.

It was good to rest and I'd left meat roll and salad on my lovely gay tea table with its snowy lace and linen cloth and bowl of amethyst crocuses. Mary had got up and had a meal of toast and egg and gone off for a walk, and when she came in sat and wrote letters so I wrote to Cliff and Jim Picken [*Edith's brother*] and it will be two less on Sunday.

Saturday, 6 March. Mary works with a Russian Jewess, daughter of a man who has always lived here and kept a furnishing shop. She likes Mary and asked her if she would like a piece of matting and today she had to go down for it. It was such an Easter like day and I said to Mary 'Let's go on in the bus to Walney and have a walk along the Bank and we can shop afterwards'. Never do I remember such a warm lovely day so early in the year. People loitered and sat about on the sea shore, the larks – such a feature of Biggar Bank – sang their little throats out as they mounted into the summer like sky. Daisies pied[†] the short grass where soldiers and RAF lay about reading or writing as they lay face downward. Happy dogs played their own little games on the edge of the full tide and made believe floating sticks had been thrown in for them to retrieve. A haze hid the Cumberland hills. It looks as if it will be fine for a day or two. Mary is such nice company and we strolled happily along and picked up a lot of rotting oyster shells and I'll pound them up and sift them and use the finest for the new chicks when I get them and the coarser will do for those I have.

Tuesday, 16 March. A queer girlish conchie came in to the shop – I'd seen him a few times at Canteen – and wanted something for his mother and his friend's birthday. He is about Cliff's age and never have I met such sweet girl of a fellow, in looks and softly waving hair, gestures, voice – and ideas! For some reason – hard to say for I felt I could not be chatty – he sat down and with his hands clasped round his knees and sweet smile he told me of his love for his job as batman, the way he tried to 'please his gentleman' – I heard an echo of 'Can I do yer now, Sir!'* – and his passion for the sea and country and his distaste to go back to London where he was a waiter. He sat and talked and talked, of recipes for 'his gentleman', his loneliness on his days off, his distaste for 'rough canteens'

---

* A line made famous by the vastly popular radio programme *It's That Man Again*.

and preference for British Restaurants, his longing to get a job as waiter after 'all was over' in some quiet spot in the Lake District. I wondered if he had been over-mothered, he was so gentle and confiding. With all my distaste of the conchie type I felt I could have taken him under my wing and said he could come to our house when he felt lonely. I had to give up hinting and say plainly that I was going to close the shop and go for lunch – and he asked if he could come back when I opened again! If there are any really nice boys at Canteen they never like me like the 'oddments' it always seems I attract.

We were short handed at Centre for Mrs Higham and Mrs Woods had to go to a Moral Welfare meeting,* and Miss Heath had forgotten her glasses so was not a lot of use in booking up. I heard more war talk than I've done since the blitz for people are puzzled because all the balloons and most of the anti-aircraft guns are away. We wonder if they are wanted elsewhere and feel a bit worried. When I think of the outcry there was when the balloon were brought 'to *advertize* us', as one woman put it, I never thought they would be so lamented.

Tuesday, 23 March. A woman came in to the shop and upset me for the rest of the day. She was a stranger and drawn faced woman with a cultured accent and beautiful clothes. She bought a little cart for her granddaughter and we got chatting about the war and prisoners and the worry of mothers with lads in the Services and I think I said something about women with daughters being on the whole happier today. Suddenly she started to cry so bitterly and I got her to sit down on the little stool by the radiator and got her a drink of water and gave her two aspirins. She looked up and said 'I feel I'm going out of my mind with worry' and told me such a pitiful tale of her daughter of 23 who is a WREN and whose husband has been a prisoner of war since Dunkirk. She 'loves life and dancing' her mother says and goes off night

---

* The purpose of the Furness Association for Social and Moral Welfare, according to the *Furness and District Yearbook for 1939* (p. 110), was 'to protect the tempted and restore the fallen'. Its concern was primarily with extra-marital sex and pregnancy.

after night in a clique of girls and Naval men from the Depot, married *and* single. She has had flu this week and it's discovered she can expect a baby in four to five months. Her story is that she 'knows nothing about it – it must have happened when she was "tight" some time' – all the parties she goes to there is 'everything to drink'. Her father, an officer at the Fort, says she is a 'slut' and 'that be hanged for a damn fool tale'. Her mother says 'I don't know *what* to believe'. I said 'You *must* believe her, my dear. She has no one but you to turn to. *Do* believe her and if that is too much don't tell her you doubt her story.' The poor woman said 'Her husband's a prisoner – who is to tell him, or that proud family of his?' I said 'Well, if it was my girl I'd find some way to shield her and that poor lad in Germany should never know till he was back and she could tell him herself. What good will it do to torture him while he is so helpless?' Her grief was distressing when she had to 'let go'. I persuaded her to go in the passage behind the shop and rest and dropped the latch and went for a taxi to come the back way.

I told Mrs Higham and Mrs Waite and was interested with their reactions. Mrs H is getting a really bitter 'jaundiced' outlook on the girl of today through her work as Secretary to the Social and Moral Welfare. Mrs Waite is a magistrate and sees the seamy side and tells me I am 'soft' and 'sheltered' and don't know what a rotten lot the youth of today are at heart and when out of sight of home. Yet I cannot believe it. The boys knew such crowds of nice boys and girls, ordinary busy happy young things who never talked of 'getting sozzled'. Why poor Jack Gorst, whose nerves went after the accident which killed his mother and who drank heavily at times, stopped it when he was drawn into happy company. People said 'I'd not let a boy of mine go round with Jack Gorst' but Cliff never suffered from his impulsive actions of bringing him home. Mrs Waite thinks young things want more discipline. Mrs Higham thinks the same and in addition would like corporal punishment by parents more general. I believe in treating children as 'people' with responsibilities to themselves as well as others, and felt in my heart 'Well, I've made lots of mistakes but my boys *like* me as well as love me. They are my friends and I am and always will be theirs.' 'Odd ways' of upbringing are sometimes better than 'You-sit-there-till-I-tell-you-to-move – and keep *quiet*' ...

Luckily my husband was a bit late for tea and I got all ready by the time he came in. We had whole meal toast and cheese and egg scrambled together, strawberry jam and bread and butter and gingerbread and Mary went out as she had only had her meal at 4 o'clock when she rose. My husband said 'I suppose I'd better get into the garden' and something made me say 'I think I'll do a bit at the borders', for I've got 2s 6d of sunflower seed and *must* find room for every one. I'll need everything I can grow for my feathered folk next winter. He looked so happy as he said 'Righto, I'll help clear away and wash up and we will get an early start'. I dug and raked and got the soil a bit finer and the cat and dog of course came to superintend and the hens lined up inside their fence begging for any stray worms and we laughed quite a lot about nothing at all. I like to be gay. We worked till dark and when we got in my husband said 'What a pleasant night. It flew past and I've got such a lot done. It's nice to have company when gardening.' I'll try and go out more. He used to have that 'Now-don't-do-that, leave-THAT-alone' attitude which kept us all out of the garden and made the boys feel that they would not even cut the lawn if he was about ... I was not a lot more tired and the air was fresh and sweet. I never remember so fair a spring, *never*, not in the golden happy days we look back on as 'faery times, when we were young'.

Saturday, 10 April. I rested awhile before tea, after Mary went, and I had such a passionate longing for Jaffa oranges, for golden juicy fruit, that I decided I'd open a tin of sliced peaches – and went reckless and opened a tin of cream too. It made such a lovely surprise for my husband and he teased me and said 'I'm going to have a turn out some day and see what you *have* tucked away'. I felt rewarded for not using my little store recklessly for the golden fruit tasted like sunshine itself. When I felt so picky and ill, it felt like a tonic. I could not help but chuckle as my husband went to make sure the garage door [*to the house, giving access to visitors*] was locked before we started tea. Anyone would think I'd stolen it! All the same, nowadays things are too precious to share as at one time.

Thursday, 29 April. The rush I had to get home made me more inclined to pity war workers who rushed home for their meals and I thought of women with children and shopping to do as well as part-time work. Lunch was hot and I only had to heat the soup. I decided to get some shoes at the weekend and by what I see – and hear – there is not a lot of choice in Barrow shops. As I cleared the table I thought 'Market day or not, I'll go to Ulverston'. It meant taking the town bus into town and standing 20 minutes for the Ribble instead of picking it up at the corner for lots of housewives go shopping there from Barrow, particularly on market day. Everything seems plentiful there and the shoe shop where I went much as usual. I was 'hailed with choice' actually! And got such a nice pair of Killic shoes, only utility, it's true, but not any different to what I'd have chosen for I wanted plain ones. I could have got a very good pair of brogues and was tempted, but they were heavy walking ones and now summer is here I felt I'd like a lighter pair. They were only 26s and a few coppers – I forget whether it was 8d – and I felt my trip out justified. Such a different class and grade of vegetables – lovely big white cauliflowers and piles of carrots and I've not been able to get carrots for a fortnight for what was in the shops were sold before I got down. Cooked meats and sausage and nearly all cakes and pies had gone, but with the hundreds of Lake District folk who throng the town on market day that could be understood.

A kindliness and courtesy, rare nowadays, lingers among the country folk. I looked at them, weather beaten and wrinkled with sun, with good clothes built for hard wear and mellowed by rain and sun, battered shapeless hats on the men and women alike, at the features which seem such a type of the hills and fells – rather big nosed, clear cut features, wide mobile mouth with rather thin lips – rather like comedians and as if they found plenty to smile at if not actually laugh. A strange feeling of kinship woke in me. I saw old men so like my Cliff will be, God willing. I have thought at times in my life that I loved London and the bustle of cities, but I know plain as I grow older that my heart and roots are in the quiet places, that although I like people I love places.

While holidays for the Lasts were few and far between, they were able in August to go to Spark Bridge and stay for four nights in a cottage attached to Aunt Sarah's. They travelled there by bus and were accompanied by their dog, Sol. Arriving on the 9th to 'the perfume of wood smoke hanging over the whole village', they settled in to the 'beautifully furnished cottage', feeling that 'frets and discords seemed to melt – or take their proper places'. They went for a walk and in the evening visited the Farmer's Arms to listen to the nine o'clock news, then retiring so that Nella could 'scribble by candle light'.

Tuesday, 10 August. The papers come on the 12.35 bus into the village but there are no extra ones so we waited till Aunt's old cousin had read his *Mail*. There is no wireless except at the two inns and it makes the war so far away. We can have a quart of rich creamy milk each day – as much as we like really, there is no shortage. The milkman would have let us have a *pound* of fresh butter if he had known we were coming but the milk all went in before he knew he would want extra on churning day. The peace and courtesy, the dignity of life, seem to linger in this quiet spot. The traveller from the Ulverston grocer's where our family has traded for several generations, and where I would certainly go if I'd time to go to Ulverston, called. His country drawl came through the connecting door of Aunt's two cottages and his patience as he repeated remarks to Aunt Sarah, whom time makes more deaf, the way little goodies like corn-flour, shredded suet, cust' powder were checked off a list, and seemingly she was 'in the running' for mint humbugs this month! They have a 'no grab system'. Everyone gets 'something extra' with each order, no one is missed because they live far from the shop. I know I'm prejudiced about small town ways but often I wonder if all the clever city ways have killed something special that after the war we would do well to re-capture. I sat and listened while Aunt Sarah made the traveller a cup of tea and they gossiped. It made me smile as I listened to the old time 'broadcast'. This one had started well with harvest, another had got 't rat catcher in, aye, and caught dunno *how* many "king" rats', which left alone would have led a band of females off and started a colony somewhere else! ... I heard of births and deaths mixed up with the merits of fine versus medium meal for porridge, and a debate on fire lighters. He wanted Aunt Sarah to try them – 'grand for a quickly lit fire'. He was tired – but had to go up the hill when he left. Gran's old traveller had a raw boned hack and wore a caped coat that must have been older than himself. This one has an old but powerful motor bike.

The rain cleared and we went to pay a call on a friend from Barrow who bought a house in the country after the raids. She lost her husband recently, one of the cleverest men in the Yard. Poor Walter Machin. He was a dreadful sufferer from duodenal trouble and yet worked like two men. We were sorry to find her out and I left a card with a scribbled message – I don't think we can get that far again this week. We sat over our simple tea of cheese and whole meal bread and butter, strawberry jam and cake. We don't seem to do anything and yet the day passes quickly. It seems to be doing my husband some good for he is not as moody and talks quite often. After a rest we strolled up the hill to the Farmer's Arms where all the visitors and many of the locals go for the evening. It's not a large place – run by two Manchester business men who retired to the country and decided to keep a pub. This one, over 400 years old, was an old time brew house and only nut brown ale, posset[†] and sack were on the original license. They had rather a struggle to get a wine and spirit license and I believe their cellar holds wines and liquors for all palates, however exotic. I asked one of them if they had many visitors and he growled 'Far too popular – 22 this week'. He said 'This place is too darn popular and it's getting that something will have to be done. We take only "friends of friends", so to speak, but the problem of help grows more acute – and we don't *want* to make money.' I chuckled as I thought of the guinea a day – and all drinks extra. I thought it one of the best paying propositions I knew just now.

'I feel quite a lot better for my little holiday', Nella wrote from home on Friday, 13 August, 'and ready to start off again next week at the shop and Centre. I'd hate not to have my settled work to do. When I feel so tired sometimes I feel it such a blessing I *have* it that it would be a sin to grizzle over aching back and feet.'

* * * * * *

When Nella was on foot in Barrow, she occasionally remarked on the signs of a nation at war. On Sunday, 2 May 1943 she and Will were out enjoying the warm day and saw groups of Dutch and French Canadian soldiers from nearby camps 'strolling along' the roads. 'I looked at the ugly Nissen huts, at the training planes overhead, and at the gorse, so brave and gay. I felt "There will be golden gorse and larks when all the ugliness of huts and torn up country roads are past and when khaki is not general wear". I'd a queer sadness on me somehow that not even the sunshine could dispel.' But the battles that were being fought abroad rarely came up in conversation – 'Not one word of the war', she might report after a day spent in the company of others. On 24 June she remarked in her reply to M-O's Directive that month, 'it's surprising how little the war is discussed – even mentioned.' Among her WVS colleagues 'the chatter is of everything but the war. If war *is* discussed it's in that personal way – sons and daughters in the Services and their needs, leaves, parcels etc., points' values, Home Front recipes', and similar close-to-home concerns. 'Beyond saying "Aren't our lads doing well?" or "We gave 'em it last night again," or occasionally a queer wave passes over the town and an "It won't be long now" attitude is taken up', war news featured little in conversation.

On those infrequent occasions when Nella did dwell explicitly on war, optimism failed her.

Thursday, 19 August. A shadow falls over me somehow. Maybe the weather, maybe the thoughts of this dreadful invasion of Europe starting. I often think 'It will indeed be a "new world" after the war. All and everyone seem hell bent on destroying everything in the old one.' Sometimes when I sit quiet a chaotic montage whirls through my tired head, the 'civilization' we boast so much about, and where it has led us. Fabulous riches found to train men to destroy each other, to equip them with more and more death dealing weapons, when such a fraction of the thought, energy and money could have done so much good. The world *is* 'coming to an end' indeed. If all the bad cruel Nazis and the 'wicked' Japs were being wiped out, we could think it for the betterment of all, but it seems so many of the flower of all races are going. Two women have sat side by side for four years at Centre sewing at bandages. One has lost two sons at sea – and now learns her airman son has to be 'presumed dead'. The other one's three sons work in the Yard – have good jobs. The daughter of 28 is 'reserved' as she is considered necessary as a secretary to a boss in the Yard. The other woman's daughter had to join the WAAF. I look round the big room at faces I've known and loved for over four years. My heart aches. Even in that small circle, the bravery and courage, the 'going on' when only sons have been killed, when letters don't come, when their boys are taught to fight like savages if they are Commandos, when they are trained and trained and trained for bodies to be made to endure, to go kill other women's lads, to wipe all the light from other mothers' faces.

PART TWO: PEACE
1945–1955

CHAPTER ELEVEN

CHEERS AND TEARS

May–September 1945

After a prolonged hiatus, Nella's diary resurfaces in the Mass Observation Archive, dated Friday, 4 May 1945. Hitler was dead, although many people did not believe he was; Germany was in a state of complete collapse and largely occupied by Allied forces; and the end of the war in Europe was obviously imminent – peace arrived officially on 8 May. While war in the Far East continued, many – perhaps most – Britons were by now thinking a lot about life after the war, and what sort of peace they would confront. 'There will be no spectacular change to sweep things away on V.E. Day', Nella thought on 4 May.*

During the war Nella had often imagined the post-war future, usually gloomily. She had felt (when she thought about the matter at all) that the extraordinary upheavals of wartime were bound to leave an unhappy legacy. 'They talk of the "world after the war"', she wrote on 27 October 1941, 'I wonder how much effort it will take to clear up the mess before even beginning to rebuild.' Would future generations 'see a clear path out of the morass' (11 October 1942)? On 22 August 1942 she was talking with a Mrs Clarke, who 'went on dreamily "I wonder when all is over and finished, will people have a deeper sense of values, or will it be only a race again to make and sell for money alone?"' When Nella worried about Cliff – and whether he would return safely – she was a realist and recognised that, even if and when he and other young servicemen eventually did come home, 'We will never see them again as we knew them. Life will have altered them for good or ill' (17 October 1942). She often anticipated hard times, even chaos, when peace came, just as the years after the First World War had been marked by unfulfilled promises aplenty. 'I look ahead', she mused on 28

---

* Substantial selections from the week just before and after VE Day are in *Nella Last's War*, ed. Broad and Fleming (2006), pp. 265–75.

December 1942, 'and see rationing for so many years. In fact I often argue that the worst periods will be after the war when the help we talk of to the starving people of Europe will be a fact. Every possible thing will have to be shared, not just food. I often think when I hear people talking how few have any idea of the mighty problems and adjustments ahead.'

There was, then, a lot to worry about – the plight of millions of refugees, the revengeful feelings of the victors, the prospect that 'we will be more or less poor' (DR, 29 August 1943) – although she was enthusiastic about the Beveridge Plan, a blueprint for the welfare state, and she both hoped for and expected improvements in education and welfare services. She also anticipated with pleasure the renewed possibility of driving with Will to their Lakes (not possible since severe petrol rationing from mid-1942) and 'sit all afternoon, so quiet and still, and leave all frets and worries in the peace of the quiet hills' (25 December 1942). Now in 1945, with hostilities in Europe concluded, she was to start experiencing post-war changes directly, and in all sorts of ways.

Friday, 11 May. It's been a real heat wave day, sultry and thundery but with a clear blue sky. I had to tidy round and go shopping. I hoped the oranges would have been in, but it will be tomorrow. I left a casserole of the two little chops, onions, carrots and potatoes cooking and a sponge pudding on the same heat, and made sauce when I came in. I had no soup and was only sorry I had to cook a hot meal. I'd have preferred salad. I'd not time to go up to Mrs Waite's but I rang her up and she said she felt a bit better. She is worrying now for Centre to be closed as quickly as possible. She cannot bear to think another would take her place, even for a few weeks!

I had to be down early at Canteen, to get the dried eggs scrambled and the marg beaten up with milk, a tiresome job in the heat. We were not too busy to have little friendly chats to the boys who came in, several of whom were POWs who had returned. They could not know of our efforts in the little shop, but to hear them talk of the Red Cross and parcels brought tears to our eyes. They said it was not just the food, but the looking forward to something that kept them going. I've always felt a blessing rested on that little junk shop. I felt very happy. An American lad was on leave, from Germany. I felt surprised, wondering if we would yet see Merl and Brin [*American soldiers*]. The camps are all being dispersed and done up and all huts made spruce. It looks as if they will be used soon. New Zealand sailors and our usual Polish airmen came in and one of the latter brought us a 6d ice each from a nearby ice cream shop, saying it was a 'peace celebration'. One whom I know well, with coming in for over a year – he has been instructor to his fellow countrymen – was telling me he intended to settle in Canada, 'get his citizen papers' and never return to Poland, for his home is now part of Russia and he says 'home no more'. He says his father and mother are well and 'maybe will die in Poland as they know it', but he and his brother will make a new home. His sister committed suicide with many more highly strung girls when the Germans drew near to their town. He once said simply 'They preferred to die virgins'.

I felt my aching feet and ankles would hardly carry me home, and I felt sorry for the girls who came into the stuffy smelly place for the evening shift. I had a cup of tea with the window open to catch the little breeze, and read the paper and rested, and then Margaret came in and we talked. She had a 'chameleon's hump'. I said 'Anyone would think the war had started instead of finishing' and she said 'Well, things *are* flat somehow. It's not a bit like what I thought the end of the war will be.' In Barrow no heads of anything did any planning. I really think wolf had been cried so often, people's hopes raised and then died so often, that no one could grasp the fact this time that it *was* nearly over – and then suddenly over. The poorer more demonstrative people in little streets seemed to have parties planned. Odd how a little bit of ground in front of a house and a garden gate – and even more so a real garden – seems to have a different effect on the occupants of a house. It seems to breed more aloofness. I've noticed it in quite small Council houses. If people are moved from terrace houses they have soon lost that 'gossiping round doors' habit. Sentimentalists call it neighbourliness, and I suppose up to a point it's good, but beyond that point it's a breeding ground for much of the misery of the very poor. Lack of privacy, wasted time, and gossip leading to quarrels are a few things not taken into account when speaking of the way they have parties and celebrations and the snooty suburbanites don't bother. Personally I hate to have my actions supervised and dragooned!

Margaret hopes the Americans come. She says 'There was more life in town then than even when the Scotties were here so long'.* She talks of 'clearing off' as soon as she is 21. She has had to 'pipe down' for her mother told her she would not go till she was 21 and Margaret at present rather wonders how far parental authority *can* go! For once her vitality was quenched a little. She is at a loose end. I said 'Well, you're not blaming the end of the war for that, surely?' She said 'No-o, but somehow everything seems altered. I've never known anything but war plans and talk. It's upsetting somehow, like coming to the end of a long journey and not knowing what will happen and where to find lodgings etc.' She will not be alone in her reactions. It seemed another little sign of the chaotic state ahead. The peace will have greater and more difficult problems than ever war had. This war will have such 'roots' it did not grow up in a night.

I wonder sometimes what is happening in Germany, where slave workers are in numbers strong enough for brigandage and reprisals on their hated masters, and in places where any authority by the Allies is not near enough to make for law and order. I don't think the end of bloodshed has yet come for the German people – or the misery and death. That American lad who had come on leave spoke of Cologne as a gigantic rubbish heap which could only be tackled from the edges, working inwardly as roads had gone altogether. I thought of the hundreds of people who might have been trapped in underground shelters, to die a lingering death, and the pestilence and death which might result from the bodies and lack of drainage and sanitation. I wonder what will

---

* A woman in the American Red Cross, Elizabeth Richardson, was for a few weeks in late 1944/early 1945 posted in Barrow, because of the presence of US servicemen, and wrote a number of interesting letters and diary entries from there: James H. Madison, *Slinging Doughnuts for the Boys: An American Woman in World War II* (Bloomington and Indianapolis: Indiana University Press, 2007), pp. 107–37.

happen when the aggressive German POWs are released. I feel I'd like one *huge* V bomb to fall on Grizedale Hall where I hear all the big wigs of the German Army are being brought! It might solve a few problems in the future.* I thought Steve Howson's theory that the next war will be against Russia with Germany as our allies was a figment of his imagination, largely due to his phobia about Russia, but I've been really amazed to hear little remarks with the same trend – trivial remarks like 'Russia will have to be watched', 'Look how Russia is trying to upset things at San Francisco', 'After all, our Royal Family are descended from Germans, you know', 'Russia will take generations to be *really* civilised – they are only bossed now and the majority never reason or think anything for themselves'.

Saturday, 12 May. It would have been a gorgeous day for July today. I rose early and began to pack things away in the bathroom. We can manage to get to the wash bowl and must do till Monday night with a sponge down. In small houses when a general upset is made, there is so little place to put things. My husband brought up George, the apprentice, again and lifted all carpets and I got all my odds and ends of soiled tablecloths and woollens, overalls and a folk weave bedspread washed and on the line. I did chips, cabbage and sausage for lunch and made a cup of tea and we had stewed bottled gooseberries and a piece of plain cake. I felt about all in and had planned a rest as my husband intended to write, but he said 'I don't feel like staying in – let's go on the bus to Millom'. It was a bit of a rush but it was one of those journeys when everything fell into place. We thought it best to go down by town bus to the starting place, but could have got on as it came past the street, and at Ulverston there were only a few waiting and we got a seat. Although in sight across the estuary, the winding hilly road took nearly 1½ hours by

---

* Grizedale Hall, south of Hawkshead in the Lake District, was a POW camp for German officers. In mentioning a 'V bomb', Nella probably meant a V-2 rocket, invented by the Germans and first used to attack southern England in September 1944. There was no defence against it.

bus, and they had had a very heavy thunder storm in the night and the green of grass and trees was dazzling after the rain.

There was a group of boys rather hard to place sitting near, but when one began to hum 'Mairzy doats' I knew one of them – and remembered the London evacuees I'd taken by bus to Millom last autumn. I began to talk to them – such charming boys – two of whom I'd gladly have brought home myself. They had the keen intelligence my own lads had and when I reminded them of that Friday and our chat about stone walls and roads built yet as the Romans did when here they remembered me. I bet their people will get a shock when they meet them, if they have not seen them! Their quite good schoolboy suits looked two sizes too small, their hair was like springy grass and partings seemingly abandoned, but it was their speech which really amused me – 'summat', 'lile', 'yon', 'gitten' for 'something', 'little', 'over there' and 'got' and the soft Cumberland dialect mixed with the quicker London way of speaking. I asked them if they were wanting to go back. One lad of 12–13 said seriously 'Well, yes. I've begun to worry a little, thinking of my future. I'm all set to be a doctor in my own mind. Dad says it will depend largely on what scholarships I win – and I feel I'm losing time here in the country.' I looked at his keen young face. I thought 'Nothing would make you lose time, my dear. You will have gained something by your six months stay, if only in health.' One thing they all liked – being able to run and play on moor and field and 'no one saying anything' and 'it being so nice when you fell down, to smell the grass and heather'. They had seemingly all had good homes and spoke as if their friends had been happy and of one little boy and girl who were staying altogether as they had lost both parents and grandparents in London raid and the little girl was 'chesty' and needed care. The wise way he spoke of 'papers going to be signed and all done properly, you know' made me smile. Two didn't like the hills, said 'All was ever so nice and flat' where they lived, and none seemed to have seen many hills before coming north – I remembered their reactions at the time. They are going back very soon. It must be unbelievable to the Londoners that all their terrors are past.

We had time for a Cumberland tea – sandwiches of homemade potted meat, new rolls split and made into open sandwiches with a thick layer of chopped hard boiled eggs, a huge plate of warm buttered tea cake and four large cakes – for 1s 3d each, after they had 'checked' what was eaten and expressed surprise at our small appetites! We had to go back to the bus stand and we queued for about 15 minutes as the timetable had been altered. Such an odd collection of folk for sleepy out-of-the-world Millom. A good sprinkling of evacuees, their once smart city clothes rather shapeless and smart costumes worn with peasant handkerchiefs or no head gear, gloves or stockings. Land girls, two Polish airmen, ultra smart girls who looked as if they might be barmaids for their accent did not quite match their Hollywood getup. A couple with two children fascinated me – foreigners of some kind. I heard two women discussing them. The man, strangely enough in a khaki service battle dress, was a Russian and the mother a Czech. The children were really lovely with dark curling hair and smoky grey eyes. The father's head would have interested a student of heads – unless it's general to a type of Russian. The back view was a quite normal shape and size, but the side view was so sloped [*she drew a picture*] that he had less forehead than anyone I've ever seen. His features seemed so small and compressed that his curling hair stood out like a wild halo. I thought 'If the brow is the sign of a thinker, you cannot do much reasoning or thinking' and wondered again if it is typical of a type of Russian. The mother looked like a goddess. Later her splendid framework might grow heavy looking, but at about 30 she was a delight to see and watch her effortless grace when on leaving the bus they had rather a steep path to climb. Not a couple to find in out-of-the-way Cumberland – another sign of the general mix-up today.

The sliding roof was off the coach. The sun shone like a blessing. The cool sweet breeze smelled of sea and country as we rushed along. I never recall a nicer day out. We were home just after 7 o'clock and I rang up Mrs Higham to arrange about the morning, when we go to church in the parade the Council have hurriedly arranged. It's a good walk for me and twice that for Mrs Higham so my husband said he would 'chance the car out' – I think he is feeling reckless when 'basic' petrol is in sight.

Mrs Higham was delighted and said 'We have got a lovely weekend for it'. Me – I'm not sure. The sunset had a thundery look, black clouds all over the horizon line. I wish it would pour all night. The gardens are looking very parched. The dining room was cluttered up with all movable light things from the front room. I'll cover up all the other things for it's only the frieze and ceiling and the one wall to paper in there. I laid down on the settee with the sun on me and we listened to *Music Hall*. I think Josephine Baker must be better when seen as well as heard or else her style is more suitable to French audiences. I noticed she got the least applause of any on *Music Hall*, and she left me very cold. Mrs Atkinson was not very pleased we had been off. She said 'You might have told us. We would have liked to go.' And I could see she thought us a bit unfriendly. To her, being alone is a penance, and Mr Atkinson was painting and the girls both out. I had to come to bed early. I'll get no letters written in the morning. I'll have to be up by 9 o'clock.

The town's thanksgiving service on Sunday, 13 May was marred by poor weather and, according to Nella, it was ill attended and badly organised. Later 'We listened with interest to Churchill's speech, very good and comprehensive – except for his omission of Civil Defence – but his remarks about the munition workers dropping at their benches with fatigue was more than amusing unless they act differently from any I've come across. Even my husband noticed that Civil Defence went unnoticed and the brave firemen and wardens would feel slighted when the Home Guard was so gloriously mentioned.' Then she looked ahead. 'At 9 o'clock as Big Ben tolled out its strokes I said my altered prayer, not for peace to come but that it should stay, that the Allies should be strong and not weaken, that a blessing should rest on those who love peace enough to realise it was active and not negative and must be worked for as strenuously as we did for the war.' Like most Britons, she had little sympathy for the recent enemy. 'I felt very glad to hear the Germans were not to be pampered', she wrote on 16 May. 'Making them be self-supporting is the best. We must not be soft or let them forget easily the Belsen camps and the slave murders. When I think of what our fate could have been, I would be very strict. I think the very best primary step will be that of freedom of the press and radio. The Germans as a race have had the blinkers of an isolated village shut off from the outside world, their self-importance growing in consequence.'

Wednesday, 11 July. I've had a busy tiring day, but a letter from Cliff set my day in tune. He seems so happy and busy – and happier than he has yet been in the Army. He says he has more responsibility. I think the spells of inactivity in the desert, and all the weary meaningless courses which led nowhere before he left England, made a great drain on him. His restless spirit needs action to feel he is achieving something. I'd quite a deal of shopping to do, little things like Andrews liver salt and a ball of twine, and to try and get Cliff a nail file to replace one he lost. The one I lent him has had its day. I saw electric kettles and irons, plenty of heavy bottomed pans for gas or electric stoves, children's skipping ropes with turned handles, fine lisle stockings – in a shop window, openly displayed – and some *flannel pants*!* Granted the latter would only have fit a youth of 14–15, but there *were* grey flannel bags,† which seem to have disappeared entirely. I was at Centre by 10 o'clock and Mrs Higham and I settled down to jungle jerseys and worked busily. With no interruptions I got the tricky shoulder bit fixed and tak tacked† on five jerseys before I made lunch. I'd left soup, a good salad and a little cold meat, and a wee dish of egg custard and jelly, and I brought the two latter to Centre. We feel we must make an effort to close before September for the whole building gets so damp now there is no heating. If it's a wet spell it is damper and more dank than in winter when the heating dries out the walls. Mrs Woods had promised to come but did not turn up. I did not feel sorry, and still feel a bit snooty about the way she let me down over the shop closing and then gushed over me so for my 'cleverness'. I suppose now that her bridge friends will have got back from their holiday we won't see her again on Tuesdays. I got ten of our last bundle of 35 jerseys back, but Miss Heath could not get them all examined. It's surprising what slapdash work we have had to rectify, yet

---

* On several occasions this month Nella gushed enthusiastically about the sudden availability of goods that for long had been hard to obtain.

everyone knows the wear and comfort of the jerseys depends on exactness of measuring slots for equipment and of making any cut in the material well bound and stitched. I often wonder when I see slipshod voluntary work if in their homes there is the same slackness.

The evacuees are all away. Mrs Fletcher's two were amongst those many from Workington, Millom and the Cumberland villages and farms who cried bitterly at 'going home'. Mrs Diss said if it had not been pitiful it would have been comic to see so many woebegone faces at the carriage windows. Mrs Fletcher's boy evacuee *begged* to be let stay; he is a big strong lad of 12–13 and said 'I know you would get my allowance stopped, but I'd work hard in the garden and help look after the hens and I'd not eat as much, and as soon as I leave school I'll come into the joiner's workshop and work. DO let me stay. Let Ethel go back. Mother doesn't want me and I was always in the way in our flat. *Please* Mrs Fletcher, write and tell Mother you will let me be your boy and always live with Michael and Mr Fletcher and you.' Mrs Fletcher had already approached the mother – it's been a great disappointment when acute thyroid imbalance made having a family unwise [*beyond their one child*]. Michael has been a lonely child in spite of them always encouraging children to throng the house. John has been an ideal companion, ready for every bit of fun, and as Michael said happily 'not going home at bedtime'. Mrs Fletcher said when the mother came on holiday she made no secret of the fact she 'disliked boys – they were so rough and could not be dressed as nicely as girls', but she said that he would 'soon be earning' and she was going to 'have the good of him'. Mrs Fletcher was very unhappy about it. She said 'Our Michael will never go in the business – and besides, we want him to be an architect. John would have had a good home and had good prospects, for my husband had already begun to rely on him in those little ways you rely on a son of his age. The way that lad was up to open the greenhouse in the morning, collect the eggs and "cheek" Granddad into a good humour was a pleasure to see. We all liked him and he liked us. It's dreadful to think he will not be wanted. Before we took him to the station he was missing and we found him down the garden, staring into the meadow where the ducks are, and

as he turned to leave he said 'Ain't ducks *kind* things'. Mrs Fletcher said
she was going to laugh, thinking it was a joke, but saw his lip quivering.
She is very understanding of small boys. She said 'You know, I didn't
know *what* to say so I talked quietly of all the kindness there was really
in the world, far more than cruelty if people only knew it and would
look for it, and how even things like ducks, old Tib the cat, and last
but not least that old crab of a Granddad of ours liked kindness and
was eager to return it'. We worked on till it was a rush to get the last bus
before the Yard came out.

On Sunday, 15 July she heard a very different story about evacuees from a
boatman in Bowness. He had had four children from one family, ranging from
five to eleven in age, billeted on him for three and a half years. 'They were children of people who worked in a munitions factory and who came every holiday
to see them, staying at an hotel or good boarding house, dressed in the best of
clothes, boasting between them they earned over £20, never gave the children
a penny to spend for pocket money or sent any extra for their keep, even when
they had childish ailments. Clothes had to be "wrung out of them by the billeting officer" – and at the end the foster parents were asked if they would like to
adopt the younger two, as they were girls and not likely to be earning for awhile.'

* * * * * *

During the war Nella had thrown herself into work outside the home – at the
WVS Centre (usually two days a week), at the canteen on Fridays and on many
days at Barrow's Red Cross shop, for which she had prime responsibility. While
she had once made light of her volunteering – on 5 November 1940 she had
written that her work at the Centre 'is largely gossiping and coaxing 3d tickets
out of the women for my everlasting raffle' – her volunteer work (and it greatly
expanded after 1940) actually had meant a lot to Nella. It gave her a sense of
purpose; it helped her to feel worthwhile – and to be acknowledged by others.
It had been a sort of anchor; it liberated her from the constraints of domestic-
ity – 'the cage of household duties alone', as she once put it (15 August 1945). In
many ways the war changed her life. After a shaky start in 1939, she remarked on

9 February 1944 (DR, January 1944), 'Gradually my busy life of today took shape. Everything I could do seemed to help me to do something else, giving me more than I gave, steadying nerves and resolve.' She no longer felt as confined – or 'repressed' – as she had sometimes felt in the 1930s. Her husband, she once said, had wanted her to live in 'the shell he liked so much', and feelings of 'impotence' had gripped her (DR, August 1942). Happily, her wartime work went a long way to change this. This work was varied, useful, stimulating, and mostly done with others. 'My job – or rather jobs – are all volunteering', she wrote to M-O in reply to its March 1943 Directive, 'but I love them and the Red Cross shop is a great pleasure to me even if a great deal of work. I don't feel I could ever settle down entirely to be a housewife again.'

Wartime volunteering presented women with new challenges. It summoned from Nella (and no doubt many other women) talents that were previously under-exercised, and which perhaps they barely knew they possessed. Nella often felt called upon to be creative, and to use her active imagination for some larger objective, whether to solve money-raising problems or to fashion her own appealing handcrafts (mainly dollies) or attractively to present items for sale in the Red Cross shop. 'I couldn't bear things if I did not feel I was helping to straighten things out,' she once wrote, 'however small or feeble my efforts' (2 May 1942). 'If it was not for my work I don't think I could go on', she confessed on 6 October 1942. 'Shadows crowd round me like gaunt dogs. I feel the shop and the Canteen and Centre are the stones I fling to keep them away.' It was important to 'get outside my home, for I can keep from thinking. It does no good at all to brood or worry and yet it's difficult if at home not to do so' (1 July 1942). Her work and her writing were two of her principal passions; they were ways of engaging with life on a deeper level. On 28 December 1942, 'When I was coming home, I thought of the little shop, so loved and cared for, to others only a tatty little junk shop, to me "dreams come true". Always have I had two intense wishes, quite apart from the two boys and purely personal. One was to write books, one to have a shop and work with people. I've written my "books" alright in the shape of letters! Now I've a shop, an extra precious one where every 10s is a parcel' (for a prisoner of war).

For a woman who felt this way about her wartime work, peace was bound to have a big impact. There was an inescapable sense of loss. She worried on 23

May about the possible closing of the Red Cross shop. 'Somehow I realised more today than ever what the shop means to me, perhaps with knowing Hospital Supply will close down in the near future. Looking back it seemed so difficult to get a start to be useful and now, after 5½ years effort, I doubt if I'd have the zeal to start over again on a fresh project.' The Red Cross shop did in fact close in June, and this was a particularly wrenching experience. 'It's like having a tooth drawn out in pieces,' she wrote on 18 June, 'instead of one good tug.' She needed and wanted to feel of use and constructively busy; she wondered what she would now do with herself, and how she could be engaged outside the home, where her unsociable and uninquisitive husband rarely welcomed visitors. Now in her mid-fifties, how, she asked, would she find ways of consuming her time in a worthwhile way?

* * * * * *

With war winding down, Nella often reflected on the changes, many of them dramatic and troubling, that the world was already undergoing and that she and others might expect with the arrival of peace. She was anxious about the challenges of adapting to a post-war existence. She worried about her sons – Cliff, who was still in the Army, had suffered serious abdominal injuries in November 1944; Arthur (now married to Edith) was still posted in, from Nella's perspective, remote Portadown, Northern Ireland. She had doubts, too, about her diary, which had absorbed so much of her time and energy since 1939. 'The thought struck me as I began my diary,' she wrote on 4 May, 'how much longer will they want them?' 'They' were the people at Mass-Observation to whom she regularly dispatched her writings – 'miles' of them, as she remarked a few months later, on 30 August. She spent at least an hour in bed most nights writing her MO diary.

Tuesday, 21 August. I wonder how long before it looks like peace in Japan – and *is* it really peace or will it all break out again, or linger like a festering corroding sore for years, like the war in China? Vast countries like that are not like we are in Europe. Little things grow dearer and dearer to me. Sometimes I feel I run the danger of 'clinging too closely' to things and by experience I know how foolish that can be. The little wood fire I made for my husband to have his supper by (for I know he always feels chilly after perspiring and working outdoors), the gleaming bits of brass I'd found time to polish tonight, even my bread and gingerbread, seemed 'real' in a world of shadows and doubts. I feel the everyday jobs and my little household gods are more real and convincing than 'big news', which my tired head doesn't seem to grasp. I said once at Centre 'I feel like a piece of elastic that has been stretched and stretched and now has no more stretch – and cannot spring back'. They laughed, but several said it was a pretty good description of their own postwar feelings and I can tell Arthur has somewhat the same reaction. More and more do I feel I must take each day as it comes, do the best I can and lay my day aside, taking up the next. Sometimes I feel so dead tired, like a burnt-out shell, craving only to relax and rest. Then my mind rises and rebukes my tired body – says 'so much to be done, so little time'. The stars shine brightly tonight. I love stars. They make me feel trivial and unimportant – and are so stable. I don't wonder the old ones thought Heaven was 'above the bright blue sky'.

Wednesday, 22 August. The dusk fell quickly tonight and there were no stars in the overcast sky. It's grand to think that this winter will have no blackout, that bright lights will be in streets and from lightly curtained windows. How remote the last six years are becoming. It's odd to realise how Cliff has lost such a slice from his life, turned from a charming if headstrong boy to a man who shows his apprehension of life and having as yet no stability of a settled place in the community, by moods, and a general look of strain. He has all his limbs. I think of the poor ones who came back handicapped so badly. I pray so deeply for real peace – for ordinary people who ask so little of life beyond simple needs, food and shelter for their families and a little for small enjoyments. I search for details of factories 'turning over' or opening, contracts received, but it's not very often I feel satisfied when I've read the papers. I read today an article written by an American armaments man, who urged America to 'go underground'. I recalled an article of Naylor the astrologist written when big underground shelters were being made in the beginning of the war. He said a time was coming when we would put all works and factories – and people would live in huge blocks of buildings – built deep down and air conditioned. It made me feel terrified at the time. I so love the freedom of fresh winds and air.

Tonight I thought of the dreadful new bomb – we will always live in the shadow of fear now. With the dawn of new and comparatively easily made and handled weapons, no country will ever be safe, however big their armies and navies. Only by change of thought and heart can civilization be saved. Old sayings are real truths – 'Put not your trust in Princes, or any sons of man' – more vitally real than ever. And what change of heart can be expected today – bitter hatred, chaos, broken faith, lost ideals are poor foundations. I feel again this world of ours has blundered into a beam of wickedness and unrest. Call it Uranus the 'dark Planet' or what you will, it's some evil force that affects all. I've a deep sadness over my mind and heart like a shadow, instead of joy the war is ended. I tell myself impatiently that I'm tired out, that I'm run down, and I rest as much as I can, coming to bed early, but it does not lessen the shadow. I go and work in the garden and leave a little of it there and when the bright sun shines I feel I 'lift up my hands' to it in delight, but cannot stir the heavy dead weight shadow off my heart for long.

Wednesday, 29 August. I used to think how happy people would be when the war was over, but beyond thankfulness that it's over, I see few signs of the brave new world. People are beginning to have that fear they will be paid off. Women are not settling down very well after being at work. I hear many cases where they have lost touch with little children who have learned to do without 'Mam' and turned to a Granny or older sister, of wives and returned soldier husbands feeling the strain after living apart. After the last slump a lot of people in Barrow who had considered their job secure in Vickers got a nasty shake-up when they were sacked. I hear odd remarks or parts of them, which show how women's thoughts are on 'whether Dad will get the sack', if this or that department is busy or likely to be. The stocks lie stark and empty – no big keels laid to make Barrow people feel secure. Only Sir Charles Craven's keenness and foresight kept Barrow being like Jarrow or similar dead shipbuilding towns. He is dead now and things are different altogether.* Little sleeping worries have risen after six years when work was assured for all comers. People ask the prices in shops lately. There's none of their 'Give me a couple of pounds of those' but rather it's 'How much a pound?' and a consideration before saying how much is required, and flowers are not quickly bought regardless of price. The moneyed folk are beginning to see that war jobs don't last forever ...

When things went wrong with Gran – and so little in her overworked life seemed to do for long – she had a funny little way of rising on her toes and drawing a deep breath as she said 'Ah well, we must do the best we can and pass on'. At times I feel her simple creed my standard of life and living. I feel like a grain of sand on a seashore, feeling and knowing my utter, utter limitations; that however I try, I can do so little; feeling a strange loss when I cannot work directly as we did in the Red Cross shop; wondering what I will do when the Centre closes with its purpose and Canteen with its service, making me feel I'm keeping things moving in the right direction, however small.

On numerous occasions Nella had spoken and continued to speak of the consolation she found in being in touch with the natural world near Barrow. 'When I feel I cannot possibly go on,' she had written on 24 March 1945 (DR, February–March 1945), 'I take a bus and steal away to the Lakes and hills I love and to which I turn to know the meaning of that Peace which is of God, which flows over moor and fell, inexhaustible, free for all. I feel recharged. I'm a very peace loving woman, who ranks peace as one of the highest, most desirable virtues or states of mind.' Now these satisfactions were within easier reach.

Sunday, 2 September. My husband said 'Would you like a run to

---

* Charles Craven was Chairman of Vickers-Armstrongs Ltd from January 1936 until his death in November 1944. He had been responsible for getting a lot of business for the Barrow shipyard in the 1930s, thus protecting the town from severe unemployment.

Ambleside?' I'd only expected to go on the Coast Road and felt a trip up the length of Windermere was a treat. I packed tea, taking a little loaf, butter, jam, tomatoes and cake, and we set off. Everywhere now there is a little hint of autumn, a golden tassel of one turned branch of beech, curled fading plane tree leaves, vivid red of hawthorn berries, and blue-black elderberry, and far up in the woods on the slopes of the hills, cherry trees gleam like a torch in the dull green. The last of the corn sheaves were being carted and they looked as if they had only been waiting for transport. The shorn grain fields have already tufts of green grass springing up.

We stared in amazement at the Bowness car and chara parks. Never did we see so many before war, for an adjoining field had had to be used and was full of private cars. The odd part was that most of the charas were from Blackpool and Preston and from the other direction from Cleator Moor and Cockermouth – twice the distance allowed for travel in coaches – but no one bothered and everyone looked happy in spite of there being no accommodation for tea as there once would have been. As there was no sign of picnic meals we wondered if they had had tea on the way. The big motor launches were packed and the small ones were doing a good trade. It's made Bowness very busy with the petrol allowance. My husband said 'What will it be like when the rationing goes and cars can be bought again?' I said 'Perhaps no more crowded. It's exceptional just now – VJ trips and little outings so long denied.'

We went on to quiet Ambleside – too far for Blackpool coaches to go. Yet it too was full of parked motors, wherever they could be squeezed along the Lake front. But we found one unused spot – had just room for us to edge in. I'm always attracted by the carriers with one child in and the fearless way they handle them, shooting cleverly about, never bothering about big motor launches or rowing boats with the two elders moving strongly. I'd taken a bit of sewing and a book, but I just sat quietly watching the boats and sailing ships, till I dozed off to sleep for over an hour. We had tea and a little walk along the shore and were home by 8.30.

Mr and Mrs Atkinson were very cool when we spoke over the fence,

although we did not say we had been to Ambleside. I know they think
it odd when we don't fill the back of the car whenever we go out. They
cannot be happy unless someone is with them. I feel my husband's moods
are best if he is quiet, and somehow lately I've felt more than ever the
need, the real necessity, to relax. Perhaps it's with being at Centre and
Canteen, and the shop when it was open, and having to study so many
people, keeping them happy, joking little squabbles away. But whatever
it is, lately I've felt glad to escape into the quiet of the countryside, or to
sit by the sea. Mrs Atkinson likes to know exactly what each day brings.
Three evenings she goes to a whist drive, and two afternoons as well. On
Saturday evenings they visit relatives, also for cards, and she has tried to
persuade me to 'make a date' every week for cards or to go to the pictures, as she thinks I need a 'bit of a life'. I feel I gain more life by relaxing
with a book after my busy days, that an evening which is good for her
after a day's housework and shopping is not suitable for me; and anyway,
beyond a pleasant neighbourliness there is no friendship, nor could ever
be, for we have no tastes in common.

Margaret is different. We have so much in common, both in ideals
and views. Her mother said one day 'Our Margaret is more like you
than me'. I thought of the lonely evenings little Margaret always had till
she began to come in our house, bringing her little problems, reading
my books and discussing them, picking up little cooking and sewing
ways. It grieves me sorely when I feel Margaret cheapens herself with
her many light friendships, tearing away a bit of her affections each time
and giving it away, feeling sure it's the 'right one' every time. She came
in tonight looking a bit dim. Her latest friend is an Australian airman,
son of a very prosperous farmer who gave all his children a good college
education (agriculture) and sets them up when they marry. While he is
in England waiting to go home, he has been given leave to go to a farm
somewhere in the Midlands where he can study artificial semination
and then he will take it up in a big way on his return, as 'the old man will
be highly delighted'. Margaret said dolefully 'I'll never see him again I
suppose, and if he had asked me, I'd have gone out to Australia. I would
make a good wife for a busy man you know, Mrs Last!' I hugged her and

1. Nella and Arthur, her elder son, at 9 Ilkley Road, 1940.

2. Cliff, Nella's younger son, in wartime.

3. Barrow bombed, 1941.

4. Home from the Yard, 1950s.

5. Relaxing on the Coast Road, 1950s.

6. Jessie Holme with her daughter, Kathleen, late summer 1948.

7. George Holme and Kathleen, 1949. The Holmes feature prominently in Chapter 15.

8. The Poker Club at the Grammar School; see 30 January 1950.

9. Ilkey Road from the back, late 1940s. On the far left is one side of the Lasts' house. The semi-detached houses belonged to the Atkinsons (left) and the Holmes (right).

10. Cliff, a sculptor in Australia in the 1950s.

11. Nella, Will and their dog, Garry, around 1953.

gave her a kiss, feeling so sorry for her. I said 'Perhaps, ducks, you are too adaptable. You know men like a girl to be a little aloof.' She said a bit surprisingly 'Oh, things are so different nowadays to what they were when you were a girl'. I agreed in my mind. I remember the tidal shock I got when one moonlight night when I was drawing the bedroom curtains, I saw a young airman kissing Margaret with a fervour generally only seen on the screen, and later found out she had only met him that evening, and was told 'Don't be silly – a boy *always* expects to kiss you if he brings you home'.

I felt so shaky and ill. I was glad to come to bed. This little epidemic going round seems to follow its course – sick and bad pains, followed by about two days of intense weariness and aching bones, and then a cold comes on with sneezing and nose running.

Wednesday, 5 September. We ought to have gone down this morning to the WVS really but it was no use. It was beyond me and Mrs Howson called in and did not know the ones working, putting up the stalls, and she is too shy to work with anyone she doesn't know. We were to have the ice cream and jelly, but the scoop was very stiff and my small hand soon tired – arthritis has sapped the strength from my 'knotting' fingers. A friend offered [*to help*] – she said laughingly as she spread her hand, 'My fist won't tire' – and because I went on to refreshments, Mrs Higham wouldn't stay on the ice cream stall. Not that I minded. We work well together and the ones in the kitchen, while well known WVS, were unknown to me by working together. We had the little buffet where people who did not want the sit-down tea of 1s 6d could buy what they wanted. All passed off well, except that we were so held up at the Mayor's non-arrival. We let the Matron open the proceedings, and then the fat ill-bred woman who is our Mayor waddled in beaming, saying she was sorry to be late but she had been listening in to the 'big race' [*the Irish Sweepstake*]. Shades of Labour Mayors of the old school – and women – ugh. I detest women in power unless they are something out of the ordinary.

We gave Matron a big Teddy bear instead of a bouquet after she

spoke, and we have decided that the Children's Ward badly needs decorating and refurnishing and our £500 target will be used for that, and
the WVS always takes an interest in 'their' ward. The Mayor got a lovely
little begonia in a pot – such a jewel bright thing, covered with buds,
which would have lasted for weeks. It did not endear her to us when
she swept it off and broke the pot, and after breaking off two bright
flowers for her button hole, left the rest lying. Perhaps she thought we
would have put it down to her 'having greenhouses full of plants', forgetting that we who were Barrovians remembered her upbringing in a
back street and knew her *very* well. When I saw the giver's face as the
little plant was trodden and swept aside, I felt I'd have enjoyed stuffing
it down the Mayor's too elaborate silk dress! When she came to office
she applied for more coupons, to 'dress the part', and got the answer that
'in her position, it was up to her to set a good example'! It's very easy
to spot people who buy things without coupons in Barrow. They have
the 'Jewish' stamp – over-decorated and doll-eyed bits and pieces of fur
and tucks. How the authorities have failed to find out about Davidson's
racket I don't know – a dress without coupons is £1 more. Quite openly
a girl will say 'I had to go for my wedding dress to Davidson's as I'd no
coupons to spare, but I got my going away costume at Ireland's. After
all, you only wear a wedding dress once and you can always sell it and if
you've not given coupons it's no loss at all.'

Friday, 7 September. Such a lovely nostalgic September morning. At this
time of the year I've always such a craving to be off and away over the
hills and far away, an urge that when I was younger used to tear and
weary me with its intensity. The smell of crysanths, smudge fires, sun
scorched grass, the long shadows on the grass, and the autumn colouring in hedges and woods was a delight and a torment to me. I knew I'd
be too tired to cut the lawn when I came in from Canteen, so went out
as soon as I'd washed up, to do it before I vacced and dusted. I seemed
to find weeds and twitch grass to take up more of my time, but I made
a real good job of it, in spite of the fact that the shears were red rust and
I had to clean them up, sharpen and oil them before I could trim the

edges. For a man who has to use tools, my husband is careless over any for the garden. Everything is let get rusty and dilapidated and I always tell him it takes more time with bad tools. I brushed all the fallen apple tree leaves off and I did feel so suited with my job and thought how glad my husband would be when I'd done it, and he never ever noticed I'd done it all! I had soup and cornflour for sweet from yesterday and I made a really tasty casserole out of the kidney, onions, carrots and sliced potatoes, and boiled a little cauliflower, vacced and dusted, packed Cliff's clean laundry and just managed to get washed and changed for Canteen before lunch.

Mrs Howson and I stared when we went into the greengrocer's. There were such heaps of things, onions, tomatoes, pears (not so good and too ripe), eating and baking apples, cucumbers, runner beans, celery, carrots – quite like a pre-war shop – and the flowers were a glory. It's not a shop I'll patronise after the war. I hate their furtive passing of bags of indifferent fruit – third-rate at top-rate prices – and their 'biggest in the window' way. It had rather that name before the war but lately everyone complains. Yet at present, unless you are a regular customer, there is little chance of getting even furtively handled goods, kept for 'customers' so they don't have to queue. Today I refused to take three pounds of apples the girl had weighed with two half bad ones and calmly insisted she replace them with sound ones, and when she had got her breath back she did so. I was always a keen shopper. One thing – I'd always a little more to do with my housekeeping money than most, with so many doctors' bills and illness. And then again, I love managing a house and getting the best of everything as far as freshness and quality go. To go round the market with a big basket was a real delight to me. No shopkeeper gets my custom who sells inferior food.

Mrs Howson laughed when we came out. She said 'Don't you feel in a good mood today?' and I said 'Perhaps not', but it suddenly struck me how darn sick I was of controls and shortages of little ordinary things – 'Do you know I've only one comb and that has two teeth out'. She said 'We have one between the four of us!' There is not a scrap of soap in town, no matches or cigarettes; even regular customers are not able to get any, and I've only had sweets off one ration book yet. When Cliff was here for ten days I let him take one emergency ticket back to London, in case he had to stay with friends, but said to send any remaining coupons back. He had not used any, had stayed two and then three days at a hotel. So I had his full rations. I thought I'd get the sugar, tea and points (5) and put it away for another time he came unexpectedly, use the fats and swap the meat for fresh eggs off Mrs Whittam who has plenty of eggs but prefers meat. I let her go for her meat herself and she had to go into five shops before she could get any. I'd made out with my rations of meat when Cliff was here, and we were never fond of a lot of meat, so the eggs will do for tomorrow's lunch with chips – I got three.

We found Canteen in a real bustle – sailors booking beds who had just come into town and some nice Americans going. It's really amazing how small town Americans come back all the way from Germany for a few days leave – and recommend their friends. This lot had been somewhere in the Midlands, but heard so good a report of Barrow they came here and stayed at the tatty Canteen to sleep, going round the country in buses and swimming at Walney. I found some string for one who needed it and he said 'It's sure a swell place. I'll come back if I ever come to England for a holiday. The folk here are just like home folk.' He gave me all his little tinned goods – jam, cheese, and a wee tin of butter. I drew lots for us all to have one, but kept the wee tin of butter for myself as well as the jam I drew ... We were kept on the go all the time, but no big rushes, and we peeled a lot of potatoes for chips, for the evening squad, before we left. Mrs Howson came in for a cup of tea because her mother was out and we sat talking idly. She suddenly said 'How lovely your lawn and garden look. Do you have to cut it often?' My husband shook his head and then took another look at the lawn and noticed it had been done, but never said anything. I thought 'You tiresome ungrateful thing', but didn't comment on it, and neither did he. My back ached and I felt very tired, so beyond ironing my one and only cotton frock to go black berrying if it's fine tomorrow, I rested till supper time, glad my busy day was done. I've often talked of the rest I'd get when the war was over, but as yet it hasn't come along.

Tuesday, 11 September. It poured heavily at our usual closing time [*at the Centre*] and everyone lingered till it was a dash to lock up and catch the last bus before the workmen's buses started. I can hear of many being paid off, some transferred to other towns to work, some just on the dole. The Australian sergeant pilots who were going to work in the Yard, and in office as accountants, etc. till they could be gradually taken home, are going off in a bunch after all. I'm glad. It has not made things better to see other lads found jobs to occupy their time when complaints of our own townsmen of 'having nothing to do at all' come by every post to wives and parents. I fear there will be trouble if demobbing is not speeded up. If we have to let America have trade barriers reduced as return for help over Lend Lease, it will be a bad thing. The country will be all supplied before our lads get back into their jobs. Whatever plans were made in the past, I fear things have so changed. We are in a worse plight than after the last war, and with the discovery of the atomic bomb, every future preparation for industry as well as security will have to be taken with one eye on its possibilities. When I think of Europe's demobbing problems, my head reels, and wonder 'will we ever get straightened out?' America again has emerged unscathed, her people at home unaware there has been a war, except for a little rationing and of course those who have had men in the Forces.

I fried bacon and sweet apples cut in thick slices and there was whole meal bread and butter, raspberry jam and plain cake. I got out Cliff's shirts and settled to unpick and tack new neck bands on, and repairing them where necessary, ready for machining. There is no real hurry to do them, but I like to finish off one job before I start another and put it away. I'll be able to settle down to my dollies without having to feel that guilty feeling of a more important job. I'll be glad when a few 'features' come back on the wireless – *Monday Night at Eight o'Clock*, for one. I don't know what I'd do without the wireless when I'm sitting sewing, when my husband has his moods, and conversations on my part peter out after vainly trying to interest him or rouse him. If I was sitting alone, my thoughts would be free to roam and wander, but it's different when 'manners alone' make me want to interest a person sitting and glumping.

Three days earlier she had said that Will 'grows more mumpish and averse from company, and alas I'm much less patient, or perhaps more awake to the fact that my nervous breakdowns were due to "repressions" as Dr Miller said … His idea of "love" is for a person to always do the things he thinks, to have no ideas of their own' (8 September).

Thursday, 13 September. I saw an amazing sight – a tall 'overblown rose' of a woman, that sallow complexion that seems to follow a lifetime of coffee drinking, a heavy greasy Veronica Lake style of hairdressing; and her clothes – a jaunty smartness and perky hat, but never have I seen such shoddy material, and on her fat calves she had a pair of knitted red turnover socks, gartered below her huge dimpled knees, from which her full skirt swung. Her costume was black, and her black hat had an upstanding red quill, and she carried an awful looking bag made of the same red 'string' as her socks. Her shoes were of a heavy cloth with wooden soles. She seemed to be asking the way and when I appeared the two women seemed to make her understand I would help her – WVS seem universal aunts. Then I saw her dog, a dirty woolly French poodle, clipped like a boulevard doggie, and his bright clown eyes sparkled from under his dirty top knot. He *was* a pet. I'm stupid with any language, but oddly enough can always get by, and I somehow understood she wanted the railway station, and off we went. The dog liked me and came quite happily and we did attract attention! I think she must have been Dutch or Belgian, for when the train came in two heavily built Merchant Navy men got off the train. One spoke English and thanked me for 'looking after Therese' – and I was not sure whether it was the girl's or the dog's name. He seemed the most pleased to see the latter! He was very sad. I gathered he had been somewhere to identify a body washed off his ship and swept ashore by the tide …

My husband does worry me. He grows more and more detached and really I often feel I'm not a good influence for him. When he is tired out I always feel so sorry for him and do every little thing to comfort him, but at times I wonder if it would have been better if I had nagged and stormed him out of his moods. I looked at him tonight as he sat – he surprised me by a remark he passed, and I thought I knew them all. I've been looking forward to going into the 'drome on Saturday when it's open for inspection when our big Savings push opens. A bus runs up to within a mile and a half. We could take the car and go nearer. Granted it's a cold windswept spot, and it would be tiring walking round, but it's a chance we will not get again to see anything like it. He spoke of a bad cold he had coming on, the need to go to Ulverston, how tiring it would be, and all the people who would be there, and we would 'have to stop and talk to them'. I had that irritable feeling at myself for my weak streak when I heard myself say 'Alright, if you don't feel like going, we will go to Ulverston and then on to Spark Bridge to see Aunt Sarah'. I felt angry with myself when I saw the look of relief open over his face. I thought 'Now why couldn't you have said "Alright, you go to Ulverston and I'll go with the Atkinsons and see the "drome"?' ...

The first chill of autumn makes me think of winter, and of winter in Europe, making me wish that America had had more of a share in war than she has. She shows very plain signs of her old grab and brag. The word 'peace' will have little meaning for them who have no shelter or warmth. The jaunty smartness, the fat unwholeness of the woman in the red stockings I met today, came back to me. She was one of the lucky ones. Diet and right food will bring down her puppy fat. Her courage showed in her eyes, her attempt to look fashionable, and her shaven poodle. I thought of the old ones, the little children, the displaced people who may be suffering for others' sins and do not deserve that they should be turned adrift, back into a homeland that does not want them. I see so little signs of the brotherhood that seemed as if, when it flowered in war time, it would come to fruit when peace was signed. Arthur's words come back to me. He said he would 'like to retire to a desert island with a handful of congenial souls'. I feel at some time, in some former life, I've been a nun – sought the cloistered life – or maybe I'm the type who seeks it. I feel as if I withdraw within myself more and more in my mind. I feel so useless and little, my efforts so futile and feeble. Nothing I can do or think or say can really help the poor ones. My heart's-ease and feeling of being worthwhile in the scheme of things passed when our dear tatty Red Cross shop closed its doors. When I could gloat over the week's taking, thinking 'so many poor men made happy for a little while', it was always like oil in the lamp.

Maybe I'm war weary and a bit debilitated. Certainly things have rather got me down lately, try as I may. People seem to come too close to me, bruising my mind, tiring me inside. Little things annoy me. My worries go to bed with me, sleep lightly, wake at a touch, and are ready when I rise to keep pace with me all day. In spite of all my gay chatter and nonsense, I have no one with whom to talk things over. Come to think of it, the only one I can let me back hair down with is Arthur. We grew up together, poor kid. He helped share burdens from a very early age. Letters are not satisfactory. Beside, it's not fair to worry him with formless little worries and fears. He has his own. My husband's health, little half-formed worries about Cliff, a vague mist of fright and fear, a feeling of chaos all round, fret me when I sit quiet. I feel a feeble 'lifting up of my hands' rather than words when I pray, a feeling that God just knows how I feel and any help would be received with gratitude by me – renewed faith, a chance to help, serenity of mind that seems to have fled me for the present.

One great feeling though – I can read a book, taking interest and losing myself. The Herries[†] books to me are always a delight, beyond their style, bringing alive the places I love in the Lakes, peopling them with what could be the family of Rawlinsons instead of Herries, tracing resemblance and thinking of our old ones lying quiet in Hawkshead churchyard, who lived when the Herries folk lived, feeling akin.[*] It *is*

---

[*] Nella's mother was born a Rawlinson; and the family 'were known as the "proud Rawlinsons" – a name that has been associated with Hawkshead and Lake Windermere as long as there has been written records. Yeoman farmers, independent and free thinking people … The women were always the stronger-minded and more go-ahead, the men folk were content to dream and plan' (DR, May 1946). Nella was an admirer of Hugh Walpole's regional fiction the 'Herries Chronicle' (1930–33), which comprised four historical novels (one of them was *Judith Paris*: see below, 6 October), featuring narratives of violence and romance, and set in the Lake District in the eighteenth and nineteenth centuries.

a blessing when I can read. I do my duty writing and then read on into the night, when I don't sleep, and if I wake restless, put on the light and read awhile, blessing my room to myself, the fact I've not to lie staring into the darkness, afraid of disturbing my husband, who needs his sleep when he has to work so hard.

Friday, 14 September. I felt exhausted [*after a day at the canteen*] when we were going home, but it was my own fault. I'd only had a very little lunch and nothing but cups of tea. The flies seemed to be over the food and the sink smelled till I went out and got some disinfectant. I felt annoyed when I had to pay 1s 6d again – really mad. I thought 'I bought this and I'll use it', so poured nearly half down the sink, some down the staff lavatory, and gave a sailor the rest to use in the men's lav – then found out the pong came from the pig tub rather than the sink! I rested and ate some bread and butter when I got in, thinking of the announcement that the WVS will go on for another two years. When we have got through all the material, and Matron's work at Hospital Supply, we will close down, but there remains still the clothing to bale and pack and dispatch to the Red Cross Headquarters – garments sent from the American Red Cross. Then there is Canteen, and when Hospital Supply closes I will do more there if necessary, but none of us will agree to be 'exploited' in any way. We have worked constantly and uncomplainingly all the war years, but we will not 'blackleg' or do work someone else would be paid for doing.

Tonight as I sat I thought of six years ago when Cliff went off in the second lot of Militia – such a lifetime ago it seems; so many who went about then will never return. I had a sadness at the utter stupidity of war, and the blindness and complacency which allowed us to look on while Hitler armed and prepared, chuckling at his antics as we would at those of a clown's, telling ourselves silly things like 'the rolling stock of Germany is so outworn it could never stand any big strains', shutting our eyes to the huge strategical arterial roads being made. My dad was an ardent admirer and disciple of Lord Roberts, never trusted the Germans, and after the last war worried over the 'muddled peace'. It's a terrible thought that so much can hang on the way things are handled now, and what dreadful results may come in another 25 years.*

---

* Field Marshal Earl Roberts (1832–1914) had advocated a robust British rearmament to defend against (as he saw it) an understandably expansionist Germany. In a speech in Manchester in October 1912 – when Nella was young and recently married – he had declared that 'there is one way in which Britain can have peace, not only with Germany, but with every other Power, national or imperial, and that is, to present such a battle-front by sea and land that no Power or probable combination of Powers shall dare to attack her without the certainty of disaster' (*Lord Roberts' Message to the Nation* [London, 1912], p. 9). A street in Barrow is named after him.

CHAPTER TWELVE

A SORT OF PEACE

September 1945–January 1946

Thursday, 20 September. The years slipped back to six years ago, when war had only started and we were sewing cloth rugs, in very spare moments. When our minds were half crazed with fear for the future I loved talk. Men were being called up. Now it's over, the fighting and killing part, but it's dreadful to read of the food and fuel shortage and the winter coming on. Poor gay Vienna again facing famine, and all the Balkan states, which are only a name in the paper to us. Greeks, French, Dutch – all the same, hungry and cold. I've had to pinch and scrape at times, economise the rest, to make things go round, but have always managed to serve a tempting meal if it had only been baked potatoes and herrings, when the boys rushed in 'simply starving, Dearie' from school. There has been always a fire to welcome them home, a door to shut out the worries and hurts of the day, a bed for tired heads to sleep and wake refreshed.

When I think of those poor women who suffer twice – once for their families and then for themselves – my heart aches. I'm rather glad that Mrs Woods has not been with us all these last weeks. Today she jarred on us badly when she said that half Europe *should* die out including the treacherous French who had 'let us down and didn't deserve help in any way'. I thought as I looked at her 'Well, after all, if we all got our deserts you might be in prison for bribing shop girls to give you extra rations and buying everything you could in the black market'. She thought Mrs Higham and I had 'no sense of proportion' when in answer to some girl about sending the baby bundles which might be used for a traitor French baby, I said there was no such thing as a traitor baby and Mrs Higham said if there were a thousand bundles and she knew they were going for German babies it would be all the same! I felt a row was very near. We don't think alike on a lot of subjects and Mrs Woods has that hateful air which many teachers have – that 'Be quiet, silly ignorant child, don't you hear me speak'.

Margaret brought some magazines back. There is a decided coolness now between us. I think my remarks about the Australian pilot have offended her out of all proportion – several times she has got in a dig about such a girl 'seeming to be good enough for so and so'. Useless to say anything. The cap has been crammed down over her ears and not just fitted. I wonder in my heart if I started a train of thought that night, if Margaret suddenly sees how many 'friends' she has had, how many 'heartbreaks'. Her friend Linda is married and very sedate, rather snobbishly and slavishly so! She pauses to think how her husband – now left town – would like every little action. Margaret asked her to go to a show the other night and Linda said 'Oh NO Margaret. Eddie would not like it, for I know you would be sure to meet some of your boy friends and they would string along.' I looked at Margaret's gay vital face tonight, suddenly seeing why Cliff and she didn't draw any nearer as I'd hoped. They have both that lack of stability, that 'snatching' at life, always wanting the next thing. They are too much alike. I hope Margaret doesn't keep up her offence with me. She is a sweet girl and never takes notice of my husband's moods and silences. I came to bed early, glad my mind is settled enough to read and enjoy a book. It's a great blessing when one can lose all sense of time, all worries, if only for a short time, in a book.

Tuesday, 25 September. I feel I've never had such a sour attitude on life in general. I thought of the fun and laughter there used to be at Centre, even in the darkest days of war. Sometimes they say in the office 'You are quiet' – say it in wonder – and I just smile, but think 'I feel quiet, I'm tired out', and wonder if that is why others feel dim. There was such an eager looking forward to the end of the war. When I used to talk of still lean times till all got reorganised, I was looked on as a real dismal Jimmy. Now it's over. We look forward to a winter which promises to be short of coal and food. Women who thought their husbands would be released if their job was waiting are feeling disappointed. Husbands are coming home so changed and with such altered outlooks they seem strangers. Women are leaving their wartime jobs and finding it's not as easy to pick up threads as lay them down. Clothes coupons are beginning to seem inadequate lately when big things are needed. Meat is scarcer and nothing to replace it in the menus of harried landladies and mothers of families. Milk is down to two pints a head per week. There is so little brightness in life, and people's heads are so tired. Speaking for myself, I feel as if anyone said 'Tell me what you would really like to do', I could not tell them. I could say I'd like to go somewhere where there was no bitter winds and damp to make me dread winter, somewhere where I could lie in the sun and feel warm, but I feel too indifferent to think of anything I'd really like to buy, or do, and what I do seems only like another job – all except when I come to bed and lie reading. It's my chief joy today. I think of this tiredness magnified to the highest degree amongst the homeless ones. Sometimes I wonder if we get 'wavelengths' of their despair and depression. I wonder what would happen if anything like the Spanish influenza swept over the world like it did after the last war – people would die in greater numbers than even in the war.

Thursday, 4 October. My 55th birthday [*she erred: it was actually Nella's fifty-sixth birthday, as she later realised*] – and Centre finally finished except for a little whist drive next Tuesday and our trip to Blackpool on Wednesday. I feel a bit dim tonight. We were down early and worked like niggers. Mrs Woods came down soon after Mrs Higham and I and helped us sort out six years accumulation of junk in the way of old cardboard boxes, old letters – Mrs Waite has a Chinaman's aversion to destroying any written or printed matter! Carters trailed in and out for various lent things. The place got emptier. We were glad of our hot lunches – really hot with junk we had burnt and got the oven hot. Mrs Waite came in and Mrs Lord and Miss Ledgerwood would not have anything at all to do with her and kept out of the Committee room. I got into trouble with the organisers of the trip to Blackpool for having asked Mrs Woods to go with us. I said impatiently 'Oh, don't be daft – you invited Mrs Higham and I, and Mrs Woods is on the Committee', and got the answer 'Well, we like you'! They knew it was my birthday and teased me to tell them how old I was, one woman saying 'Well, *I* know you are nearer 50 than 40', and made those who knew my age laugh! ...

I was home at 4.15 and before I changed or washed I relaxed on the settee and read Cliff's letter – quite an 'ordinary' and newsy one. I need not have worried so with visions of him being ill. He is so happy just now in his work, he says. He would make the Army his career if he had a small private income! I've been astonished to hear many remarks which show the same trend – married men too who speak of living in occupied countries with their families later on ... Aunt Eliza came in with some pears and a wee buttonhole of two flat clover-coloured daisies which will be the making of my clover flannel frock. She has such an eye for colour as 'form' – surprisingly so for an old country woman. We sat and talked. She will be 80 this December but her mind is as keen and clear as Aunt Sarah's and her memory like a book whose pages can be turned back for reference. Surprisingly enough, tonight she talked of mother, who died at 52 – poor mother whose heart broke at 21 and for the rest of her life had little to give her second husband or her three children; who, looking back, seemed to live in a world entirely her own and pre-ferred shadows and might-have-beens to real people. My husband said 'If Nell doesn't stop losing weight she is going to grow very like her mother in figure and general looks'. Aunt Eliza was shocked. She said 'Oh No, Will – why Nell's mother was a beauty. I'm sure Nell takes after Grandma Lord', which, considering I've heard Aunt Eliza discuss the short stature and the all-round worthlessness of a family who had lived for generations in Woolwich – 'which they tell me is London' – I thought it a bit comic. She looks well for her change of air and speaks of trying to get a cottage in the country next summer. I thought of the way mother and her sisters had squandered money, just lately letting it drain away. I thought in that respect I was like the Lords' family, and of course I never had any to squander. My shillings have always had to go as far as eighteen pence.

I made some little felt shoes and got them on seven dollies. They are coming on very nicely. I've a pile of odd bits of material from Centre, too, I can piece up for very wee ones' nighties and I'll make some little dressing gowns of crazy patchwork from my good scraps of pastel-coloured crepe de-chine and silk. I'll find plenty to do alright, but I would like to find something where we could work in company. It's no use worrying. I had a job to 'break into the war' but I did it.

Bed seems pretty good to my aching back and wretched bones and I'll read when I've written two letters.

Saturday, 6 October. It was such a queer foggy morning and when I went to the hairdresser's for 9 o'clock the cars and buses all had lights on full. I cannot be in a good mood with myself. For the first time, getting my hair permed irked and fidgeted me, but it's a very good one and will last. It was my husband's birthday gift so cost me nothing either. When I came home at 12 o'clock, the sun was shining brightly and people thronged the streets. The sun, the heaps of celery, pears and apples, tomatoes and boiled peeled beetroots, and meeting so many children and young people happily munching apples or pears as they walked in the sun, seemed to give such an air of happy prosperity, quite like the pre-war days.

It always seems odd to me to see queues for shoes, but an incident I heard the other day made me wonder if it was people's greed that was partly to blame for the shortage. Favoured customers get a ring when Joyce or good branded shoes come in and one woman who, before the war, would never have had more than three pair of shoes was heard to boast she had 15 pairs of shoes that had never yet been mended and were 'as good as new'. My husband, who never in his life owned more than one fountain pen, now has three. He had one from Arthur as a present and passed on the one I bought to Clifford and was heard to say he 'could have done with a spare one' and was offered two at different times and took them. I said 'You cannot use more than one pen at once' but he seems to like to see them! I've noticed many little incidents like it at different times and feel it's one of the chief sources of everyday things being scarce. I had enough soup to heat and we had potted meat, celery and tomatoes, whole meal bread and butter.

We decided to go to Kendal for our last little outing before the clocks were put back, and have our tea out. It was a glorious day for motoring, bright and clear and golden brown leaves softly falling like snow and drifting along the roads into heaps. I dearly love Kendal, its old hotels and buildings and its general air of peacefulness, only marred by the heavy North Road traffic thundering through. I think it should be by-passed from the narrow streets. I could have bought fat hares and rabbits, trout or mackerel, and the shops were so well stocked. I saw china and crockery I never thought to see again, and the antique shops had things of beauty and usefulness, not ugly museum pieces. I looked at chairs and presses, gay china and lovely glass, thinking [*Hugh Walpole's*] 'Judith Paris may have owned things like that', and laughed at my whimsy when I realised they would have come from every corner of England. I saw my first television set but was not very thrilled. The screen was so tiny, any performers would have looked like dolls ...

Mrs Howson came in for a chat. She got home last night and looks a bit down. She has had a nice time in Portsmouth. She says she doesn't know what she will do when all the clothing job finishes at the WVS. She is a very lonely and somewhat aloof woman, and at times gets notions that everyone and everything is against her. I feel concern at times when she is in that mood, recalling how her father with no 'real' cares felt the same – and one day was found hanging from a beam in his paint shop.

Tuesday, 16 October. Sometimes I've a cold fear on me when I look at my husband. He never had a very firm hold on realities. Now he has an interest in nothing. At one time I grew frettish if I was not 'bright and amusing'. Often now he never speaks for the whole evening unless it's a grunt or 'Yes' or 'Oh'. I think of his parents and shudder. Beyond breathing and eating, they have not been alive for years, say quite frankly they 'don't want bothering' when their sons or daughters call. No memory, no interest in themselves or the outside world. I'm heart thankful the boys are not like that. I'd rather never have their company than they should grow so afraid and indifferent to life. All my wild rebellion seems over. Strong people don't dominate like weak ones. In a strong person there is something to fight, a chink in their armour somewhere. Everyone has something. I count my blessings and find I've a good many, and most of us walk alone. I often envy women with a big family. I look at Margaret often and wish she was my girl, though lately we seem very apart. I think my words about the Australian were a 'cap that fitted' and for the first time she began to think.

Saturday, 20 October. I've a great sadness on me. Perhaps the grey day and the thought of winter contributed to my mood, but somehow the dockers' strike, the worldwide unrest, the widespread misery made me wonder how long it will be before we can say 'Peace in our time, oh Lord'. The only peace is that there are no active hostilities, but the corrosion of the war years is eating deeper into civilization. People have time to think, and their thoughts make them afraid. In the chaos that follows war there seems so little to grip. Things alter and move so quickly. Sometimes I feel I'm on a slide – and a greased one at that. In the simple code in which my generation were reared there was right and wrong, good and bad, things which were just not done, examples we strove to follow. All gone. Freud pointed out that behaviourism [*restrained demeanour*] could be excused on the count of inhibitions and repressions. In a world where mass murder by bombing was looked on as necessary, where life was as little valued in the Western as the Eastern world, when young men went off on suicide expeditions by air and glider, where clergy had ceased to hold people by doctrine or natural dignity, where no hero lasted for long and where home ties were broken, and 'Mother' or 'Dad' as always handy to turn to impossible, there seems none of the stability so necessary for each and all, if we have to have peace of mind at all.

I often feel as if the whole world had been a heap of compact bundles of sticks, and all the strings binding them were going and sticks lying round or floating downstream, blown in high winds, breaking each other or pressing the ones underneath into the ground to rot. I wish I could find some work which had to be done – a job to do outside my home, working with and for others. As I sat tonight I visualised all the piles of mending, my hospital dollies and garments, books I'd planned to read – and found them wanting. I don't want 'leisure' to feel creeping tides of worry and unrest come nearer. I want to feel I am helping, in however small a way. I want the laughter and fellowship of the war years.

Tuesday, 23 October. My husband rang up and suggested going to the pictures tonight as he could not get home early tomorrow night. I scrambled an egg for him and I had cheese and tomato and there was loganberry jam and whole meal bread and butter, and plain cake and gingerbread. I enjoyed the picture, *Roughly Speaking*, though it bordered somewhat on fantasy to English people, in its opportunities and ups and downs, but I thought it would be grand to be married to a man who hit back at life without whining and complaining. I had a letter from Cliff today. It looks as if he has made up his mind to go with the Glider Pilot Regiment if he has a chance when they go to Palestine, although he says they may have one of their own flyers as adjutant. Things may work out for the best if he does. I've always said he needed discipline, and up to now he has kicked against everything, seeing authority as only to be flouted. Another year in the Army may make him more sure of his own capabilities. He is not lazy and if he can concentrate on a job where he will be happy it will be all for the good. I *do* miss Arthur sometimes, and long to talk things over and over. I sit and turn things over in my mind as my fingers fly over my sewing. The humour I've been in lately recalls six years ago, when I honestly think my rag dollies helped me to hold on. There's a great satisfaction in seeing a thing take shape and form under one's hands, especially if they are made from oddments into something worthwhile. I often have a sneaking wish I was strong minded like Mrs Atkinson and could say I was going to a whist drive a few nights a week. She tells her husband quite frankly, if he's too dull to talk or play cards, she will go where she *can* be amused. Yet cards never interest me for very long. It would be more of a penance than amusement if I went to play so often. In spite of my busy day I got two more dollies finished, little black girl dollies in gay dresses and a big bow in their mop of hair.

Saturday, 27 October. I thought I'd have all nice for Xmas when Cliff came, but if as he expects he will be in Palestine by then, I think I'll make all gay for his leave – that is, if he comes. Surely he will come for a few days, dull as he finds home. I often wonder what queer kinks he has deep down, when he finds so much fault with all at home, with its size and set out, my decorations and 'old fashioned ways'. I look round and think it's a very nice house really, and kept as well as anyone else's. Sometimes I tell myself it's a kind of twisted love of both home and me that makes him lash out. When he was younger he used to get cross at my 'weak streak' and say I gave in too much for peace sake, but by Gad I've had to give in as much to him as anyone. I've known the impulse to strike him flat, to speak cuttingly and to the point, to strip him of some of his conceits and silly values – and that streak in me that made me always insist that home was a place where you came to recover from the knocks and pricks of life and not receive them laid a hand on my lips. Then again, I have a feeling hard to define that in spite of all I stand for *some* anchorage in Cliff's life. If Cliff knew how clearly I saw things, his way of thinking and acting, the worthlessness of so many of his 'friendships', I feel something would go. It's better I should let him think I'm 'sweet and dumb', seeing and understanding only what he thinks fit, knowing nothing but what he thinks fit to tell me. He forgets – or ignores – that talk and gossip filters through.

Tuesday, 30 October. It was a fine morning and I decided to go shopping and get rid of my heavy headache in the fresh air, and I wanted to see if my dress had come in to a shop where a consignment was expected. I got a really beautiful one, a real 'dream dress', and by Gad my diary and I will be the only ones to know what I paid – 8 guineas. I told my husband it was 'over £5' and he nearly had a fit. I felt peeved when I thought how little I'd ever spent on clothes, always making them myself till I got my two last coats tailored. He never realises the days of cheap remnants have gone, and he is so unobservant he never sees changing prices and supplies. It's a soft turquoise blue that blends perfectly with the russet of my coat. I thought at first it was too young but the shop girl said 'It's exactly your dress in style and colours are never considered "young"'. Silly old thing – I don't remember feeling so excited over a dress since I was a girl. Cliff will understand. Maybe I'll whisper my 'sin' to him when he comes!

Friday, 2 November. It was such a fair, sweet morning – hard to realise it was so near Xmas. I'd a pile of best tablecloths and napkins, doyleys, and overalls, and I decided I'd take advantage of the fine morning. I had such hindrance – phone calls and people paying bills who lingered to chat and I felt I didn't get near done I'd planned. I had good soup to heat and enough meat roll and I boiled potatoes and carrots and made a good steamed raisin pudding and a little marmalade jam. I felt tired and it was such a nice pleasure to be shut up in Canteen. A ring just before I went told me the result of the specially convened meeting last night. We cannot get a night porter – the one who applied last week only stayed one night – and it's been decided to close the bedrooms this week, or until we get a porter. If the beds are not let I only give the Canteen till Xmas to stay open, for it's an expensive place to run now we don't have as many for meals and snacks. I'd a little shopping to do and Mrs Higham picked me up at the corner and we managed to get all done before going into Canteen. I was glad to see 6 lb of sausage I'd had promised and we had the breakfast bacon but no potatoes for chips, after me getting the fat.

We felt vexed when we had to refuse nice lads a bed, but Mrs Goode, the bed-maker, was talking to us and she said it's not only that we don't pay well, but she says that since VE day the Canadian 'behaviour' worsened and since VJ day it's been growing worse. Quite decent fellows come in dead drunk and wet the beds through and are sick on the floor – often all over their bed – without the least trace of shame. In wartime there was nothing of that, but now it's as if, she says, they don't fear 'reporting' or have any decency when they have drink. She says that two night porters left for that, saying there was more decency in a common doss house. It will be a pity if that element is the cause of the Canteen closing, for we get older and more stable men and fellows on leave or who cannot get train connections. We were very busy all afternoon, for with it being cold we made toast and put cheese or scrambled egg on top.

We came home in the Highams' car, and I had a cup of tea and did some mending as I sat by the fire. Margaret came in to show me the material she had bought with the coupons I let her have. She has got black for she says it's such a good standby when she can use different accessories. She is going to make a long dress after all. She says they are coming back very quickly and she will have it long till after Xmas if not for after March. She looks very thin. She says she 'has no time for Barrow boys – they are all dull after RAF and Americans'. I held my tongue this time. I could have repeated remarks Cliff had passed about girls who liked Americans better than our own lads!

Sunday, 4 November. Last night I was kept awake by fireworks going off, as if those kiddies who had been lucky enough to get any had not the patience to wait till Monday. I had my usual rest and before I had my bath I slipped down in my dressing gown and popped a little dish I'd prepared last night in the oven. I put my soup on to heat on a low heat. I had sausage in a flat dish and stewed apples and made apple sauce and put it on the sausage and added a layer of mashed potatoes and it made a very tasty lunch. It was tinned soup – with not cooking my meat – but I added a little Bovril for flavour and extra 'goodness'. We had a cup of tea and piece of cake for a sweet, and having washed up we were out by 1.45, for it was such a lovely day we planned to go to Ambleside, feeling there would not be many more fine days. The beech trees are still a golden glory and the sun turns the bracken clad moss and hillsides to russet. As we passed under beech or oak trees their leaves fluttered down through the open top of the car, bringing in their scent, like withered apples. At Bowness they had little motor launches and sailing boats out, and even rowing boats for hire, and each big chara park had a good number in

– and I counted them in one by the Lake, 27. I've never known so long
a season and the Lakes, and cafes and sweet and ice cream shops were
doing a good trade. It would be dark for the charas going home. It was
dusk when we got in at 5 o'clock. There was bottled pears and unsweetened milk for 'cream', whole meal bread and butter, parkin* and plain
cakes, and a leaping wood and coal fire. When I'd washed up I put a
rather damp piece of oak log at the back of the fire and it lasted all right
as we sat, and the wood smoke seemed to go through the whole house.

My husband was writing for awhile so I sat quiet and stitched busily
at one of the little cot quilts and got one finished. It's a really worthwhile
little thing – both sides very good silk and neatly and strongly sewn on
to a pad of cotton wool. It will do fine for the two tiny cots when they
have poor babes of a few days old who need warmth of cotton wool. We
listened to *Lorna Doone* and then the news. My husband has been very
moody and quiet lately. I sat wrapped in my own thoughts and surmises
– a montage of speculation about Cliff and if Arthur has got his nomi-
nation [*to sit a Civil Service examination for promotion*] and if I'll see
them this Xmas skimmed through my mind. I'd like to see the girl Cliff
speaks of. He has spoken so often of never marrying that I think she
must be exceptional!* I went into the garden just before I came to bed.
The stars were bright as if it were going to be frosty. All round fireworks
popped and in one garden they even had a bonfire. Children of today
have little restraint. They want what they want right now without that
careful preparation for a given festa. It's part of the 'take the cash and let
the credit go' of today which creeps in everywhere. 'Fish is in Jones', you
think rapidly. 'Will the sausage I had got keep till tomorrow? Better get
fish while I've got a chance.' You see cold cream in a shop, and although
you have quite half a pot you buy another while it's there.

Unconsciously we are all changing in little ways. I thought tonight
as I sat how hard I'd grown these last six years. No one would fret me
into a nervous breakdown now. When my husband gets his moods,

---

* Cliff had proposed marriage to a young woman in the WAAF. She later turned him
down (which was just as well since he was gay).

beyond seeing he has nothing to annoy him further, then a tasty meal, and warm fire waiting if it's cold, I let him alone with 'Ah the back of my hand to you' feeling. No coaxing and worrying – and he doesn't get the black moods he used to do. When he does, I don't even notice them. Somehow I've learned – or gained – serenity. I've come at long last to that place where Gran walked, and know what she meant when she talked of 'laying her burden down before God after she had done what she could to bear it'. Knowing too the Rhythm and Strength she spoke of – all there if we 'reach out'. She had big worries and came through. My little worries fade before hers, but they are ever present. I feel too that now I don't go out two days a week I don't throw things off the same.

Sunday, 18 November. We went to Spark Bridge. It was such a lovely bright day, like we get at the end of December when we have 'crossed the line'. Aunt Sarah was baking bread and they had chops done in the oven for a treat. The stock pot bubbled and, adding to the smell of baking bread and wood smoke, made a smell of home and comfort. They are as bright and cheerful as can be, happy in all their little blessings as if they had money and every of their hearts' best wish – maybe happier! It grew dark rapidly and we came home, giving a lift to a very odd couple. He was a very young RAF officer; she was a pretty, very silent girl of perhaps 18–19. They were walking along with heavy suitcases and I know they had a very long way before they could catch a bus to take them to Ulverston station. They didn't speak one word to each other, and he had a very pettish manner when he spoke of 'hanging round Ulverston till the 6 o'clock train'. I suggested spending an hour in an ice cream cafe over a cup of tea and said 'Perhaps they will have fires in the waiting room'. He gave me a look as if I'd suggested he pass the time singing in the streets. A more haughty spoilt infant I've not seen for awhile, in spite of his RAF uniform. I tried to talk pleasantly to the girl but she was either very shy or afraid of him.

My husband said when they had got out 'Perhaps a honeymoon couple'. I said 'I hope it's only an unofficial one. That girl looked too nice to make a mistake and be punished all the rest of her life. She could live down a stolen weekend.' I could often giggle wildly when I see the effect of a lawless remark of mine on my husband. Poor lamb. He is really unique. His mind clings to the catechism and prayer book in general. He thinks marriage means utter possession of body and soul, thoughts and interest, of a wife by a husband. That I should say such things of a lord of creation shocked him to his soul case. He would get a bigger shock if he realised my whole impression of men in general sometimes!

Christmas was approaching, and Nella decided to put austerity aside. 'I'm not going to save and scratch ever again', she declared on 5 December. The immediate beneficiary of this resolution was her husband, for whom she bought an extravagant Christmas gift – a lovely oak framed electric clock (costing almost £3) which she thought would go nicely with the oak trim in their dining room. Hard times had gone on long enough, she thought, and in her view the restrictive policies of the new Labour government were decidedly objectionable. 'This government is going to rob us of all individuality. I'll not live to see the reaping of the whirlwind, but I'm not going to help them. For the rest of my life I will spend any little surplus I get' (5 December). As if to underline this determination, later that day, when her husband asked what she would like for Christmas, she indicated that a fur coat and a diamond ring would be much appreciated.

Monday, 10 December. It's been a really evil day of icy fog, and maybe it was partly the cause of a really nervy day all day. I felt depressed and sad. I pictured homeless cold people, little children and old ones without fire and warmth. My snug little home and glowing fire seemed both lonesome things – and a reproach. I baked bread and some plain biscuits to put in a tin for when Cliff comes. He loves biscuits for supper and I've still half a tin of parkins so he will not have to worry about eating out. I had a bit of pastry in a bowl from last baking day, and I made a nice damson tart with a jar of bottled damson. I made a very good suet pudding and there was some to send down to the old ones, with a little new cob of bread and a few biscuits ...

As I grow older I grow more convinced in, if not reincarnation exactly, that our life here is incomplete, is only a tiny paragraph of a long book, which will have to be taken as a whole. I feel the truth of so much of my old Gran's sayings and teachings, wondering where she learned them. Her 'do the best you can and pass on, leaving the rest to God' might well be a teaching for today's problems. As I sat tonight I had the feeling of frustration I had before I got into war work proper – so much to do and no one wanted my services! Europe and its terrible sufferings might be on the moon and out of reach of our help, for all the 'aids' it gets in Barrow. Perhaps when Xmas, our first peacetime Xmas, gets over, it will be different. Mrs Diss said 'Trouble of it is, you know, if we do start a "make and mend" as you suggest, we might only be helping black market crooks'. I think the Red Cross could give us a lead, for everyone could do a little and it would help as the shilling a week fund helped. So many people take the view that 'Germany has brought it all on herself'. I said to Mrs Woods 'Well, there is France, and little French children'. Her big blue eyes rolled and flashed as she said 'And for what are we to thank France, pray?' I feel we should leave 'punishment' to the clever ones. The ordinary simple folk should hold out a hand to anyone in trouble or want – we are not God – and little children feel cold and frightened whatever their country or colour. It's a very remarkable thing that amongst the people who think Germany has brought it all on herself, that France is traitor and should be punished for giving up – Belgium too in some people's opinion – and these are the best church people I know. I shocked Mrs Woods terribly by saying 'The kindly pitiful Christ you sing about would have been in the Belsen camp and in all the worst bombed places. He wouldn't recognise his churches as "holy" places.'

My husband said 'You look very sad. Are you worrying about anything?' I said 'I've got a real attack of the blues. I think I'm worrying more than I know about Cliff, and Arthur and Edith having to move, and it's opened the door to a whole battalion of worries and sad thoughts.' I'm glad I'm going to the little reunion whist drive tomorrow and meeting all the Hospital Supply lot. Mrs Caddy the caretaker died very suddenly. She was in the best of health and spirits when we had our last drive and disappointed because we planned to have this one in the ARP Club. She was upset a few weeks ago when her black cat dear Dinkes was run over. She cried to me as she said 'You know, I'll miss that cat this winter when the door is shut and the evenings are so long. When you live alone you grow so attached to your cat.' It's as well now he went before her. He followed her like a dog and his excited rush to greet her when she had been shopping made me hope he was waiting for her. He was a very nice cat.

Wednesday, 12 December. When Mrs Cooper went I finished off the shirt I had tacked and then hunted out all my Xmas bits and bobs, carefully packed in boxes. Cliff's little tree carries its age very well – 25! Perhaps the great love he had for it and the fact it would not be Xmas without it has helped preserve it! I put all the little glass ornaments on and the big star and two strands of tinsel I bought out of Mrs Waite's little hoard she gave us to sell at the Hospital Supply last Xmas. I bought a box of tiny crackers only thumb length for our last party, seven years ago. I caught my breath at the thought that only my own two and three of the girls were left. One girl died of TB – that was the outcome of going in the WAAFs and sleeping in a damp bed. One died when her baby was born – poor dear, she was the wife of one of the Boots crowd. And one was killed in our raids. The other two we lost sight of completely when their family moved to Australia. I'd forgotten Jack Gorst, though; he was there, for it was the crackers he brought in – made like little dinner rolls – that made me forget to pull the wee ones off the tree. I said 'Never mind. I'll save them for the next party' – and '39 brought something else but parties and I said to myself 'I'll keep them till the next party as I said'. They look a bit tired and dusty, but then, aren't we all? I think they have little whistles or jewellery in – something hard. Mrs Atkinson said with a little sniff 'Trust you to have something that no one else has, or can buy'. I was glad really that no one came in as I unpacked my little oddments, of paper rolled up from, I think, three other Xmases – two anyway. I trimmed the little tree with the feeling that every little tawdry chipped bauble was alive and was glad to be on the tree again, for when I'd finished I felt myself musing and gently laughing over a remembered incident, and the tree twinkled and winked in the firelight as if to say 'Go on remembering. Memory is the one thing that no one can break or tarnish, soil or destroy. It's your very own.'

Under my well thought preparations and my plans I've a sadness which takes keeping down. Perhaps it's because of Cliff and his future. Perhaps thinking of Arthur and Edith flat-hunting. They talk of young folks having families. I see no chance as yet of Arthur starting a family in any reasonable comfort, and he is 32 and life passes so swiftly. Just as a clock often begins to go fast as it nears the end of its spring, and needs complete winding or it will stop, I feel we all are going faster. I'd like to talk over, or rather listen to clever competent people talking about, this loan from America. I feel America has not acted like a good neighbour at all. My husband says that when travellers come round so much is 'written off' their catalogues and they tell him 'all is for export'. The New Year is going to be a shock for people. Things will be very tight and on the whole more difficult than in the war years, for there will be so many more civilians and so many less things to buy. I feel America is laying the foundations of resentment which will recoil on her, whereas she could have laid those of real comradeship, and in life there are 'no rewards and no revenge – only consequences'. I feel it's the fact we have a Labour Government, that if Churchill had still led, things would have been a lot different. Rightly or wrongly, the USA Government fear Attlee and despise Harold Laski.* It would have been better if he had been in the hotel in Barrow when a bomb demolished it. He is that most unfortunate of men – one who does not know when to speak and when to hold his tongue, and in a public figure it's the unforgivable sin. The fact too that he is a Jew is unfortunate. I've often been astonished at the mistrust and real hatred of Jews in quite ordinary men in the street.

Friday, 14 December. I was talking to such a nice lad in Canteen today,

---

* Harold Laski, a forceful and outspoken socialist, was Chairman of the Labour Party at this time – and much reviled by non-socialists (and not entirely popular in his own party). Clement Attlee had been Prime Minister since the end of July.

well spoken and with that indefinable air of 'background'. We spoke of demobilisation. He hopes to be out by next June. He's 24. He joined up at 17½ because he was out of joint with the jarring course he had embarked upon, and the Army offered a grand escape. His uncle has since died – his father died when he was small – and he has absolutely no idea what he will do. He thought he might 'go in the building trade' for he will have to help his mother. A boy in a nearby street was a ticket collector on the railway. Now he is demobbed a Major – acting Colonel when he came out – with a dainty expensive looking wife he married when a Captain, and they have a little girl of two and another expected any time. I thought of housing problems as well as work and 'adjustments'. I felt the Saturnalian 'Lord of misrule' was in charge of this lovely earth and its misused treasures. The dire feeling that lies like a bank of heavy snow clouds in my mind seemed to deepen. When Big Ben tolls I feel my heartfelt prayer urging 'Please God, bless the young ones' ... We older ones have had our day, have made or marred our lives, but we did have chances. Any courage we possess was rooted in 'security' of some kind – home, Church, or faith in the 'clever ones' who seemed omnipotent.

Till I die I'll remember the morning after our worst raid, when roofs and windows all went aground – tiled roofs. I felt I walked about in a daze. With a curious lack of any noise or talking or movement, except a persistent tinkling sound, like the little temple wind bells we once would buy, it was falling shovelfuls of glass as everyone swept it up and put it in heaps. Sometimes in my mind I feel and hear that tinkling noise, when I think of the shattered lives of so many, of the senselessness and the utter folly of war, when no one wins. America has won this war, but in a short time she will have a bigger depression than ever before. She has no soul and is too young a country to understand the problems of the old world. And there's a thing people tend to forget. One of the strongest cornerstones in American society as a whole is bitter resentment, either to their own country or another, which compelled them to seek a fuller life overseas. There is a deep hidden fear in Americans. That is why so many of them bluster and brag. They are not 'used to things'.

Prosperity hurts them as much as the poverty and hardship which sent their fathers wandering, but shows in their love of being top dog.

I rave. It's after 12.30 and time I slept!

Cliff was now at home.

Tuesday, 18 December. Cliff looks a lot better. He had been working hard before he came and I feel he is worrying a little about getting a start when he is demobbed. I hope he gets into interior décor and likes it. He has a queer streak of instability that has stayed from childhood and not been outgrown with his somewhat artificial life in the Army. Seven years nearly out of his life by the time he is demobbed – six and a half at any rate – and at the most important time. Maybe he would have had somewhat muddled values if he had not gone in the Army. He is very like my father's family. I see it very plainly when he is talking – that under their circumstances he too would have saved the world, to ride the crest of the waves, or sink below them.

I told him a few things of my father's family as we sat yesterday, more as a hint of where his footloose fancy can lead than anything else. They were all East India men, sailors or traders, up to my great grandfather's day, who 'saw these new fangled engines being used freely – even put in ships, maybe!' – and advised his sons to learn all about them. Some made good. My grandfather was one, but never happy. He married early and got tied down with responsibility. I recall him as a darling old man who loved to read of foreign parts, and his collection of oddments bought off sailors were a joy to us children and a curse to his wife and daughters. One of my father's brothers 'rode the crest' and crashed, and spent 20 years on the Cape breakwater for illicit diamond-buying, a savage sentence only possible those days of DeBeers' monopoly in South Africa. I feel my Cliff has so much hidden conflict from his ancestors. I try to be patient when he gets difficult, praying always he will be 'true to the best in himself'. Beyond that, there is little to be done. Any influencing has been done when he was growing up and any lessons learned then may be remembered.

For Nella, December was to be a month full of sociable pleasures. On the 17th
Cliff had a visitor, Jacques, a French-Egyptian friend, who delighted his mother.
'I felt my laughter and the feeling of happiness in my little gay decked house had
recharged me,' she wrote that evening, 'making me more vital than I've felt for
a while. I like bustle and happy people round me. I don't mind work, and dearly
love to see people round my table enjoying the food I've cooked.' She enjoyed
the fun and 'happy faces'. 'I felt the war years and worry had rolled back like a
soiled curtain and let sunshine in to flood my little house.' Then, on the 20th,
Arthur and Edith arrived from Northern Ireland, bringing all the family together
for this first peacetime Christmas.

Sunday, 23 December. My husband had been writing as usual on a Sunday
morning and as the sun shone, Cliff said 'You all go out, I'll get the table
ready', and knowing how he loved arranging things I went off gladly
for I felt a bit whacked. We went round Coniston, always my choice
if I'm asked. The Lake lay remote and grey, but a strong sunset drew
tearing red fingers of pinky red across it as if trying to rouse it to friendly
movement. Its light touched the hills to gold where the bracken dried so
valiantly this year. Arthur said 'The bracken must have been a glory this
year. Even now it's more colourful than I remember it.' Somehow I felt
it was the last touch to our happy Xmas, to take that little loved run out.

Everything was ready. I had only to brew tea and cut bread and butter
and scones. I felt all the war years – my anxiety of last Xmas – and
dreams that it could never have been. The little tree in the corner, the
lights lit round the arch of the bay window and the plentiful spread
would have all been pre-war, only my lads were men and only Edith's
and Margaret's faces fresh and girlish. I had a bit of sweetened milk for
cream, rum butter and loganberry jam, Xmas cake, chocolate biscuits,
mince pies and shortbread. My cloth with the embroidered holly hocks
picking up the red of the little tinsel baubles on the tree. Happy laughter and gay voices. Even my little cat purred extra loudly and blinked
happily from someone's knee. He is growing too heavy to nurse for long
and gets passed round! We pulled the little crackers – and everyone
who did not take sugar in their tea insisted on a sugar lump to suck,

saying it was 'the next party'. I'd saved my crackers, as I said. Seven years old or not, the tiny things went off with quite a loud pop, and wee lead charms were in each – tiny horses and spinning wheels, squirrels and horseshoes. Everything was soon cleared away and we started to play Pontoon[†] for a while, but got so interested we played till 10.30, when I made supper as Doug had ordered a taxi for 11.30 ... I love parties – best in my own home.

Monday, 24 December, Christmas Eve. Mrs Whittam was very upset. Her best friend's daughter had been cut to pieces on the railway line and she was going to her funeral. Such a bright clever girl who worked in our Public Library and whose fiancé shot himself a few weeks ago. He was in the RAF and badly injured but they 'repaired' his poor face and his other injuries mended, but later he found himself going blind. A letter, not published, was to her mother, begging forgiveness but saying she 'could not face things without Bob', saying she knew she was acting wickedly in killing herself but that she chose that way to be with him – that 'it would never be Heaven unless she was with him'. Another of war's tragedies – one among many that we will not hear anything about ...

We all felt we would like a breath of good fresh air and went in the car over Walney. I walked along the beach. The huge waves rolled and crashed. Suddenly I felt my old love of the sea return. I felt as I looked that in spite of mines yet around in some places it was sweet and free, that the fear and menace of death had passed, leaving the ordinary risks and turmoil natural to it. I had a few calls to make – two on old people who visit Aunt Eliza and are over 80 ... I called on Mrs Waite, taking her some mince pies and a piece of Xmas cake, but though I could see movement in the dining room as I went up the path, I was not let in. I scribbled a Xmas message on the wrapping paper and came away. They are very odd and must be a great trial to their sons' wives ...

All the buses are stopped for Xmas. They refused flatly to even run a skeleton service to enable people to visit or go to church. It's odd how high handed public servants like dockers and bus people can be. They say NO and that's that.

The following days featured customary seasonal celebrations, exchanges of gifts (including a single banana for the whole family from Australia, 'which had ripened perfectly'), socialising with family and friends, and a lot of time preparing food and eating it – detailed accounts were provided. The Lasts enjoyed a goose for Christmas dinner, and Nella got 'a really lovely diamond ring from my husband' – he probably valued her, in his own way, more than he sometimes let on. On Christmas afternoon she visited the hospital where she had volunteered during the war, and later had fourteen people for tea, with even more visitors in the house in the evening, many of them people of her sons' generation, and very much in a party mood. 'I felt I could have sat down and howled for sheer happiness,' she wrote on Boxing Day morning, 'for joy that in spite of everything young things could laugh and be gay.' Later that day they had 'a little run in the car' and at five o'clock were entertained by the Atkinsons for tea. 'Not a single thing has spoiled or marred our Xmas', she thought (written early the next morning); and during that day, the 27th, she prepared a hearty breakfast for Cliff, who was taking the morning train to London, saw *My Friend Flicka* at the cinema, and in the evening saw Arthur and Edith off on their train and boat to Belfast. Returning from the station, 'I felt as if my little house still vibrated with love and happiness, laughter and gaiety. I felt as if all my little worries had been sorted out tidily … I feel I have got things a little more in focus. Perhaps I've laughed a few mulligrubs away!' Nella, while introspective, liked to be with people and to feel socially connected. The next evening, 28 December, after attending a party that included a concert, she noted that 'Me – I'd rather talk and listen to people talking than any "amusement"'.

Sunday, 30 December. I felt really thankful it was Sunday. I could hardly bear to stand on my right leg. [*She had twisted it at the canteen the previous day.*] After I'd had the tea and toast my husband brought up, I knelt in very hot water in the bath and bathed in it, afterwards rubbing it well with wintergreen, and it was a little better. I had a very busy morning with letters and rose at 12 to make lunch – good mutton soup in which too were some goose bones. There was cold mutton, as tender as chicken – a nice chunky bit of chilled mutton, and much better meat than I've had lately – chutney and whole meal bread and butter, egg custard and bottled apples and then a cup of tea when I made some to put in the flask to take out. All was white with frost. It never lifted all day, and we went to Spark Bridge to wish them a Happy New Year and take a jar of good dripping, a bit of marg, a glass of sherry each and a big slice of Xmas cake.

We went on for a little run to Coniston Lake, and I never saw my dear Lake lovelier. The bracken clad hills were mirrored on the silver surface till it was a fantasy of gold and grey, with patches of blue sky in the mosaic. My husband stopped the car to pump up the tyres as he thought the pressure too low, and I sat with the windows wide open with the sun on my face. Such utter peace and beauty. I felt it was enough for all the troubled world. No sound save the gentle murmur of a wee beck as it hurried to lose itself in the placid Lake. I could have sat all afternoon just listening to the silence, caught in the Rhythm I always feel in that quiet spot, nearer to God than anywhere else I know. I sat so quiet and still, thinking of the New Year, longing for a job of some kind. There seems so little to do in Barrow and so many to do it. Women like myself who have been busy and useful, feeling they were helping, cannot find a way to help the peace as we did in wartime. With 2,000 women on the Labour Exchange, it would not be right to do anything they could do, yet I know many who, like myself, long to do something. I felt I 'put my name down' as I sat – my New Year resolution formless but willing.

We were home by 4.30. All was white and lovely with frost. It looked as if the trees and bracken clad slopes were sprinkled with a powdering of snow. I had left a good banked fire. I put slippers to warm and made tea while my husband covered up the car. We had been eating chocolate this afternoon and so did not feel very hungry. I had some good Kraft spreading cheese a friend had sent from Canada and passed on to me, and I made sandwiches and we had rum butter. My husband can always eat cake, particularly Xmas cake, but I felt I did not want any more sweet stuff. We settled down quietly by the fire. I had a good detective book I had started last week, and my husband had some bills to make out. The cat settled on my knee and all was quiet till 8.30 when we listened to *Man of Property* [*by John Galsworthy*].

I keep wondering how Arthur's back is, fearing he is letting himself drift into the rheumatic state which so tormented my husband and his father and really clouded their lives for years. When he was home he told me he didn't want the piano after all, that he wanted to sell it and spend the money on something he would need for the going into their new house. Secretly I felt vexed. I'd certainly given him it years ago and often wished when they left home and there was no one to play it that I could sell it and buy the china cabinet I needed but had no room for in this small house. I could have done with the money for many occasions, but would never have thought of selling it when I'd said Arthur could have it. He said 'Cliff can have half the money' and I'll see he does. Sometimes I'm appalled to see that Arthur and Edith are waiting for their money every month. Arthur never had any financial sense at all. I feel Edith could budget better if he would let her.

Monday, 31 December, Hogmanay. Such a bitter morning. My leg ached but was quite a lot better, and I went downtown early for my rations and to pay my bill at the wine merchant's, and was offered a bottle of whiskey and one of rum, both of which I accepted for whiskey is my standby in either gastric attacks or flu colds while my husband prefers rum, and there's no telling what we will need before winter is over ...
I took the bus and went up to wish Mrs Waite a Happy New Year – and got in this time! Poor old dear. She is so disagreeable and is worried about her husband who, the doctor thinks, has something rather malignant at 82. I looked at them both. They are so difficult and aloof. No real love or friendship. No interests. I hope and pray I don't live till I'm 80, unless I can be like Aunt Sarah or Aunt Eliza, whose mind seems to keep their body in check and who plan ahead as if they had years and years to live. I didn't stay long. I hurried home gladly to do my ironing and some mending with my machine ...
We listened to the wireless. Mrs Howson and her husband came in for a few minutes on their way to a party, but we were in bed by 10 o'clock, feeling we would rather sleep the New Year in for we plan to go to Morecambe for a run out tomorrow and get lunch at a hotel. My

husband has not used the car for business lately and he loves a good
run.

Tuesday, 1 January 1946, New Year's Day. Winter has come, very decidedly. It's been a day of heavy frost and really bitter wind. We set out
about 11 o'clock and in spite of my fur coat, rug and woollen stockings I
didn't feel very warm. We stopped for lunch at the Carnforth Hotel and
had a surprisingly good lunch – turkey and plum pudding and as good
soup as we would have had at home, roast and boiled potatoes, carrots
and sprouts and an excellent cup of coffee, for 5s 6d a head. We passed
three cars and a big lorry that had been smashed up recently. No doubt
the roads were bad last night. Everything was quiet at Morecambe
except for people going off to a football match and children being taken
to a pantomime matinee. I didn't see one place offering hot lunches.
Generally if they are, a board is placed outside hotels. We were back
home at 4 o'clock, and wanted to be off the narrow winding roads of the
Levern before the sun went down and frost seized on the roads. We had
banked the fire with slack† and it soon was poked to a large blaze, and
I'd left our slippers by the side to get warm ... All round sounded quiet
as I made tea ... I think all the festivities were over last night. Never in
peace time before the war were so many people about in taxis, cars and
on foot between 2.30 and 5.30.

I keep wondering and wondering what will be the effect if the loan
to Britain doesn't materialise. Prospects didn't look too rosy with it. I
always thought a few bombs should have fallen in America – real big
ones! Last war the same. They lost men like all countries but as a per-
centage it was not proportionate, and again they seem to have 'all the
money in the world'. All the brave talk of a 'new world' seems to be
dying slowly. People have not changed one bit. Many in fact have turned
selfish and self-seeking, and grown hard and bitter. Me – I never put a
lot of reliance on 'uplift' talk. We *could* start something, plant a tiny
acorn which we might not see beyond the seedling stage, but that it is
the best we can hope to do ... Nowadays many talk as if atomic energy
was kind of philosopher's stone to turn everything into something

new and wonderful. It may well be so – in material things. But that prayer 'And renew a right spirit within us' is the real and only solution in human relationships. I'd hate to live in a world where I had only to press a button. If I had a job to do outside my home I'd be grateful for any help, but the world is largely made up of everyday folk like myself who have to weave their lives and jobs and efforts for home comfort into one whole pattern, and not only have bright tinselly bits all over but the solid yarn of service and the joy that comes from a job you have done in your own particular way. 'Beauty', 'the Arts' and 'appreciation of literature' etc. come after. They are the parts that show – the simple things the foundation.*

---

* A few weeks later (2 February 1946) Nella again voiced her sense of the limitations of modern materialism: 'When I feel the most blue, I feel Nature is beginning a war now, as if man's stupidity has roused some destructive force – and there is always the atom bomb and its dire possibilities' (DR, December 1945–January 1946).

CHAPTER THIRTEEN

DARKNESS AND LIGHT

February–September 1946

Saturday, 9 February. It was bright sunshine this morning, and when I looked out of the dining room window I saw a little flash of gold in the border and I put on my coat and went out to look at it – my first crocus – and beside it three frail snowdrops danced and nodded in the keen wind. The crab apple tree plainly shows tiny buds, and the rambler roses have had leaf buds for awhile. I felt as always the miracle of spring, of life from seeming death. All was quiet except for the crying gulls overhead. My little garden seemed a precious thing as I walked down the path, already in my mind's eye seeing the colour and beauty of what will soon be. The stirring life shows in little weeds and tufts of grass in the crazy paving, the bulbs pushing through and that uplift of bare branches before the buds break through ...

Inside me I'm growing very old, and it's as if I feel a 'wide vision', less tendency to worry and fret, to 'tell God all about things' rather than to pray. There's a lot of truth in the old saying 'It's the happiest time of your life when your children are round your knees'. I feel I would have been a happier woman with a 'long' family, with young things still to love and cherish and not just a little mog of a cat, wise and kindly as he is. As I lay back in the chair tonight I felt a great sadness on me, not altogether flu after effects. I don't like the blueish patches on my cheeks and lips if I have any exertion. I hope I am not going to have to step aside from any little I could do to help. There is so much to do and life slips so swiftly by.

I tried to talk to my husband and tell him what was in my mind, but he only looked blankly at me. He said 'I cannot see what you are worrying about. You have done more than anyone else I know. You should be glad when you can take things easy.' I suppose he is right to a certain extent, but I feel torn in two sometimes when I think of the frightened, homeless people, of hopeless mothers with little hungry children, of homeless cold old ones. I feel I've a wailing wall in my heart. If I could only feel I was helping. I realise more and more the goodness of God when I was able to work steadily through the war, through the worry of Cliff's illness, and the weary weeks when he was so out of joint with life. My husband said 'You must start going to the pictures in an afternoon like other women', but I feel when it's warmer weather I'd sooner work in the garden than go to see pictures I'd no interest in. It's alright if it's a good picture, but we do seem to have had poor ones lately on the whole. Unless anyone was in the habit of going they would not have been attracted.

Tuesday, 12 February. I had a little weep over Cliff's letter today – a bright somewhat impersonal letter with the 'sting in the last' when he signed himself 'Your wabbit'. The years rolled away and I recalled the first time I'd called him that. He was an infuriating baby, and my husband never had any patience with children. I was ill after a major operation and Cliff had grown really beyond them all, only good on the occasions he had been brought in the Hospital. That particular night the wild shrieks and my husband's loud angry voice had distressed me terribly and I could not rise and go downstairs. I'd only been home a few days. Suddenly the bedroom door opened with a crash and a wildly yelling and kicking baby was hurled on my bed – poor lamb, he was only 19 months old – and my husband shouted 'I can do nothing with the little devil. I feel like killing him.' I reached down and patted my angry baby and said gently 'He is not naughty, Daddy. He is only a tired little wabbit who wants to cuddle up to Mammy wabbit.' He stopped roaring, looked a bit surprised, and then nodded as he crawled, slippers and dirty play overall, into my bed, and cuddled up. Later I drew his clothes off and he slept all night as he had first laid down and somehow I'd found the way to quieten his tantrums. I think he found things too much for him at times. As he grew up there was always a mood he had called 'wabbitish' and I always tried to plan a little outing or try and find his 'worry'.

Wednesday, 13 February. My husband and I had a little laugh when we recalled the time Cliff was born and I was so ill for weeks, unable to get my strength back at all. I had a queer eccentric doctor, who relieved other doctors and lived in one of the loveliest old houses I've seen, with a charming wife quite twenty years younger than he was and two clever children, one at Eton and the girl at Girton ... He said [*about Nella*] 'She should have champagne, oysters, beefsteak – tempting food. These nervous patients are the devil you know. Give me a person who likes to eat, every time.' As I lived in the New Forest, had no pull with any tradesman or knew no one likely to be able to get any extras, we just dismissed the whole idea but out of his own cellar he brought all kinds of wine beside champagne! – and all kind of little dainties, crisp red apples and grapes from his own growing. He said 'I like North Country folk – they always put up a good fight', and then used to sit and tell me of his years as an Army surgeon ... He had everything in life, but looked back wistfully to, and clearly enjoyed, his war work – and I never got a bill. He said when Cliff was so tiny 'Oh, he will grow; we'll make a soldier of him yet', never realising how true his words would be.

Norah's husband, who had served in the Navy, was about to return from Australia, and the couple were to move into a house at 24 Ilkley Road.

Friday, 15 February. Margaret came in for awhile. She seems to have lost a lot of her gaiety somehow – like most of us lately! Norah and Mrs Atkinson are cleaning Norah's house up the street. They have got a shock to realise it might be months before Norah gets her furniture. She has not got her dockets yet and then there is often a wait of up to six months. None of us had realised that. Norah thought of being able to have all ready when Dick comes home at the end of March. My husband was busy book keeping and all was quiet. I've got out a piece of Jacobean embroidery I started before the war and had forgotten about. Its gay wools are cheerful to work with, but there is a great deal of counts in it and my hands tire of close stitching and holding the frame. I wish it had been a tray. I could do with a new one.

Arthur and Edith are finding how tiresome it is to be waiting for builders to finish a house. They relied on their word it would be finished by the middle of February, and the roof tiles don't seem to be on yet and then there will be a lot to do inside. The prefabs at Barrow are a laughing stock. If they are all like these in the country, there's a deal of time being wasted. The plumbing arrangements which were supposed to be so simple that one man could assemble them and connect in eight hours have taken a man three weeks for the first one and he is still at it.

Tuesday, 19 February. Everything seems to have conspired to irritate or worry me. No letter from Cliff to say whether he had yet got his washing, gramophone or his watch he should have received yesterday morning. I'd one phone call after another, two tedious people to pay bills, and my milk boiled over – all over the stove – and then to put the cap on things I put some garden rubbish on the fire my husband had left to blow over the rockery and set my chimney on fire! Luckily no policeman was about and the thick cloud of smoke blew away, but I got palpitations so bad I felt I'd choke and had to lie down. Luckily I'd got my casserole of mutton out of the weekend meat, leeks, celery and potatoes and had made the steamed date pudding yesterday so I'd only soup to heat and sauce to make. I sat and cleaned my bits of brass and silver so that tomorrow I could bake a cake and work with Mrs Cooper a little.

I was down town for 1.30. I left my lunch dishes in water so as to have plenty of time to walk slowly to the bus stop. My hairdresser has another girl and is booked up for weeks except for odd appointments. No more perms can be 'pushed in' for three weeks. I said 'It's odd, after Xmas and so long before Easter. You are generally slack, aren't you?' She said 'Yes, but don't forget women are getting ready to meet demobbed husbands and many certainly need a perm. They have put off and put off, often if working, with not much time.' The heat of the cubicle made me realise how much better it was to be first customer in the morning. I booked my usual appointment for Saturday morning week but had to take it at 10 o'clock instead of 9.

This time I have needed house slippers for months and the ones I made have got completely done with wearing them so much lately, so I bought a new pair today, deep blue leather ones with a bit of black fur round, and at one time I'd have got better ones at Marks & Spencers for their 'ceiling price' of 4s 11d – and [*now*] paid 14s 9d and five coupons. The awful felt and cloth things for four coupons made me realise how valuable a coupon was when people would buy gay trash for 23s 9d if they could spare one wee coupon! All the fish had gone, but when I saw the huge cod heads and kipper boxes I felt I didn't want either herring or coarse fish. I'd have liked a bit of plaice or a Dover sole. There was lots of sweet biscuits about, but I didn't get any. I've only 14 points left after getting raisins, for most of my points go in tinned milk, beans and peas, cornflakes – since I've had a little with my Bemax† for breakfast and supper – and dried fruit. I was lucky enough to get a box of Braggs charcoal biscuits. I used to always have them if I 'felt my tummy'. Little things like charcoal biscuits and rest after meals did more good than anything.

I was glad to get back home, and I had a rest till teatime, glad indeed I had got in when I did for a shrill wind sprang up and brought heavy rain showers. I did cheese on toast for tea and there was baked egg custard and bottled damsons, malt bread, whole meal bread and butter, honey and plain cake. There seems a lot of misunderstanding about the clothes coupons – amazing the people who think they are extra, not having listened properly to the broadcast. Even Mrs Atkinson had it wrong, saying what a 'good help' it would be, when underclothes are simply 'fading away'. I wangled a few coupons off Cliff, thinking of Margaret, but before I could spend them – with being ill – he sent for his book back, but I told him I'd like a few later if he could spare them. I badly need a few new towels. Wartime ones have not the wear in them that the pre-war ones had, and perhaps the laundries don't use the soap they did, relying more on chemicals which would rot fabric. Giving our Lakehead Laundries every credit due though, they have been marvellous. They are a big firm, travelling the outlying districts, but the van men and shop (receiving) people never leave them. Several have been [*employed there*] all my married life and it's like the small business, which I prefer. I can tell there will be a pretty good change over of grocers and butchers when rationing cards are issued again. Due to general unrest and memory of wartime unfairness – often no fault of the shopkeepers – women seem to have reached the end of their patience and feel any change will be better than going on.

The laundry service that Nella remarked on this day had been lauded several years before, in her DR for May 1939. 'Here in this district', she said, 'we have the most wonderful laundry I've ever struck. It operates all over the Lake District from Carlisle to Ingleton in Yorkshire. Generally a monopoly makes for indifferent service but not in this case. Clothes are beautifully and carefully washed and there are three services to pick from. I choose the middle … They are washed as well as the first class but only flat ironed. At that the shirts etc. are better finished than high priced services in most laundries I've used in different parts of the country. By this service I find it cheaper to send the bulk of my wash rather than have a washerwoman.'

Thursday, 28 February. We settled by the radiator, I thought for a quiet evening, until my husband began to wonder what he could hang on the wall in place of the picture I would not have up again. Then the balloon went up. I felt something snap in my tired head. He got told a few things – not altogether connected with the picture! Yet through all my anger and annoyance I strove to control my tongue a little. With so many of his uncles and his father ageing so soon, he has always feared it. At fifty he had the worn out physique and mentality of a man ten or fifteen years older and any energy of mind or body has gone in his day's work. I feel such a deep pity for him. It's made me give way so much but I wonder if it's been altogether wise. I think of the real squalor of mind and body of his people's home. I see the writing on the wall as I strive to keep things together, try to interest him in outside things – in the boys and their affairs – making excuses for him always, that he is tired or worried or busy. Tonight I could have run out into the cold wintry night and ran and ran till I dropped. 'Boyishness' which is engaging at twenty can be childishness at thirty, and each ten years grow more hard to put up with. I came to bed, feeling things work out. I felt lost and a little adrift when he decided he would like to sleep alone, but it's another oddity of the family and now I'm glad of it. I feel my bed is a peaceful haven where I can relax alone and read or write, try and sort out my values, and count my blessings.

Friday, 1 March. Mrs Howson called for me to go to Canteen and I posted a little parcel of 'bits' for Aunt Sarah in case we couldn't get up this weekend – a tin of soup, a scrap of marg and dripping, a slice of bacon left from what I'm brought, and a bit of cheese. There is so little to give nowadays. It often gives me a sadness.

Somehow so much of the 'sweet' of life has passed. How can we teach children to be unselfish, to 'pass the sweeties', 'give a bite of their apple', or 'break a piece of cake off and give a bit to the poor doggie'? It used to be said of a greedy adolescent, 'Well, he was the only one and there was no one to share things with'. A generation is growing up who don't know what it is to have many little goodies themselves, and even tiny tots know the value of points and what is rationed. Sometimes I think all the colour as well as sweetness is dormant, if not dead. I see Norah Atkinson borrowing oddments for her new home – and she is so grateful for my old curtains. When I reflect that I bought them in 1939, had them always up at my front windows, mended the glass cuts after the raids, turned them so that the faded side was inside and then altered them for the dining room where the remaining colour was almost bleached out by the sun – I feel they are no treasure. I wondered whether to cover two old thin blankets with them, and wondered if it would be worth the trouble. Little things annoy, and on the other hand, delight women. If bright gay curtain material could be coupon free – say four yards on each coupon book – it would mean such a lot. If it only meant one window bright – there doesn't seem much hope though, and everything grows shabbier and more down at heel.

Saturday, 2 March. It was a lovely bright morning, but cold enough to keep the snow wherever the sun did not melt it. I was not feeling too bad with myself, just going slow, when my husband came in. Then the fun and games started. He was determined that all pictures should go back on the walls [*which had just been painted*]. I was as determined they should NOT. Knowing my hatred of a scene, I felt he played up, thinking I'd give way when the painter and Mrs Cooper were about, but this time he was quite mistaken. I'd got to that pitch of nerves when jumping on them would have been the mildest thing I'd do. I've won, beyond my two good little oil paintings of Wartdale Lake and the Tarn above Hawkshead, the mirror over the fireplace and the little carved garden mirror facing the window. My nice new wall papered room is not cluttered. Of all outlooks to live with, the Victorian cum early Edwardian is the darndest – always to bring back mementos from a holiday and buy useless dust traps for presents, and never part with anything.

Sunday, 3 March. Norah and Dick came in for a few minutes. He is delighted with the house, but rather taken back at the thought of Norah having to work for two years. He will not be able to pay £2 out of his wages for a beginning, so there seems little to be done if they want a house of their own at first. It's so dreadfully hard on young people setting up a home. It strikes at the very root of happiness. He had brought a piece of coconut matting – from Woolworths at Gibraltar. It made me laugh when he spoke of shopping there, with all the shops in Sydney and the glamorous East. We went to Spark Bridge. I don't feel happy about them if I don't see them fairly often. They had not expected us with me sending the little parcel, so it was a nice surprise. Food seems scarcer than ever in the villages. It's only with shopping in town there are any little extras, and just now there is so little in the gardens. I wish people would not keep saying 'Well, *you* have had no surprise when things worsened', as if I'd gone round like Cassandra![†] Joe said 'You always said, lass, that things would be worse for a while after the war finished'. I said 'Well, maybe, but I didn't see quite the shortages and muddle, or take into account the Allies themselves would start to fall apart' ...

We were back early. I made up the fire and soon had tea ready. Toasted fruit bread – I put raisins and a little honey in one of my little loaves when I baked – bottled pears and unsweetened milk, lemon cheese and whole meal bread and butter and fruit cake. The table looked so gay and inviting, and still I did not feel I cared whether I had any food or not, and what I ate soon satisfied me. I could have giggled wildly at my husband's attitude, barely speaking when spoken to, glancing at the changed walls pitifully like a ham actor. Odd how little his reactions affect me nowadays. I cannot believe at one time I worried and worried and let his monkey shines drive me into a nervous breakdown. Now any breakdown would not be mine. I feel often I look at a rather tiresome stranger, wonder at my own weakness of attitude, which led me to be shut up like a dog, only taken out on a chain, called to heel, petted and patted but never let out of sight or off the chain. I must have been a fool. I feel it has fostered something in me that would have been better not. I was never dull or bored that I can ever remember. If I could not do one thing, I turned to another, while longing for friends who would not notice if they were snubbed or let see they were not welcome. My war work bridged that gap. I loved working with people, feeling 'I'll never be shut up again', and when I'm well enough I hope I can find something outside my home.

I sat and embroidered my cushion cover, feeling tonight I'd be well to start my blouses this week and then I'd have a bit of useful sewing on the go. I'll have to take my curtains down too and let the hem down. They have shrunk 1½ inches, and it fidgets me if a thing is not right and I have to keep looking at it.

I keep thinking of Cliff. He is always at the back of my mind. I wonder if he will get a start soon [*in interior decorating*], feeling the real calamity it would be if he had to come back to work with his father, knowing how impossible it would be, feeling I could never stand the strain nowadays as I once did, when they were so totally different in every possible way, in every line of thought and action.

Monday, 18 March. The heavy rain and hailstones seem to have broken the back of winter. I woke to birds twittering and chirping, and the garden looked as if spring might be soon here. I felt tired when I rose, and my back was bad to start the day, but I thought fresh air would do me good and I went downtown to get my rations. There was a real Monday look about the shops – no fish or meat, sausage or cakes. I met several women I knew well. All complained of the poverty of Barrow shops compared to Ulverston and the Lake towns. All but two were worried about returning sons and their jobs. One who has been so high hat about her son being a captain – she has been shunned a little – today was especially worried. I'd not known the son or his job before he joined up, but was surprised to learn he had only worked for a newsagent who had asthma badly and could not meet the early train for his newspapers or deliver on cold wet days. Somehow I had the idea her son had been in a bank. She is desperately wondering how he and his wife and baby will fit into life on their return. She seems in awe of her daughter-in-law, who seems a 'captain's lady'.

Cliff, who had just been demobilised, arrived in Barrow on 20 March for a brief visit. Nella found him in good spirits, although she admitted the next day that 'I sighed as I noticed how slow he was in his right hand – but checked myself when I thought it was only a finger gone after all.'

Friday, 22 March. I had to rise earlier to cook breakfast and pack sandwiches for Cliff. I made him a nice breakfast, half a grapefruit prepared overnight, a little rasher of bacon, two sausages and an egg. The potted meat I'd made from the sheep's head made nice sandwiches with chutney and cress, and I kept two slices for my husband's tea. I packed a slice of cake, two buttered slices of malt bread, an orange and a flask of tea in the thermos I bought him at Xmas. The taxi came at 8.30 but I didn't go to the station. I felt a bit shaky with rushing about and laid on the settee for half an hour. I had to take Cliff's watch back to the watchmaker's. The repair I'd had done a few weeks back had gone wrong again.

Why *do* newspapers print things before they are official? Every knot of women I passed seemed to be talking of the marg and soap cut – then tonight on the wireless there was 'nothing sure', as if women haven't enough worries. There were no queues for fish, and plenty of variety, but I never can have fish for Fridays what with going to Canteen. The bus conductors are quickly replacing the clippies[†] and it's a real pleasure to be spoken to politely. So many of the girls gave one the feeling they were completely indifferent, whether you rode on the bus or fell off it! ...

I had half an hour's rest after lunch for we were going down in Mrs Higham's car so had no waiting or walking to the bus stop. I've felt so out of joint with Canteen since I had flu. Somehow the gaunt nearly empty place, short supplies of food, cutlery and crocks, and the type of soldiers who come in, seemed to repel me. Gone are the friendly nice lads, and rather curt and sometimes insolent fellows come in now, as if instead of friendliness they work off annoyance on us. Today two of them did upset Mrs Fletcher. Poor Marjorie. She is so big and strong looking but her thyroid makes her very nervy and frightened. We had such short supplies of cakes and could only eke them out with cheese sandwiches, buttered teacakes and hot dogs. I like to be fair to all the boys and said to the helper 'We will only let each lad have one cake'. These two piled up four on one plate, six on the other, and gave Marjorie cheek. I'd been sitting down resting and she served for me. I went to the counter and one of them snarled at me and told me he would darn well please himself – they were for sale, weren't they? I tipped the cakes back on the dish and I said – he was over 6 feet and soared over me – 'Little man, what a shock you are going to get in civvy street after your life of luxury in the Army'. If I'd been as nasty as I felt it would have done little good. I felt the roars of laughter of his friends were better than any sharp remarks. Mrs Whittam said 'You can get under anyone's skin. That lout said "please" when he came for his cup refilled.' ...

Mrs Whittam *is* an oddity. She has always a huge roll of notes in her bag from selling something – horse, cow, etc. – or looking for something worth buying, and we thought nothing could surprise us but she certainly did today when she fished out of her sleazy leather bag 100 clothing coupons for which she had paid £10! It was more of a bombshell than once when she had over £300 in her bag and I revolted and trotted her off to the bank with it, fearing at that time, when we were always so crowded, someone could hear her – she has a loud voice – and rob her as she went home. I saw Mrs Higham's mouth open and shut like a fish's and felt mine did the same! I said 'Now what on earth are you possibly going to do with those? You naughty old thing. You know you have stacks of good clothes you say are "too smart" for you.' She beamed all over her very weather beaten face and said 'Well, I badly want a new hat', and joined in the burst of laughter. She has a very good velour hat that wind and weather has altered and which she puts on her head with the delicacy of a cow stamping in the mud and which we always call her 'creations'. I said 'Silly, you don't need coupons for hats, and I know you have some nice ones. Pass that one for keeps to your cat. I know she must have had kittens in it several times.' Crude remarks like that are priceless wit to Mrs Whittam. She shook and rolled with mirth till she nearly fell off the chair. Dear knows what she will do with all those coupons if, as I pointed out, she kept out of jail.

Saturday, 23 March. I've had a maddeningly tiresome day. I don't remember worse. I had a hair appointment for 9 o'clock but missed two buses which were crowded and when I got down it was 9.10. I needn't have worried. I had to sit waiting till 9.30 and then the water was not as hot as it should have been, for something had gone wrong with the thermoset in the tank. I got fish for lunch – nice haddock fillets – and a nice piece of smoked cod for Aunt Sarah. It's such a problem nowadays to get a little tasty bit for them.

When I got back there were two real tinkers mending jute doormats and I said they could mend mine. I could have done it myself with a packing needle and coarse string, but they looked so lost and hungry, and they talked in such sing song Welsh they were bad to understand. I made the mistake of not asking how much it would be, and I'm sure I look soft, for when they brought it back they demanded 15 shillings. It's a very good 'has been' for I always believed in buying the best, or else I'd have said 'You can have the mat'. They came in the garage and were half in the kitchenette before I realised they were there, and both neighbours were out. I don't remember being so frightened of anyone, but I stood firm. They would not let me have the mat, but on the pretext of examining the work – very badly and sloppily done – I seized my potato knife off the stove where I had laid it and said 'NO – I'm going to give you your valuable jute back', and made to unpick it. They agreed to take 5 shillings – for about ten minutes badly done work and 6 pence of jute string just caught round and not oversewn as usual, and I told them I was ringing up the police and laying a charge of trying to extort money. They believed me for they gathered up their bass bag† and left the road hurriedly.

It upset me badly and I shook from head to foot and felt glad when I heard a ring – till I went to the door. A queer eyed untidy woman who might have belonged to them stepped up on to the top step and began begging, for food, coppers, and clothes. I felt it the last straw. I said 'There is a telephone at my hand. If you don't go away I'll call the police.' She looked very surprised and stopped cursing me and began to whine. I said 'The police of this town are very severe with beggars', and off she went. I'm sure they were all together. I cannot recall beggars at the door for years.

During the next couple of months Nella travelled much more than she had in the previous year – day trips to Lancaster and Kendal, drives to Ulverston and the Lakes, Easter weekend in Morecambe and a weekend in London to visit Cliff. In London she shopped and on 27 April 'went to Derry and Tom's lovely roof garden' and later to the theatre, and did lots of sightseeing, although not as much as she had hoped to do (her 27-year-old son did not approve of his 56-year-old mother going out on her own). Cliff, she felt, put on some big-city airs. 'I tried not to act country cousins and only slipped up a few times,' she wrote on the 29th, 'and was only reproved once, and anyway the little waitress did look tired and the aspirins I gave her and the sniff of my smelling salts did her good, for her head ached. She was a really nice little girl but annoyed Cliff when she stood talking and told me she had a baby of three and twins a year old and worked every Sunday in the Richmond café to help out while her husband minded the babies. Cliff said "Londoners don't talk to people. You would be looked on as eccentric if you lived here, you know."'

Saturday, 1 June. I looked round at the shoppers. A casual glance would have said 'so well fed' but the too fat young and early middle aged women, to a keen observer, would have confirmed too big a starch diet. If bread and potatoes are cut, women will be the hardest hit – those who just buy a pie or cake and who make do on that for themselves, especially. I'm always so thankful we like soup, odd savouries, and vegetables. One confectioner had a great idea – little trifles set in paper cases, the prices ranging from 3d to 1s. Mrs Higham brought in four for tea at Canteen, saying they were quite good. Granted I've a picky, finicky appetite and prefer a very small portion of anything nice than double the quantity if it doesn't appeal to me, but I thought I'd never tasted such trash. It had synthetic jelly at the bottom, tasting and looking like red ink, and then a tasteless layer of yellow custard sweetened with saccharin and topped with a flavourless dab of something like soap suds. Politeness alone made me swallow the nauseous concoction and I managed to palm most of the jelly in the bottom and put the paper container in the pig bin. I felt more grateful than ever I could look after Cliff's food for him. I believe in good wholesome food well served as one of the chief essentials of life, from both a physical and mental standpoint.

I reflected how things work themselves out. I come of a clever family, whose girls dance, sing, roller skate or go in for sports effortlessly, and of whom many are really beautiful. I was lame when a child. Only some-what crude methods of sleeping with a heavy weight on my right foot while lying on a hard mattress stretched my right leg out after a hip and pelvis fracture. I was never very active. My father scorned a good education for women as unnecessary. I always felt a sneaking envy for my clever cousins. Now I've no envy of any cleverness, not even for people who can add up well. I've a *superiority* complex instead!! I'm never at a loss for a meal. My husband says he has 'never known there has been a war' because he has always had tasty meals, has never been without some little tastie of bottled or preserves for a little treat, and my thrifty country ways of always a bit on the shelf rather than a feast and then a famine has been after all a gift that is better than a cleverness.

We went round by Ulverston and then sat all afternoon on the Coast

Road, my husband writing and I had my books and dipped into them, mended some stockings, and had a nap with the sun on my face. We were home for 8 o'clock and made a wood fire and we listened to *Music Hall*. Mrs Howson came in with her husband who is home on leave, and they had a drink and a chat. I feel sorry for Steve. He will soon be 40 and is a Warrant Officer whose time is up about February. His pension will not be enough to keep them – he has only been a Warrant Officer a short time – and he says he will be up against young, well educated men in the wage market. There is a possibility of him staying on till he is 50, but that means he would have to give up his dream of a real home of their own for over ten years. I feel Mrs Howson has not been as careful as she could have been. She could have had a well paid job all the war – she is a very expert dressmaker – and saved money instead of spending all on non-utility materials and making lovely unnecessary things, always for herself. They haven't by any means enough to set up much of a home, and she whines about it a lot, blaming poor pay and treatment by the Navy for them not having more money saved. I wondered as I looked at her tonight what she would do if compelled by circumstances to live on Steve's pension.

Wednesday, 5 June. Down town I met several people I knew, and they and the women who hurried from shop to shop looked so harassed, all speaking of 'more difficult to get things than in the war when U boats were sinking our ships'. Not one word about V celebrations. No one seems to be bothering in Barrow. My mind went back to last Peace celebrations. We were in Southampton. Cliff was only a few months old, Arthur 5½ years. I recall the happy feeling, the wonderful parade where Southampton history from prehistoric to 1918 were wonderfully portrayed, the lavish decorations, the fire works, the fun and gaiety. We went out before lunch and came back about 3 in the morning, with Arthur curled up asleep in the big pram by Cliff. I'd taken flasks of tea and Glaxo for Cliff, lemonade and sandwiches and fruit. We bought ice cream and hot baked potatoes, and hot Horlicks as we trailed home to where we lodged. Such a wonderful day. I recall my happy heart as

I looked at my sleeping boys, the feeling of deep thankfulness that the war was over, that 'we will never have another war'. Now no one feels gay or happy about this one being over. People feel suspicious about 'war to end war' and no one talks like that now. Rather there is that feeling that discord is spreading, that given the opportunity, there would be an even bigger war, where 'nerves' and atomic bombs would wipe everyone out. We have so little to look forward to. As I came home I felt my little loved house more welcoming than ever. I closed my front door with the feeling that not even the raids ever took from me, as if I shut all discord out and entered a little corner of peace. It's such a nice house somehow. I feel it likes me.

Thursday, 6 June. Mrs Higham said 'I hope I'll not begin to grow old as well as fat'. I said 'Steady on. What about me? I'm ten years older than you and never had your good health.' Her answer gave me a little sadness. She said 'You will never be old. You have your two sons and are too wrapped up in them to notice such trifles as passing years.' She and her husband would have made such good parents and could have done much for children, both with their understanding and money. It's been a great grief to them. We had buttered malt bread and shortbread and parkin biscuits by the fire, and she went at 5 o'clock and I made my husband tea, savoury sandwiches, lettuce, baked egg custard, honey and whole meal bread and butter, malt bread and shortbread. He said he would cut the lawn in spite of it being rather too damp, and I got a bit of ironing done and some mending. Margaret sat down for a chat when she ran in to show me some lovely Fair Isle gloves and berets she had knitted – at work, of course! – and I took down our small suitcases and laid them on the back room bed ready to pack at leisure. I cannot think that we will be in Ireland this time next week. I'm not looking forward to the journey. I wonder how my wretched tummy will stand the sea trip and a week is not very long to get over any upset and enjoy things, and my husband is NOT a good traveller. It seems to bring out the worst possible in him! He doesn't like a change in any habits, hates strangers, especially if they talk to me, gets excited about things left undone at home, and is sure he left a light on or a door unfastened, etc! When he goes anywhere in the car it's not so bad. But memories of holidays by train come back – after weeks battle to go at all. I'm glad we are going to Arthur and Edith, though, for the boys never stand nonsense.

Whit weekend was approaching, and Nella and her husband had plans to enjoy themselves (drives to Morecambe, Ambleside and Kendal), although on Friday morning she had another reminder of the war when 'I woke in terror at a loud bang which shook the windows, wondering what it could possibly be. Later I learned it was a big sea mine that they had exploded and as the crow flies we are not far off Walney beach on the Irish Sea side.' Then they were off to visit Arthur and Edith in Northern Ireland, and spent a happy week there.

Friday, 21 June. To our surprise, Cliff met us [*on their return to Barrow*]. He had travelled all night. I think his main object in coming was to bring me a Siamese kitten [*to be named Shan We*]. He always promised me one after the war but I always put him off, for I didn't want to hurt old Murphy's feelings – he is a very odd cat. Between his running wild for a week, Cliff and Mrs Pattison being about, and the kitten, he has held aloof and sulked in the garden all day. I've left the garage window open for him and his supper on a plate. I had to set to and do a biggish wash for Cliff – he goes back tomorrow night again …

This wee kitten is like a baby. He cries bitterly if cold or lonely, but in spite of only being eight weeks, uses an old tin lid with ashes sprinkled as if very accustomed to a 'lav' of his own. I felt so sorry for the little lonely orphan, I put an old tea cosy in my basket and tucked him up nice and warm. I brought him upstairs and put him on a chair by the bed. He was quite happy till I got into bed. Then with a joyful whoof he sprung onto the bed and settled himself close to my side as I write, beaming up happily through his slitted blue eyes and purring loudly. I hope the two cats settle down peacefully. I don't want old Murphy to feel pushed out for the little newcomer.

Cliff wants to 'buy everything you have ever wanted, Dearie. I'm going to see you never stand aside again for any of us.' I looked at my little cat with mixed feelings – he is a darling wee beastie, perfect in every way – but I had old Murphy. I wonder what Cliff has in mind – about things I've wanted in the past – and have I rather outgrown them if I get them now, I wonder? I cannot recall a real 'crave', except to travel and see the world, and who would want to do that just now? I've my little modern house, shabby it's true, but things like carpets, etc. will come round in the ordinary way – be bought. I've simple tastes and little clothes sense. If my clothes are reasonably good I wear them long and carefully; I loathe 'amusing' styles. I've the garden – and the car, which if it is 1934, to me is as good as a new model, and gets me to my loved hills and Lakes. A Rolls Royce could do no more. I'm puzzled to put a name to one thing to add to my content, unless it's a fridge, and that's for family comfort on the whole. As to denying myself, it was never a hardship if it was for my two lads. It was a pleasure and privilege to help them in any way – and still is. Old Cliff over-rates me, I fear, but I looked at him in slight surprise when he spoke of 'making up to me' some day. I felt very touched.

Sunday, 23 June. Margaret came in with a friend who married and whose RAF husband has just been demobbed. He was going to be an architect but 'thinks there would be more in photography' and plans to set up in business, and he has only a small folding camera, and never handled a studio one, done much developing, and no touching up. I felt amused as I thought of another young fellow – also married – who has bought a horse with his gratuity and plans to begin a riding school and teach people to ride, running by the horse and rider presumably till he gets another horse to ride himself. I often feel a sadness when I hear the many cases of unreality this war has bred in young fellows – girls too – who have lived a sheltered life and had no chance of trying out their mistakes as they went along. I felt glad Cliff has a vein of practical common sense. He told of many ex-servicemen who had lost their gratuity and very hard earned savings in get-rich-quick methods, toned down till they sounded genuine in the ears of men who had not been in the rough and tumble of life for a few years.

Another thing which Cliff was very bitter about – he says ex-servicemen are being exploited. 'You cannot expect a real wage till you get into civvy life and you have your allowance for a few weeks', and then are only kept for a few weeks and another 'mug' comes along. He said 'I never realised myself how dear things were, or the many food problems. I honestly don't know how I'd have managed if it had not been for the way you shop and plan for me. Money goes nowhere in London. I've a good stock of clothes too, thanks to you keeping them free from moths and dodging new collars onto shirts and letting out the jackets. Some fellows I know have no civvies but what they get when they come out of the services and have to build up a wardrobe, both for work and "best", and I don't know how they manage for that either.' Cliff is like Arthur in that he thinks that the danger spot in human relations has yet to be reached; that high hopes and joy at being free again is carrying men along, but when they realise the scraping and pinching to start a home as well as keep on, men will grow bitter, and if things don't quickly stabilise will tend to turn to anything that holds out more hope, from crime to Fascism or Communism. Arthur is convinced that we are on the road to inflation; that already there show plain indications of it; and the news in today's *Sunday Express* that inflation in America will cut down the loan granted so niggardly is not good hearing. It seems a sorry business altogether. The seeds of ill feeling are not only being sown but show signs of sprouting.

Sunday, 30 June. I never saw so many people at Bowness and Ambleside even before the war. Hundreds had come by charas, more by trains and then steamer and even motor launch. Boat and rowing boat were reaping a good harvest of half crossings as at one time it would have been 6d or 1s an hour and 1s a shot per trip with the boatman. South Lancashire crowds don't behave 'tripperish' in the Lakes as they do at Blackpool. The quiet dignity of the hills and Lakes seem to welcome and impress them. There never seem loud raucous voices raised in song. Perhaps, though, that type don't come. It may be that they who come have a love of calm serenity. Some who sit on seats in the sun look one with we who feel the hills and fells holy ground, where all the peace and wisdom of life lie, ready for us if we can only reach out for it and claim it.

The heavy rains of yesterday had been a blessing to the little streams and falls. Everywhere the sound of running water, and cattle and sheep never lifted their heads as they busily cropped the sweet damp grass. Keswick was full of visitors. Moneyed foreigners always make for there. When we stayed at the Royal Oak last year, there were many who had been all winter. We picnicked in a quiet spot. Shan We had water and some minced cat meat and romped happily in the grass. This golden day will pass into rain. The purples and grey, green and brown of hills and bracken moors were too sharply etched against the blue of the sky for it to be fine for long. It was even lovelier motoring back than going. All was quiet on the roads. The charas had left. Only holidaymakers sat about and boatmen dressed up rowing boats and covered motor engines, and the two last steamers down the Lake were crowded to capacity. As they passed I felt a God Bless in my heart, a wish that the memory of peace and beauty would linger through the busy week of bustle, queues, and general worry.

My deep love of the Lakes never makes me want to shut out trippers. I feel 'Come and share it. Hold up your arms to the everlasting hills and draw their peace and beauty and healing calm into your tired minds.' To many heedless people I feel 'Go to Blackpool – you will be happier there', but I could never shut people away. My uncle is a rabid 'Friend of the Lakes' man. He would put a wall round if he could, so high that no one could see over. I would be very stern with people who wanted to build jerry houses, make wide motor roads, build factories or works, or run a railway through, but I don't understand or agree with him in other ways. People who are shut in ugly soulless towns need our Lakes and fells. I know I'm not consistent for I wouldn't 'tear down the ugly pylons' as he and his friends would. They are not too obtrusive, and I can only see the beauty and comfort they take to people whose lives have lacked much in amenities.

People have to live and work in far-off places. The farmers who are so important should not have to live like medieval peasants, their women folk slaves to hard work and having less comfort than the people whom they feed. I can see beauty in a tractor's moving its way over a hilly field as much as a horse straining out its heart. School buses to me are only a blessing. I never would long for the 'good old days of the village school'. My Gran as a Quaker was well educated by Friends and believed in her children being taught at home and then sent to school, but mothers of that day could not always teach their children. My husband's grandfather, who was reared on a lonely sheep farm, could not read or write till he was 18, and only his insistence and the fact he had a little money to pay for an adult school run by a retired school master in Bowness 'educated' him in about 18 months. Everything must be shared in tomorrow's world, beauty and peace, education and all that goes to make a happy child and good citizen.

Wednesday, 10 July. I didn't feel too good when I rose and 8 o'clock brought a lad to the door with a request I would let five men have some boiling water. I looked out. It was a gang mending holes in the road with tarmac! I put on my kettle, reflecting there must be secret signs on our gate. It cannot altogether be Mrs Atkinson's idea that they know I'm soft! I had a cup of tea and some toast. I cleaned away and decided I'd make an early start on my bedrooms. The phone rang repeatedly. I had two garrulous callers to pay small bills. Shan We was a great attraction and I thought they would never go. Another start. The dustmen came. 'Please could they have a drink of water.' They are such decent kindly men, and always shut the gate. The kettle had not been emptied; I switched it on and made them a jug of tea. It was such a hot morning and they looked tired out. The coalman came, and said joyfully 'TEA', so I made him a cup, and started again. More phone calls. No butcher. Luckily the fish came, and I fried two nice hake steaks, and did cauliflowers and potatoes, and fried up a real good gingerbread from the beef dripping Mrs Picken sent, and made malt bread, to bake at the same time. Then the boy came for hot water again. I felt worthy, and said 'Everyone else are in the street', but he grinned cheerfully. I'd enough soup for my husband and milk sweet from yesterday. I'd a little fish and vegetables, and a cup of tea.

I'd said I'd go down to the bank for my husband and I'd to pick up my bacon, or else I'd have relaxed quietly for the whole afternoon. It was hot but a lovely breeze from the sea, which made it pleasant. Two encounters gave me lots of reflections. Both women I've known from girls. One was a bar maid, and a very gay bohemian who met an Admiralty man a lot older than herself. When he announced his marriage, several took him aside and pointed out she was not a girl anyone married. He gave the answer 'She will suit me – a virtuous girl would bore me to death'. He was Harbour Master at Hong Kong and they had four of the nicest well bred sons anyone could ever have. When she returned, no one would have any more to do with her than formerly, and she was a bit lonely, and always glad when I met her in the Park and talked, when we had the children out. Her husband died. They must have had lots of money, for all the lads had good schools and the eldest is a naval architect and going back to Hong Kong where she plans to go back to make a home when the two youngest boys make a start. They all adore her, and it's the happiest family possible.

The other woman has never trod the primrose path, prides herself on her respectability, and whined about her son getting married after being a POW and 'worrying her to death' – she considers he 'owes his mother something for all the worry he has been'. She came up in the bus with me. I felt she was the last butterfly on my wretched tummy. I came in and was very sick and had to lie down for an hour, wondering what was virtue and what was not! The first woman's gay, vivid personality, too young dress, rather brassy dyed hair – and adoring family; the second's sour Puritan face, whining voice, holier-than-thou attitude. Life is odd, and seems to grow more so!

Thursday, 1 August. Mrs Whittam brought a jug of tea and we sat on the little wall of the garden. Some German prisoners passed, glum and miserable but thoughtful, ordinary men. They glanced at us. Mrs Whittam and I smiled and I said 'It's a lovely day'. One replied in well modulated

English 'It is indeed'. I wondered where he had learned to speak so well. We talked about the difficulties of life today when they had passed out of sight on their way to the fields, of all the unhappiness and frustration, heartbreak and misery, though we didn't use exact words. There's such a streak of wholesome sense in Mrs Whittam. I wonder if cows help country people to have it – or sheep? I've noticed people who have much to do with tending them have a clearness of vision and ability to think, however slowly. Both of her daughters rant and rave about German 'beasts'; she quietly talked of their homes and little children growing up without them. We talked of the misery underneath, the heartbreak and despair that passed unnoticed, little things in human relationships that meant so much, security in the love of home, planting things with the serenity of seeing them grow, of seeing days come and go without anything happening, of laughing without cause, just because you felt happy. Mrs Whittam's red jolly face, with its flying wisps of hair like a halo, saddened. She said 'Never long for grandchildren, Mrs Last. What's in front of mine?' I thought of my baby of 27 years ago and my heartfelt relief that war was over, never to return. People don't feel that sense of hope and thankfulness now. It's more a 'How long before it starts again?'

Wednesday, 14 August. There was great excitement at North Scale – 'squatters' were moving in to the RAF huts in Mill Lane. I feel shocked at the good Army and RAF huts that are going to waste while people are wanting homes so badly. Nissen huts could be made as comfortable as the hideous prefabs, I'm perfectly sure. One quite good camp seems to have got into bad repair altogether, yet it was ideally situated for, if nothing else, a holiday camp, for it was right on the Bank, only across the road from the sea. I felt 'Jolly good luck to all squatters. In these days when we are anchored down with ration books and restrictions and growing into a nation of "yes men", it's good to find someone yet with pluck and spirit.' I really enjoyed my afternoon. It nearly blew us away as Mrs Whittam and I strolled up the Lane to the fields for the cows ...

When war first broke out I used to feel wildly 'Dear God, where has all the fun and laughter gone?' It crept back a little, if dressed in battle and service dress. I wish it could get demobbed too. The lack of bright sunshine is, I think, the cause for fretfulness and gloom; a sunny day seems to wave a magic wand. Mrs Whittam said wistfully to me 'We did have good times at Canteen, even if we had to work hard sometimes, didn't we?' They were such nice people to work with always. Yet now we are all like an untied bundle of sticks, all tired and busy with house-hold tasks and worries we took in our stride, or made them fall into the pattern that was our life for so long.

Saturday, 7 September. The morning flew past. It poured with rain but my husband had to go down to a bungalow on the Coast Road to see about some windows repairing and we all went. [*Arthur and Edith were visiting.*] It cleared up as the tide went out and we got as far as Grange. We had a late tea and lingered talking. Arthur seems to be confident he will get his Higher Grade next year, with a rise in salary of £250 a year. I listened to their plans. When they had a little surplus money, they are going Youth Hostelling every fit weekend, buy a little car as soon as they can afford it, have a fortnight in Switzerland in the near future. No talk or plans of beginning a family. I sat quiet and listened and watched their faces. Arthur seems to have a poor view of prospects of peace for long. He seems to think Britain has dropped to a third rate power, and Russia and America the ones who will decide the future for some time. Without him actually saying so, he gives me the impression he thinks it folly to have children nowadays. Yet if they don't, their happiness will have no roots. Edith is very 'primitive' and wholly natural. Her home is her delight and, to her way of thinking, children *are* home. It will be a sad mistake if they don't choose to have children, and, I feel, a tragedy if they cannot. We live in our children, try and help them avoid our own mistakes and failures, pass on the torch of faith and trust in God's good-ness and Plan. They are our standard to carry on and on, when we would sink and fall if we only had ourselves to think about. My Cliff was not a very lovable baby. He was nervy and difficult, with a tendency to fight and scream beyond belief – or patience! I used to be so ill after a major operation when he was 18 months old, my one prayer was that I would be spared as long as my nervy, cantankerous scrap needed me. I had so little money. Life was a struggle, for my husband was never very strong. It was the need for my baby and my faith that kept me going. I'd have been unable to do it for myself. My longings for a grandchild recede. It looks as if my little cats will have to be my only pets! ...

We were all tired, and came to bed early. We plan to go to Keswick if it's fine tomorrow and show Edith a bit of the Herries country. How I'd have loved to work with Hugh Walpole, covering ground for his fine Herries books. Of all gifts I crave, that of 'expression' would be my dearest wish. I've met such interesting people, and always heard unbelievable stories about people's lives. If I could put all in written language and sequence, I *could* write books, I'm sure. Maybe I'll get my wish in some future reincarnation!

CHAPTER FOURTEEN

EVERYDAY SCENES

November 1946–October 1947

Saturday, 2 November. My head felt so heavy and I could hardly sit up straight, but it was worth the effort to go to Kendal to see that it was doing my husband good and helping him forget his business worries. It's so difficult to find comfort for him, but I did point out there was only the two of us, and dear knows I've always had to manage on little, and as I pointed out a bit heartlessly when he talked of a slump being inevitable sooner or later, that by then he might not have to give his parents £2 10s out of his business profits. When I think of his well-to-do chemist brother and one who left the business in resentment of what he called 'carrying a couple of passengers', and realise how my husband has it all to do just because of an argument when the business was turned over to the two of them – and the chemist brother can make his son a doctor, he has so much money – I feel I detest that family more than ever. I think as always how my husband has been the complete mug for them all his life. Some part of him never matured. He went into the workshop at the back of the house, never went away from home, never mixed in company if he could help it, never reads, never listens to anything he calls serious on the wireless, and has carried the domination of his parents all his life. Instead of making him more understanding towards Cliff, he goes on and on about 'If Cliff were only like other businessmen's sons' etc. Quite useless for me to point out so many sons who have not followed in the family business. Nothing wipes the look of injury off his face once he starts off.

All my life people had wanted to change me. My mother wanted a boy – or a blue eyed, golden curled child like the one of her first marriage, who died a gentle being of two. She could have forgiven my dark eyes and hair if I'd been a boy, but as it was I always felt her disapproval in everything I did, or how I looked. My husband was attracted to me because I was 'always so gay and lively' but has always disliked any gaiety himself, always pointing out that *he* was satisfied to be with me alone, *he* didn't want outsiders etc., always wanting me to be different. It bred and fostered in me a real horror of trying to make people alter to please me – I'd not try and alter my little cats beyond training them to be clean and agreeable.

Cliff must live his own life. I stood it till my tired aching head could stand no more and then I said as I held out my left hand, 'Before I would dominate Cliff's life in any way, I'd thrust this hand into the fire, as God hears me', and then smiled wryly to myself at the futility of my remark. Cliff would never be dominated, by people, or circumstances. Anyone who tried to do so would find they only held shadows. If circumstances held his body, the real Cliff would go. Oh dear, I could have shrieked 'Shut up' like a fishwife!

Monday, 4 November. Cliff's letter came telling me he was spending Xmas at home and would be off to Australia by the end of December – dear knows how he has got his passage. I wonder if he will be better away from the London he so loves, and a lot of the silly useless people he calls his friends, and who don't seem of any value to him. Perhaps in Australia, where he will have to stand alone, my poor laddie will get his values finally sorted out. Weak tears streamed down my cheeks, I felt so very unhappy. My husband thinks I'm a fool not to put my foot down, for Cliff says he would never go if I was very set against it. I cried till I felt all life and vitality was drained out of me, and as I bathed my face I felt I prayed in my heart that I could keep in my mind how unimportant my little troubles were, that we were all part of the Plan, that all would work out some place, some day. 'I am the captain of my soul' is feasible but 'I am the master of my fate' is not true.

With peace came little in the way of plenty in 1946–7. The lights had indeed come back on – to reveal a worn and shabby people inhabiting a nearly bankrupt

nation. There was an impressive litany of woes, many of which got Nella's attention: a colossal national debt; housing shortages; thin or even virtually non-exist-
ent supplies of consumer goods; and austerity policies from Westminster that
continued or even increased wartime rationing and added new regulations that
constricted daily life. The burdens of existence fell heavily on housewives, for
it was they who did most of the mending and making-do and queuing, and it
was they who dealt directly with new restrictions and unpredictable shortages.
Bread had never been rationed during the war; now it was. In 1947 about half
of consumer expenditure on food was rationed, and non-rationed perishables
such as fish, fruit and vegetables were often in short supply or to be had only at
alarming prices. Rations of some coveted items, including bacon, ham and fat,
fell below wartime levels. The widespread shortages of consumer durables were
exacerbated by the government's drive to revive Britain's exports of manufactured goods, at the expense of the domestic market.*

Tuesday, 26 November. When I went downtown I thought I'd never
seen so many angry, baffled women – all except Co-op members! – who
lately have been so well served. Tinned fruit was the bone of contention. 'Strachey [*John Strachey, Minister of Food*] said there was 2 lb per
head for everyone and it was in the *Daily Mail* and the *Sunday Dispatch*' – yet my grocer, with hundreds of customers, had four small cases
and we were told we would have to queue in the morning if we wanted
one. If Cliff had been home for Xmas, I might have considered going
downtown at 6.30, though at that time I'd have had to walk, but I'll not
bother. Someone with kiddies might get the tins I'd have got.

I stood among the women waiting to be served. Well dressed or
otherwise, they all had one thing in common – a kind of look in their
eyes and compressed looking mouths, as if they had closed them tightly

---

* Portraits of life in post-war Britain are presented in two highly informative books: David
Kynaston, *Austerity Britain, 1945–51* (London: Bloomsbury, 2007), and Ina Zweiniger-
Bargielowska, *Austerity in Britain: Rationing, Controls, and Consumption, 1939–1955*
(Oxford: Oxford University Press, 2000). Andrew Marr, *A History of Modern Britain*
(London: Macmillan, 2007), part 1, surveys the period admirably.

at times to keep back sharp words of irritation. I was covertly watching their faces through a little strip of mirror, rather badly lit, and one mouth looked particularly set. I looked again at the bit of chin that showed above a row of tinned pears, feeling pity as I thought 'You *do* look repressed and irritable', till a corner of the hand woven scarf under the chin caught my eye, and I recognised it for my own mouth, and wondered 'Do I often look like that? Where, oh where is "Lasty's gamin grin" that seemed to amuse in those far-off Hospital Supply days, the "sugary smile" which at Canteen was said to spread over my face when Naval or Merchant Navy boys came in tired and hungry?' My face so fascinated me I went into a chemist's shop next. I felt I must really see myself as others see me. I walked to the cosmetic counter and under pretence of selecting rouge under the daylight lamp, I looked closer at myself than I remember doing and was rather shocked to find how 'unlit' my face was, so tired and shabby, so resigned, as if gaiety and laughter had fled – a November face. I bought a little box of rouge, feeling I needed it inside rather than outside, realising with a little shock how dead and heart-a-cold I really felt, knowing suddenly what makes a man get quietly and steadily dead drunk!

Christmas was 'a very pleasant day, if rather quiet, after last year', and since Nella had persuaded her husband to close his workshop for the better part of a week, they had time to relax and to take day trips.

Friday, 27 December. It was actually a fine day, and after a slap happy tidy round with vac and duster, we set off at 10.30 to go to Ambleside to pay the bill for towing the car when the crown wheel went. They were very off hand – said they would have sent it sometime but were very behind with all book keeping and bills! It was a lovely day. We lunched at Ambleside at the White Lion, quite the best place we have been for years, and on to Kendal. The hills toward Scotland were covered with snow, but the sun shone like a blessing. Everywhere men worked at tidying hedges and ditches and road borders and carted huge drifts of leaves away.

To me it's really terrible to see German and Italian POWs, as well as Poles. Why oh why are they not sent home to work at repairing their own land, building up family relationships, and doing a man's job? Whose idea is it, I wonder, to keep men in semi-idleness, destroying initiative, making them soft with regimentation and pampering? They cannot all be Nazis and two wrongs never yet made one right. I look at their brooding sad faces with a great sadness. Human beings have no right to treat their fellows so. Hope deferred doesn't only make the heart sick, it withers and kills. My husband says I've always some bee in my bonnet, but nothing would make me feel it a right thing to do. I'm not 'sloppy' about POWs but you cannot punish a nation. What's the use of scraps of rations and old clothes in helping folks? Give them their men folk. Help in things like material to repair, seeds, livestock. Make all Germany on the same footing, not zoned so that one fares better than another. Help decent Germans and back them to accept authority – and start afresh ourselves. My husband says they must be kept for harvesting our food. Then how can we pray for good crops and fair weather if we use slave labour, and anyway how expect them to work 'worth their keep'? There may be Italians and Germans who, like many Poles, want nothing more than to settle in England. That's different, and surely work could be found on the land or in the mines, though from what I hear they are not wanted in the mines by the men who don't want their own sons to be trained for mines.

Whenever I've my WVS uniform on, it's almost certain at least one Polish soldier will speak to me. Last week I solved a mystery of quite a few weeks standing as to whatever the Poles could buy to pack into parcels they are always sending home – it's second hand clothes. They haunt the cheaper wardrobe shops in a rather poorer shopping street, and I feel sure the Pole was telling me of his family and their footwear trouble. His companion seemed to be telling me of his desire for work in a woodwork factory and insisted on showing papers – I could have read them if I'd had my glasses, the ones in English – and he drew a tangle of carved wood from his pocket and it was a chain cut out of a solid piece of wood, like Norwegians and Danes make. It's a very great problem no doubt, but it must be tackled; it's not good for anyone to have numbers of men herded together, growing bitter.

Saturday, December 28. I took my little Shan We [*on the drive to Morecambe*] – he refused to be left behind. Such an odd cat. He either loves motoring, or my company, enough to conquer any fear of the traffic noises, and when we had lunch at the Royal at Bolton-le-Sands, he was tied to the table leg, but showed no signs of wanting to stray. He had his lunch and bottle of water in the car, but so strong is habit, I've to take a scrap of ashes in a newspaper – he must have at least one forepaw on familiar ground.

The shops at Morecambe were very attractive, and like Kendal, still had tinned fruit like apricots and golden plums. Either people had no points or there had been plenty. We walked round the shops and along the Prom. There was a surprising amount of visitors sitting in the windows having late lunch and a lot of huge new cars about. South Lancashire people like Xmas Holiday always. As I looked at them I thought, as often, how silly and futile to lump people together and say 'I don't like Lancashire people' or Germans or Poles or any country. There were two South Lancashire men staying in the hotel where we had lunch, and no one could have been favourably impressed, and I thought 'I'd hate to be classed among those men and typed as from Lancashire'. They looked as if material things were their god; too well fed and too fat, too loud mouthed, far too expensive clothes and car for the feeling of black market not to come into my mind, and I'd have liked to slap one of their faces as he leered at me and kept touching my hand as he petted and played with Shan We. A really horrible man. We were back home for 4 o'clock, both feeling better for our little trip.

Wednesday, 1 January 1947, New Year's Day. It was such a lovely bright morning. We decided to set off at 11 o'clock and have lunch at Ambleside at the White Lion again. I took Shan We and nearly lost him – if coaxing could have made me part with him, he would be lording it in the White Lion, with several cat lovers at his command! He loved it, particularly when he got scraps of turkey brought to him. It was an 'extra' lunch – turkey and a choice of trifle or plum pudding but I preferred cheese and biscuits. We would have gone off to Keswick, but snow powdered fields and roads and lay on the hills and heavy clouds threatened more, so we turned back and came home by Kendal. Ploughing, hedging and ditching, and dung spreading were all going on busily. Even the heavy water-logged land was being turned by tractor ploughs. Farmers are more behind than last year for the wet autumn was bad for planting winter seed. We were in by 4 o'clock, and I made up a good fire and we sat down to get warmed ...

We sat talking of the coming year. He said 'I wonder what it will bring?' I said 'I feel changes all round somehow', and to amuse him I began to talk of 'If I won the Irish Sweep', or rather the share of a ticket I have. I feel so sorry he has lost Norman [*a reliable workman*], for it means he has to work harder, and he did plan to take things easier after the war. His condition rather than his health gives me concern. I notice a big change in him – an aging far more than his actual years, and he says he feels he is growing old quickly. If only he could take things easier, and think out his work better so as to minimise effort. He should have had a son to help him, though few sons would have been content with the muddling ways of that workshop, and he would never change in any way of anything; and it's difficult sometimes in the house, where I do insist it's *my* place, and as I don't interfere with the shop, tell him he should not interfere in the running of the house. I've fought my way to that stand, and anyway he cannot really prevent me giving things when I have to help his old ones. Never a day passes but a wee taste of some kind goes down [*to them*]. I never open a jar of jam etc., bake or make anything, but they get a tiny share. I hoard my sweets or chocolate and they have little cheer-ups when they feel dim and have often eaten their share.

My husband needn't have been so short today when I gave some POW all the sweets I had with me – they *were* mine. We had stopped to have a drink of tea out of a flask and two fair-haired lads – stupid 'peasant'-faced children – came along. I let the window down and beckoned them and said 'You boys like toffee?' I felt a little twinge of real fear at the wolfish [*look*] in their eyes when they saw the handful of sweets I held out and, knowing boys, divided them equally. There was two coloured tinsel-wrapped chocolates – they were 'Quality Street' mixture – and the anxious look on one boy's face till he got his would have drawn a rebuke of 'Now, greedy' from me when Cliff was small. I could only feel pity for the two grown children. They spoke quite fair English, but very slowly. I said 'A Happy New Year, boys, and good luck'. They gave a funny little bob and one said 'And to you, good madam' I thought, till a little while after I realised it was 'müdder'.

Gradually a feeling of pity rather than let-them-suffer towards POWs seems to be creeping into people's attitude. Mrs Whittam is very kind to those at a nearby camp. They made rope slippers very skilfully and asked three packets of cigarettes for them, and Mrs Whittam gave everyone a pair for Xmas so that those poor lads could feel they were capable of earning something if it was only cigs! Yet at Canteen she was really bitter against all Germans, and very angry with me for the notion that there could be any good ones. What interests me is – nobody has a good word for the Poles and I never see anyone talking to them. Yet any I've had speak to me are quite nice friendly boys or men, and if our eyes have met and I've smiled they have seemed eager to return it. They walk about like shadows, rarely conversing, and the look in their eyes, sometimes of far horizons, grieves me sorely. Someone once said to me 'Those Poles might have fought against us', yet I know that same woman feels sorry for German and Italian POWs.

'Today I was approached again by the Secretary of the Women's Unionist Party, and asked to take the Chairmanship of a Ward', Nella wrote on 3 January. 'I held it for two years before the war, and did quite a bit of speaking, but always shied from a real political speech, feeling I was a sad "wobbler" and had no hard and fast conviction or the real bigotry necessary.' Two weeks later, on 19 January, she said of this political overture 'I don't feel a good enough Tory to do it'. Later still, on 18 February, she allowed that the Labour government, which she usually criticised, 'are trying to work to a goal, where no one will be hungry, and all will have work to do. I've a deep admiration for their ideals and aims. If I began to speak or work for the Conservatives, I feel I'd have just that sympathy to opponents that would make anything I said or did of little value.' This sort of open-mindedness tended to moderate her Conservatism. 'I've a fatal gift of seeing both sides of a question', she confessed in a Directive Response from October/November 1948. Still, she was decidedly not on the left. 'I'm a Conservative,' Nella wrote on 18 October 1945, 'or maybe a Liberal at heart, like Arthur says. Anyway, I'm *not* a Socialist.'

Nella's sympathies were clearly with individualist rather than collectivist values: she wrote in her DR for October 1942 that 'I'd rather live in a hut of my own than share a palace with others'. While she championed prudence and personal responsibility, disapproved of those who lacked foresight and was hostile to bureaucratic controls, she also possessed empathy for people stung by the misfortunes of life, and this sometimes steered her thinking leftwards. On 21 December 1948 her friend Mrs Newall said to her, 'You crack on about being a Tory, but you are an out and out Socialist sometimes.' This remark touched on Nella's eclectic and flexible ideas about politics.

* * * * * *

'What a day', Nella wrote on 7 January 1947. 'We woke to find all covered with snow and a cold wind that seemed to drive into the house and take all warmth away.' The rigours of this exceptional, almost unrelenting winter persisted for weeks, with various consequences. On 18 January, en route to Spark Bridge, she noticed that 'The flooded fields and meadows were pitiful. No dung spreading has been possible – the heaps either lay in islands or washed away. So little ploughing was possible last autumn and now, when the ground should be getting into shape, it's under water.' 'Bitterly cold' were the words she often used to describe a day's weather. She kept only one fire going in her modern house, in the dining room; and she saw how her Aunt Sarah struggled to keep the cold at bay in her small cottage. 'I shuddered to think of the squatters in the RAF huts over Walney', she wrote on 29 January. 'They could not keep fires day and night as the servicemen did – and still complain of cold and discomfort.'

These were grim weeks. Coal was in short supply – some women were routinely going to movie matinees in order to save on fuel – and from the second half of the month there were intermittent power cuts, which meant, among other things, that these cinemas closed. On 24 January, 'When the laundry man brought my fortnightly parcel, he said "Go as slow as you can with laundry – if we don't get more coal this week we will have to close down".' On 29 January Nella found that 'water spilled outside glazes into ice almost at once, and when Mrs Salisbury [*home helper*] was doing the step, her cloth kept freezing to it!' It was all rather dispiriting. 'It seems as if Nature herself is part of the out-of-joint tenure of our lives', she wrote on 6 February. 'When blinding snow was swirling down yesterday afternoon', observed the *North-Western Evening Mail* on 10 February, 'Barrow Park resembled a scene in Switzerland' and 'tobogganing was in full swing'.

Friday, 7 February. The cold has been arctic – glassy roads and a bitter south-east wind that swept through unexpected crevices and doors. The screaming gulls fought over my boiled vegetable scraps and wheeled and swept overhead all day, and the starlings, tits, thrushes, blackbirds and robins fought over the sheep's head bones I threw on to the lawn. I felt I'd no clothes on under my cotton overall. My wretched bones felt they creaked and my hands swelled with the pain when they got chilled. I was thankful I could stay indoors … The news of the cuts in electricity was a shock. I thought of the poor people who were in all electric houses or flats. As it is it will mean cinemas, hairdressers and many confectioners at a standstill in the day, and be a problem to housewives with only an electric stove for cooking.

The next day her husband joked about her fondness for making plans, saying '"You should have been married to Shinwell. You would have seen he never landed us in this mess. Your love of planning would have been of some use there."' (Emanuel Shinwell was Minister of Fuel and Power.)

Almost every day this month was a struggle – a struggle to keep warm (often not possible), to prepare food, to keep the pipes from freezing, to get out and about. (Nella was house-bound most of the time.) People's spirits were low, their energy was sapped and physical complaints were commonplace.

Wednesday, 26 February. It was a very wild night and I heard the heavy swish of snow, but I wasn't prepared to see it as high as the front palings. I always bring in the garden spade and the stiff brush I use for the paths if it looks like snow, so my husband dug himself out to the middle of the road where it wasn't so bad and then got a bus to work. The snow plough had been out all night so men could get to work all right. I was surprised when Mrs Salisbury arrived, all bundled up in scarves and a big coat. I said 'I hardly expected you this morning'. She scowled from under her ragged scarf and said 'I nearly didn't set off and then I thought "she'll only try and shift this bloody snow and make herself bad" and I thought how good you always were to me', and she grabbed the spade and brush and went snow clearing. I went on working inside and she stayed for lunch before going on to another place.

Saturday, 1 March. My husband had to go to Ulverston and we decided to go on to have a look at frozen Windermere, if the roads were not too bad. We felt a queer awe at the steel grey sheet that was the friendly rippling Lake of summer – it looked austere and remote. The sun was smiling behind a shoulder of a hill, and its slanting rays seemed to lick out every shorn hillside, every ugly gaping gully where trees had been dragged to the road. There was not a sound anywhere. An awful stillness seemed on everything and that queer atavistic desolation gripped me. I felt I wanted to lift my voice in a wild 'keen', if only to break the silence. We seemed the only living and moving things left on the earth. I felt thankful to leave the unfamiliar scene. The hills around were patched rather than crowned with snow. The fields were white instead of freshly ploughed as they should have been by March, and heaps of dung stood frozen and useless. I wonder if it will mean a bad crop and harvest, with so late a season. Heavy sullen clouds rolled in from the sea, looking as if we would have more snow, and we were glad to get home to a fire and our tea, with the table drawn close to it.

Friday, 7 March. The blizzard reached us last night and we woke to find all snowed up. While my husband dug a way out, I rose in my dressing gown and hurriedly packed soup in a jar for him to heat at the shop, and made beef roll sandwiches for him. I opened the door and passed out the milk bottle to put on the window sill 'in hopes'. Shan We seemed to lose his head – he took a header into the deep snow and disappeared, except for the tip of his brown tail. I leaned forward and heaved and we both fell backward into the hall, bringing a pile of snow. The cross-eyed look of reproach he gave me and the anxious look he gave his tail, as if surprised to find it still on, nearly sent me into hysterics of laughter – helped by the same 'Why should this happen to me?' look on my husband's face as he shovelled snow. He said 'I don't see there's anything to laugh at', but as I said, he wasn't standing where I was! Snow ploughs kept the bus routes open but two cars were stranded in our short road. I was surprised when the Co-op lorry came but the driver asked to phone for a motorised lorry to come as it was too much for the horse. Poor beast, he was getting snowed up, and I persuaded the driver to unyoke him and bring him into the comparative shelter of our path. He had a tarpaulin over his back but I offered the kitchenette matting to cover his neck and head a little, and Mrs Atkinson and I fed him bread and apples. He was a nice old 'spoiled' horse – he raised his shaggy hoof to shake hands. I made tea for the driver and boy and Mrs Atkinson and I had ours, and later the lorry driver.

Friday, 14 March. More snow, to add to the piles of frozen snow on the roads. I rose feeling tired to begin the day. I'd not slept very well. I gave all a general tidy and dust, cleaned silver and brass oddments, and took the worst of the snow off the front paths and had an early lunch. The sun shone brightly and I was downtown for 1 o'clock, to keep an appointment at the hairdresser's. The roads were a horror of slush and melting snow. It poured off roofs where gutters and spouts were still cracked and broken after 1940's bad winter, and queues of women stood nearby on the curb to escape the dripping eaves. That meant passers-by had either to walk under the drips or step down into the flooded gutters. I didn't bother. I'd Wellingtons on so just splashed along, but women with only low shoes on complained to a passing policeman. The women in the queue lost their tempers and everyone shouted angrily. I thought the policeman acted really well. He said 'Now, now ladies, it's not my fault the gutter leaks or the sausage and black pudding is late, but you cannot expect to have these others ladies get wet – now *can* you?' If he had taken a high hand, I felt the angry women would have been capable of rolling him in the slush and snow.

It was only after the middle of March that the harsh wintry weather retreated. However, flooding presented new perils; some land was under water, and many farmers were struggling to contain the damage. 'Townspeople cannot realise the devastation of floods that take off good top soil and utterly ruin rich pasture and crop land', Nella wrote on 22 March. 'My husband's insistence it's the atom bomb that has caused the dreadful winter makes us at times wonder.' In the evening on 28 March she and Will drove to Spark Bridge. 'It's pitiful to hear of small farmers I know well, who have lost over 100 sheep and lambs, and one young fellow who built a little house on a hillside had to take his children to a barn higher up, as the snow, melting, washed through their home like a river.'

* * * * * *

With the arrival of spring and summer, Nella's spirits improved. There were enjoyable holidays – a week in Belfast (she went on her own and by plane), a fortnight in Scarborough in July – and the summer of 1947 was as sunny and warm as the winter had been bitterly cold.

Sunday, 22 June. We set off to Silecroft, at the foot of Black Combe. The hot sun after the shower of rain brought out the scent of new cut hay, honeysuckle and clover till the air was drugged with sweetness and the larks seemed singing in competition, so sweet and shrill they sounded. The sea rolled up with little waves, flopping on the shore. Bathers and happy paddling children were everywhere. A lot of German POWs strolled about, a surprising number on their own and quite plainly letting any of their countrymen know they preferred it that way. I never saw such a mixed lot, a number had such brutish faces. I felt they were the type that would look on at the Belsen camp, so utterly insensate their expressions, their huge outstanding ears and flat backed heads making them look subhuman. Yet amongst the group were men who looked like musicians, thinkers, scholars – and aimless boyhood. One, perhaps on a farm, had a working dog with him and I bet it had never known such fondling and affection. They sat in deep content, looking out to sea. They were better dressed – in dyed service clothes, but quite good fitting – and only a few had small POW patches stitched on. A number had jungle jerseys on. I thought of the WVS who had patiently put on the shoulder patches, never thinking Germans would wear them. It brought back Hospital Supply days, now so long ago. Our work and effort seem only a dream that has faded. So too has my family dream – that I had little happy boys around me. I've often longed for Arthur and Edith near, but a growing suspicion makes me feel it would never bring happiness to either Edith or I, unless Edith has children of her own. She will grow very jealous. I've always tried so hard to make her feel a daughter, but I fear she would get the music hall idea of a mother-in-law and resent Arthur's deep love for me.

Thursday, 26 June. Mrs Higham had been down to the Social and Moral Welfare this morning and was a bit downcast. She spoke of two 'wasted' young lives and blamed mothers going out to work and their not having a home life. She is like me and bigoted about the importance of home and mother for young things. The curate came. He is so deaf he wears an ear appliance and has odd mincing ways and affectations. I looked at him as he girled and gushed, with the feeling I could 'throw up', and when he said 'What is the matter with *dear* Mrs Last?' I could have leapt in the air. I felt he was the answer to 'Why Christianity has failed'. Thank goodness he didn't stay long. I shuddered to think he was going to a living of his own shortly. He is called 'little Tom' in the parish. I prefer dignity and someone to respect. I looked at him and thought of the dignity and reserve of my two cats! When he had gone, we talked of the lost dignity of the clergy, wondering if the 'jolly good fellow' attitude had been the cause of a lot of the casualness of today. Mrs Higham

always causes a little resentment in me when she insists I *am* a Christian.
I say 'I'm not, you know, and haven't been since I was a girl of 12–14',
but again today she said 'Nonsense – you are one of the best Christians I know', and went on to talk of our war years together and said
'Only a Christian could have said that – or done so and so', as if conduct
depended on any creed.

Wednesday, 2 July. I went down town for some cat bits, the last I'll be
buying for some time, and then went on to Walney. Talk about salons
and witty and interesting talk in them – I'd back Ena Whittam's tatty
untidy kitchen against *any*. If it's not politics – Ena is Secretary of the
Women's Unionist branch for Walney – it's a discussion on clothes or
domestic economy, and there is always her sister and several friends
drifting in, and Wednesday afternoon, when they expect me, seems
their At Home day. I was later today and found them deeply discussing
of all things – Lesbianism! I sat and laughed and my amusement and
my 'Well, well, and all respectable married women' didn't offend them.
Maisie, one of Olga's friends, had had a book on sex sent from America,
and a chapter was given up to the subject. I could add little knowledge,
beyond knowing several 'kinkies' and having a strong suspicion of a few
more. Maisie spoke of a 'somewhat unhealthy curiosity about private
parts' – she is a solemn eyed little mother of two children and her
husband is even more solemn and is a Youth Club Head – paid post.
She said 'I don't quite see why you laugh, Mrs Last. It's a very serious
subject.' And when I said 'So are the Pyramids' she stared. I could tell
she thought it a phase of modern times. I thought of the utter ignorance
of my young days, and the horror there would have been if such subjects
had been discussed openly. I thought how much better it was nowadays
when curiosity was not a crime.

Sunday, 27 July. After the 9 o'clock news we went and picked the raspberries that had ripened and I got a 1 lb jar and ½ lb jar filled and covered
with sugar syrup to sterilise tomorrow. I felt I didn't want to leave my
quiet fragrant garden to come to bed, and my little Shan We felt the

same. He had been out with me, but plainly showed he loved the cool grass to roll on and the mystery of shrub and bush to play his own little games of hide and seek. The evening seemed to carry on the sweet nostalgic memories called up by the lovely music and opening tune of *To Let*.* Were Edwardian summers warmer, times more gracious, or only so in memory? To each his own.

My earliest Victorian memories are of being a somewhat spoilt crippled child, of plump women who seemed to jingle with what they termed bugle trimming, a vague smell of caraway seed, quite a few parrots at different houses where we went – how I hated and feared them, dear knows why – of lots of men with beards, of flannel petticoats and the weirdest washday articles on the line, too much to eat, and horrendous stiffly starched pinafores which were a stern test of a little girl's niceness in keeping them clean. I was nice once for quite a while, till my horrified mother found out I was leaving it folded on a shelf in the pantry as I went to school, and donning it as I came in. Perhaps the fact I could walk without a crutch when I was 11, began to go off on business trips with my father when I was twelve – five years or so after Queen Victoria's death [*Nella was actually eleven when Victoria died, in 1901*] – made for a 'lightsome' outlook, a quickened interest in life. The hoof beats in *The Forsyte Saga*, the perfect, perfect productions of a land where it was always summer thrill and hold me as nothing ever before on the BBC. Did fires burn more brightly, people always sing sweetly old ballads when asked out for the evening? Were the new fangled Viennese bands that were brought from London to big garden parties in the country so very good? Were there so many raspberries, damp fragrant mushrooms, juicy blackberries – and so many wild sweet chestnut and walnut trees? And do children now ever discover the rows of Dickens, Thackeray, Dumas, Harrison Ainsworth, Scott or Brontë on the higher shelves of the bookcases?

---

* Earlier that evening they had listened to an episode of John Galsworthy's *The Forsyte Saga* on the radio. Nella admired Galsworthy – and disliked Anthony Trollope: 'I always feel Trollope portrays a period from which sprang "socialism" in its more rampant form' (28 December 1947).

When the boys were small and begged for stories, they loved best to be told 'when you were a little girl', of life on Gran's farm, of trips to London and Ireland. Arthur said as he grew older, 'You had something Cliff and I never had', not realising they too had different memories than their children will have, that time speeds by, and only by comparing can we see how swiftly, so swiftly that as we grow older there is a little confusion. Sometimes when I've had a sadness, I look at my treasured snap album, often feeling my little boys nearer than my grown sons, often, alas, feeling I've dreamt it all, now I see them so rarely. All the striving and worry, the anxious love – all passed. Only two wise kind little cats about now.

Saturday, 2 August. I feel a sadness when I look at my husband. He was so different on holiday. I began to feel it had done him lasting good, but now he is back his little worries have piled up into an overwhelming flood. I often wish I was clever and could help do books and bills but know in my heart, however clever I'd been, it wouldn't have been really practical. No one could work with him. It's best I'm good at cooking and housekeeping perhaps. Today as we sped along in silence I built a little dream – that we went to Australia and made a home for Cliff. I feel often so useless, so selfish; there's so little to do in Barrow in the way of any voluntary work and it's pounced on by women like myself who have learned the real joy of service and working together. If we could go to Australia, I could make a home where Cliff could bring his friends and work happily, and I know well, if my husband could potter in the sun, his health, mentally and physically, would be better. Some people need a certain amount of stimulus of routine, but others, as they get older, love best to just sit. It's always a deep seated worry in my mind, and rarely lifts for long.

There was a constant stream of holiday traffic, and, to me, more huge transport lorries on the road than ever, and our narrow winding roads are not really suitable. Before long this question of roads will have to be really tackled – bypass roads through narrow country towns like Kendal and Ulverston. It's a marvel how the huge industrial loads get through.

I've seen loads from our Yard that must have only got over some bridges, under others, and round narrow awkward bends with inches to spare.

Tuesday, 5 August. I met Mrs Thompson, who was the Canteen manager. She is one of the unlovable type of Scot, and we often had little wrangles, but I felt sorry for the way she had been ignored in the winding up of Canteen. What bitches women can be, especially if they have snobbish daughter-of-a-bank-manger, wife-of-a-Rotary-member views like Mrs Diss, the head of the WVS, and Miss Willan, a retired school teacher who comes from Ulverston, that little town of snobs and worshippers of 'the county'. I've come to a very catty conclusion about Rotary, if our town is any guide – *super* snobs, the lot of them, with a more feudal manner, a holier than thou, that is very at variance of its brotherhood policy. Mrs Thompson says they have wound up Canteen affairs in their own way, which puzzles me, for after all there would have to be auditors and she holds all the bills and several of the books. Her husband, an Admiralty man, is in poor health – he has 'cardiac debility', the result of war strains. She is still teaching and they plan to go to her people in New Zealand, who went out in a family of eight, and the parents, and who have all done well. She said 'Wouldn't it be nice if we could go out on the same boat?' I thought 'Yes, if it was a very big one'.

Sunday, 10 August. We were out before 2 o'clock and went to Arnside. It was scorching hot and a lot of people were there, mainly visitors. Scores of German POWs sauntered about, looking so happy and well kept now they can buy hair oil and blacking, light shirts – and ice cream. I looked at them, many such pleasant healthy lads, and thought if I'd to choose between them and 99 out of 100 Poles, I'd choose the German every time. I'm really getting a prejudice against the loutish unmannered Poles who lounge in the buses, while women and old people stand, and walk three and four abreast on the pavement. Why don't they either send them home or let them work? They slouch so aimlessly about as if with no hope – they are 'dying' slowly. If there is a risk of what the Russians will do to them! – well, all life is a risk. They are *men*, and we have no right to spoon feed anyone. What was once 'Britain's sheltering arm' and so forth tends to be interference to a degree nowadays. I often wonder in a 'maze' why on earth we don't get out of Palestine and leave Jew and Arab to batter each other instead of using our poor soldiers as 'in between'.

The tide slipped silently in, as it generally does in Morecambe Bay. Soon happy bathers were playing and swimming round. We had our tea, and left for home just before 7 o'clock to travel slowly to be sure to be home for 8.30 to hear *To Let*. Somehow I felt as if I was part of Galsworthy's 'golden age' tonight. I felt sun soaked and the westerning sun still warmed the dining room and made for that feeling of well being when all is glowing and warm. The very music is a triumph, a mental magic carpet to carry me back, and the tempo of their lovely voices is perfection. I got my husband to carry a bucket of water for each of the little fruit trees and I watered my leeks and broccoli and the little rockery walls and rose trees at the top of the garden. All seems very dry and it looks set fair for a day or two.

Wednesday, 13 August. Mrs Salisbury didn't come. She said she might be having a day at Lancaster with her sister-in-law, so I began to do the bedroom. There was a ring and Mrs Whittam's agitated voice begged me to come over early and give her a hand. She didn't know where to turn. The harvesters had come two days before expected and Ena had been up all night with a cow that had developed mastitis and there were sandwiches to cut for eight of them working in the fields ...

What a mix-up and mess they were in, and Olga does get cranky. I persuaded her to take her little girl and Ena's three children off to bathe. I simply couldn't have done anything today with them all squabbling round me. Mrs Whittam and I make a grand pair – I love to plan and 'boss' someone round, she loves to be told exactly what to do – and then she works like two. She said I could do what I liked and there seemed lots to go at, so I said 'We will bake for two days and then it will help Ena tomorrow'. Mrs Whittam looked after the coal oven. I got all ready. Two big tins full of date cookies, three of cheese scones, three of plain to have cheese between – Ena cut into a 12 lb cheese she had saved for harvest. I beat up a batch of dough for little crisp rolls, using new milk, made a four pound gingerbread, two big tins of jam pasty and two of apple, and then the rolls were ready for the oven. A pleasant Jewish looking POW came from the field to carry the big enameled bucket of tea, and he took one side of the big basket of food with Mrs Whittam. We had washed crisp lettuce hearts and there was a bag of dead ripe tomatoes and we didn't forget to put in a little box of salt.

I took Ena some tea into the cowshed. She was so upset over the cow and the vet didn't come. He had left pills yesterday and it seemed a bit better, but as I told Ena, she shouldn't have let her drink. The POW came and I asked him to go gather an armful of marshmallow and we boiled it and laid big poultices on the cow's swollen udder and we all helped to bathe her all over and put cold compresses on her poor hot head. They call the POW 'Youbie' or something like it. He had real kindness and patience with that cow. I said 'You should have been a vet' and he said quietly 'I would have been by now if the war hadn't come'. He spoke very good English. I looked at his intent face as he bent over the cow and at his long sensitive hands, and felt I'd have liked to know all about him. Oddly enough he knew Gran's way with mastitis in a cow. He prepared the marshmallow as I'd have done myself, and I could see he thought the cow had been neglected. Ena *is* slapdash. Kindheartedness is not enough with animals. As much common sense is required as with children. My husband called for me, and we sat on the seashore for awhile, but I was tired out and I'd my potted meat to make.

'I cannot recall such lovely prolonged weather for many years', Nella wrote on 15 August, 'not since the first year we were married.' There had indeed been day after day of sunny, warm, often hot weather, and Nella was feeling decidedly better and keenly soaking up the benefits of nature. As she put it on 18 August, 'This golden life giving weather makes one able to resist colds and sniffles or aching bones. I'm sure it will help us all for the winter.' This prognosis proved to be over-optimistic. One day in the following winter, 28 January 1948, 'when a stray sunbeam fell on my face, I felt I wanted to clutch and hold it. Sunshine is life to me. Last summer I felt the years and my aches and miseries roll off me – to bounce back in the dull winter days.'

Saturday, 16 August. We had all windows, the windscreen and the top open, yet it was only when we were moving we felt it bearable. Harvesters, road menders, bikers and hikers and drivers of heavy lorries looked very un-English with only singlets and shorts – many only the latter. Their golden brown bodies gleamed with perspiration, but they looked as happy as I felt in the lovely sunshine. I never saw so many tramps. They shuffled along, the only overdressed people about, for most wore tattered overcoats and had heavy packs that could have been a makeshift tent on their backs.

We went to Arnside, thinking to find it cool by the estuary, but it was very airless. We had tea. The ice cream made our simple meal very festive. Scores of POWs from the big camp nearby sauntered about or sat on the wall. I felt really happy for them, to see how getting a little money nowadays had turned them from sad sullen prisoners into ordinary citizens. Granted this life giving sun would lift up anyone's spirits, but the gleaming oiled hair and polished shoes, light open necked shirts, and some odd looking white linen caps they had bought from some queer source made them look usual in spite of coarse POW pants. Some had sunglasses, many ate ice cream – but it came to me suddenly that I rarely saw them smoking. A wide mouthed lad with gleaming teeth and long sensitive hands sat near, so like my Cliff when he went overseas – even his burnt orange shirt made the likeness more plain. Cliff loved to feel different ...

My husband said suddenly 'This weather agrees with you – you look ten years younger'. I laughed and said 'Only ten years – I feel as gay and light headed as a girl, and feel like buying a bathing suit and going swimming again'! I feel my body is soaking up sunshine like blotting paper. Work is a pleasure, simple well cooked food a banquet. I feel it will build us up for winter and help us face any crisis.

We wouldn't have come home as early, but wanted to hear Churchill's voice again. I'd a queer little sadness when I heard him. I felt he was worried and heart sick, and baffled when he had no authority to sound the clarion call as formerly. Bless him for his faith and courage that we *will* pull through. I share his concern about so many who want to go abroad, but what can we do? Youth is so fleeting. This generation has lost so much, and dear God they ask so little – just that chance to work and see something for their labours, a share in those simple good things in life in the way of food that the colonies offer. I've never yet heard anyone speak of making a fortune or of big wages, only the chance to get on.

Sunday, 17 August. We were out by 1.30 and got round Coniston Lake, over to Ambleside, on to Keswick, and picnicked by Derwentwater ... I've always said there is very small litter left about the Lakes. Today I saw that if you are litter minded you can ride in a Rolls or motor coach or tramp the roads. Few little streams are running into Thirlmere, and only one where there was any coolness from its wetness or enough to bathe sticky hands. A very big car with four well fed adults and a chauffeur were just pulling out, and I suggested we park awhile. Thrown carelessly out, presumably from the car just left, were paper drinking cups, a small cardboard box which had had sandwiches in, two empty chocolate car-ton-boxes, and crumpled paper napkins. A passing tramp paused shyly as if hoping there would be something he could pick up. I smiled and picked up the sandwich box, which had two in it, and said 'This box might be useful for you'. He came across and we looked down at the litter and he shook his head and then picked all up, and said something about 'being kept busy', as if he held himself to be the salvage collector of that piece of road, but when I looked at his grubby, shabby appear-ance, I thought he had a finer 'inside' than the untidy ones.

Monday, 18 August. Another lovely day. I seem to have packed in two days work! I decided to go downtown shopping before it got too hot and put some clothes to soak, dusted round, and was downtown by 10 o'clock. I bought 4 lb tomatoes and 2 lb pears to bottle, left my grocery order, and got fish bits etc. The town seems full of strangers, and scantily dressed women and children in bright colours made such a happy note.

I stood waiting for the bus and met an old Barrovian, whose family
and my father were connected with the railway when it was local and
called the Furness Railway. He is staying at a nearby hotel and I've often
chatted to him going downtown or waiting for the bus. He seemed
lonely, for he has spent his life abroad on tea plantations. He is older
than I am. He married a friend of my father's youngest sister, who was
not ten years older than I am, and she died years ago and they never
had a family. He has always asked after various relatives and friends
– if my husband had been more sociable I'd have made him welcome
and invited him round, but it's no use denying the fact I'm giving up
the struggle as regards visitors. The bridge was evidently up and buses
delayed. Mr Jefferson suggested strolling on to the next stop. I remarked
how I loved the sun, and how happy and well I felt in sunshine, spoke of
when I lived down south and of envying Cliff in Australia – just talked
idly as we strolled. He said something about me going back south to
live, perhaps Devon, but I said if I made a change, I thought it might
be Australia. I recall something about going for a long visit to Australia
and coming back – 'After all, you have your own life, and interests in
England' –and then I couldn't believe my ears – he asked if I thought I
could consider marrying him!!!

Such a mix up. I've had a suspicion sometimes he was getting me
mixed up with Aunt Mary, whose husband was killed in an accident in
Abbey Road in the blackout in the war. I can remember telling him I
was going to Ireland on my own, and how he teased me about 'always
being independent'. It was such an embarrassment to us both, and he
apologised so sincerely for his mistake. I could see how lonely he has
been these few months, for I've often seen him round town and always
alone. I was so upset I got a bad attack of hiccoughs when I got in. I
wish I knew some lonely friendly soul who could marry him. He's a dear.

The next day she saw Mr Jefferson from a distance at the cricket field and 'thought
of all the uprooted Anglo Indians coming back to England where memory had
distorted friendships and associations and disillusionment followed quickly on
their return'.

Wednesday, 20 August. I've been nattering about the lavatory seat and lid ever since war ended. I hate shabby things and try and dodge some way to make them better, if I can. My husband never had that pride in his home to make the best of things and says 'Ah, don't bother – it's right enough' as long as it holds together. I wanted him to have the seat and lid French polished, but today I got on my top note and decided I'd do the darn thing myself. I unscrewed it off and partly stripped off the polish with a piece of woollen material, wrung out of warm water and ammonia sprinkled on, and I'll sandpaper every scrap off. It's mahogany. I think I'll just oil dress it, giving it repeated stains of linseed oil and then Mansion polish will finish it off. I love a Chippendale polish on wood, or beeswaxed oak, far before a hand gloss ...

I was washed and changed before lunch, and off to Walney before 1.30 to Ena Whittam's. The cow is better and out in the field again and today they were not so busy, for it was a little spell off in their harvest, for the two north fields are not ready till Friday or Saturday for cutting. There's a lot of chinks in any scheme, rationing especially. Olga and Billy, two of Mrs Whittam's family, have bought a pig between them to fatten and kill about Xmas, to ensure they have plenty to eat all winter. Olga has one little girl, Billy as yet no family. The pig weighs 22 score pounds, and they paid £25 and will feed it till killing, and there is all the waste weight. Ena says she estimates their bacon will work out at at least 3s a pound before they get it, and they will only have to give up their bacon ration!! I helped pick pears and beans for two orders besides my own, and then we stacked up a pile of untidy raspberry prunings and potato tops, which, to Ena's mirth, annoyed me as they lay around. She said '*You*'d never make a farmer. You are too nasty particular about dirt and untidiness.' I smiled, but thought of Gran's farm, tidy to a degree and as sweet and fair, in its own way, as a well-kept house.

Monday, 25 August. Another lovely day. A pleasure to get up and face the day's work. I decided to take all my curtains down, wash them, and left them in water to soak while I went downtown shopping. I met Mr Jefferson and quite simply got to know how he had got me mixed up with Aunt Mary. On the boat coming over, Amy was talking about people and families she knew in Barrow and the district and Mr J. and she found they had many mutual acquaintances. He asked if she knew anyone called Lord – Mary Lord, who had been a young friend of his wife and her sister. Amy said 'Ah yes, very well – wasn't it dreadful about her husband, but it's a happy release' and told of Uncle Jim's death, and how very lonely Aunt Mary would be now her family were either married or, in the case of Molly, working away from Barrow. Then he said 'I was walking down Abbey Road and saw you laughing and talking to someone and your whole appearance in your summer frock brought back a memory of before the war, when we were over. You looked so like Mary, and when I met you the first time and said "I'm sure you were a Miss Lord" I never thought of any other Miss Lord, or of the years between my visits.' I told him about gentle sweet Aunt Mary, who, through all her bitter troubles, married to a brilliant clever man who was a dipsomaniac [*an alcoholic*], loved and shielded him and only 15 months after just stopped living and laid back in her chair without a word and died.

Wednesday, 1 October. My husband came rushing in excitedly and said 'How would you like a fridge for your birthday?' and said a shop had four in and the proprietor, an electrician who often works on big jobs my husband has, had promised him one for a long time. In fact, he first did nearly five years ago, but any that has come in has been either 'shop' ones or priority. I feel a bit dazed and a bit indifferent, as I think if I'd been let have one and paid for it myself by instalments when the boys were home, it would not have cost so much – £29 10s – and I would have had it when most needed. I've done so long without it I could have gone on doing so. I didn't voice my thoughts. If we have another hot summer it will be grand for we both like ice cream, as well as the advantage of well kept food, hard butter and marg, and crisp salads. It's my birthday and Xmas present, so I'll buy my shoes, and if I decide on a costume, out of my year's income – this year only £19 odd.

Poor Dad. I'm always glad he died before he saw his investments dwindle and crash after the 1914 war. They had begun to weaken in 1919, when he died suddenly. In a queer expansive mood on the cold wild March day before he died, when I sat on a low stool with my sleeping baby on my lap – Cliff was 15 months old – he said he knew he would never realise his dream, to retire to Cornwall, and live retired, but he said he realised it was 'much better to journey than arrive'. He had had a queer unhappy marriage. Mother should never have remarried. Her thoughts and heart were forever in the never-never land of her idyllic short marriage. She thought married life would always be like those few months.* Dad puffed at his pipe as he rather shyly said 'You were always a blessing and interest to me. You know I've only really had two women to mean anything in my life, you and my mother, and it makes me very happy to know I'm leaving you comfortable. I can see Will will never get far, and I know you want to help the two little boys.' If he had lived to see how money and investments went down so rapidly, it would have grieved him.

---

* Nella's mother's first husband died shortly after their marriage. On 16 December 1947, when Aunt Sarah was speaking of her (she died at fifty-two) and 'of her sadness and inability to take life as it came', Nella 'had a vision of the sadness and aloofness of my mother's face – Dad always said she should have been a nun'.

CHAPTER FIFTEEN

HIGHS AND LOWS

October 1947–August 1948

Thursday, 2 October. Mrs Higham came in to see my fridge. Like Mrs Atkinson, she has that feeling I have – that we could have bought it years ago ourselves out of housekeeping money by instalments. 'When things pass, both good and bad go' – by the wee man.[†] I'd not go back, wars, atom bomb threats, or anything else. I'd like the more leisurely days, the plenty of simple amenities, of quantities of plain food like butter, milk, coal, etc., cheap. I'd like the ignorance that really was bliss, when war was something in the history books for ordinary people. The South African Boer war only touched a few deeply. To the rest and especially to we children it was a confusion of flags waving and 'Soldier of the Queen' and happy cheering, cakes in bags and mugs of tea sent to outlying fields in beer barrels which made the tea taste very odd.

But under all the freedom, women could only speak and write, and *all* men were tyrants, however loving.[*] I see red when a silly song out of I think *Annie Get Your Gun* is sung, 'The girl I will marry', is drooled over the wireless. It sums up the Victorian–Edwardian attitude so thoroughly, and I was one of the unfortunates who 'looked like a doll'. I've always looked incapable, or something, for added to my weak streak, I've been over ruled by first my father and then husband, 'taken care of', 'far too attractive to give much education – she will only marry and it will be wasted'. Men folk of my day had a very 'Man of Property' outlook, 'I earn the money, I must know where it all goes' attitude. No housekeeping savings could possibly be spent on anything not liked or

---

* 'My father was absolute monarch and the house was run for him', Nella had declared in her Directive Response for July 1939.

approved by the lord and master of the house, father or husband. A woman's place, unless sickness or loss drove her out to work, was, except in districts where women worked in mills, decidedly in the home. When my husband had such a lot of rheumatism and was off work six months at a stretch, he would never let me have boarders to help out – there was only men boarders in any quantity in Barrow at any time, with there being no work to bring women into the town. I was not let take advantage of my father's offer to put me into a little shop of whatever line I chose. Every idea that didn't coincide with his was condemned utterly. If the boys had not backed me up more or less by their outlook on life and their ambitions I couldn't have gone on – and I saw to it they had no false ideas of lordly superiority toward women!

Mrs Higham and I talked idly of our girlhood, of men's really harem outlook. She said 'I often wish I'd stayed in Liverpool, you know. I could have felt in things as I grow older.' We talked of Hospital Supply, Canteen, and Red Cross shop days, when we felt worthwhile. Now there only seems the daily round, and to take each day as it comes and do the best with it. Neither of us are the 'Housewives' League' type who could fight for causes.

Wednesday, 15 October. Mrs Whittam and I sat and talked. She has had a wonderful lot of things sent from America lately – it cost her nearly £6 for duty! Her daughter has sent shoes and a dress, stockings and rubber overshoes, and stacks of food – dried fruits and chocolates, meat, milk and jam. She is wisely putting some on the shelf. We had a good grizzle as we conjectured about the austerity ahead, wondering how long it would last. She had backed Firemaster and it came in second – she never seems to back a loser in a race ...

It's a fearful and wonderful thing the way the Russians have emerged from serfdom in so short a time, but virgin minds like virgin soil, and can nourish quicker than old. The Russians are unique in this swift moving modern world. With that clear-cut opportunity to go from night to day, they are not cluttered up with the perplexities and complications of mind the rest of the world have accumulated in the last

200 years. I always have a feeling that Russia is a potency of good or
ill, and can swing civilisation as never before, I've a feeling, for right or
wrong. Communism is THE force in the world, and the worst of it is
that it is one of the few creeds (?) or beliefs (?) – perhaps force is the
right word – that in this world of inertia of mind and muddled thinking
is a living urge. Just as Christianity took a deep hold on people by the
sincerity and belief of people who would go to their deaths in Rome,
making them feel 'it must be right', I've a feeling that the very fanaticism
of Communism is like a torch on a dark journey for a lot of people.
Sometimes I feel as if life baffles me. I sit and think and think, trying to
fit things together, feeling I look through a kaleidoscope that changes
before I've seen the last pattern and making little sense or cohesion at
that. Ordinary people can do so little.

During the next dozen weeks Nella wrote of various matters. Scarcity continued
to be a nagging worry; manufactured goods were more and more costly; housekeeping money was 'ever shrinking'; renovations dominated several days at 9
Ilkley Road; it rained a lot and was sometimes very cold; and there was at least
one power cut. 'People *do* seem gloomy and depressed,' she wrote on 8 December, 'and I've noticed those who rely on pictures or whist drives for their pleasure get far more so than anyone who sews or reads.' There was some winding
down of WVS business, and on 5 November Nella and other WVS members
from Barrow went to Preston to hear its Chairman, Lady Reading, speak. On
Saturday, 29 November she made a rare reference to football. 'Barrow won, so
all those thousands of Carlisle supporters – 2,000 alone came in coaches from
the surrounding district of Carlisle, and then there was the long line of cars and
the trains – had their long journey to see their side win in vain, and they drop
out of the Cup final.'

Babies were much mentioned. Aunt Eliza was to have another great grandchild in the spring; two new neighbours, both reckoned to be in their thirties,
were expecting; and Edith announced that she was again pregnant. (She had had
one miscarriage.) Nella was a great admirer of babies. She saw a lot of Norah's
baby girl, born in mid-November, although it was Norah's younger sister, Margaret, not yet married, whom she was particularly drawn to. On 22 August, before

her baby's birth, Norah had apparently suggested that Nella might help her with some sewing – but she was reluctant to oblige. Norah then 'said "If it had been our Margaret, Mrs Last would have sewn from morning till night" and got the reply from her mother "Oh, if it had been *Margaret*, Mrs Last would have had the baby for her".' Occasionally Nella thought back to her own babies, although she rarely spoke of the one who did not survive: 'I buried my first baby on a Boxing Day', she recalled on 7 December (and said no more).

Friday, 9 January 1948. Jessie Holme* came in for the afternoon, and Mrs Atkinson came in, *so* distressed. Her sister-in-law who went back to Canada sent parcels and a whole ham to be divided between Mrs Atkinson and another sister. It looks really perfect but is salt as brine and curiously tasteless. Even Norah and Dick hadn't eaten two thick slices Norah cooked, and when I tasted a wee piece I couldn't wonder. I could only suggest she boiled the whole piece after soaking well, with vegetables to add flavour. She had looked forward to it coming so much. It could have been such a grand 'standby'. Jessie was so delighted with a dressing gown we partly dodged up some time ago and finally fixed this afternoon – a few hours sewing will finish it. She had a very good but shabby raglan camel hair coat. The cuffs and collar were worn, and she had only worn it about the garden when she lived in the country. Her sister had a nice wine coloured one, with an 'overcheck' in fawn, equally good but old fashioned and worn. Between the two, after we had had them cleaned at cut price, we've made a dressing gown both smart and better than money could buy nowadays. It's got a deep border, wide deep cuffs, and roll collar of the check material as well as the big patch pockets Jessie wanted and made from the fawn front facing which we discarded, with a band of check material. She didn't want a belt, so I fitted it slightly with darts.

She is tall and stately. I said admiringly 'Jessie, you look as if you had stepped straight out of *Vogue*', and she was delighted as she prinked and

---

* Jessie and George Holme, who were expecting their first child this month, lived in the house adjoining the Atkinsons', two down from the Lasts.

preened. Suddenly I realised why I had liked her as soon as I saw her. She is 'my kind of folks', perhaps because of her country origin, for she has always lived in Broughton, a very small market town just up the coast from Barrow. I gave her a piece of Xmas cake with her cup of tea. I wished suddenly Edith was as friendly and showed signs of liking me. I couldn't imagine Jessie showing resentment or jealousy in *any* way. Her husband's mother is coming to be in the house, and she has a good 'visiting' nurse, and Mrs Atkinson and I will see to anything she needs till her mother-in-law gets here from Whitehaven. I opened a small tin of salmon for tea. Jessie had to go to make her husband's tea for 5 o'clock, and I gave her a tin of cheese and macaroni out of a parcel from Australia. She has an appetite like Norah and a good digestion. My goodness but I hope baby Holme is a boy. It's not that she 'hopes it will be a boy'. To hear her talk, there's only one sex! I recalled my own calm assurance – I wanted boys myself – so hope she too has boys. She wants two or three children.

Tuesday, 13 January. Jessie Holme came in. She feels restless and unsettled, now her time is near. She looks very drawn and ill. I looked at her in pity today – 34 is not the time to be having a first baby. Apart from the physical side, babies and young children need the patience, or rather the joyousness, of youth, to rear them. Jessie would be sedate, though sweet, at any age. Young wives of today have a lot against them, if even they are born home makers. Jessie has some good bits of furniture from home, but her house has such a cheerless look, so few rugs or carpets, and poor skimpy curtains. The polished lino looks so cold and bare. I thought of the houses that are going up now with concrete floors. Some very nice maisonette type of flats are going up nearby, on the main road. I look at them every time I pass – concrete floors and stairs, and all woodwork eliminated that is possible. I thought of stepping out of the bath, or warm bed, for I cannot see any floor covering making concrete 'warm'. We sat and talked of babies, and little children and their odd sayings. It was a pleasant afternoon, and after a cup of tea, Jessie went at 4.30. Her husband has such odd hours for work.

In 1948 Jessie was to figure prominently in Nella's diary. Her baby – a girl – was born on 21 January. 'Even allowing for Jessie's exhaustion, she was indifferent to it. I asked if she had thought of a name and she shook her head and said "We never thought of a girl coming"' (22 January). The next day Nella visited her again. 'I felt concern for her listless, languid look, all vitality and humour drained out of her smiling face. The baby is thriving but she doesn't take much notice of it.' Jessie continued to be uncommunicative, and talk persisted of her and her husband's longing for a boy (24 January). On the 26th things were looking up. Nella was 'really delighted to see the change' in Jessie. 'She looked her old self, and quite happy with wee Katherine Ann, as they have decided to call baby, and she seemed to have got over her deep disappointment.' On the 29th all seemed well. 'To hear Jessie talk now, she got her dearest wish when she had a baby girl! She is such a sweet person. I knew she would come round and love it.' Jessie was often mentioned in the following weeks, for Nella was regularly doing shopping for her, and sometimes caring as well for 'wee Kathleen', as the baby was finally named. Jessie's baby tended to be sickly, unlike Norah Atkinson Redhead's robust baby Ann, who made frequent appearances in the Last household.

On numerous occasions in late February and March, Nella remarked on Jessie Holme's fragile health, which was a big concern for her husband, George, whom Nella thought very well of – he was said to be attentive and considerate. George 'is so worried', Nella wrote on 1 April, 'when Dr Miller says she is so bloodless, and needs meat, liver, and kidneys. When doctors know well it's impossible for them to give permits for extra, they should be careful about giving orders. Poor George said "I wish I knew where I *could* buy some" – and he is a railway detective!'

Monday, 5 April. I called at Jessie's but she was not back. George left word with Mrs Atkinson she was coming back this evening. She had been so ill on Sunday they had to bring in a Broughton doctor, the one she always had before coming to Barrow. It was a kind of fainting attack and George was badly frightened. The doctor confirmed Dr Miller's diagnosis but prescribed some kind of liver tablets as well, and said she was in very poor health and *must* relax and rest, feed up, and have all the fresh air possible. George looks worried to death. I feel they are realising the difficulty of a big rent out of his wage. He is only a plain clothes railway policeman. I don't think he gets a big wage, and I can tell all extras for the baby and its arrival have been taken from savings.

Tuesday, 6 April. A cold wet morning. I didn't feel like going downtown for 10 o'clock, to meet Mrs Higham at Boots, to buy a few prizes for Thursday, and had to hurry and knead bread and tea cakes and leave them to rise. I'd packed Aunt Sarah's little fortnightly parcel of odds and ends, and when I missed the bus decided to walk. I wished I hadn't. Halfway down Abbey Road I heard such a dreadful cry not far away and on reaching a corner saw a man lying in a big pool of blood, and two workmates kneeling by him. I asked a man if they had phoned for the ambulance and he said someone was doing so. Nothing could be done by us standing staring – we walked down the road together. I felt sorry for this man. He had actually seen the poor fellow fall off a 50 foot roof. In tonight's *Mail* it said he died two hours after admission to Hospital …

This Easter [*the end of March*] I felt my mind go back so plainly to Easter spent at Spark Bridge. Oddly enough, Arthur spoke of the same memories, and on Easter Sunday Cliff wrote 'Do you remember when we all used to stay at Spark?' and walk down the field to church on Easter Day. Often a feeling of awe creeps over me, to hear little things I've said or done so long ago recalled by my grown men. It's rather a terrifying thought to realise how a child's mind can be influenced, but perfectly true. In my child-life, my mother seems a rather vague lonely shadow, my father very remote, till I was old enough to realise he was an unhappy man who had a magic key he was anxious to lend me, into a land of books. Odd vagrant thoughts of life and people. But Gran – my prim lipped Quaker Gran – at 58 I find my life shaped by her maxims, her faith, and never failing kindness, and a goodness that was part of her very fibre. If Gran said a thing, you could steer by it. If she said a thing was 'not done', it lost any charm it promised. When you are young you don't realise this 'power' or else it would have more importance. I always try to impress young mothers with the power of love, the importance of seeing the good behind the naughty, and most of all, letting a child see good in a mother, never telling them untruths or breaking a promise ...

It was my day for shocks. I heard the committee talking amongst themselves about Mr Jefferson, who went back to India last November – he is dead. He has left over £12,000 and has no near relatives. Speculation was rife as to whom it would be left, and hopes he had remembered the Club. It's a good thing he won't be unhappy any more. He was of so friendly and kindly disposition and when he was in England so lost and alone.

Wednesday, 7 April. Mrs Salisbury is a treasure. Her passionate love of a 'good turn out' far outvies any little odd ways and slapdash methods of ordinary routine. We looked at gleaming walls and ceiling, and she asked anxiously if 'Everything was OK?' I said 'Yes indeed, it's perfection'. She said 'I said to my boss the other night "I could take a job anywhere now. I know all the right things to use in cleaning, and the proper way to go about things. Mrs Last is *very* particular."' I said 'Not thinking of leaving me though?' and she shook her untidy little head and reminded me again she had only left me before when little Billy was coming. She said 'My boss said if ever you went to Australia we would sell up and go, even if we didn't live near you. We would feel we had someone, and he thinks with us both being workers and three lads and a girl growing up, we would stand a good chance of getting on.' I felt a family like the Salisburys was ideal for Australia. I'd lettuce in the fridge, and we had it to corned beef and toasted tea cakes, and there was whole meal bread and butter, jam and cake. I felt very picky. I wished I'd had some of Cliff's lovely honey. I hope another tin comes soon.

I picked up the local *Mail* to glance through, and felt my blood chill with horror and pity. A lad I'd known from a baby had been 'found hanging' in his cabin on his ship at Chatham. The father was a grammar school master when both boys were there. Arthur was a favourite with him because of his interest and work in drama. The only son, he was their idol, and brilliantly clever. They wanted him to be a doctor, but gave way to his wish to go as a cadet at Dartmouth. The mother went back to teaching so there should be plenty of money for Kenneth's career, and now at 26 he is dead by his own hand, after all the horror of war. I felt sick with pity to think of the agony of mind and shattered nerves that would make anyone of 26, with the career he loved before him, and all his life to enjoy, choosing to end it so dreadfully.

Friday, 9 April. I had to go down to the hairdresser's, and did a little shopping. I went out early so didn't go into Jessie's, for I intended going out this afternoon and thought I could have done any shopping then she needed. When I called in on my way back, I found her brother had come from Broughton, in answer to a phone call from George, who is distracted about Jessie's nerves. She walks about all night and complains she cannot breathe if she lies down. Her eyes looked so wild and furtive I felt alarmed, and she wouldn't let either Mrs Atkinson or I do anything, or get ready. Luckily George came in and I could see he was determined she should go to her mother's again. I felt upset to see the change in the poor thing. Mrs Atkinson and I have tried in every way to be kind, but she didn't even say goodbye and wouldn't let us offer to do anything about shopping or looking after George, etc. She has suddenly developed a grudge against everything and everybody, and George the most of all. I hope she stays till she is thoroughly herself.

Saturday, 10 April. My little attack of acidosis flamed up into a bad gastric attack. I felt feverish and ill when I came to bed, and woke at 1 o'clock, to be sick and ill till after 6 o'clock. I felt so shaky when I rose, but a cup of strong tea and bit of toast pulled me together. Mrs Atkinson came in looking upset. Before she was up, the phone had rung and Mr Atkinson answered. It was Mary Easton, Jessie's friend at Broughton, who said in an anxious tone 'Could you contact George, please'. Mr Atkinson has off every Saturday and George had told him last night he too had a day off and intended 'pulling up a few neglected jobs in the garden' before going to Broughton by the teatime train. Mr Atkinson brought him to the phone and after a few minutes talk George told Mr Atkinson 'Mary thinks I'd better come at once', so we are wondering if Jessie is worse in some way. Her furtive eyes worried me. She seemed to let them glide vacantly over everything and everybody, with no interest or focus.

Sunday, 11 April. When Mrs Helm was giving me the sunflower roots she said 'What did you think of Chislett?' – Mr Helm is a magistrate and often met him, as Clerk to the Magistrates.* She said 'He has never been a happy man, and I think would have been off before, but he thought a lot of his old mother. She died last year and there was a lot of money in the family, so it looks as if he had waited to realise all before he went.' Mrs Helm is a very religious woman and said sadly 'It's a great pity – and even more for the mud it has stirred up', and she named a string of prominent townsmen who were unfaithful to their wives, some just visiting different rather shady women, two who travelled rather out of the town, where small children were growing up, suspicious like their wife's family. She said 'There's no goodness or honour left anywhere. Clergy and doctors are so changed. They are no different to ourselves. There's no one to look up to.' ...

As we strolled slowly up from the cinema, a big Wesleyan church door opened, and the congregation came out. I knew most, if only by sight, and suddenly Mrs Helm's rather whining voice came back to me as she said 'You don't know who's who nowadays. Mud is everywhere, only waiting to be stirred up.' Amongst the ones coming out were two she had mentioned as well known visitors to a 'doubtful' house. Two girls I well knew had been 'fast', to put it kindly, with both our own RAF and the Americans – I knew of two weekends spent at a quiet hotel near Spark Bridge – and could tell the girls knew most of the hotels of the Lakeland. Now they are married and look settled. There was a knot of men talking together. My husband said 'There's three of the "Forty Thieves"' – a name given to a few businessmen who buy and sell houses

---

* The well-paid Magistrates' Clerk for Barrow and Ulverston, a married man in his fifties, had recently left his wife in favour of a woman in her thirties, also married. The scandal was a major topic of conversation in Barrow, and his picture was reproduced on the front page of an issue of the *Daily Mail*.

etc., and it is said force prices up. I thought 'I suppose in every gathering of people a similar "bag" could have been made nowadays'.

Tuesday, 13 April. I've felt wretchedly ill now for a week, nothing settling when I eat it, however simple. I was undecided whether to go to the whist drive, but finally decided I would, and spent a pleasant afternoon. I went into Mrs Atkinson's when I came in to see some curtain patterns she had got, and the phone rang. It was Mary Easton, Jessie's friend, who had been trying to get both of us in the afternoon. Her news shocked and distressed us. Poor Jessie is in a very bad way, though after last Wednesday, when I'd seen the furtive aloof stare in her eyes, her news didn't surprise me. Jessie's parents are old – 74 and 76 – and past worrying, and they don't like the idea Jessie may be like her two uncles, one of whom died in a home, and the other drowned himself in a nearby tarn. On Saturday night her father and brother took her for a walk, to try and make her sleep. She got away from them, and after a search they found her kneeling in church, sobbing bitterly. Mary took the law into her own hands and begged the family doctor, who knew poor Jessie from a child, to 'Do *something*'. He paid a casual friendly call, and has sent for George for a talk. George is one of those 'fine big' men who often are so negative. He doesn't seem to bother, not even when he woke suddenly and found Jessie dressed and going out. Jessie has turned against everyone, even her dear little baby. She won't even wash or feed it. I've a great sadness on me. She was the gayest, kindest and most gentle creature. She does need love and understanding.

Wednesday, 14 April. I woke dull, after a broken night. I couldn't sleep for thinking of poor Jessie. I'd just finished breakfast when the postman came, and Cliff's letter made me hoot with laughter – he is growing a beard! I felt whatever else that one is or has been, there's never been a trace of dullness! Mrs Salisbury changed her day this week – she comes in the morning – so I did all my little odd jobs, and dusted and vacced. I was washed and changed by 11 o'clock, so I could go round to Jessie's aunt to see if she had heard what the doctor had said yesterday. She cried bitterly – she is 73, a year younger than her sister, Jessie's mother. She said 'Oh Mrs Last, what can I say? We are all so stunned. The doctor says Jessie must be watched day and night, and the baby kept out of her way, and that the next move is up to George.' I thought of that wireless programme *Lamentable Brother*. I felt the doctor could have stressed the importance of the poor woman having the benefit of skilled attention and care as soon as possible and not merely thrown the discussion on poor George to have her put away. The doctor says it is 'nothing that will pass', and that it is too complete a breakdown for that. Her aunt said 'I once had a bad breakdown after an operation and had to go for a month's holiday with my sister to Southport. Perhaps if it could be arranged, it would cure Jessie.' I could have wept as I came home, to think of the dreadful cloud on poor kind Jessie, and that dear little baby.

Thursday, 15 April. Mrs Salisbury came. Yesterday she had been to the Women's Clinic. She has rather a bad prolapse, and they want her to go into the hospital – book now, for July. It's a private ward, run by the Maternity Home doctor. The town pays part for all woman patients, who only pay £2 a week, and I think another 2 guineas for the operation. Mrs Salisbury wonders if the Government will take over and she could come under the new scheme. It's so muddling, it's difficult to know these things.

George called with a big bundle of laundry, to send when the van man called. He looks nearly dead with worry and loss of sleep. He said Jessie had stood against the wall in the kitchen since Sunday, never moving or speaking, eating or drinking. The doctor says she must be taken to a brain specialist at Lancaster, but I can see that George is hoping that the few days leave he has been given will see a change in the poor dear ...

My husband looked tired out. He has had a lot of worry lately with his work, and his mother takes all her troubles, real and imaginary, into the shop. Of all her family, she only turns to him, and when her ration books were lost again this week, it was an added worry for him. I've put my foot down. She shan't have them again. I took the bus down to see her after tea, and told her I insisted on doing all her shopping in future.

I've offered many times and been refused, but when I took a firm stand
tonight she said 'I'd be very grateful'. I was so taken back by her gratitude I looked closely at her. I feel she is perhaps failing quicker, since
Grandad had his accident. I'll go out in the morning and see her shopkeepers. She gets groceries from the shop where I deal, and shopkeepers
are always kind and considerate to arrangements affecting old folks ...

In the evening I walked down the garden path with my little cat. Such
a heavenly sweet night, with the smell of growing things, spring flowers,
budding trees. Jessie and I planned to do our sewing on the lawn this
summer. She said 'I'm going to live outdoors all summer. Perhaps that
will be my best tonic.' I looked across Mrs Atkinson's lawn to the half
made rockery they had started, poor Jessie, and poor, poor George. I
wondered who would look after the little baby. I listened to *ITMA*,[†]
relaxed on the settee. I didn't feel very appreciative. I didn't feel in the
humour for 'nonsense'. I felt as if Jessie's illness had broken the little
ring fence round me, that it showed clearer and more focused the strife
and chaos all round. A real good cry would have done me good, but I
felt beyond tears. I felt a blanket of futility smothered me, mentally and
physically. I'll be very glad when Edith has had her baby and they are
both well.

Friday, 16 April. Mrs Howson and I had a very pleasant afternoon. She
hadn't one 'rave' about anything, and our grief and pity for Jessie was a
common bond. Everyone in our short road liked Jessie, who had a coun-
trywoman's friendliness. Norah left her baby with us and went shopping
by bus. She is a lovely baby, and the most placid one I've ever known ...

I made a cup of tea for when Norah came back tired and I'd some such
nice biscuits, with raisins in and tasting as if sweetened with honey. As
I got my tea I kept thinking of our conversation, which Norah broke off
when she came back. Mrs Howson was so shocked about capital punishment being abolished. Somehow poor Jessie's illness has swung me for
all time to the side of this decision. To see that gentle sweet woman so
alter, to hear of the pitiful state she is in now, made me realise how little
– *none* at all – 'badness' there is, only pitiful twists and warps, and that

'only by the Grace of God' do any of us escape. Bad people must be shut up safely. Doctors could study them, and perhaps help others 'afflicted', but punishment can only be revenge, which is evil. Mrs Howson said 'You have some very queer ways of looking at things, but Steve says you are always sincere, and that word used by Steve often means "You've got something there".' But she feels murder will increase now that people will not think 'It's not worth swinging for'.

Saturday, 17 April. I was shaking my duster out of the stairs window, and I heard Mr Atkinson call 'Will you come down a few minutes, Mrs Last' and found him talking to an elderly woman, the mother of a nearby confectioner. I felt my breath catch as I looked at her parcel, remembering suddenly today was Jessie's birthday and that she had taken some marg for a birthday cake to be made. Mrs Waugh knew poor Jessie was very ill, but not just how ill. I peeped in the folds of the paper at the attractive little brick shaped cake, snowy iced, with a spray of violets at each end and 'Happy Birthday Wishes' written between. We talked it over. George and Jessie's brother are taking her to Lancaster on Monday – she is no better, and her physical health is failing rapidly. We decided the gay cake would only be another distress to poor George, and Mrs Waugh said her daughter could easily sell it and would credit the marg and make another cake when Jessie came home, if I could let them know when she was expected. As I resumed my dusting I felt I wished I knew ...

George called with the key. I don't quite know why – there won't be occasion to go in their house. He looked distraught. It's a dreadful thing for a man to have to take his loved wife and leave her in a mental home. I longed to ask who had the baby. He said Jessie hadn't spoken, cried, or eaten for a week. When they coax her to sit or lie down she looks blank and vague and fights so desperately if they try and make her. The doctor gave her some kind of injection and they laid her down and took off her clothes, but in less than two hours she was up, had got some clothes on, and was standing against the wall in the kitchen again. The doctor has stressed the fact he could do no more and wanted them to take Jessie to Lancaster for last Thursday. Now it has to be Monday to see this particular doctor. George seems incapable of thinking he will have to leave her. He seems to have a hazy idea of some 'magic' which will bring back the Jessie he has always known. When I phoned to the laundry, I asked for the manageress and explained a man neighbour had left a huge pile of washing, and I'd be very obliged if a van man could make a detour off Abbey Road as our delivery and collection was over for this week, and added 'It's a case of rather desperate illness. Will you please return it as soon as you can?' It was only lifted Friday morning – and returned before tea today. I thanked the van man and expressed surprise, but he said 'We are human beings down there you know, and try to please our customers'. Just a week tonight since Jessie was found in church, kneeling and sobbing wildly, as if she felt all human help was failing her.

Monday, 19 April. We went out in the car. My husband dropped me at his mother's home, while he made various calls. I looked round in desperation, wondering what will have to be done. My husband and I are the only ones to bother at all and beyond always paying them £2 10s each week tax clear, he doesn't really feel concerned. His quite understandable reply to anything I've said is 'Surely the other four can take something on their shoulders'. Trouble is they don't want anybody round, and are happy in the dirt and disorder. In the dining room there was a little heap of coal in the corner – 'it was handiest there'. I said 'You are not fit to do any housework at all, mother. Let me come down with Mrs Salisbury, who will scrub through'. She said 'I never do any housework. It never wants doing, and I won't have anyone in the house poking about, you or anyone else'. What worries me is what will be done soon – very soon if I'm not much mistaken. They are both failing fast. I've neither strength or endurance now to tackle taking them over. As we came home I said 'Would you agree to shutting up our house for a few weeks and moving down into your mother's house to take charge? I would do, if I could get a competent woman to come in every day.' He shook his head and said 'No. You have done more than your share for my family. I've not been as blind as you think. One of the girls must take charge and we will do our share.' What puzzles me is where all their little private income goes, but wonder if my husband's remarks about 'money going where the clothes coupons go' is correct. Flo was always a 'grab', though if she is getting them, she should do something in return. I can see we will all have a share in the big problem ahead.

We were back by 9 o'clock. I don't know whether it was the peaches or the feeling of worry I came back with, but I was sick again. My husband actually said tonight 'Why don't you go to the doctor's?' But as I pointed out, I had the stomach mixture he gives me, made up by my brother-in-law, and know well what he would say – 'You must stop worrying, lie down after every meal, and cultivate that sense of humour you are in danger of losing'. I don't consciously worry, but it's times like these I realise how nice it would be to have a little social circle which didn't depend so on my own efforts. No one drops in. They come with that 'Where's Mr Last?' if they come in, and if he looks busy or 'quiet', they never stay. For one reason and another, I've fought rather shy about making a close friendship. Jessie was an exception. I felt as if I opened barriers, didn't care whether my husband would approve, and felt Jessie 'belonged' with me. She used to say 'Kathleen, we will have such a lot of kindness to repay, but we will, my darling, won't we?' and smile so sweetly over the wee thing's head, lovingly. The baby always seemed to know me, even when I'd not seen it for a day or two when they went to Broughton for weekends. Its wise dark eyes looked widely. Its wee hands clasped in a little gesture all her own. She had such 'pleading' always in both eyes and gesture, as if begging to be loved. Poor George. It's so difficult to understand why this heavy blow has fallen on him.

Tuesday, 20 April. George called early. He had come down to tell Jessie's aunt that he had left her in Lancaster, and was very cut up at the brief, not to say callous, reception they had got. A woman friend of the family went with them and Jessie was perfectly docile and allowed them to wash and dress her and get her ready, never speaking a word to anyone, but she took notice of the signposts on their journey. When they got to the mental asylum, Jessie was led into another room and they were asked to wait. A little later all her clothes from her vest to her coat were handed out, with every little toilet requisite, even her comb and tooth-brush, and they were told they would be communicated with by post ...

I had a pleasant afternoon at the cricket pavilion, and not a bad game of whist, and hurried home to make an early tea, for my husband had said he might come home early enough to go to the pictures. I wanted to see *Mrs Miniver* again. I only made a simple tea, peaches, new but-tered tea cakes, whole meal bread and butter and jam and sponge sand-wich. I often get so out of patience, knowing so well we both need more 'gadding about', but he *won't* go to last house shows. He insists if he is not in bed before 10 o'clock and gets 8 or 8½ hours sleep, he feels too tired in the day. I say 'Well, I don't and never will see how you cannot plan *one* evening so we can go to a show'. Now the variety doesn't start till 6.30, it's alright, but mainly owing I think to the stoppage of the last bus service before the 'old' time of coming out, we stick to the wartime picture showing, 5.30 first house, and the second always starts before 8 o'clock.

Last time I saw *Mrs Miniver* was in wartime, when we had worry and fear, but high hopes and courage – hopes of all the good we would do, the feeling we could do as much for peace as for war, never realising the queer frustration – frustrating everything – everybody would find when the ceasefire sounded in Europe, and certainly never thinking of the flare-up in Palestine, or that Stalin would replace Hitler in his bid to rule the world. I loved every minute of the picture, wondering again just why futile silly pictures are made, crime and sex glorified, slime and mud flaunted, when a simple picture of nice people packs the cinema, as I'd not seen it for a long time – first house at that! My husband enjoyed it thoroughly and had that 'we must do this often' air. I bet if he could see a few comparable pictures he would! We have booked for the variety tomorrow night. The first week was a triumph for the promoters. The second, with the all male cast and memories of the queer set up of some of the leads when it was in Barrow once before, must have made them wonder if it would meet expenses. Yet the Five Smith Brothers and a goodish support packed both houses in that big place, and it looks as if

Sid Millward's 'Nit Wits' is going to do even better, for those who went last night are saying 'You mustn't miss this show, it's a yell'. Barrow is unique in many ways. If word goes round the Yard a thing is good, or bad, men seem to rely on their workmates' word, and a failure or success relies on the huge Yard crowd.*

Mrs Howson brought in such a lovely little worn coat for Mrs Salisbury, who is always glad to give coupons if she can get good clothes without money. I looked at this non-utility coat – I recall the material was very expensive, and Mrs Howson insisted she '*must* have silk lining, as she had always been used to it'. She went to Manchester in her search, and it's a coat little worn, and younger than either of mine, yet to hear Mrs Howson talk is 'quite unwearable'. She was in such a queer prickly mood tonight. I bet she will be difficult to live with. The jealous skitty way she always had in a pawky malicious manner, that once made us laugh at Canteen, is settling on her, and like a bag of pepper on a piece of meat, tends to utterly spoil any goodness or niceness. I saw my husband stare in blank amazement as she talked so shrewishly of anyone who had pinched and scraped to buy houses while their men folk had been at war. She said 'I believe in enjoying life while I can. Doesn't it make you sick to think of the way women worked and saved every penny, and grew old before their time?' My husband rubbed the top of his head in perplexity. I know he was searching for words. He said 'Well, I cannot say much. I know it's what Nell would have done. She was a grand manager in the last war and managed to save £100 for us to put on our house.' I felt the glare she gave us both. I could have giggled wildly. As long as I've not to work or live with her, I can see a funny side.

Someone of my own blood will die soon. I had Gran's old dream of carrying flowers for someone. As I didn't feel very sad, perhaps it will be one of the old ones. It's a long time since I had the flower dream. Poor

---

* This show was apparently a bit disappointing, for the next day Nella wrote that 'there was a very good variety bill, but Sid Millward's "Nit Wits" wearied me, the brass was so piercingly loud, and two good comedians who gave two turns – "The Finlay Brothers" – seemed to exhaust the humour of grotesque clowning'.

Dad joked about it, when I told him, and said 'For goodness sake, don't get the same silly ideas your mother had about dreaming of flowers', but he died very suddenly, and the daffodils I'd carried in my dream were in the wreaths heaped on his coffin. I've not been sick once today and [*had*] only faint butterflies. Perhaps my rest after meals is helping.

Wednesday, 21 April. Mrs Salisbury came, and we had a busy and unhindered morning, and I found time to slip round to Aunt Eliza's before lunch and took her a little bottle of damson, some papers Cliff sent, and a bunch of such lovely spring flowers out of the garden. She was looking bright, but felt neglected – nobody loves her. I said flippantly 'What the heck ducks, you've got your parrot', and to my horror she said 'I've decided you must have Colchester when I die'. I said 'Now you know darn well I detest birds in cages', but as she pointed out he rarely went in his cage. I said 'He wouldn't have much fun with my two cats' but really meant my poor cats would have none at all if that wretched bird was round. He delights in biting their tails or tweaking their ears, and his raucous voice and really terrible laugh has always kept any of Aunt Eliza's cats well under his claws. I said firmly 'Now *don't* wish that bird on me. You are worse than my mother-in-law. She wants me to promise to look after granddad if she goes first, and no arguments made me falter. Have that nasty parrot – I WILL NOT.'

I had tinned soup to heat and sausages to fry and I did steamed fish for myself, cooked cabbage and potatoes and made a semolina sweet to go with bottled apples. Mrs Salisbury washed up and I got washed and changed, for I wanted to do some shopping before going to a big Social and Moral Welfare meeting in the Town Hall. Two bishops, Lady Fell, and most of the clergy in Barrow and Ulverston, as well as a good number of subscribers, made the meeting a big success – and me feel like a fish out of water. I nearly disgraced myself by falling asleep, as [*the Bishop of*] Carlisle's sonorous voice boomed platitudes. To my embarrassment the Bishop of Penrith thought he recognised me, warmly shook me by the hand. I'm sure he mistook me for someone else. I've only seen him twice when he was at Hawkshead and we went to church there in wartime. I didn't feel at all interested somehow, good cause or no, and I looked round at the best workers and thought how dull, not to say sour, some of them looked. I'd a little game with myself, trying to pick out the ones I'd turn to if in 'trouble', plainly recognising that much as I like and respect Mrs Higham she wouldn't be amongst those I'd feel would understand passion and temptation.

Sunday, 25 April. It's been such a lovely day – we longed to be off in the car.* I'd my usual rest till lunchtime, and got letters written and had a nap. Lunch was soon ready, mutton soup, cold mutton, salad, yesterday's remains of a milk sweet with jam, and a cup of tea to finish. I packed the laundry, went into the garden, and did a bit of weeding. It was so warm and lovely I took a chair out and sat in the sun. I could see George and Jessie's cousin busy in the garden and later he came in, looking a little happier. He had a letter from Lancaster, saying Jessie had spoken to the nurse, and asking permission for some electrical treatment to be given. He gave me the address so I could write each week, saying letters were allowed but didn't know about flowers or papers. He said the baby was unbelievably good, and Jessie's mother was having no trouble at all looking after her, and he will travel from Broughton each day. He said sadly 'Eight years married and I've only been able to look after her for less than a year, and a sorry job I've made of it'. I said 'You may find that Jessie is better sooner than you expect. They said she was in such poor physical condition, you know, and she will get the very best of care for body and mind.' I prayed my words could be true.

Friday, 30 April. Early this week I heard the cuckoo, and the Howsons

---

* Often in the first half of 1948 Nella and Will took car trips on Saturdays, for he could usually find some business-related excuse for these journeys, which was not possible on Sundays. 'I *do* long for the time petrol can be used', she had written the previous day, after an outing to Ulverston. 'Even to go and sit by Coniston Lake would be good for him, and now there is the wireless in the car, he would settle happily.' Since the petrol ration was about to be restored, initially at a lower level, Sunday motoring would soon be resumed. Petrol rationing was not entirely eliminated until mid-1950.

disputed it, but this morning both she and Steve had heard it. We talked of when the nightingales sang so sweetly from somewhere near. The gun batteries seemed to frighten them away, and the last time I heard one round here was the night after our heaviest raid. Cliff was home unexpectedly, and we had just heard that little Kath Thompson had died in the hospital from bomb injuries. It was the first death like that that had touched us closely. I was standing listening to the liquid bird notes, in the still sweet evening dusk, and Cliff came out. Perhaps something in my attitude kept him from his cheery 'Come in for your supper'. We stood quietly till the bird moved away from the nearby tree, and he put his arm round me, kissed me lovingly, and we came indoors without a word. Both of them had such an 'understanding' way. We didn't need words ...

Margaret and I talked of poor Jessie, and when she went I listened to *The Clock*. I think the productions dealing with mental kinks and illness the wisest, most worthwhile features ever put on by the BBC, *Lamentable Brother* especially. To unthinking or ignorant people, who had never come into contact with breakdowns, they give an insight and understanding. Years ago I had a very bad breakdown after a major operation and a lot of worry. I said to my doctor 'Do you think I'm going mad? I feel I'm losing some kind of protecting "sheath" off my mind, and feel people's emotions, thoughts and fears, have queer "clairvoyant" dreams, and can tell fortunes in a really odd way.' He said 'No lassie (he was a Scot). You are not the type to have melancholia.' But it made me realise deeply how minds *can* change and grow perplexed. I once told him a dream I had, so queer and arresting it did me as much – perhaps more – good than the long sea voyage he said he would like to prescribe. I thought I was standing leaning over a low parapet, looking at a wide, strangely green river. As I looked closer I saw it was closely covered with leaves of every possible shape, colour, condition and variety. I stood dreamily gazing, growing more conscious of each separate leaf. Some were jostled by others, some sailed calmly and effortlessly, some were battered and bruised, carried in cross currents, some actually seemed to be trying to flow upstream against the stream. For one I felt real contempt – it seemed to be so determined to be bruised and broken and to go any way but to glide serenely. Then I knew *I* was that leaf, broken at the edges, getting nowhere at all. I felt conscious of a pulsing Rhythm, of the countless leaves sweeping by me. I lifted my hands off the parapet where I had gripped so tightly and, not praying, not conscious of any plea, held them outstretched for help. So moved was my whole being, I felt strength flow into me. He *was* a nice doctor. He didn't laugh or make fun at all.

The next several weeks were unremarkable, although there was some warm, even hot, weather to enjoy. Jessie Holme, though absent, was often in people's thoughts and conversations. Nella picked some lily of the valley to send her, regretting that 'there's so little I can do to show my loving sympathy, beyond writing gossipy letters … George has had another "normal" little letter, again saying how sorry she is to have been so much trouble to everyone. I feel a bit of wholesome selfishness would be an asset to that gentle loving creature' (6 May). On 10 May George 'told Mrs Atkinson that Jessie was fretting badly to come home, that she looks perfectly normal, and worried about her house getting dirty and dusty, and the house being too much for her mother. I felt again that the poor girl should never have got to beaten state she did. Most people I've heard visited for the first time in a mental home have either not known their visitors or bitterly reviled them for "shutting them up".' On the 21st Nella was buying film so that George could send Jessie photos of their baby, and the following week (29 May) she reported that 'Jessie is worrying and pining to come home, but the treatment is for three months. Someone told George that he had not to build up *too* high hopes on the sudden recovery Jessie had made – it could only be temporary. What cruel people there are. It took the light from poor George's face.'

Tuesday, 24 August. Margaret had sent to Hutton's of Larne for a catalogue and then a piece of linen for a big tea cloth – she likes the way I always lay a 'nice' table. Mrs Howson came to see what she had got and to see the catalogue, and we were sitting happily discussing linen, 'bottom drawers', etc., when there was a ring and I went to the door. A radiant, laughing-eyed woman seized me in a loving hug, saying, 'I've caught you in this time'. It was *Jessie*. I looked at her and couldn't speak. I felt tears brim and fall down my cheeks as I said 'Jessie, my dear – I'd have passed you on the street and not known you'. George was with her. They came in for a few minutes. She had been to get her hair permed. She said 'I'm going to try and repay all your kindness, though I shall never be able to tell you how much your letters and papers meant, even more than the flowers and tit bits. The sister and doctor used to be interested in all the cuttings you sent and we all used to read them, and once the doctor said "Well, it seems the papers *do* still have happy bits of news" – and he bought his wife a Siamese kitten because he said Shan We seemed such a pet.' Mrs Howson is very tender hearted, and Margaret too got weepy. George looked at us all and then at my husband and said in deep disgust, '*Wimmin*', and it made us all laugh. I said 'It's all right for you. You remember this happy-eyed Jessie – we don't.' He shook his head and said 'No, I never saw her like this. I think I'll keep this one instead of the Jessie I used to know. I feel we are going to have such lots of fun together.'

We seemed to laugh and talk nonsense, and a remark of Jessie's made us laugh out loud, as she said seriously 'George said you gave him the most comfort and hope of anyone when one day you "snorted" at him and told him that the only thing wrong with me was that I was *buggered* and you laid down the law about one thing piled on top of another'. Mrs Howson looked a bit startled, but no one knew how worried poor George was that day, or that he had such a deep fear Jessie's mental trouble would mean she would have to be kept in Lancaster for a long time, perhaps years. I'd forgotten what I had said to comfort him, poor dear, but it was certainly an odd way to comfort a man, and I laughed with the rest. She said nothing about giving up her home, and I don't think she will do so. It would be a tragic error. Jessie begged us to go up and see them at Broughton if we can. I've hesitated to call. I don't know the mother very well, and felt I might have intruded, but Jessie was shocked at such an idea. They hurried off to catch the 7.30 train, and soon Margaret and Mrs Howson went and I began to iron, a feeling of such deep happiness in my heart since my Cliff began to walk [*after his war injuries*] with only a slight limp.*

---

* George and Jessie Holme, who moved to Preston in 1953, both lived long lives: he to eighty-eight, she to ninety. According to their daughter Kathleen Emery, whom we met in March 2012, they were devoted to each other, their long marriage was harmonious and strong, and her own upbringing very happy.

CHAPTER SIXTEEN

LOTS TO TALK ABOUT

January–February 1950

While Jessie Holme's struggles ended happily, Will was not so fortunate, and his distress was a frequent and growing concern to his wife. He had always been unwelcoming of company, needy, insecure, lacking in friends and interests, and prone to anxiety, and these tendencies became more pronounced as he entered his sixties. Sometimes he caused Nella no little frustration, at other times much worry. His depressive moods sometimes took centre-stage in her diary. For this and other reasons, 1950 was a year of often intense and volatile emotions.

* * * * * *

'Such a heavy dull day,' Nella wrote on 31 December 1949, 'with the feeling in the air that the old year was actually dying ... Ever since I can remember I had a sadness on me on New Year's Eve. Cliff always teased me about my "Hogmanay Blues".' The next day, the first of the New Year, she and Will visited Aunt Sarah and Sarah's cousin Joe in Spark Bridge and then returned home, to spend the evening alone.

Sunday, 1 January 1950, New Year's Day. The fire soon blazed when poked. I had banked it with slack and coal dust dampened, and I made tea, meat sandwiches (tinned), crushed pineapple and whipped cream, Xmas cakes and mince pies. I wished there had been someone in to share, as we sat by the fire and I stitched at my crazy patch work. I felt the 'blues' I'd missed last night enfold me like a mist, helped no doubt by an article in an American magazine the Atkinsons sent in, speaking of war as *inevitable* after 1951, and hinting at atomic bombs being puerile when compared to the germ bombs Russia was concentrating on. All

my fears and conjectures of before this last one rushed over me. I felt if
I turned suddenly I'd see some of Arthur's friends' faces as they argued
against such a thing as 'too inhuman' etc. I thought of the unrest of
today, the state of affairs in Egypt, hoping if King Farouk did lose his
throne for 'romance', it had as little effect as it had when it happened in
England.* I felt, as I thought of one upset or worry, it brought its fellows
along. I heard my husband ask me something and looked up to see him
waiting for an answer. He was 'thinking how neglected we have let your
parents' grave get – we will have to go up and clean the marble stone
as soon as the weather gets better'. I felt it was the limit, and tuned in
Palm Court, which he had earlier refused as his head ached, and then
we listened to the first instalment of *The Virginians* – sounds promising.

Tuesday, 3 January. Though it still rained heavily I persuaded my
husband to go to the pictures to see *The Hasty Heart. Such* a well acted
picture. It's a long time since we have enjoyed a picture so much. It
had stopped raining, we walked home, and I soon had the fire blazing
warmly, and did cheese and toast. Before we settled down, Mrs Howson
and Steve came in, with the air of staying the evening. I *did* feel so glad.
Then there was a ring, and an old school friend of Cliff's came in, one
I'd never met when Cliff was at home. He is a 'fridge' engineer on a
line of steamers that take frozen meat from Australia and America and
bring it to England, and while in Adelaide had seen Cliff's exhibition
posters the week after it had closed, and read the notices of the 'clever
English sculptor', and tried to track Cliff down in Melbourne without
success, so called for his address so as to find him next trip. We had a
real merry party, laughing and joking. Steve and he soon got yarning.
I opened a tin of Australian chopped ham, and there was rum butter,
chocolate biscuits and Xmas cake, and the table looked like a real party,
and the cats were as delighted as I was – they *are* nice animals – to see

---

* She is referring to Edward VIII's abdication of the throne in 1936 in order to marry
Mrs Wallis Simpson. King Farouk (b. 1920, king from 1936) was notably corrupt and
incompetent, and was overthrown in 1952.

them happily being 'one of us'. Their heads turning as if listening and enjoying everything was comical. Alan was so taken with Shan We, and I begged him to tell Cliff as much as he could of my little cats' funny ways. Shan We blinked understandingly and shared tit bits of chopped ham offered. Alan had to rush off to catch the last bus to take him to Walney but is coming again if he can before he rejoins his ship. Steve said 'Well, we didn't think we were coming to a party when we came across. It *has* been a jolly evening.' I looked at my husband, sitting so quiet, who had refused even to sit at the supper table or eat anything in case it made him have a wakeful night, and sighed. But I *was* so grateful for my happy evening. I feel sometimes as if my face is ceasing to fit me properly, as if it creaks if I laugh. It's not good to get into a deep rut of passive acceptance of sickness of any kind, yet it is so difficult at times.

Wednesday, 4 January. Mrs Salisbury came earlier and didn't stay for lunch. Her eldest boy has started at the Co-op dairies, helping deliver milk – at 34s 6d a week! It's only a put-on till he can find somewhere to serve his time as a joiner or wood worker of some kind, but it means he is in mid day and needs a hot meal. We worked busily, only stopping for a cup of tea and biscuits at 10.30, and I was glad really she wasn't staying for lunch, when the butcher didn't come before lunch, for we managed with a slice of chopped ham fried with an egg. I heated tinned tomato soup and added milk, cooked cabbage and potatoes and heated some raspberry blancmange left from yesterday for my husband. I had a cup of tea.

It was such a nice afternoon and we went out early and got as far as Bowness. Shafts of sunlight fell on fell and hill like magic fingers, making golden patches on the greyness when lighting up faded bracken. Little white capped waves slapped on the shore, and there was a keenness in the air which hinted at snow on high ground. I got some locally made butter toffee, and met an old friend who lives at Greenodd, and she said she did all shopping in Bowness, registered there, and when the weather was bad got her groceries put on the bus. When I went in the front door I found my Co-op quarterly dividend cheque had come.

Coal and milk, cat biscuits and compost maker are about all I get generally, making a total of about £6 I spend each quarter. Lately I've often had to count and recount my housekeeping, feeling sometimes I *must* have lost 10 shillings. There's been Allenbury's Diet, Sanatogen,[†] Sloan's liniment, Disprins,[†] Frugoclone [*possibly a tonic*] bought every week, or when needed, and I've got into the habit of calling in the Co-op chemist's as it's on my way home from the Library. I felt 'No wonder I've felt so hard up at times' when I saw I'd spent over £13 this quarter, though that included extra milk – I always get two pints a day left lately.

I fixed some fillets of plaice and we had just finished tea when the phone rang, and it was long distance. It was Robert Haines, to say he would come this weekend if convenient – arrive off the mid day train from Euston which gets into Barrow about 6.40 – and leave for Leeds on Monday afternoon. I felt so happy he could come. I've only to change the beds – he can have mine and I'll make the small one up in the little front room. All is aired. I'll only need to bake on Friday and we plan to take him out to The Heanes for lunch Saturday if it is fine, and somewhere else on Sunday so he can get a glimpse of the Lakes. I put down the receiver and turned away, and then realised we wouldn't recognise each other unless he sees some resemblance to Cliff – or in odd snaps! I've never even seen a photo with clear enough features; any I have had have been taken at a distance. As I sat down I thought suddenly and with amusement of the time I went to meet a girl Arthur knew – Agnes Schofield from Blackpool. Off my mind galloped on memory lane. I wonder where she is, if still doctors' secretary at the dental clinic, still so dependent on advice from outsiders, always searching for someone 'to love me'. If we could only have as fair and sweet a day – or days – at the weekend as we have had today. Robert could have a nice look round, though I'd have really liked to give him an extra good time. If he doesn't have to return to Australia till March, he may possibly be able to come again. Train fares 'off his schedule', though, might be expensive. I wonder if his grant is a good one from the British Council of Arts.

Friday, 6 January. The train was only five minutes late, and I stood by the exit wondering which of the men walking alone from the train towards me would be Robert. From the end, as the crowd thinned, a slight, rather diffident looking man approached me and with a slight stammer said 'I hope you have not been waiting long in the cold, Mrs Last', as if we had met before! Robert is 35 – odd how Cliff generally has friends about five years older. I wonder if it's the case of the difference in his and Arthur's age. Could be, I suppose. He is extremely likeable and walked round touching or looking at different things, saying 'Cliff so often thinks of home and you. It's his deepest concern at times when he feels a bit down that he cannot pop in and see you, and talk things over. You know I think the chief attraction of Cliff is his love of discussing every and anything. He is so interested in life from every angle.' I sighed as I thought 'No one knows better than I do that attraction possessed by my two sons'. I'm thankful little Peter [*grandson, born June 1948*] shows signs of that same interest. All this 'strong silent men' talk leaves me cold. Any I've met have been too dumb – or two short of interest in things – to be anything else.

During the weekend Nella and Will showed Robert around the Lake District – Kendal, Windermere, Bowness, Ambleside, Hawkshead and Coniston Water. Late on Sunday afternoon they were back at 9 Ilkley Road.

Sunday, 8 January. Robert fits in so well he might be one of the family. He so loves to talk, as we discussed conscientious objectors, Russians, Americans – whom he seems to detest, saying most Australians do! – flying saucers, Australian way of life, the possibility of him living in London, even washing socks to keep them from shrinking – and things like central heating crept in. The day seemed to fly. My husband said it was just like when Arthur used to come home weekends! We settled by the fire, looking over old photos of Cliff and Arthur and a pile of odd snaps and cuttings of the war I'd kept, though tonight I did have a clear-out, feeling many more are for scrapping. I gazed in wonder and a little sadness at some of the earlier war snaps of myself, feeling that these last ten years have drained vitality and humour. Each I handled seemed to bring a train of memories of different little incidents and events and people I'd worked so happily with. Robert had a few chuckles over snaps. He has a few leg pulls for Cliff on his return!

My husband went to bed and Robert and I drew up our chairs. Even for an Australian, he is naïve and boyish for 35, and I had a little sadness as he spoke of future plans as if he was only 18, with golden youth ahead instead of past. He spoke of his fear of the future, whether he should marry, have children in today's chaos when to thinking people so many problems and difficulties beset youth. As I pointed out, they always did to varying degree. I pointed out the quiet leisured peace of *The Forsyte Saga*, which we had discussed as a little cameo of life earlier in the evening. I drew a word picture of the countryside as I'd known it, before motors and planes, and earlier still before trains when Gran was a young bride – earlier still in *Rogue Herries* pack horse and bridle path days. I said 'It was said trains, later motors, would poison the air'. Every generation has its bogey, and fears of the future, but we who have lived through found compensations somewhere, and did live through.

Friday, 13 January. Wherever I've been today there's been little remarks about the loss of the *Truculent*. Barrow people always feel they own a bit of the ships and subs they make. George came in and he had been talking to someone who had grown old in submarine building and had said 'If those lads were in reach of their equipment, they would be up and floating like ducks'. I shivered as I said to George, 'In the dark cold water, no ship near to pick them up, it would only prolong the agony.' Such a dreadful senseless accident, no combat, no 'they died gloriously', as much an accident as if crossing the street and been knocked down by a bus.*

---

* On the evening of 12 January the patrol submarine *Truculent*, which had been built in Barrow and launched in 1942, collided with a Swedish ship in the Thames estuary and sank. Sixty-four men lost their lives. Building submarines was a specialty of Barrow's shipyard.

Saturday, 14 January. The Yard pays wages on Thursday night now. I'd not realised how women's shopping habits had changed, partly with having money to shop on Friday, partly through rations making shopping as such somewhat of a lost art, and again with men folk being at home Saturday. Every now and again there seems an urge by Chamber of Trade to close most if not all shops on Saturday afternoons. I was really surprised to see grocers' and butchers' shops empty of customers, and assistants just standing about. Grocers as well as butchers had geese, turkeys and chicken, their flattened shape showing they had been packed in boxes and in a fridge. While I don't like poultry or meat too fresh, I don't think I'd have liked to buy any this morning unless I'd smelled them thoroughly, and I smiled to myself at the look there would have been on the shopkeeper's face as I sniffed!

Tuesday, 17 January. I got the pantry and kitchenette cupboards cleaned out this morning, and it took me most of the morning. I had cold meat and macaroni pudding to do, and opened a tin of soup and added grated onion and a little Bovril, and cooked frozen peas and potatoes. My husband went down to the doctor's and saw Dr Miller, who is better after his operation. He told my husband the same thing – that his cure is in his own hands. It's what he thinks and does for himself, rather than drugs and potions, but added too he realised how difficult it was to conquer 'nerve' health when one got low.

Thursday, 19 January. I shocked and offended Jessie a little. They had been talking about Priestley's broadcast, and though Jessie is a real Conservative, I could tell Priestley's kindly humble puppy philosophy had affected her. She said 'Don't you like him?' I said 'Ah yes, as a playwright and real kindly man, he has no peer, but he *does* see life through rosy spectacles, which, though cosy, is not realistic nowadays. We could do with lots more like him. They are a good leaven.'* Jessie said 'Sometimes

---

* J. B. Priestley's 'The Labour Plan Works', one of a series of party political broadcasts, was published in *The Listener*, 19 January 1950, pp. 112–13. Priestley did, indeed, profess

you are very cynical. *I* either like people or I don't' and Mrs Atkinson agreed. Mrs Atkinson said a bit crankily 'Now if Mr Last had only been interested in cards we could have played whist and I wouldn't have missed going to the whist drive so much tonight'. I said 'And if he only had wings, he would be able to fly', and joined in the laugh, but thought of what a lot of things he didn't do or want to do!

Saturday, 21 January. It was bitterly cold, but the sun shone, and we went round Coniston Lake. The day had that newly washed crystalline light that Hugh Walpole so loved and described so lovingly of Derwent, Skiddaw and round Keswick. The hills seemed to drowse in veils of soft amethyst to deep sepia shadows. Swale[†] fires nursing under the whin and dead bracken made long plumes of smoke that rose up into the still air like fantastic fir trees, higher than the hills in the background. Age old grey walls were jewelled with emerald topiary[†] from little tufts of green moss, and orange-yellow lichen where the sun rays picked out the colour. Evergreens glistened as if every leaf had been washed and polished separately. Horses' coats shone like burnished metal, and the hill sheep's wool dried in the keen wind and made a little shimmering nimbus round them as they cropped the grass, or lay quietly resting. In sheltered fields fresh hurdles made folds for the expected lambs, in the rude shepherds' huts. The glint of straw could be seen stacked and piles of turnips under rough shelters were ready. I stood by the smooth quiet lake, thinking how Robert would have loved to be with us today. Nothing stirred or broke the perfect stillness. The sun sank lower and brought fresh beauty as its light crimsoned delicate tracery of birch and beech, larch and oaks against the clear blue grey of the sky. The nut trees looked strangely out of place, their fringe of catkins giving them the look of trees in a Japanese print. On the East and quiet side of Coniston Lake there's several well built, stone summer bungalows. A year or two ago a garage was built by the largest one, a telephone installed and a boat

---

political humility and a common-sense outlook. His socialist thinking was not to Nella's taste.

house built for a little outboard boat. Today smoke curled out of the chimney and the place had a generally lived-in look. I wondered what kind of people lived in that lovely peaceful place – perhaps a writer who wove the calm, serene beauty of Brown Howe and the fells into writing, perhaps only a very tired person or persons. With a companion of one's own way of thinking, life could be very pleasant, for books and the wireless could make up for other entertainment.

Friday, 27 January. Cliff sent me *Sons and Lovers* by D. H. Lawrence, and I'm deeply interested though not read much. I felt a bit nowty as I got into the car to career along cold wintry roads with my husband in a black mood when to get him interested was like trying to strike a match on a patch of damp moss. I thought longingly of the fire and my book. We went up the Cumberland coast to Millom, today so bleak and windswept, the hills beyond in grey-black silhouette against the wintry grey sky, the Irish Sea so wild. The tide was going out, leaving a wide band of snowy foam, and the sands were left in glistening swathes where all had frozen as the last wave washed over. No wonder sea gulls seek food inshore, and sit on roofs and chimneys on the lookout for scraps. It's a nice run with switch back hills. It's a bit odd when both of us tend to nerviness that we love flying up and down hills! When we stopped at Millom we had a cup of hot tea before beginning to walk round, so though it was so cold, we didn't feel it as bad as we would have done. I bought a small whistling kettle for 2s 9d – sale price. I paid more for my other before the war, and grieved when I found my husband had taken it for the shop, for on the red hot stove it soon burned through. I plan to be a gypsy this summer if it's at all fine, taking both lunch and tea outdoors whenever possible, either to Walney when warm or to sheltered Coniston Lake. My husband doesn't worry or brood as much outdoors and the fresh air will do him good.

There's a queer semi-junk jeweller's in Millom and I've often seen nice oddments – cut glass, bits of Edwardian or Victorian jewellery, like cameos or carved ivory heads, etc. There was a string of cut crystals – maybe topaz – today, and by their clasp looked good. My husband said

'They look just your type of jewellery. I'd like to buy them if they hadn't been so expensive.' We didn't bother to ask the price, knowing anything unmarked was high priced. The junk around was a guide to what would be asked for good things. As we walked back to the car I wondered why I'd ceased to long for – covet – lovely things as I used to do. Somehow in the war, I got things sorted out, and have never recaptured that 'I'd *love* that' feeling. Pity. It's an added spice to a woman's life if she can shop and think 'I'd get *that* if I had money'. Maybe it's a sign of age!

We were back well within two hours. I built up a good fire and snatched half an hour with my book while my husband covered up the car, put in the lamp and put mats to the bottom of the garage door. He has made such a fuss of this car, with it being new perhaps. I made toast and scrambled eggs. There was cake, bread and butter and honey, and warmth to take ache out of bones. When my bones ache so badly I think of homeless people, especially displaced persons, with no hope. I read the paper but my husband wasn't interested in anything tonight after he had listened half heartedly to Wilfred Pickles at 7 o'clock. I got out my sewing and just before 9 o'clock there was a ring, and it was Alan Boyd. What a friendly lovely lad he is. He was going to a nearby hotel for the Hospital Dance and had said he would drop some cutting of Cliff's through the letter box, but rang to let me see him in his uniform because his mother thought he looked better in it than civvy clothes! He does too, like all men and *no* women, unless they have clock stopping faces and extra good figures, and then it's figures that matter more than femininity. He sat and talked till I reminded him the dance would be well started. He made me laugh as he said a bit ruefully, 'Yes, and I'll *have* to have a drink to get me in the mood to meet my sister's friends and dance for the rest of the evening'. My husband said 'Don't you like dancing, Alan?' and he said 'Yes, it's alright, but nothing beats yarning and listening to folk talk'. I felt he was a kindred spirit.

Monday, 30 January. The wind howled over the chimneys. More snow is on the way. It's a dreadful kind of weather for elections to be held. A bill was put in the door tonight to say we were having a Liberal candidate in Barrow [*a general election was imminent*] – the first for many years. Mrs Howson and I talked of politicking in general. I said 'I think I lean to Liberalism most, perhaps because though my father was a staunch Conservative he had only been so over the Free Trade-Tariff Reform bill and all his people and most of mother's were Liberals'. We had not discussed our political views before, not taking any view of any beyond Labour-Toryism. I was surprised to hear her say 'All mother's brothers and sister are Liberal. Some never voted at all when only Tories put up against Labour.' It set us wondering if it would be the passive Liberal vote coming out for one of their own candidates that would affect this election. I've had a little cynical feeling as I listened to J. B. Priestley and Maurice Webb* that for many waverers and Pollyanna minded ones the *last* speaker, provided he or she insists that 'Everything is ALRIGHT, the worst is over, all our mistakes and spade work finished with, only trust US', will win. No one realises there will be any bills to meet. I've yet to meet anyone with more than a hazy idea that Marshall Aid† will cease, or be paid back. 'America has all the gold. Why *shouldn't* she shell out?' idea.

When I sit thinking, my mind often drifts back to 50, even 55, years, for I've a good memory for details. I'd not a very happy childhood and knew pain and endurance from five years old to about twelve – to be crippled by an accident those days meant effort to walk straight again. Partly through love for me, partly because he had a horror of anything marred, my father spared neither money or effort. All my pleasures were quiet, and the happiest days spent with Gran who in her busy life had little time for sorting out ages. She had the curious attitude of lumping people and animals. Her farm hands were equal to the Squire or her children in some queer alchemy of her own. She never talked down to a

---

* Maurice Webb was a political journalist and broadcaster, a Labour MP and Chairman of the Parliamentary Labour Party. He had spoken on the radio two nights before (published in *The Listener*, 2 February 1950, pp. 201–2), and Nella had described his speech as 'a triumph of wishful thinking mixed with sincere conviction. If things *could* be as rosy and serene as some of the Labour speakers make out.'

little intense girl, who was let see the seamy side of rural life as well as the lighter side. I was always conscious of troubles and strife, 'sins' in the way of unexpected babies, shortage of money, bad luck, and all the real life of the countryside. My father always talked and talked of everything. I've sat mouse quiet and forgotten while the questions and problems of that far off day were discussed and 'settled'. I try and search faithfully so as to avoid that rosy distortion that time brings to people who are lonely and growing old. There was poverty, misery, drunkenness, wife beating, lads running off to sea, dirt, more sickness – or was there now? – little money, such a lot that needed 'evoluting'. BUT, there was kindliness in need, laughter, that joy in scraping and scrounging for holidays you don't seem to get from holidays with pay to go to a noisy Holiday Camp as there was from a week in the country 'keeping yourself', only paying for rooms and attendance. People moved slower. There was more time for family life and less outside distraction. We've got a Health Scheme [*the NHS*], and less time for doctors to find out what's wrong with you.

Mrs Howson and I meandered slowly amongst her memories – at 42, of course, she is a decade behind mine. She began this 'Where has all the ____ gone?' by grieving about some sixth form boys she knew who had been found playing for money in the Grammar School Prefects' room, and the Head had told them 'He couldn't recommend them to the university as he intended'. We wondered exactly what he meant, and if that lack of recommendation would carry weight.* She always holds Cliff up as a shining light, neither knowing or understanding the problems and worry I had over that Arab† of a lad. She said in answer to a remark of mine 'Boys *had* to be boys' – 'Your Cliff would never have done such a thing'. I said 'Oh yes he would, *and* any darn fool monkey shine going, if he had had time. But my two always seemed to have so much they liked to do they never got round to antics like that, and as

---

* Norman Raby, one of these boys, doubted in 2011 that the headmaster said or would have said this. A photo of the 'Poker Club', taken shortly after they were caught, appears as Plates, p. 6. Mr Raby recalled that 'in some ways we were a little proud of our notoriety'.

girls as well as boys thronged the house, practising for plays, or talking their heads off on all subjects, girls were never that "mystery" that made for furtive conjectures and daft motives like Dennis Veal' – another headache for the Head when he found a passionate love letter Dennis had written to a girl of 15 – he is 17. We wondered if there was a deep underlying meaning about idle hands!

My husband sat back in his chair, never joining in. Mrs Howson said 'How we gabble Mr Last. You must be tired of listening.' He said in a tone of self pity 'Ah, I like it. I wish Mrs Last would be as bright and gay with me.' I said 'No monologue is as interesting as a duet. You have to have *some* response you know.' But he only looked at me blankly, in a way that gave me a little sick feeling deep down inside, as I thought how more and more he resembled poor Mother. I try in vain to find out what deep fears he has to cause such dreadful nightmares. I wish he could go to one of those clever psychiatrists seen on the screen who seem to easily bring such fears to the surface and make them lose their terror. Perhaps they only exist on the screen anyway! The trouble lies so deep it's been there since I ever knew him – when he was only 19. I thought his extreme shyness so attractive, so different. I'd never known what it meant to be shy or out of place. I was so gay and lively, so full of life and fun. That's what attracted him – and what to him was such an attraction – I could 'stand up anywhere and recite or tell jokes'. Odd he should so quickly think differently, should think I should keep all and any gaiety for him alone, to show such boredom and aversion to going amongst people as soon as we were married. If I'd not been so young and inexperienced I could have seen the danger signals. If I'd been stronger minded and made a firm stand, perhaps then he would have grown to like company.

Tuesday, 31 January. I feel so down tonight. My husband had a wild nightmare – huge men with long shining swords were chasing him along deserted streets where no one appeared from whom help could be expected, and he had 'run and run till I dropped'. He looked ghastly, and complained of feeling as if his head had been kicked. I tidied round quietly while he lay back in his chair, and then wrote two letters while he had a nap ... [*His doctor had advised him to retire.*] We sat and talked. I said 'Are you worrying about Mother? Do you dread the big change if you really did retire? You know how against change of any kind you have always been. Could it be that?' I pointed out how, when I'd really got on my top note, Harry had begun to take more on as regards Mother, and made the two daughters do the same, and it had made a great change. I said '*I'll* settle the business, and if I cannot, Arthur will come over and do it. Say the word and go to bed if you like for a week. We will see to all.' I keep Mother out of his way, feeling sometimes the poor dear has a real horror of her and her ways, as if he fears his loss of concentration and memory will worsen and he will grow like her in every way. I wondered if that could be his fear. I scolded gently and pointed out our money would last as long as we were likely to live, that he hadn't any fear I'd resent any decision. I talked gently and persuasively about the future, though I feel I won't coax him to give up entirely. It's a matter he must finally decide for himself. If I did persuade him and he one day wished he hadn't, I know so well how he would blame me, and there would be nothing could be done about it. I said jokingly 'If I win that Irish Sweep I'd whisk you off on a long sea voyage', and he half smiled as he said 'You could do whatever you liked. I'd not disagree.' ...

I felt desperate with worry as I saw how old and ill he was looking. The doctor has changed his medicine again, saying 'You will have to have sounder sleep'. I sat in the fire light, my little Shan We on my lap, and felt so worried, so alone, and so utterly helpless. I made tea when he woke, feeling refreshed. I'd minced the last of the cold meat and we had mint jelly to it, and bread and butter, and there was honey and cake. I tried so desperately hard to talk things over, recalling the brooding shut-in look the boys had had sometimes when things went wrong with their world, how it cleared as little grievances were brought out and talked over, things I'd no 'touch' with, and was no help in whatsoever. I've heard them say 'Things look different when you talk about them', as if the mere fact of putting things into words made them real enough to face – and fight. It's so difficult to reach my husband – so impossible. Any subject, person, problem, viewpoint, angle, etc. he feels upsets him and he says 'Don't talk about *that*' or 'I don't want to see so and so' – it or they 'upset me'.

I begin thinking and when I go to bed all comes back to me. With the boys under the circumstances we could have made up the fire and drank tea and talked for hours, but we would have found a solution, whether only suffering a thing or clearing it completely away. I stitched and stitched as my mind whirled in wild montage of ideas and plans. If he only had friends – but he told his brother his visits and phone calls upset him. Granted Harry wanted to talk over Mother and her affairs at the time, and Nellie is one of those feather heads who open their mouths and let every passing thought out – like 'Ah dear, you *do* look ill, and how like Mother you are growing' etc. etc. If he could be told by the doctor 'You *must* have a holiday at a Convalescent Home, by yourself', or if he had ever been on such friendly term with the boys as to make me feel he could go to Arthur's for a holiday – many men could find joy in little Peter, and *want* to see something of the pet – or if he would write to them and look forward to the postman coming. I felt 'If only winter was over and we could go out every day – if I could get him interested in the garden'. I had a vision of every day of winter, before warmer days came. Sometimes when things looked dim the boys and I had a kind of fairy story – a 'If I had £1,000 to spend' phantasy.

Wednesday, 1 February. My husband looked so white and strained and said he had slept badly. After lunch and I had washed up and we had settled by the fire, I really pitched into him. I began by asking him 'What are you so afraid of? Your wild dreams show a deep hidden fear that is sapping your strength. *Try* and talk to me dear. I'm sure I could help you if you would let me. You know what I once told Arthur when I'd helped him out of what he thought a scrape and he had said "You are a pal to understand". I shocked you when I said "It's what mothers are for. And remember whatever you did it would be the same – if you killed anyone, I'd help bury him." You didn't see it was a joking remark that was one meant to turn aside Arthur's concern and make him laugh, but I meant it in truth. I'd do *anything* to help you.'

When he said 'There's nothing I can tell you – I don't feel more worried than usual', I had that queer clear feeling in my head as I have when I get on my top note and feel facts that have puzzled me grow clear. I said 'Well, I'll tell you, you have always been a man to so dread change. I couldn't move a picture, discard outdated oddments of furniture. You never liked a pair of curtains in my remembrance till they were nearly worn out, and look how you made things so unpleasant when I altered the table and settee. You realise even what interest you take in the business is too much, but you are so afraid of taking the plunge and selling up, and making the rest of the family responsible for Mother. Tell me, don't you think *that* could be your bogey?' He thought for awhile and he had to admit it 'might be'. I said 'Well, search your mind and find out – and then quit worrying. I bet I'd settle things in a week, and if *I* couldn't, Arthur would help, and you wouldn't have the slightest worry. And remember,' I said warningly, 'things will have to be settled if you don't stop having these nightmares. I don't need Dr Miller or anyone else to tell me.' He looked so piteously at me I could have wept. I went on 'We have only ourselves to think of. Our money will last, and you know that I'm adaptable enough to take what comes, country cottage or anything else.' He nodded, and I changed the subject, and read him bits out of the paper. I felt I sighed as I looked for bits with no 'worry', what with elections, hydrogen bombs and 'snow and ice in most roads' and the like, there wasn't much cheerful ...

I feel sure I've found his hidden terror that hounds him in nightmares, shocking his whole nervous system. I recalled when Arthur would be about 14 and Cliff 9 and he had a bad bout of sciatica and had to go to Buxton for treatment – nine weeks that time. We seemed to have such a run of bad luck. I'd not had any painting or papering done for some years. I longed to be able to do. We heard of a very clever woman paper hanger, and after we had talked over ways and means we decided *if* we could do it out of what bit of money I felt I dare spend, we would begin. Our house had never had one thing destroyed or its position moved. After spring cleaning, every picture and ornament had to go back in exactly the same position, for dear peace's sake. How we planned and schemed, lived on herrings, cheese, vegetables and porridge, never spent money on any amusement, selling piles of oddments we felt wouldn't fit in our new décor, even clothes and some bits of jewellery. We painted every scrap ourselves. What paint was not renewed had a coat of flat varnish. The walls were plain cream – no doll eyed frieze or 'panelling'. We walked round the house before my husband was coming home and felt in ecstasy.

I'd not then realised how deep rooted was his aversion to change, that it was so vital a part of his make up. He got out of the taxi looking so fit and well. His tea was ready and we left the first remark to him. We had written every day and told him how busy we were, but I don't think he could picture such a change. He looked round the dining room in silence, went upstairs, and came down again, still without a word. I felt vexed to see the bright glow fade from my two boys' faces. They had worked so hard, planned and schemed and been so delighted with the result. We went to bed. My husband was restless and in the morning had a temperature. I sent word to the doctor he had come home, but wasn't so well, and I'd like him to call. When he did he asked if my husband had had a shock of any kind, and I said I didn't know. He had had little to say of his journey home. He was ill for about a week, and I began to see what the shock was, and though the doctor laughed and said 'Nonsense' I was convinced I was right. Beyond a distant 'You have altered my home so much I don't feel it *is* my home', he never referred to the change, and when friends came in and said 'How busy you must have been – everything is lovely' or words to that effect, he never answered!

Thursday, 2 February. When my husband came in I felt very glad I'd talked to him yesterday. The accountant wanted to see him about 'fast drifting into liquidation if you have another year like this'. I've known that with one thing and another he wasn't paying his way, but I'd not realised quite the position. The accountant, a pleasant friendly man who has done the books of the shop and also Harry's chemist shop for years, advised him to make up his mind to 'lock the door on it all, pay off the men as soon as existing jobs are through and all worked up, and give all a miss for about a year'. Arthur advised the very same thing but my husband dismissed such a wild impractical suggestion. Now it looks as if he will decide to give up, not selling up till he feels well enough to go into things. I felt things were rushing away with me. I've so often pleaded with him. It took a real top note of mine to get him into a reasonable enough frame of mind to agree to the accountant's suggestion, and not make it a shock!

Friday, 3 February. We settled by the fire. I read all and any bits to interest my husband, both in the papers and a *Woman's Weekly* Mrs Howson left, and then at 7 o'clock I so gladly turned on to Wilfred Pickles – that man often feels a personal friend lately. I felt so very strung up, so little would have shattered the calmness on which my husband's very well being depends nowadays. I felt as if nothing could have cheered me, my husband looked so despondent and down. Then the elephant keeper 'had a go', and in a perfectly serious voice, answering Wilfred's 'Why do elephants marching along a street hold on to each other's tails?' said 'It keeps them decent'! not pausing to realise he meant decent in the Northern Irish idiom meaning 'tidy'. We laughed and laughed. And the poor woman's account of the abscess on her tail end, and her evacuation from a hospital in the blitz in a blanket, with a 'gas mask and some papers', struck us as funnier than the most comic things we had heard for a long, long time. As I picked up my sewing and feeling as if I'd had a big glass of champagne or something, I thought 'Black bitter luck follow anyone who ever alters *Have a Go* in the very least detail. It's got something to last as long as the BBC does. Wilfred Pickles has a 'spark' of something. Tommy Handley had it, and amongst the very few who have it are Gladys Young, Freddie Grisewood – yes, and Stewart Macpherson. In such widely different personalities, I wonder if it's some very personal streak of their very own they give into the microphone. A few others have it in different, sometimes fleeting, degrees. It's a great asset.*

---

* Wilfred Pickles (b. 1904) was a celebrated entertainer and radio personality from

Saturday, 4 February. The birds have got their mating notes very early. We used to say when I was a child, they began courting on the 14th of February. I didn't feel well. My wretched bones nearly got the mastery of me. I felt a bit better after breakfast, and decided to clean the insides of the windows. The clear sunshine made them look cloudy with smoke and steam from cooking. I was in the lounge and my eyes fell on a little carved coconut wood elephant. I felt chuckles begin in my throat and a vision of five or six elephants swinging down the Strand, with their ponderous yet 'mincing' tread, so smug and confident in their 'decent' appearance as trunks gripped tails! My husband put his head round the door and said 'What are you laughing about?' and I said 'Decent elephants' and he laughed too.

Monday, 6 February. I got nice fillets of plaice for tea, my husband's favourite fish, and tea was soon ready. He looked a little brighter, but when I suggested taking my raffle tickets in to Mrs Atkinson's to see a few, he said '*I'll* buy two and you can see her tomorrow surely'. In his poor sick mind I often wonder what I stand for exactly – some kind of anchorage and security? In his wildest most terrifying dreams, he says 'And then I heard your voice' or 'You reached down and caught hold of me with your firm warm hand' or even 'You smiled at the great big man and he put the huge sword back in its sheath with a loud rattle and we just walked away'. Once he made me laugh loudly and long as he told a long rigmarole of a fearsome beast with, presumably, more than its share of heads and legs. He said 'You *were* so cross. You said "The devil toast you. Why cannot you drink a saucer of milk when there's nothing else? Poor old Murphy likes milk."' And he went on 'You patted the beast as if it *was* Shan We, and it followed you round a corner of the road'.

Yorkshire. This edition of *Have a Go* had been first broadcast on the Light Programme on 1 February and repeated in the North Region on 3 February. According to Erin O'Neill of the BBC Written Archives Centre in Reading, there is no surviving script, probably because the programme was originally broadcast live – from London Zoo, which accounts for the joke about elephants.

I got out my crazy patchwork. I thought it had been my own idea to stitch and stitch, after blending colours that in themselves were a pleasure. Tonight I felt the idea had been put into my mind as a little indirect answer to my ever repeated plea for 'All Lovely Things', as my Gran called patience and kindness, pity, courage, etc. Now as my mind clearly tells a little rosary, I find my prayer short and ever shorter – kindness and courage so much more important than anything else – and health of mind and body to keep on. I looked at the brightly burning fire and my little cats. I'd quarrel with anyone who said cats don't think. Mine do much more. They see into my sad and often so lonely mind and show *they* understand. Old Murphy will rear his big kind head out of the tight ball he has made of himself and with a queer highly pitched purr that is almost a word come to lie on my foot. My Shan We is my shadow, leaving the warmth of the fire any time to seek me if I go upstairs, his anxious face pressed against the window frame if I'm sweeping outside.

Monday, 13 February. Ulverston always seems as familiar as Barrow, which was really my home town. I'd gladly go and live in Greenodd or Davy Bridge, about three miles away, if we could find a cottage – it would have to be for sale. We were coming home and my husband said 'You're miles away again. What *are* you thinking?' I said 'The bungalow of Lakeland stone, with the room in the roof, the long living room with wide windows each end, central heating, the walls and paths of well laid stone, and so on and so on, that I'd plan and have built if I won the Irish Sweep.' He said 'What about your plan for Australia – going there?' I fell into another train of thought. I've always such an aversion to meddle with the boys, or make them feel I would cling, or interfere, perhaps because I've always had someone wanting to change me, from the days I realised my dark brown hair and eyes and excessive vitality when small were contrasted always with the child of mother's first marriage – to my total disadvantage. She had been blue eyed and lily fair, quiet and gentle always. I always felt too as I grew older I shared the place with my father in mother's mind and heart – somehow we were interlopers. Her life really ended before the honeymoon days were over, before she realised they *would* end. In the 10½ years since Cliff left home, he has grown and developed. I've grown so much older and so desperately tired. He, I know, pictures me as I used to be – ready for anything, grave or gay. I'd be a great disappointment to him now. I don't feel there would be a place in his gay vivid life for anyone who felt so depleted of all vitality. I shrugged off my thoughts impatiently. They impinged on the new philosophy in which I rigidly schooled myself – to take every day as it comes, and when things do get on top of me, count my many blessings again and again, like a rosary.

Thursday, 16 February. My husband was in a queer mood. He said 'When you ever had your fortune told, did anyone tell you I'd have to retire early?' I said 'No, I don't think so'. He said 'Well, *try* and think. You have such a marvellous memory for conversations that took place years ago.' I said 'Well, I cannot recall anything remotely like "retirement".' I added 'Remember I was told I'd not end my days in the home I'd just moved into?' – looks as if that country cottage about which we talk may be a fact! He went on 'As soon as the weather is better we will go to Morecambe – you must go and have your hand read'. I shook my head firmly as I said 'NO. I put away all and any little "gift" of my own for fortune telling when it began to worry and upset me, and as for having my hand read, I say what I said last summer – "I don't want to look ahead – much better to take each day and each problem as it comes".' Then he wanted my 'honest opinion' of his health, his prospects of recovery, etc., as if I was a doctor and a specialist. I told him he was absurd if he thought I knew more than Dr Miller. Poor dear, he looked so sadly at me as he said 'But you *do*. If I'd listened to half your advice and what I called "nagging", I'd never have gone on and on till I collapsed. I'd never have grown in on myself as I have done.' There seemed so little to say. I felt so limp and tired myself. I could only say quietly 'We will feel brighter when the spring comes. I wish often we could pack up and go to Australia and end our days in sunshine.'

Saturday, 18 February. It was sunny. We went out in the car, first to

contact the secretary of the master builder who is going to try to get
Gilbert, the apprentice, somewhere to finish off his apprenticeship.
Then we got as far as Bowness, for we had set off early. The election
apathy seems general. I thought of pre-war years as we went past little
villages and groups of cottages and saw little or no signs of posters –
except biggest ones on hoardings or walls, with notices of meetings in
school rooms or village halls. I smiled to recall the real feuds elections
used to cause, when every window showed a rosette of Party colours
on the curtains, if not a photo of the favoured candidate, when Liberal
yellow and Conservative blue ribbons were worn by every woman and
small ribbon rosettes were flaunted on every coat lapel by the men. I fell
into a long train of thought, a montage of Boer war cum elections cum
First War recollections. I thought wryly 'We all seem to have just so
much vitality and enthusiasm. Once it's spent it's gone.' But I realised I
spoke for only my own generation. It didn't explain the apathy of youth.
We all march to the sound of different drummers and music alters from
one generation to another, even heard on the wireless. Twenty years ago
I knew a thinking old man who bemoaned 'We are evoluting too fast
and "soon ripen, soon rot" you know'. I wondered what he would have
thought of the ever increasing tempo of life and discovery today.

Sunday, 19 February. If I had been in reach of Cliff today, I'd have raised
blisters on him with my tongue. [*He was pursuing a career as a sculptor in Australia.*] *What* a day I've had. Yesterday some papers came,
including an *Australian Digest*. In it was quite a good interview but it
was very journalese. Cliff had warned us about the 'smoky Lancashire
town' mentioned as the place where he was brought up. I felt annoyed
myself at the way Cliff was referred to as having 'hard working parents'
who presumably had no patience with Cliff wanting to be a sculptor,
and when it referred to my husband as a 'working man'. Nor did it
mention he had been in the Navy in the First World War – and that
was why we happened to be in the New Forest near Southampton – or
the fact he was a businessman doing his own works *and* that Cliff had
gone into it against every scrap of advice. I felt thoroughly annoyed

with the slipshod, quite inaccurate write-up – whereby my father had been a wood carver on sailing ships! I thought of the quiet shy uncle, my accountant father's brother, whose murals and panels had decorated ships of the *Aquitania*'s age! My husband had evidently worked up a real upset to his nerves when he had gone to bed, and had one of his bad turns in the night and was shaky and ill till noon, and nothing I could say in excuse or explanation of 'anything to fill up' would calm him. He was quite bitter towards Cliff and his 'lies', as if Cliff would have been so misleading, and as I was daft and rash enough to say 'unless he has been a bit tight'. Then the band *did* play. I'd not felt too good myself when I rose, and his mood so upset me I was really ill, which pulled him together as nothing else would have done, when I felt faint and had to lie down, after having brandy. I pulled myself together and began to make lunch, knowing that however he felt my husband could eat, and needed, a good meal ...

Little remarks [*later that day*] showed how hurt and resentful he still felt. I said 'You are taking it too seriously. Cliff was careless and the journalist wanted to make it a poor-English-boy-with-no-chance-at-home doing so remarkably well in Australia'. I thought of the discords there *had* been between him and Cliff, the years their opposite warring natures had nearly killed me, as I was first torn one way, then the other. I'll see before any newsprint from Australia is read aloud. I felt very little would have made me cry till I just couldn't cry. Little worries piled up like a snowball and bowled me over. Not even the real anger and annoyance I felt for Cliff's silly heedless way, and not seeing an interviewer had sensible facts on which to build, could spur me out of my weepy fit, by Gad, though if I could have had that lad alone for ten minutes I'd have felt better. It was one of the times that called for a top note, and I'd have flayed him with my tongue. My husband kept bursting out into remarks that showed how bitter he felt. He said after staring in the fire 'Put the idea out of your head I'd ever go to Australia, even for a holiday. *I've* no notion to appear as "hard working, non-understanding of a lad who wanted to be an artist", out of an industrial Lancashire town "where black smoke hid the blue skies" anyway. Where *is* such a town? Remember when Arthur was at Wigan and we used to go and see him. Remember the nice shops and the Standish Park.' Then there was a pause, and Palm Court music filled the room – the aerial has been partly repaired and reception's good at the moment.

Then another outburst. 'When I think of the way Cliff overruled and fought you when you were so ill after your last operation, when the doctors stressed you had to have no worry and your heart was so bad, and how he insisted on leaving the Grammar School and coming into my business. When I think of how quickly he saw his mistake and was so wildly discontented, when I think of how patient you always were – "no encouragement from the working man, his father, who had no patience with boyish efforts to carve and model"', and so on and so on, till I began to dread he would have another bad attack of nerves. He said 'The trouble with you is that you always gave way to people, always tried to see *their* point of view. You should have taken a stick to that lad more.' As I pointed out, any slappings and correcting always *did* come from me. A very little more and I felt I'd be telling him of all his omissions as a father, as the boys grew up.

I shook with nerves, and butterflies fluttered so busily in my tummy I began to feel deathly sick, and I went upstairs to undress, thinking I'd get washed and come down in my dressing gown to make supper. Instead I was so sick I had to crawl into bed. I slept for nearly an hour and was wakened by my husband with a beaker of milk food, and he said 'I've fed the cats and laid the breakfast table and there's nothing for you to go downstairs for again'. He looked so scared as he sat on the side of the bed, and he didn't say any more about that darned interview of Cliff's. Earlier in the day I'd written a 6d airmail, read it and tore it up. Then I wrote another, rather coldly mentioning that 'No doubt your *Digest* article makes good reading – and publicity – for Australia, but people in Barrow reading it, knowing our families so well, would no doubt wonder if *all* the article was a distortion, and your efforts and success doubted. I prefer something a little less journalese that I *can* proudly show round, and I understand Daddy's feeling of resentment at being described as a "Lancashire working man".' And I finished my letter in my usual gossipy way, with none of the sharpness of the first letter, but knowing Cliff, I know he would read between the lines!

Two days later Nella and Will were sunning themselves near the breakwater in Walney, and she made 'a joking remark' about winning 'the Sweep' and visiting Australia. This 'brought tight lips and a quiet sneer as he said "We mustn't forget our clogs", which made me long intensely for the chance to tell Cliff just how deeply he had hurt and annoyed us by his cheap journalese interview.'

The Australian article that Nella and Will had read was by Geoff Waye, 'A Place in the Sun', *Life Digest* (Melbourne), January 1950, pp. 25–7. It was probably the following passage (p. 25) about Cliff that was most upsetting: 'He worked for his father, but should a piece of putty or a strip of wood come his way, his fingers fashioned it into little figures of grace and flowing lines. But the son of a working man was not intended for such time-wasting foolishness and his talents were not encouraged.' (This Australian also wrote of the Last family living in 'Lancashire, where the smoke from the mills filled the skies', so he was unaware that Barrow was not a mill town.) Some of the dismissive views on Cliff's English background that his parents disliked are reasserted in the introduction to Max Dimmack, *Clifford Last* (Melbourne: The Hawthorn Press, 1972). Cliff, according to this author, who had known him since his arrival in Australia in 1947, was 'frustrated by his well-intentioned but ill-informed parents who borrowed from the local public library books containing reproductions of the works of the old masters which they encouraged Last to try to copy in crayons and water-colours' (p. 6). Cliff was portrayed by both these commentators as unfulfilled in his early years and misunderstood by his family.

Monday, 20 February. My husband went to the doctor's and came home very downcast. He said 'The doctor doesn't think I'm improving as I should. He asked if I was a Mason or member of any club through which I could go to a Convalescent Home.' I felt tired and out of joint. I said snootily 'Didn't you tell him that you thought paying into *any* kind of insurance for the future was a waste of money?'* I said 'You could go to

---

* Later that week Mrs Higham was visiting, and she 'was really shocked when he went on

Belfast. Edith asked us to go for a holiday when all is settled. You could even go to Australia if you only would. A sea voyage would perhaps set you up – as Mr Richardson set off on his own.' Perhaps because I felt tired I felt less patience. I thought of something I once read, 'In life there's no rewards, and no revenges, just consequences' ...

We had our first canvassers tonight, one Labour, one Liberal. My husband went to the door for the first one and told the Labour canvasser 'As a business man, it's not policy to discuss elections'. I went the second time and recognised an acquaintance with whom I'd often talked of Liberalism (then almost extinct) versus Conservatism. He said 'I'm sure *you* will give us a chance. Your views were more for us, even when you were Chair of Central Ward.' I said 'I'm anti-Socialist, putting my country before party politics, and regard Megan Lloyd's bid for power as traitorous.* Any Liberal who loves his country would vote Conservative – and I am not one you know, so cannot understand why you think I should vote that way.' My husband wasn't suited† because I'd 'spoken so plainly'. I said 'Hell's blue light. I've walked too many miles and knocked at too many doors, canvassing at General Elections, not to prefer a straight answer to a shilly shally statement, and one that showed plainly enough where your vote *wouldn't* be given.'

Wednesday, 22 February. We settled down again, talking of past elections. Once a candidate was disqualified, for buying pies for all his helpers – the opponent built up a case against him – and tonight my husband said 'Remember Mrs Marsh. She was the girl who started it all by a chance remark, and the result hung on her evidence. She had been the girl who carried the pies from the bake house.' I remember her as an old busy body till the day she died at 76! Odd how things lie quiet in your mind and

---

to tell her he had "never believed in any kind of insurance", and she learned that I'd have *nothing* from any source if he died' (23 February 1950).
* Megan Lloyd George (1902–1966), daughter of David Lloyd George and a Liberal MP from 1929 to 1951 – she later joined the Labour Party – championed radical causes in her party, whereas other Liberals were moving, or had already moved, to support Conservative positions, a trend that Nella approved of.

then pop up like a Jack in the box. I began to tell of the first Election I could remember, when I would be nearly six years old. I'd had the accident that was to make me lame for so long, and my father insisted we move from an outlying fishing village, where we had moved when I was only three months old, so I could have treatment. Nothing ever daunted my gay spirits when I was young, and I was a great novelty in a Bamboo rickshaw affair of a go-cart, and older children would always take me along. Mother, so prim and proper, would inspect them and give them strict instructions and then off we would go, generally towards the docks where the ships were such an interest. I don't suppose my mother gave the election a thought, beyond voting,* though bands of children marched with placards, yelling slogans and singing words fitted to well known songs. I had a marvellous time, rattled over rough roads, my go-cart smothered in blue streamers and bunting. I've an idea children must only have had to ask to get red, white and blue rosettes, cockades, placards to carry at the ends of sticks, etc. I ate bits of food from paper bags and newspaper, sang till I was hoarse, bewildered and delighted by all the goings-on of town life, and really frightened when a policeman took me to the police station where mother and Aunt Eliza frantically welcomed me and my father came in looking relieved. I'd been 'officially lost, a poor little crippled child, who knows what can have happened?' – for about eight hours. As my husband laughed at my first election and the little escapade, I thought with surprise 'Why, that was one of the happiest days I had? What a strange elusive thing "happiness" is, to be sure.'

My final bet for the election result is pretty much how I thought at first – a return of Labour with a small majority, with Liberals and Conservatives in enough opposition if they combine to curb them. Personally I hope it's like that. They *should* face consequences of all their 'leap before you look' actions, and though at times a balanced Parliament would no doubt be a stalemate, no fresh schemes of Nationalization could be made, and existing ones would be made to run more economically.

---

* In fact, women did not at that time have the vote, except in some local elections.

In the general election on the 23rd, Labour won Barrow and retained an overall parliamentary majority, though just barely.

Friday, 24 February. I've *blessed* the election turmoil of these two days and when results began to come in and the local *Mail* was delivered, my husband found even more interest.* We had cheese and watercress, toasted raisin buns and chocolate sandwich and then had the wireless on all evening. We once helped at a local election where a fiercely contested seat had to have four recounts before the winning candidate was announced, so we knew a little of the feverish uncertainty that there would be in some places. When I heard that at one time the Conservatives were even and then more Labour victories came along, I thought of a prophecy by Naylor the astrologist I'd read after the last election – that Mr Churchill wasn't destined to lead the Conservatives back to power. He is the most wonderful, the most inspiring leader any country has known, but I've always a sneaking remembrance of Mrs Waite and her utter dominance at Hospital Supply. She towered above us all by her work in the First World War, and could see little good in any of us. Yet it was a *good* committee – each of us had 'something' – which, till the worms turned, was useless.** I couldn't help but wonder if there *were* strong men in the Conservative Party who, given their head, could lead. I wasn't surprised at Labour losing some seats and the Conservatives gaining, but not as much see-saw, or the Liberals losing so many deposits. What troubles me is that *no* one will do any good, and just when so much outside interest and endeavour is needed, bold ventures and ideas so essential, it looks as if it will be stalemate, the Socialists proposing and the rest saying NO. I wonder if there will be another election soon. One thing, there could never be any coalition. There's too wide a gulf

---

* 'This interest he has taken in the election has been a pleasure to both of us', she wrote the next day. 'I wish something else would come along.'

** She means that the somewhat meek and reticent committee members, who had been pushed around by the domineering Mrs Waite, retaliated by being active, assertive and effective.

now between Socialists and the rest. I listened to Mr Churchill's brave but broken voice with a pity so deep I began to cry bitterly. I don't cry easily, or often. My husband said 'Now fancy you upsetting yourself so over so small a thing'. But somehow that brave gallant old voice got tangled up with my own worries and fears. I couldn't have separated them as I cried till I felt sick.

Monday, 27 February. Aunt Sarah *does* miss her little cat. It was such a clean, faithful little thing, and died as it had lived, at her bedside on its mat, peacefully and cleanly. She says she is too old to have another. I could see today she was upset because a picture had fallen from where it hung over her bedroom fireplace and broken two treasured old china figures. She said 'Are *you* superstitious about pictures falling? Your mother and mine were, you know.' I said I'd never had any experience of falling pictures, but a magpie on the lawn made me feel really ill, though in the country I never bothered. She nodded as she looked in the fire. I felt sorry for her – till her next remark sent my lips twitching. She shook her head sadly and said 'You know, Joe has never been *really* strong. That's why he never married and I promised his mother to always look after him.' (He is her cousin.) As Joe must be about 80 to her 85, I thought there was little fear of him being cut off in his prime! ...

Mrs Howson brought Cliff's papers across and stayed awhile and her first words were 'Well, what did the doctor say today?' He began about the Convalescent Home proposal. Our eyes met. I knew she wondered, like I did, if he *would* go when the time came. He used to go to Buxton Hospital for six to nine weeks at a time, but under great protest. He hates things more nowadays that in any way upsets his routine. Mrs Howson looked curiously at me and said 'What will *you* do with yourself?' I had a passing idea I'd have had a little holiday in Belfast. I so long to see little Pete and feel a change would do me more good than a tonic. Then another thought had crossed my mind – of doing all the Spring cleaning, and having the back bedroom papered – the man said he would come soon after Xmas – and of having lazy afternoons after a busy morning, relaxed on the settee with a book, and no reading aloud.

Luckily I didn't mention going to Ireland, for my husband said quickly 'Ah, Nell can have a good rest. I'll soon be back and she will have to write *lots* of letters to me, like she used to do when I was at Buxton. She wrote every day and told me all she had been doing.' I sniffed as I said to Mrs Howson 'So, if you see a cheap line in chastity girdles, let me know'. He wondered why we both set off laughing. He said 'You've just got new corsets. What do you want another girdle for?' Which made Mrs Howson laugh till the tears ran down her face. She wiped them away, powdered her nose, and said 'You *are* a pet Mr Last'.

CHAPTER SEVENTEEN

PLEASURES AND PERTURBATIONS

May–December 1950

Wednesday, 3 May. We decided to go tonight to the Coliseum, mainly to see Albert Modley's brother Allen, who was a comedian – very good too and a well balanced show [*billed as 'Strippingly Saucy'*]. I often think I must have a queer kink – the turn that interested me above all others was judged by most standards revolting! A supple limbed man with a toupee, but with the rest of his hair long, and with unmistakable air of perversion, did little more than 'dress the stage' and join in generally. Then came his scene – two Chinese immobile opening curtains, a pallet bed piled with cushions on the floor, in a corner a table with a life size silver idol with contorted limbs, silver mask with stiff upstanding spirals of hair. The curtains parted. A golden haired girl came through and was helped off with a gorgeous fur coat, and led to the divan where she was given an opium pipe and settled herself to sleep and dream. The idol quivered into life and stepped down. His supple silver body only had a G-string with silver fringe. Few realised the utter perfection of his writhing as his arms wove bonelessly in what looked like a true altar dance. His body had lost the perfect sinuousness of adolescence needed for perfect interpretation. The music was marvellous and puzzled me at first as it whispered and throbbed with the true temple beat – a gramophone record of course. I heard a man behind say 'You see a lot of this kind of thing in India, you know, but generally in back street shows'. The dreamer on the pallet bed tossed and moaned. The 'idol' with the perfectly masked face – like a real idol, so impassive, sexless, ageless – bent over her, and then sprang silently back onto the table as she stirred to consciousness. The attendants brought her coat and firmly led her to the curtains, which parted. She went through. They fell in silent folds. The 'Chinese' attendants tucked their hands in their sleeves and bowed their heads slightly. The spotlight flickered on the immobile silver idol, and the curtain fell quickly as the music died. A real gem of production, timing and performance. I suppose it *was* revolting. It was perhaps a 'wonder it had been let escape the censor's eye'. The half whispers round showed that people recognised what the man was by inclination if not an 'accident' of birth, but somehow the perfection lifted it above all else for me. Allen Modley is good. Pity he models his toothless grimaces on Norman Evans, and his witless type of humour – 'gormless'[†] is the Yorkshire word – on his brother Albert.[*]

Thursday, 4 May. The sun shone. I persuaded my husband to go to Ulverston market and felt glad we did for I got such nice fillets of sole and a halibut head for my cats – 1s 8d for the fish and only 3d for the good meaty head. Beside two country lorries drawn up in the square, a line of women queued. Feeling curious I went to the top of the queue to see – then hurried back to the end to wait my turn for cauliflowers when I heard the price – 1s for bigger and cleaner looking ones than for 2s 6d in Barrow. When it was my turn I said to the pleasant faced girl 'I wish you came to Barrow market'. She said 'Nay. Dad and Mother say it's wasted time and petrol, and it means we can sell them cheaper here in Ulverston. We sell all we grow direct so our prices are generally about half.' She told me they had had plenty of young spring greens at 6d each but all had been sold. I saw onions on several stalls at 1s a pound, but they found few buyers. Women bought green scallions at 6d a pound. Though not so strongly flavoured, they were better value. Plenty of nice fowls, huge whole salmon, and every kind of 'good' fish in the fish shop where I got mine. I felt shopping was easy with a full purse! We had a cup of tea at a snack bar, and then were home by 11.30.

---

[*] Albert Modley (b. Liverpool, 1901) and Norman Evans (b. Rochdale, also 1901) were variety entertainers and comedians.

'I love to wander round on market day in Ulverston', Nella wrote on Thursday, 22 June 1950. 'Born and bred in a town, so much of my childhood's happiest memories are of Gran's farm on the hills, coming to market in the gig, meeting kindly country neighbours. The smell of freshly cut and dug vegetables or the sight of a patient shaggy horse is akin to the feeling I get by Coniston Lake – not exactly an escape as much as a reality, something firm and strong in my life.'

Friday, 5 May. Mrs Howson came in after tea, in one of her very worst 'I've no time for *that*' humour, and sat waspish and bitter tongued about all and every subject that cropped up. I felt puzzled and wondered what had possibly upset her. I've not seen her quite so nowty since canteen days. I think I found what was the root of her bad humour. I asked if she had filled in her Civil Defence form, and she snapped '*Yes*, if there's any decent job going *we* might as well have them and not the folks who have only been in WVS five minutes'. She and I differ widely on WVS policy. She 'doesn't want strangers poking into meetings and dinners – folk that never helped when there was work to be done'. I feel we who have gone through the war have had enough and should encourage and help others to take over in the dreadful event of being needed again. Perhaps because I myself feel so depleted nowadays, I think others will feel the same. She said suddenly 'What do you think of that newcomer, Mrs Todkill?' I said 'I don't know much about her at all. She was a stranger. Her husband is an Admiralty man, and she came to the WVS to try and make friends and when introduced to me I pounced on her and asked her if she would take over and help Mrs Higham in the trolley scheme, and be stand-in for me at the hospital outpatients' canteen.' I got *such* a look as Mrs Howson said 'So *that's* how she got pushed into things – and now she is going to be organiser for the Civil Defence. *I* was asked but felt *I* wasn't smart enough, but *she* took it without demur.'

I laughed to myself at Mrs Howson's being asked. At Canteen she gave frantic signals for help to the counter if a coloured man, a foreigner who couldn't speak English, or a lad who showed the least signs of having had drink came up. She got offended and was so touchy she had to be handled carefully, and disliked people at a glance. I wondered what job on her own she could have held. As for lecturing, she has no idea of speaking coherently, even about clothes and fashion. It's difficult sometimes to grasp the idea she wants to convey. I said without thinking 'Mrs Todkill is a quiet little thing – but have you seen her firm decisive mouth? To me she looks as if she has been used to authority – perhaps been a teacher.' Then I got Mrs Howson's opinion of teaching, folk who were stuck up because they had been to college, etc. etc. I felt so out of patience. I felt she needed a sharp slap and a dose of syrup of figs like a disordered child, and I felt too I'd all the whims and moods to cope with that I was capable of doing. I often realise with a little sadness that I must have had a lot more patience in the war. Maybe, too, I felt more balanced. To make up for little annoyances and frets, there was the purpose, the laughter and the wide companionship, and the feeling you were helping – a pretty good feeling.

Wednesday, 10 May. Such a lovely summery day, and the sun so warm. I got Mrs Salisbury to do all the windows and she seemed pleased to be outdoors in the fresh air. She had been to the Co-op dairies to find out why her eldest lad had been sacked, and was told it was because of his 'poor educational standard'. The manager *had* held forth about the lads he had sent from the Labour bureau. He told Mrs Salisbury the bulk hadn't the standards of a lad of 9–10 of the old days. He said 'Twenty years ago boys took milk out, or papers, or took basket meals to the shipyard. There was no cheap meals of free milk yet youngsters were bright and intelligent *and* mannerly when spoken to and didn't pretend to know it all.' He told Mrs Salisbury she *must* send George to evening classes and see he sticks to it. He said 'whatever he is, at least he wants to be able to count beyond 12, and write plainly, and at least spell simple words'. Mrs Salisbury said 'I told you my lads were only workers and the extra year was no good to them at school' – and I could only agree. [*The school leaving age had recently been raised from fourteen to fifteen.*]

Thursday, 11 May. After tea my husband ran Mrs Higham home and then said he would like to go for the last time to the Coliseum, which goes back to pictures next week. I looked at the orchestra – such good musicians but all grey headed. There isn't any hope they will get another similar job. Two I know gave lessons and I suppose still do. Life must be cruel to all musicians – *and* stage people – unless they are on the top. A good comedian, several good turns and a 'Title' trained team of eight chorus girls didn't compensate for the rest of the bill, which would have been more suitable for the Windmill! I never saw quite so little worn on the stage – and the really comic part was the pudgy starch fed girls which instead of allure radiated bath night. Two had definitely lost any virginal curves.* It was a shame to be in on such a lovely night. We walked slowly home, the sun still shining.

Saturday, 27 May. I heard Mrs Howson come in and knew she had come to tell me all the news of the wedding. I made a plate of mixed sandwiches – tomato, cheese and lettuce, and cheese and grated onion, a favourite of hers – and there was sponge sandwich and bread and butter and strawberry jam. The bridegroom was a cousin of hers, a year widowed, and we knew the bride from childhood. She is older than Cliff but not quite as old as Arthur. There seemed to have been a little shadow cast by an unforeseen muddle at the church. The groom and best man and big taxi cab of guests had arrived at the church before a very sad little funeral was over – that of a three year old baby who had been drowned last week. The mother's wild cries of 'My baby, oh my baby' had echoed round the church as she was half carried out, to meet on the steps another lot of wedding guests. Mrs Howson said it was surprising what a gloom was cast, and the pouring wet and cold day

---

* The Windmill Theatre in London was famous for its (more or less) nude performers. Two years later Nella made her views on nudity clear. 'As for people who have little or no clothes on, well, they haven't, and that's that. I never could see anything shocking in nude or semi nude figures, always provided they weren't gross untidy ones' (12 June 1952). By the standards of her time, Nella did not hold particularly rigid views concerning sexual propriety. On 1 February 1951 she borrowed from the library a copy of D. H. Lawrence's *The White Peacock*, although she did not report what she thought of it.

didn't help, or the fact that ten more guests were squeezed in to the tables originally laid for 50 at a not too convenient cafe. I felt glad of her prattle about what everyone wore, how they looked, who had aged – or not – in the few years since they had been out of town. It helped hold my husband's interest without effort on my part.

Wednesday, 31 May. We relaxed and listened to *Twenty Questions.* I wondered as I sat if all the gossip in the papers about the effect television was having on the home life and make-up of American people could be exaggerated, and if we were in for a general change in amusement and entertainment, as in the rest of things today. We seem to have got into a whirling mad hurry that *could* carry us over the rapids to smooth strong waters, or draw us into a deep whirlpool. History seems to be 'made' in deeper and deeper swathes and spasms as each upheaval comes. I felt a sick shock to realise Australia is taking over in Malaysia, that there's a growing need for action if peace is to last our time, never mind the next generation. Such a dreadful thought.

Saturday, 3 June. Bowness was a throng of milling people being decanted from coaches and seeking hotels and cafes where tea had been ordered. I don't think there would have been much chance of a meal without ordering. We went along to Ambleside Road. There was no chance of parking the car in Bowness, except in the big park, and we sat awhile, and then strolled along the tree shaded road by the Lake. Our 10 horse Morris was the poorest car in a group of bigger and newer cars when we returned. We had parked in a little clearing where several big trees had been recently felled, and it looked as if it was a well known spot for car picnics. We felt very surprised at the type of people who like ourselves had brought tea, and the good stoves and little collections of picnic oddments showed it was not just a sudden idea but they were used to taking meals. One big car that held three abreast was full of luggage and wraps in the back seat. I felt amused at the couple who began to light the stove while the third (looked like the son) got out folding chairs and cloth and laid out the meal. They looked more the type to roll up to a super hotel and demand a good meal. It made me look round and notice similar well-to-do types contentedly picnicking and contrast it with the definitely working class types getting out of the coaches or eating in the top class hotels where beautifully laid tables and men waiters could be seen through the windows from the road. It was 9 o'clock when we got home. I quietly made excuses for leaving till all the heavy traffic had gone. That sweet quiet peace was over all – residents out, yachts stealing out like moths, or bright red butterflies, replacing motor and steam boats, white clad chefs outside back doors of hotels, tired walkers returning to hotels and boarding houses for a bath and meal. We came down the quiet still Lake as in a dream, hardly a soul on the road. It compensated for all the rush and noise and I could relax and not wonder what would rush round a hidden bend and upset my husband.

Monday, 12 June. There's a lovely sailing ship in for repairs. It was made nearly 30 years ago in the Yard for Brazil, to be used as a training ship, and has come back for some refit or repairs. The youths on it fascinate me. They look cultured and assured, as if from good families, and have the manners and deportment of well educated and poised people. Their clothes are cut so perfectly – ordinary sailor rig, slightly musical comedy in detail. The mariners have scarlet tunics. The officers I'm sure had their uniforms made by a tailor-artist. They have this and that all over – cords and medal ribbons, chevrons and rings – and are in grey-blues as well as navy, and all of superlative material and cut. But it's their faces and colour that so fascinates me – deepest chocolate, through every tone of café-au-lait to pale ivory, and all are young enough to have haunting adolescent beauty, or the smiling candour of a happy child. It's plain to be seen that where they come from there's no 'colour bar' as we understand the word. I look at each couple or group and wonder what mixture of race and colour, tribe, 'aristocracy', way of life and thought, and religion have intermingled to form their perfectly cut features, the different noses, mouths and brows. It makes my theory that some day there will be one race with no warring element of barriers that fear and greed make, and understanding of each other's ways and thought.

Saturday, 17 June. Margaret Atkinson [*now Procter*] came in. She seems to be looking forward to beginning housekeeping in a house of her own, but said a bit thoughtfully 'It's going to be a bit strange having to ask Arthur [*her husband since August 1949*] for money. With working a year after marriage, it will seem worse than if I'd began being "dependent".' We talked of the queer unrest in the Yard. [*Managers were being laid off.*] She said 'No boss feels safe. I can tell the way they talk they wonder round our office who will be next.' Margaret is near enough the Cost Office to know the real undercurrent of worry for the future for work. There's no more lines in view, and we don't build the cruisers and submarines now that made up the orders before 'private' ships were built. Within two years, unless other big orders are obtained, or fresh subsidiary lines are developed, it looks as if Barrow will have had it. We will be worse than Jarrow in the big slump, for beyond the steel works – working at a loss and on the borderline of being closed within a short time – there's practically nothing. What few small industries there are rely on the Yard's prosperity.

Nella sometimes remarked on the state of the wider world, and usually with alarm. There was a lot to be distressed about, not least the threat of atomic weapons. On 17 May – her wedding anniversary – she was thinking about 'the account of 70 foot atom proof shelters being built at Stockholm, recalling a forecast by Naylor the astrologist, quite 15 years ago, that humanity was approaching an age when they tended to go underground, and build deep in the earth to work, live and "play"'. These were, once again, and so soon after a world war, troubling political times. On 29 June she and Mrs Higham 'talked so sadly of the news, both with a sick feeling that *anything* will happen, wondering if Korea will start the war in the East that is to destroy civilization as we know it, talking and conjecturing about Russia and what she may have behind the Iron Curtain, recalling half forgotten memories of our war work together, or air raids, blackout, shortages.' Once again, civil defence became a major concern.

Talk of war was much in the air, particularly because of the crisis in Korea (a country that many people had barely heard of and probably could not locate on a map): on 25 June the North invaded the South, and the United States responded through the United Nations by organising resistance to this aggression, as the North Korean action was widely perceived to be. At the end of this first week of crisis, on Sunday, 2 July, she and Will drove to the Coast Road. 'A group of elder people sat near where we parked, not near enough for me to hear clearly their conversation, but sentences with "Korea" and scraps of conversation about the Navy and RAF and "our Robert", and their expressions of concern, showed their thoughts were on the future, and what it would bring. I wonder if this "firm gesture" *will* put a stop to Communist drive and urge.' (Perhaps she had in mind the words of John Gordon, 'Why America Must Not Fail', in that day's *Sunday Express* (p. 4): 'Britain responded with inspiring swiftness to the call of America and the United Nations. It was a tremendous gesture we made. But, in fact, no other course was open to us. And in the crisis every man in Britain stands behind the Government.' Britain had, among other things, promised immediate naval support to the Americans in the Far East. In response to the Korean crisis, the period of National Service was soon to be increased from eighteen to twenty-four months.)

Monday, 3 July. It was a glorious day for the seaside – the tide at full and a land breeze. The cadet training camp is full of boys 14 to 18, some from Bolton and some from an approved school. It seems the policy to mix the latter with ordinary youths. In healthy windswept Barrow-in-Furness we are too young to have history of any kind, especially industrial. I looked at some of the young badly built youngsters with real horror. They looked as if they had been badly bred for generations of tired warped parents, few really nice looking, some who shambled along with dull eyes and aimless limbs looked subnormal. I like boys. One group were throwing stones for an eager little dog, and I suggested a stick so as not to chip the dog's teeth as I'd often seen. I said 'No national aid for dogs' teeth and when they cannot chew their food they die young'. I expressed surprise they went swimming or bathing and was told 'Want us in jankers,[†] I can see. But I wish you would talk to our sergeant. He doesn't like water himself and hates to see anyone else have fun there.' The crowd who were unable to bathe seemed to just lie round and I was horrified to see how some of them chain smoked, with the ease of long practice. Others bought mineral water of the colours of red ink or a hideous greeny lime, ice cream and sickly cakes from a trailer 'cafe' that was stationed. A penny was charged on each bottle, but many who sat fifty yards or even less from the 'cafe' set the bottle on a heap of stones and aimed till broken, and left the glass scattered.

I fell into a train of thought as I wondered where the curious lack of responsibility to others began. Our generation taught children 'Don't leave gates open or the poor little moo cows will get lost and not find their mammies and be cold and lonely at bedtime', 'Let's bury this nasty sharp glass so no one will cut their feet', '*Such* lovely flowers, but we will only pick some for the glass jug and leave the others to grow – they like growing as much as little boys and girls', 'It's ugly to be dirty – look how pussy washes herself and then begins to purr and sing because she feels so nice when she has washed herself'. Now they talk of 'repressions' and 'fixations' and hidden things in children's minds. I'm old fashioned enough to think a child is less complicated than the clever ones think. The security of comforting arms, a sharp slap when needed, busy hands and minds and the example of elders would be better for growing children than all the new and clever ways.

Tuesday, 4 July. Mrs Howson and I both had shopping before going to the WVS Post War Club meeting. I got potatoes, pears, tomatoes, apples, apricots and a quarter pound of mushrooms – only 9d today – and so my shopping bag was full and rather heavy. We had *such* a good speaker, a local farmer's sister who joined the YMCA at the outbreak of war and went overseas. She told of her experiences in North Africa, the desert towns and northern Italy. She had had a wonderful experience. She is a most attractive woman, now about 35 but looking less, for she is so gay and vital and must have met thousands of eligible men from all over the Empire as well as the British Isles, but in spite of all hasn't even an engagement ring. I wonder why. I'm sure she must have had *some* offers of, if not marriage, that 'understanding' that leads that way. I wondered if 'Clogs weren't good enough and shoes never came her way', as they say in Lancashire.

Before the war she kept house for a farmer brother, who got married and left her rather at a loose end, and she had never been far from the district so it was a wonderful experience. She gossiped about people and places and her work, and made us rock with laughter at her 'most embarrassing moment'. In a very full YMCA in Italy, a slightly tipsy soldier lurched up to the counter, stared hard and shouted 'Hallo, aren't you going to speak to me?' His friend asked if he 'knew the lady' and he bellowed '*Know* her – she was my last mistress in England'. She said 'The silence that fell on the group round the counter could be felt. I leaned forward and said – making matters sound worse – "I'm afraid I've forgotten exactly who you are, or where we met". He said "I was your brother's cow man and was there the year so many heifer calves were born. You *must* remember me, Miss Coward. You used to laugh at my checked shirt."' Miss Coward said it sounded as if a sigh of relief went up!

It's the first Civil Defence meeting to arrange training classes on Thursday evening. As we moved into groups for a cup of tea, we began to talk of the beginning of the last war. With a half humorous, half dread of tomorrow, Mrs Higham and one of her neighbours made us all laugh as they related their experiences with a very 'superior' lecturer. He had everyone so in line, doing every precise action with stirrup pump, moving limbs to allow 'full action of muscle' etc., while others trotted up with full buckets of water for 'chain' service. He said 'Now I want you to watch this carefully so as not to leave a gap in operations while the empty bucket is changed for the full one', which entailed a finger put in one place and the stirrup pump clasped a certain way. The homely little woman who had hurried up with the full bucket of water looked at him and said quietly 'Wouldn't it be better if I just poured this water out of my bucket instead of fiddling with the stirrup pump being lifted out of one bucket into another?' Mrs Higham said the look on that man's face as he agreed was 'something to see'.

Thursday, 6 July. I got ready to go to Civil Defence meeting, and was down for 7 o'clock. With the exception of about half a dozen women, all the rest were WVS and we feel a bit put out and bewildered to find we will have to go through the whole Civil Defence training – gas, bomb training and disposal, rescue, fire fighting, etc. etc., and do a *three years* course! There's no WVS member in our lot who can either stand up to such a course or feel it necessary before they can do all the homely jobs they did all the last war. In fact many very valuable members blinked at the notion of jumping out of windows, going through gas chambers, working in 'teams' at rescue work, etc., and everyone, including myself, said we would never have joined if we hadn't been misled! Mrs Diss looked dismayed. WVS Regional had told her we could take our training in the afternoon. There was an air of complete dissatisfaction on every hand. As a whole, none of us were capable of such rough, tough train-ing. The two youngest women were Mrs Howson and Mrs Fletcher. The latter has asthma bad if there is any untoward smell and said she 'would leave it to chance' whether she got gassed, but wear a gas mask and 'play around' she wouldn't and couldn't. Mrs Howson even surprised me by her outburst in the porch as she talked of 'Did you ever hear such darn rot? Anyone would think war was coming *any time*.'

Friday, 7 July. My husband was busy clipping off dead roses. When I see him occupied in any way I feel so happy for him, and he had cleaned two pairs of my shoes I'd put out to clean when I came back – so beautifully too. I wonder why men often get such a much better shine on shoes – more weight behind their rubbing, perhaps. I had vegetable soup to heat, and potatoes and peas to cook, to eat to corned beef. I made custard and stewed some prunes I had, and when I packed tea of cheese, lettuce, tomatoes, a loaf and butter, I put in a jar of fruit salad by adding a few prunes to the stewed apricots and segments of apple. I wanted to change our library books. I got a 'Crime Club', and one of Muriel Hines' novels for my husband, feeling another little thrill of thankfulness when he has settled to reading more, and got used to his glasses better. We went to the Coast Road and sat on a rug on the shingly shore. The tide crept slowly in, no wind at all, and the air heavy with the scent of hay going past on carts and lorries, so lovely and 'green dried'. We had tea and walked on the sands – it was only low tide – and I settled to read awhile.

My husband seemed so much less despondent. He said suddenly 'Do you remember anyone called Clamp? The wife came several times about air raid damage and I once heard her tell you her daughter was getting married. Mr Clamp worked in the gas showrooms.' I knew then who he was referring to and nodded. He went on in such a queer thoughtful manner. 'He went past when I was in the front garden when you were out. He too has had to retire through nervous trouble and he is younger than me.' There was a pause and then he went on, still in a wondering tone. 'He spends most of his time in the park. He says if he stays in, he and his wife quarrel fiercely and she isn't a bit sympathetic. She dislikes sickness of any kind and loses patience when he has no memory for anything.' I said 'Well, it takes two to make a quarrel. Perhaps he is bad to do with. You cannot judge till you hear both sides.' I thought a bit grimly of the many quarrels we two could have if I didn't keep self-control, didn't pray so earnestly for patience and kindness, but felt tears rise in my eyes as the poor dear went on. 'You've always been so understanding, such a *pal*. It's good when sex dies to feel there's something even better.' I nodded, and realised as often, it's always been a mother he has needed as much as a wife.

Thursday, 13 July. To say my feelings are mixed is to put it very mildly. My husband has found an interest!!! Wood beetles. Nasty little brown 'woody' bugs that bore round worm holes. We had a basket chair in a bedroom, and last year when Arthur and Edith were here, they carried it on the lawn and broke a leg as Edith sat down heavily when it was wobbly against the rockery. Such a train of minor destruction seems to follow Edith and she is so 'unlucky' with electric irons, cups and saucers, etc. I didn't think much when Arthur said 'The leg is worm eaten. No wonder it snapped.' Later I noticed little clusters of round holes at the top of my good oak panelled doors, and used Flit, and nagged gently on and on, finally saying I'd get someone in to see to them if my husband wouldn't tackle them. Still he didn't bother. He had that 'couldn't care less' attitude, till there was something on the wireless last night. He had done the tops of the doors with Cupressol, a mild form of creosote, but after hearing the seriousness of neglect, I got really on the war path today, and the house looks as if stirred with a stick. He found signs in a wardrobe and a dressing table back, and both have been ripped off and are waiting hardboard. He says three ply is the wood that encourages them. Clothes from two wardrobes strew the bedrooms, mats and carpets are rolled up or askew, there's litter as if for removal. BUT, I heard my husband whistle for awhile!! ...

I packed tea, raspberries and a little evaporated milk, a loaf and butter, cakes and two flasks of tea, and we went off to Walney, though black clouds were rolling up from all directions. Few had gone to the beach for the half holiday. We walked on the sands awhile, before it rained, and then had tea. On the way home, I got off at the schools where Civil Defence classes are held and found the rain had held up a lot from coming where a bus wasn't handy, and it made a late start. It was more of a 'settling in' than learning anything, and *seven* gas masks were fitted. The sergeant said 'More will be available lately, but I don't know when.' I felt faintly sick as he talked of 'zone' and the possibility of Barrow being considered as such, and I watched the gas masks being fitted with a sick pity as I thought of all that had happened since I last was at a school where we got ours, that fateful Munich year, wondering 'Is this another Munich warning?' It's the dreadful acceptance of many people that chills me most. When the sergeant spoke of the effect of an atom bomb on a place like Barrow – destruction with a 5½ mile radius, and the evacuations to a 'cushion' belt – and the remarks of the morbid, pessimistic London man who sat beside me, a queer 'sooner it's over, sooner to sleep' feeling stole over me. Ordinary people can do so little – only pray.

Saturday, 22 July. When I was coming up in the bus I noticed some nurses from the Hospital sitting opposite me, in the long seats by the exit. As the bus stopped at my bus stop a smartly dressed, coal black African girl rose from the front of the bus and prepared to alight and I idly wondered if she was visiting the African oculist on Abbey Road. As she reached the three nurses sitting opposite one said 'Hallo – thought you were going shopping. We would have waited if we had known you were coming this way.' The black girl murmured something and the nurse said 'Always changing your mind, daft cat' and gave her a friendly slap – a *chummy* slap – on the rump of the girl, who laughed so jolly and happy in return, as if colour and race were one.

We walked side by side. There's three or more African nurses and I don't know one from the other, so speak to all. I was really surprised when the beautiful honey voice said 'Beginning to think about your rag bag babies yet?' Granted I'd met them twice on Xmas Days I'd gone to the 'visit of Santa Claus', but was surprised when she had remembered I made them. She said 'Matron often speaks of you when she gets a hoarded dollie out of the cupboard. She likes to keep a few back. Last week she found a cowboy for a badly burned little boy and gave it to him. If you could see how your dollies are loved you would think your work worth doing.' I felt tears start to my eyes – dear knows why. I said 'How nice of you to tell me, my dear. Are you still happy in Barrow?' She paused at the gate where she was going to call at the African doctor's and her wide mouth split into a huge happy grin as she said 'I've never known such happiness I've found here. The memory will linger all my life.' I said 'Matron is the most wonderful person I know – and I've known her for over 30 years.' She nodded as she said 'Yes – but we have found happiness and kindness everywhere. The children love us, and we had been warned small white children might fear us because of our colour'. I said 'Children are the best judges of people. They would soon realise your kindness and love. Matron told me she wished she could have a full African staff of nurses, if only for the warmth and love of nursing you all had, as well as your sunny dispositions.' She said 'Now it's *you* who are nice to me'.

The house door opened and my little happy feeling seemed to sour. A lily pale woman [*wife of the black doctor*] stood in the doorway, with a tiny coffee coloured baby in her arms, a darker skinned little kinky haired girl, and a really dark, goggle eyed 'nigger' little boy rushed excitedly down the steps in welcome. Whatever the views I hold of 'some day, one colour, one creed', the sight of half caste children seems to strike at something way deep down in me. I *say* I've no 'colour bar', but wonder if really I've a very deep rooted one. I could work with coloured people, enjoy their society, attend their wants in canteen, fully admit them to positions of trust and service, but know, *finally*, I'd have *died* before I could have married one, or borne coloured children. So perhaps I *have* a 'colour bar'.

Nella had earlier disclosed some of her racial prejudices and mixed feelings, when she made her usual Christmas visit in 1948 to the hospital and encountered two African nurses, one of them the nurse she spoke with on this July day. They were, she wrote, 'the Basuto type – their uniforms intensify their really frightening ugliness. One was helping the one time little patients into coats and scarves, her huge capable hands seeming to attend several children at once. They looked up so "inaffectedly"[†] as if a hideous black face was the one they would have chosen to hand over them. She passed where I was standing and impulsively I put out my hand and said "A very happy Xmas, nurse. I hope our cold grey skies don't make you homesick for your lovely sunny land." A soft, rather guttural but very pleasant voice said "Oh no, madam. We *love* it here. England is a wonderful place and we have met nothing but kindness. No one in Barrow seems to have noticed we are coloured."' Nella and this nurse agreed on Matron's virtues, which led Nella to write that 'the enveloping clasp of that huge black hand, its firmness and warmth that was not only physical, made me say "Why my dear, you have something Matron has always had – perhaps it's what is called being a born nurse". It was such a feeling of strength. I'd have felt every confidence in the little black thing.' Later Nella spoke with Matron, who said '"It was kind of you to talk to nurse. She is a really splendid person – they both are. I'm amazed to find such understanding and quick intelligence in people who have so recently been 'civilized'. They put a lot of the rest to shame"' (25 December 1948).

Three and a half years later Nella again pondered her confused feelings about race after visiting this black ophthalmologist at his office in his home, whom she portrayed as 'clever, patient and well liked', and who was married to a French woman. 'I felt what wonderful people the Africans – and coloured people – were.

In one or two – three at the most – generations, they have bridged such a gap between primitive and civilized ways. I'm not consistent. I've *no* colour feeling, no shrinking from black hands touching me as head was turned and lenses fitted, no feeling of revulsion at all; yet when those really charming half caste children leaned against me – the little girl of three climbed on my knee – I felt something in me shrank away' (1 August 1952). It was the 'mixing of blood and race' that unsettled her, and which she found hard to digest (5 January 1950). In the same passage she had written of 'the shock I got the other day to read how many half caste children were the result of the American negro soldiers' short stay in England'.

Friday, 4 August. We went down the Coast Road again. It was a lot cooler, and looks set for a change. The fields were being prepared for the reaper and binder to begin harvest. Down the edges, two sides, men cut and tied a swathe – it does look a poor thin crop, and I can hear it's much worse over the Duddon estuary in Cumberland. The incoming tide was dotted with bathers. Happy family groups round little tents everywhere on the grass verge looked as if they had been down all morning. Cars with numbers from every part of Scotland and England passed or paused awhile. The number of Scottish cars increases each summer. The other day when my husband was getting petrol at the garage where he generally deals I said 'The news and situation in Korea makes us wonder how much longer petrol will be off ration'. The proprietor said 'I think it's found its level. The trade say only 10% more was sold, and that includes part of the holiday traffic, you know. My son says our sales haven't gone up a lot, but people will be buying petrol further afield, as they take longer journeys.' We walked along the sands before the tide was full. The air was sweet and fresh. We met several people we knew and had a chat, and had tea in the car ...

The news of retreat and yet still retreat in Korea is bad. It seems to play right into Stalin's hands and give him such cause to crow 'America – pooh – why *Koreans* can send them packing. They would never have a chance if they struck at ME', and it's not good Westerners should lose face. I had a fearsome little remembrance of "The last war of all will start in the East' and vague oddments of revelations that were 'being proved every day for those with eyes to see' and such like – hangovers from a nosy childhood when there was nothing for curious children to interest their minds as now, and a street orator *was* a treat. I can see plainly as I write a figure I'd forgotten long ago, only coming back now as his wild prophecies of the 'end of all things' was shouted at indifferent adults and enthralled children. Not one corner of this lovely world is safe or secure. I wonder what this dreadful H-bomb *is* like in its effects. It will be a fearful 'adventure' to set off a trial one. I wonder if America *will* set off the atom bomb in Korea. To do so could set the whole Eastern world against us. As Stalin *would* be able to say, 'This is what the West means to you, death and mutilation or a wholesale massacre'.

The war in Korea had attracted Nella's attention on several occasions recently. On 26 July 'When I heard the 6 o'clock news I felt faint shock – that we were sending troops to Korea'. Hundreds of thousands of British families were bound to be alarmed, as their boys of military age faced the prospect of being sent, once again, into battle. 'Fear and concern is coming to mothers of boys who will be due for National Service', Nella wrote on 28 July, 'for now it sounds as if they will be soldiers from the start, liable for overseas, and all it can mean, by the time they are 19.' Moreover, the current crisis raised for the first time since 1945 the potential use of atomic weapons, and Nella was gloomy about Britain's post-war weakness in a world dominated by the two superpowers. 'America has the A-bomb – and is young', she remarked on 27 July. 'We would have little or no say whether one had to be dropped in Korea, and if such a dreadful thing *did* happen – and Russia *has* them – all hell could be easily let loose. A terrifying outlook.'

Saturday, 19 August. I tidied round quickly after breakfast and we sat waiting about 15 minutes for the taxi. Being such a big wedding [*of a cousin's son*] and so many to bring from a wide district, even with a fleet of taxis it was a rush to get everyone to church in time. The bride lived at Rampside, a small village on Morecambe Bay, five miles from town. The church was beautifully decorated with pink roses and tall pink spikes of gladioli, and I don't remember seeing a lovelier bride and attendants.

Nancy had a medieval plain cut dress with long tight sleeves, flowing train in stiff corded silk, and wore a family veil. The bridesmaids had stiff striped brocade of blending pastel shades with a silver thread between each delicate hue. They were simply made but cunningly cut and so different from the usual bridesmaids' dresses. We knew nearly everyone. Miss Ledgerwood, who worked with us at Hospital Supply, is an aunt of the bride, and there was the usual big turn up of relations rarely seen between weddings and funerals. Mary Rawlinson was there, beautifully dressed, serene and aloof, parrying enquiries about the break between her and Cliff Crump, after a long drawn out courtship of nearly ten years, when she had kept putting off her marriage, saying 'There's plenty of time', and now he has tired of waiting. Perhaps because I asked no questions, she told me 'We grew to have less and less in common, and anyway Nell, I think I'm like your Cliff – too content on my own'. I said 'Well Mary, you are so like my own mother in looks and ways. I think it's as well for either a husband or any children you might have had that you don't marry. I know Mother would have been happier if she hadn't married my father, but put it down to the fact that the "real" life of her died when her first husband did. Now I wonder if she was like you – a kind of Rhine maiden.' She wasn't at all pleased, but she knows well I've known several of her half finished romances in all their details. It's as if she seeks a perfection in human relationship almost impossible to find, and the comic part is that she is more full of whims and whamseys[†] and more difficult to understand than most.

We didn't go to the station to see the bridal couple off, first to London to spend the night, and then to Newquay on the Cornish express. It was too late to make the journey in one day from Barrow.[*] Instead we went to Spark Bridge to tell Aunt Sarah all about the wedding. Other days, others' ways – she was so disappointed her share of the 'wedding feast'

---

[*] On Monday the 21st Nella was back in Rampside to view the wedding presents. There was no sign of austerity – 'I never saw such a collection of "covetable" things. It looked as if the cream had been skimmed from every good shop in town' – and she proceeded, admiringly, to list the gifts in copious detail.

and a glass of wine hadn't been sent. Useless to try and explain the difference of hotel catering and that of the old time personal attention to everything. I recall country weddings when I was small when any old or sick who couldn't go had their share of goodies put aside – someone took it and told of every detail. Ruth [*Tomlinson*] is staying in the cottage next door. She came in to hear all about all that occurred. I felt shocked to see how suddenly she had begun to look her age. Her lecture tour in America was so strenuous and she did so hate New York, saying 'Never go there if you can help it. It has the least soul of any place I've known.' I can tell she feels gloomy about the way things are going in Korea. She seems to have got atom bomb and total destruction of civilization pretty bad. I said 'I've got past it, Ruth. I've a growing Sayonara – "if it must be so" – a feeling we are all in some great and intricate "Place", that "it's not life that matters, but the courage we bring to it"'. She thinks I'm a 'visionary', 'a perfect *sweet*', that I 'must be delightful to live with', etc. Knowing dear Ruthie, I knew she was trying to convey that I wanted my bumps read!

Saturday, 2 September. As we ate lunch I asked my husband 'What would you like to do, short of putting your head in the gas oven?' He looked aggrieved at my flippancy, but wouldn't give any kind of answer. But when we got out, he perked up and said suddenly 'Let's go to Kendal'. I felt surprised. He has never suggested going since Robert was here just after Xmas. I said 'I'll be delighted if you feel up to it'. We went slowly. It's not much more than an hour's run from Barrow. Everywhere in the high wind and fitful sunshine farmers were busy. I saw many ricks being covered with tarpaulin as if some grain on higher ground had dried sufficiently. Hay too was being cut, and quite a good crop if it only dries. Two hikers hailed us for a lift. They had huge packs on their backs but my husband wouldn't stop. He had read an article or letter by a motorist in the *Express* the other week saying 'Why should motorists, who are taxed have to pay so dear for petrol, pander to some people's desire and determination to get a cheap holiday by hitchhiking?' My husband pointed out that there was a very good bus service, and just before we came along a service bus half empty had paused to pick up passengers, and the two hikers had not bothered though it would only have been a few coppers to go as far as Kendal.

There was the usual life and bustle of a county town. Kendal has been as unfortunate for weather as the rest of Lakeland. In two shops where I went – one for a lettuce and celery, one for elastic – they spoke of the 'terrible weather for August'. We came round by Bowness and parked by the Lake to eat tea, from where I could see into cars round about. Most of them were having a picnic meal – and some really large expensive cars. Perhaps the price of petrol hits more people than one realised! Fewer cars and only a very short line of motor coaches in the big car park. Perhaps Morecambe illuminations will take most coach trips now. We were home by 7.30, already foam over the Irish Sea. Banks of rain were rolling in. It's only been a 'borrowed' day.

Thursday, 7 September. There was wild confusion of piled furniture and carpets in some side streets of Ulverston, brought hurriedly from houses never been flooded in living memory, and a great deal of damage to two bridges and roads had been caused. A 'river' surged through Ulverston station, washing all before it. Passengers from Whitehaven to Euston were taken off the trains at Dalton and travelled by road round the Bay to Carnforth, and we didn't get papers till noon as all had to be brought by lorry or bus. Low lying fields were lakes. Others I never remember seeing flooded were under water, any stooks of corn that didn't float submerged altogether – a pitiful sight. I'd not dared to look at the poor garden before I left, and hardly knew where to start when I got home. I had a promising crop of pears and James Grieve apples – half were on the ground – herbaceous plants flat, rose branches torn off completely, the lawn was covered with branches and pieces of Michaelmas daisy, chrysanth plants, etc. With the dry spring and too wet autumn, stems and stalks were too spindly and thin to stand up to much. I looked at apple blossom, spring rock plants, aubretia and polyanthus in bloom, and could not remember so freakish a year. I felt spent and exhausted long before I'd made much tidy, so left it to heat cream of chicken soup and fry fillets of hake to make a handy meal.

My husband I could see didn't want me to go down to the Civil Defence meeting. I felt if I didn't get out for awhile, I'd be really ill. I felt like an old glove – nothing but the outward shape. I couldn't eat much but had a rest. He nattered about 'being glad when this silly fad is over and your Civil Defence lectures finished', and wondered 'what can I do all afternoon'. I lost patience as I pointed out the lecture was an hour, and another 30 or 40 minutes to go there and back, and suggested he went to the cinema or go over Walney. I can never understand his attitude to the car. Most folk use a car as a help to get about. He won't take it out if he thinks it will get wet, or leave it in a car park, however public, in case someone scratches or damages it. He wouldn't hear of going down to the pictures and leaving it unattended, but with one of his most hurt expressions decided to go over Walney and sit and watch the sea. I said 'Well, that *will* be cosy and uplifting – enough to give anybody the miseries on a day like this', but I went off thankfully on my own.

Odd how differently people look on home. To me it's my real 'core' of life and living. I can always relax and read or sew happily if I'm on my own, and would like to have people in rather than go out looking for change. My husband has his mother's deep horror of being in the house by himself, and only wanders around unhappily, looking out of windows, watching the clock and timing my return. I often feel I took a wrong course of action somewhere or he wouldn't have got quite so bad … Mrs Higham 'wonders how on earth you keep so serene and calm. I'd go mad if I was you, cooped up as you are' – and says 'You will pay for all this, you know', as if life was all ruled in little routines with rules made for every condition. I said 'Well, things *do* get me down at times, but I firmly count my blessings, and I've a lot you know, including my queer intelligent cat friends, who are unbelievably good company'. She said 'Cats! – fah!' I said 'Well, add books, my letters and the regular arrival of the boys' letters. Many women don't have even that link with families, you know.' She said 'I repeat, you lead a most unnatural life, and will pay dearly for it some day'. I began to argue. As I pointed out, nothing or no one could hurt you if you didn't allow things to eat into you, and she got out of patience with me and said 'Only visionaries and cranks talk like that. I repeat, you will pay for repressing yourself. Much better to begin to face it.' I felt sardonic amusement as she talked and reminded her that we 'all march to our own drummer', and thought secretly that, when done, I'd not change places with her. It must be very bleak not to have a family when you grow old.

Wednesday, 13 September. I noticed my husband get up from reading the paper and begin to chop some wood we didn't really need. I baked bread and turned out the pantry and kitchenette cupboards. I keep wanting to get curtains and two blankets washed but couldn't dry them indoors with my husband always about. I'd made vegetable soup with a little scraggy end of the weekend mutton, so it only needed heating, and I cooked potatoes and turnip to the cold mutton and made a baked custard. I felt tired yet longed to go out. It was no use suggesting the cinema. Every picture this week seemed too 'thrilling' to suit my husband. Luckily I'd got him a novel by Berta Ruck which I'd skimmed through in the library to make sure it had a happy ending and no deaths or partings, and he settled with it. I got out my dollies but felt too tired to sew for long and relaxed on the settee. I wish the appointment for the interview with the psychiatrist would come soon. Times I feel desperate as I look at my husband and see him aging and letting go of so much, shuddering to myself as I wonder what he *would* be like if I didn't sternly remind him to use his handkerchief etc. I insist on him changing his clothes or I'll not go out with him, and keep an anxious eye on him altogether, and try and push all memory of his mother out of my mind, though she poor old thing is 83 and not 62. Shut in day after day, when he thinks and thinks about every symptom, every ache and pain, he hasn't the chance of fresh ideas and interests, and he does get despondent. By tea time today I felt I could have climbed the wall. My hands shook – I sliced tomatoes for a salad to eat with cheese, and I cut my finger. Mrs Howson came in with her knitting. I breathed a heartfelt sigh of relief as she settled to talk about clothes and shopping. I'd have welcomed anyone who read the railway timetable out, and she is the only person whom my husband doesn't resent ever. I think he sees always the little girl she was when we first knew her.

Mrs Howson was twenty years younger than Will. Four days earlier Nella had remarked on his unsociability and how 'people don't like it. Mrs Atkinson has stopped coming in. If she wants me, she calls me to the back garden fence, and if he is in the garden never pauses for those little "aimless" chats that can help brighten women's daily round' (9 September). 'He has an unfortunate way of making people feel unwelcome,' she later lamented, 'though I know well he doesn't mean to be as rude as he seems and would often now like people calling' (7 October).

Will's persistent dark moods, reclusiveness and hypochondriacal fretting led to a consultation with a psychiatrist.

Saturday, 18 November. We had to be at the Hospital for 10.30. I hurriedly dusted and shook the rug, washed up and made beds, and we set out by 10 o'clock. I felt far from happy. My husband rose looking ill and was in one of his silent brooding moods, and I knew he dreaded going. After he went into the smaller room of the annex with the doctor, the nurse-receptionist and I settled silently, she with her knitting, I with a rather tatty magazine off the table. Our silence contrasted with the noise of all kinds of traffic noises, cars being reversed or started in the Hospital quadrangle, shouts of children. After what seemed a long wait, Dr Wadsworth came out and spoke to the nurse, who hurried off and returned with a pillow. She mouthed at me 'Can't get him off'. Then followed another long wait till the door opened again, and looking across at me the doctor said quietly 'Will you come in please, Mrs Last'. I had that awful feeling when the blood all seems to drain into the feet and makes them heavy as lead, and the rest of the body feather light and giddy, and for a split second I felt incapable of moving. It was only a few steps to the door of the inner room, and I saw my husband in one of the worst nervous shaking attacks he has had. I crossed over and took his very cold hands and rubbed them. The doctor got some kind of tablet and dissolved it in a glass of water, and I soothed and 'petted' my husband until the dreadful tremors passed, knowing so surely there was wild terror and some kind of memory behind them. I'd seen my poor old Cliff like that often, when he was first home, and the horrors of war hadn't faded out of his mind.

Dr Wadsworth said 'We will leave Mr Last to rest quietly till his tablet takes effect', and he took my arm and gently propelled me from the room to a chair by the radiator in the anteroom and began to talk. He said 'Does your husband get so easily upset at home? He was only being asked a few routine questions, and he reacted so badly it was impossible to hypnotise him.' He seemed to be able to put leading questions so simply. I recalled afterwards he must have been able to build up a very clear cut picture of my husband's habits, moods, and approach to life in general, not only now but for years. He said 'Would you agree to bring your husband to the Moor Hospital at Lancaster some evening?' I said 'Doctor, I'm beginning to feel so desperate I'd take him to China if I thought it would help him'. He said 'Something *will* have to be done. I can see he is worse than when I saw him first. His life cannot be worth living – yours either if I may say so.' I said 'Tell me please, doctor, am I right to give way to his moods to avoid such attacks of nerves, or should I, as his doctor suggests, "rouse and stimulate him, and quarrel with him if it's the only way to jerk him out of himself"?' Dr Wadsworth pursed his lips and slowly shook his head as he said 'Any course at present that helps to avoid such distressing attacks is your best policy, but rest assured, everything in my powers will be done to help him'. Once an attack is over, my husband seems himself, often better, seemingly, than I feel after one!

Thursday, 30 November. Mrs Higham spoke of vague unrest in the WVS office and offices. As I get little chance of going in the office I hear little – and feel I care less. When a prim old maid school teacher, fast getting a little 'woolly', grabs the news, I feel *anything* could happen. I feel sorry and understanding for Mrs Diss and her somewhat weary attitude. She wanted to give up long ago, and it's a mistake to persuade people beyond their feelings or wishes. People got so tired after the war years. New ones were needed and should have been sought. I'd expected a power cut for tea, and prepared candles in my brass as well as glass candlesticks, but the cut must have missed our part of town. Mrs Higham went early, and we settled to listen to the good Thursday evening programmes, but Mrs Howson came in and stayed till 9 o'clock. I felt I'd rather it had been Mrs Higham, for you can discuss any subject with her. Mrs Howson utterly refuses to talk of any war worries, the effects of rearmaments, anything she considers deep or worrying.

Sunday, 3 December. Everything was thick with snow this morning, and soon after breakfast it began again. I never remember such an odd effect. Big feathery flakes the size of pigeons' eggs stuck to the windows till the heat from inside melted them off. Poor Shan We sat on the window sill chattering like a monkey, and looking so distressed. I'm always puzzled with the gulls and rooks on really bad mornings, and cannot but think they have a 'memory' and also a way of telling other birds they know a place where some kind of a bite will be given them. Always they sit round on the trellis and fence waiting, while none can be seen in the surrounding garden ... I felt so bewildered and depressed by the news from Korea. What *can* we do against such hordes – and such cruel ruthless 'savages'. I shuddered to think of poor wives' and mothers' feelings in America who read of GIs wounded being burnt. My deep fear that another atom bomb will be dropped grows daily as I can see no other weapon against such odds.

Nella had read John Hershey's *Hiroshima* (1946), a gripping account of the ruinous impact of one atomic bomb. On 4 December she heard another opinion about the crisis in Korea. 'My hairdresser is a young married woman whose husband works in the Yard. She was full of the conviction of the men in the Yard that the atom bomb – or bombs – would be certain to be dropped, that unless they were used American and British troops would be pushed back into the sea, and there would be no Dunkirk rescue.' The following day, with her sister-in-law, Flo, 'We talked of the black shadow of war looming'. 'It's a queer and mad world when prices rise and rise,' she wrote on 22 December, 'and the only things

we *do* seem to be able to afford as nations are armaments and atom bombs to
further destroy and kill, not only peoples, but the gracious lovely things of life.'
As a result of the war in Korea, there was to be a major increase in military
expenditures, to the detriment of the domestic economy; Britain was under
heavy pressure from Washington to rearm.

Wednesday, 6 December. It's been an evil day of sleet and rain and North
wind and all turning to slush. Mrs Salisbury came round by the bus,
which cost me 6d extra, but I felt so glad she came I didn't grudge it. She
has never complained of being so hard up – says, too, that she years ago,
when she had two small children and her husband only had the dole, had
more in her purse that wasn't 'condemned' and could be 'spent' instead
of just for weekly bills. A lot of her troubles even now are of her own
making. As I often tell her, if she made soup and porridge and baked more
instead of tinned soups – for six of them – and didn't rely on cornflakes
always and silly little bought cakes that were stale the next day, she could
economise on her Co-op bill. Where she lives there's only one other shop
on the estate and it's easiest to get all 'on the bill' and pay each Friday. I
washed a few oddments so as not to have a real wash day with a lot of wet
woollens etc. drying in the house, for my cough still keeps bad ...

I'd remembered in the evening that Mr Attlee would speak and
Mrs Howson asked if I 'would bother to listen'. When I said 'certainly',
she went with something about 'No time for that'. I listened with real
respect for the dignity and restraint of Attlee's speech. He couldn't have
said less – or more. I felt that never before in the world's history was
so difficult a situation facing men, or countries. Whether to leave all
our gallant soldiers with no hope either of more troops to help, or a
Dunkirk, or withdraw and lose face but 'live to fight another day', always
with the sick fear that whatever we did would be wrong, but with the
certainty of Stalin's deep laid plans to engulf Europe, and, if Europe, the
whole of the world. Beside Stalin, Hitler seems a boy scout. *He* is the
Anti Christ and not Hitler.*

---

* The Prime Minister was in the American capital for talks with President Truman and

The following day Nella and Will were at the Howsons with another couple. 'We spent a pleasant if a bit grim afternoon discussing Korea and our fears. Jack Hammond is certain the bomb will have to be dropped – "the only way to stem the onrush of Chinese, drunk with power, who otherwise will wipe out our troops mercilessly; and remember those self same troops may soon be needed in Europe". I see every argument for dropping the bomb, or bombs, yet I grow sick and cold with horror when I think of the results on the innocent as well as guilty – and "guilty" in that soldiers are pawns in a game, hardly considered as human by the ones who wage war.' She usually balked in horror at the prospect that these weapons might actually be used. In replying to MO's Directive for early 1951 she stated that 'I firmly believe that any atomic or H-bomb knowledge should be kept very much to some kind of [*international*] "control". It's a dreadful knowledge and should never be in any way regarded as part of warfare, or come to be considered lightly in any way.'

senior American officials. Britain was striving to contain the increasingly dangerous conflict in Korea (China had actively intervened in November) and discourage the use of atomic weapons. The script for this speech, broadcast at 9.15 p.m. on the Home Service, is not held in the BBC Written Archives Centre, presumably because it was transmitted from abroad and no copy was deposited with the BBC. It was probably the speech that Attlee gave at the National Press Club in Washington that day (*The Times*, 7 December 1950, p. 4b).

CHAPTER EIGHTEEN

DEFINING MOMENTS

June 1952–August 1955

In June 1952 Nella and Will left Barrow to visit Arthur and his family, who had recently moved from Northern Ireland to London. It was their first train trip together for years.

Monday, 23 June. I don't feel I am the traveller I used to be. I felt wearied by the train journey, even more, apparently, than my husband felt. Arthur and Peter were at Euston and we got a taxi to New Southgate. We were agreeably surprised by the really lovely house Arthur bought, and Blake Road all seems to have owner occupiers, which shows in well tended front gardens. Built only 26 years ago, it's on a 'modern' plan, with nice sized rooms, and a French window leads to a long, rather wild but pleasant strip of garden, quite cultivated enough for where two small lively boys need to play. They *are* little loves. Christopher at 18 months promises to be as 'old fashioned' as Peter. They seem little people with ideas and views, pursuits and occupations to busy them. We sat and listened to the wireless before going to bed fairly early. Peter slept with me, my husband in his small bed in the smallest room.*

Thursday, 26 June. We went out, taking a trolley bus as far as Holborn. All transport seems so easy, but there's a lot of walking to be done. I set off with a swelling ankle and foot and when I rose in Lyons felt I'd have to be a bit easier on it if I hadn't to crock up.† We went to Greenwich by boat – a lovely trip as we met a cool breeze – and then sat on the pier,

---

* The younger Lasts' home was at 64 Blake Road, N11; the nearest tube station was and still is Bounds Green, on the Piccadilly line, about half a mile away.

watching river traffic, feeling we *were* on holiday. Every oddment I've read of the Thames' history seemed to flow through my mind, whirling in a montage of peoples of every nationality and colour, American and German – or Swiss in leather shorts – docks, cargo ships, and the hundreds of school children in parties being taken by steamer. In one huge party I heard at least four names of schools through the megaphone – the proportion of half caste children, or at least with a very strong trace of colour in their parentage – and so widely different. It's amazing the lack of difference in school age and adolescents there is between South and North – just the different accent. We were in Woolworths about the lunch hour, and the things they chose! I only hoped they got a decent meal when they got home. I'd have awarded top place for oddity, though, to a gentle old world type of man who could have been a country parson or doctor. In Lyons he had a glass of lemonade with ice cream dropped in, and a double portion of ice cream, with four wafers, and by his look enjoyed his odd lunch. I wrote my diary and a letter to Cliff as I sat on the pier. My husband went for a walk. The cool breeze seemed to lessen the swelling on my foot, taking a little of the worried feeling I had, and we had a simple tea at a cafe on Greenwich Pier before setting off for Westminster again ...

As we walked down the hill to the Tube this morning my husband was full of wild plans to sell up as soon as we got home, and buy a house down here. Because he feels lifted out of himself so much, he feels a London suburb would cure him of every ill, not realising we so live in ourselves. I pointed out he hadn't the energy to take advantage of all the little functions at home – wouldn't visit, go to a show etc. He maintains it would be different if he lived in London. My remark was that New Southgate was not 'London', that going up the river would always mean a journey as far as Lakeside – *and* home again. I made him pout and he became so moody as I said **NO**. I've not altered my view always held – London means a 2d ride, or higher now of course with fare increases, to Kensington, Forest Gate, Chelsea or the like, not even Hampstead, Chiswick or Putney a second choice, and housing problems *terrible*. In his present mood he 'will make a change as soon as we go back – I *want* to get out of Barrow'. As I've always maintained, it was what we should have done at first when we knew he would have to retire, but reminded him how much more money we were spending in Barrow. Any move would have to be down scale, not where we would need twice as much if we were not to be more restricted than at present. I began to feel glad it was my own house as I listened. I'd a growing conviction he would have gone a bit haywire otherwise.

Saturday, 28 June. Arthur had off work this morning and we went down to Kensington, really to go and see Derry and Tom's roof garden. A bad day, really, for we didn't have time to look round much and have our lunch before the shops closed. Still, I'd talked of the lovely 'unexpected' place so much to my husband and he was satisfied, though we would have liked to spend more time. We got a really good, well cooked lunch, at just under 6s a head – cream of vegetable soup, two *huge* portions of fillet of plaice and more chips than could be eaten, and a strawberry ice and coffee – and Arthur and his father had a light ale and Edith cider. The two little boys had a 'special' – there was a good choice of children's meals. Peter was good, but to see Christopher in his high chair, blue eyes blazing and golden curly hair drying in the draught after the heat of his hat, seize his fork and begin was a joy. He had his fish cut up, but refused to have any long chips touched, even if they did need spearing on the fork with his fingers. His look of ecstasy at his strawberry ice in the goblet, with the biscuit still in, amused the waitress and manageress who was near ...

I love Kensington, and was astonished to see so many large maisonette type of houses for sale, and so many dirty, neglected ones as if owned and just shut up. I'd like a good small flat overlooking the gardens, though my first choice would be a small house in one of the unexpected quiet streets off Kensington Church Street. The types, colours and languages which swirled round were a joy. I'd have liked to linger, but Edith wanted to come home and wash! – such a *huge* pile. We had tea. I'd been on my aching right foot and ankle too much to go strolling round the neighbourhood with my husband, and knew I'd better finish Edith's sun dress. She looked so nice today – a new navy moiré silk dress, small white hat and gloves – pity she hadn't a pin in her hat; it blew up an escalator and was only rescued when it had got nearly to the top – and she didn't bother to change to wash till I tactfully told her my sleeved overall would perhaps fit and she could have it. After 10 o'clock I helped her hang all on the line. I'd washed my dress earlier and ironed it. I'd a sneaking wonder what the neighbours thought of our garden of washing on Saturday night – they seem very conventional.

Early the next morning, a Sunday, 'I looked down at the untidy line of washing, and crept down in my dressing gown and brought all in, smiling to myself at my deep conventional streak which made me feel so horrified at the sight.'

Monday, 30 June. It's a real heat wave. I think longingly of sea breezes in the rattle and noise of the Tube.* We would have been content to sit in the garden this morning, but the little boys were cross and screamed. Christopher was tired for he had been up before 6 o'clock. I thought of children in flats and closed-in streets. We went down by Tube, already feeling hot, men in shirts and pants and girls in topless sun suits, ladies waving little paper fans, looking as if the two last lots *could* have been going to the Sales; breaths of coolth and sweetness at Covent Garden station when boys brought huge bundles of green forms, presumably for fish shops, and women and men had even bigger sheaves of gorgeous flowers. We had a light snack of tea and a sandwich at Lyons and got on a boat to Kew – in blistering heat, when to rest arms or back unexpectedly on the rail was to jump suddenly. We had a nice Australian sitting by us – we met him first the other day. He lives in the 'back blocks' 100 miles from Melbourne. When he goes on to his verandah he can 'see two lights and likes it that way'. I felt I understood. The masses of

---

* Will was not always sensitive to the protocols for using the escalators in tube stations. 'My husband has been unpopular a few times', Nella wrote on 1 July. 'In spite of my warnings – and given by Cliff – to keep always to the right, he will use the left, and has been bumped as well as told curtly "keep to the right".'

perspiring people and the cross children around and the 'breathed' air everywhere stifled me. I'm constantly amazed at my husband's seemingly inexhaustible fund of 'go' and think of Dr Miller's 'out of patience' with his complaints of 'no strength' and 'going all to pieces' and saying that most nervous illness was no physical illness – it could be thrown off.

We had a very nice tray lunch at Kew – good salad with ham, a roll and butter and a fresh salad of pineapple, orange, cherries and sweet apple with a little wedge of ice cream. The shade of the trees drew people, the lovely flowers and hot houses only being noticed by parties of people who seemed to have come by motor coach, and dozens of children, with harassed looking teachers seeming bent on telling them everything. A huge though shapely figure moved majestically along alone, a negress *really* black as coal, in the hottest most shrieking shade of zinnia purple. Our eyes met and she smiled in so friendly a fashion as she seemed to flow down the path. Such interesting people you see – the lovely flower like Eastern women in filmy saris, beautiful as houris,† fascinate me, as I wonder if they are on holiday, knowing their mothers would have been strictly purdah,† making me realise as nothing else the mass movement to 'freedom' of today.

Monday, 7 July. We had the most enjoyable day of our holiday and at the last place I'd have imagined – the Food Fair at Olympia! I knew the right bus to take from Piccadilly for Cliff – I used to use a No. 9 or 73 to go Richmond way and passed Olympia. I'd never seen a big Food Fair, but used to like the travelling Exhibition that came to Barrow. We were in at 11 o'clock and didn't leave till 4.30. Being Monday, there was no crush, and till mid afternoon not many people at all. We had lunch at the best place of Lyons yet – quite good soup, roll and butter, and good choice of sweet, with a salad extra, made up at the counter ... I *love* gadgets and new ways with food. I use Soreme cream and watched new ways of icing and piping, and a kind of 'baba' made out of a piece of cake, small block of ice cream 'insulated' with a thick layer of the whipped cream, and scorched rather than baked in a very hot oven. But

I pointed out to the two nice young fellows that they hadn't anything as nice as the 'butterfly' cream bun I make, or the sandwich with raspberry jam and thick cream between – 'Ordinary no doubt, but after all, ain't we all?'

It grew hot. We rested frequently in comfortable chairs, watching the ebb and flow around. Even since my last visits, six years ago, there seem a more cosmopolitan crowd, and India and her peoples, with South Americans, make the biggest difference. I dearly love perfume, and nowadays there's no 'lasting' fragrance, even in simple things like lavender, when once handfuls strewn in linen kept it fragrant till lavender time came round again. Some of the expensively dressed, dark skinned ladies in saris have the most beautiful clear oil perfume. I coveted a big bottle. I bought wee oddments of 3d jars of jam, crisps and biscuits for the little boys, and three small 9d jars of Brand's meat paste for Edith, and I will make sandwiches of one to eat on our way home. We sat in Kensington Gardens till the rush had gone in bus and tubes.

The next day they were exposed to a different slice of London life. 'We went down to Euston to book two seats on the train, seeing our first real "working" part of London. I realised the hopelessness of behaviour and decency of many evacuees was the result of such drab places, where ordinary standards of cleanliness were impossible in the smoke and squalor of railways and big concerns which made smoke and soot.' Then, on Wednesday the 9th, they were back in Barrow, and 'I was surprised to find our house seem so small after Arthur's'.

* * * * * *

There were some local happenings to catch up on. Mrs Salisbury, at her first Wednesday visit to Nella's house, had alarming news to report about one of her boarders, 'a very odd type' whose 'great hobby was model airplanes. He always seemed to have young boys of 14 and 15 around, but they were all interested in model making, and he always seemed busy developing photos'. One day 'Mrs Salisbury was turning out his room and saw some of the photos and to use her own words "I felt I could have died of shock". They sounded not only beastly but dangerous. The naked boys in acts of perversion and masturbation were plainly recognised from the group he went about with. Mrs Salisbury was the most shocked by photos of a 15 year old Grammar school boy, a member of the Scouts and choir and one of the two sons of a widow Mrs Salisbury knew. After thinking things over, she took the photos to her, saying "I'd have been glad if anyone had let me know about the dangerous friendship if it had been one of my boys". There was a big row. The widow wasn't without the advice of sensible friends, and a condition of not going to the police was that he had never to be seen in boys' company – and the photos are retained by the one who gave the advice as "guarantee"' (16 July).

Saturday, 19 July. If joyous days should be called red letter days, today is a black one. My little Shan We died suddenly, apparently of a heart attack. He ate his usual good breakfast, went to play on the lawn and ran in hurriedly when it began to rain suddenly, and sat on my husband's lap for the rest of the morning. I'd tidied up, and machined† for an hour. There was good beef soup, cold brisket beef and salad, cornflour sweet and stewed raspberries. Shan We coaxed a meaty bit of gristle and ate it, and then sat on the rug till I'd finished lunch and then jumped on my lap as usual, his paws on my chest, his clear blue eyes lovingly on my face. I remembered again how much more loving – if that was possible – he had been since he came home [*from the boarding kennel*]. I rose soon saying 'I'm going to wash up, and then you can relax till 2 o'clock' – we had an appointment at the Hospital with Dr Wadsworth, the visiting psychiatrist. I'd lifted Shan We down on to the rug, and my husband passed back and forward clearing the table. It couldn't have been more than five minutes when he said 'Come quickly, Dearie'. I saw my little cat lying on his side, his tongue hanging out, his head lolled helplessly as I put my hands under him and raised him. I'd once brought him out of a similar attack when he was only a few weeks old, with whiskey and holding him pressed to my warm body till I got a fire going, but today half a teaspoon of neat brandy poured into his open mouth was no use, or warmth and massaging his heart, which had ceased to beat before I lifted him. The light died in his jewel blue eyes.

I felt stunned – and so terribly worried at the way my husband took it. I never saw him so distraught. I wanted to phone to the Hospital and say he couldn't come, but he roused himself a little and we went. Dr Wadsworth was shocked at his appearance, till he knew about our little friend, and then was so understanding. I've always found Ulstermen to be insensitive. We came home. I'd laid my pet in his bed and covered him warmly in the forlorn hope a miracle *might* happen. I could not believe he would never rush to meet us again. My husband dug his grave in the flower border, and we made a soft cushion of lawn grass clippings and laid him on – he looked peacefully sleeping. As we covered him with more grass I murmured 'Goodbye, little cat. Thank you for your love and affection. It's been grand knowing you.' And I wondered how many people were buried so sadly.*

I made tea, but beyond several cups of tea and a little bread and butter we couldn't eat. I had a lost feeling when no eager little blue eyed cat jumped on my lap. The moment I'd finished I looked at my husband's face and shaking hands and thought of Dr Wadsworth's advice 'It would be as well to get another Siamese as soon as possible. I don't like *any* upset for Mr Last.' I asked him if he would like another, but he said simply 'No, it would never be Shan We'. I said coaxingly 'Wouldn't you like a little dog? You could take him out.' Nothing could rouse him. I felt I pushed my own grief deeper and deeper till I was choking. Kipling was right – you should 'never give your heart to a dog to tear'. I felt I hadn't to keep anything I loved. I looked at poor old Murphy with near loathing as I thought 'Oh *why* couldn't it have been you? At turned 15, you are past much sweetness of life.' My dear Shan We was only 6, loving life and living, radiating love and affection. With Cliff buying him and the trouble he was to rear, he never seemed 'just an animal'. I'd a feeling I'd lost a real link with Cliff.

I coaxed my husband to take two codeine tablets and gave him some brandy and water, feeling really afraid he would collapse altogether, wondering what I should do. Often he has said half jokingly to Shan

---

* 'You carried flowers for Shan We as if he was a person', Will had remarked (20 July).

We 'I wish you were a little dog and could come for a walk'. I felt wearily
I didn't want to face training a puppy. I like cats best, but realising how
on the edge my poor man is feeling I'd undertake to train a hippo if it
made him happy or gave him an interest. We went for a little walk. I
suddenly thought of my hairdresser – she bought a Cairn puppy some
time ago, an adorable beastie. My husband saw it and wondered 'if Shan
We would agree with a puppy if we got one'. I rang her up for a chat. She
lost a much loved dog at about seven years old and said 'A friend advised
us to get another one straight way'. I asked her if she thought there were
any puppies at the breeding kennels where she got hers, and she said
'Ring up and see. The number is in the phone book – a place near Carnforth'. When my husband came in, looking wild eyed and nervy, I said
'Now if you *would* like a puppy, I know where I might get one'. He didn't
speak. He didn't seem to hear properly. I thought wildly 'If I could go
tonight and get one I'd gladly go – *anything* to take that lost expression
off your face'. I felt my constant prayer rise to my lips – that I could live
longer than him. I felt little bargains in a montage of wild pleas. *Whatever* happened to me, I'd never complain if only I *could* live longer, to
always look after him.

Following their adventures in London, Nella and Will resumed their (mostly)
quiet lives in Barrow-in-Furness. There were changes in their household, one of
which was the acquisition of a dog to replace Shan We. Nella had mixed feelings
about dogs, and clearly preferred cats. Still, a dog it was to be, and on 21 July
1952, after inspecting a litter of seven puppies, Nella wrote that 'I'd not have
known where to choose, but one little fellow was determined to be chosen – he
made such a fuss over my husband. I was delighted. The colour came back into
his cheeks. There was no doubt from the first.' The puppy was named Garry; he
and Will hit it off reasonably well and in due course regularly went out together
for walks. Nella, an exponent of firm discipline, thought Will over-indulgent with
Garry. In January 1953, 9 Ilkley Road became a cat-free household when old
Murphy, aged fifteen and a half and seriously ill, was put down.

* * * * * *

On the night of 31 January–1 February 1953 there were monster storms in parts of the British Isles (and elsewhere, especially the Netherlands). A car ferry went down off the coast of Northern Ireland, and 128 people lost their lives; and there were over 300 other deaths as a result of the massive floods that night, almost all of them in settlements in, on or near the Thames estuary and in coastal areas of East Anglia (Essex and Norfolk were very hard hit). 'Thousands were rendered homeless,' according to the *Illustrated London News* of 7 February (p. 193), 'and from every quarter of the flooded districts poignant stories were recorded. Some were drowned in cars on the roads, dead were found on roofs or caught in trees, and families were marooned in flooded houses, crouching in lofts and upper storeys in their night attire. Public services were disrupted and fear of epidemics was an added anxiety.' Some 32,000 people were flooded out of their homes.*

This was a major disaster, and it summoned up the sort of relief efforts that Britain had witnessed a dozen years earlier. 'It is "like the war all over again"', wrote Tom Driberg in the *New Statesman* (7 February, p. 141), 'not only because of the troops, but because of the spirit of comradeship and hospitality among the thousands of voluntary workers who have "mucked in" – the hotel-keepers and yachtsmen at Burnham-on-Crouch who have looked after evacuees from Foulness and cooked meals day and night, the boat-builders who have crossed to the islands dozens of times every twenty-four hours bringing off boat-loads of the homeless, the ladies who have made the Royal Corinthian Yacht Club a model rest-centre.' Help also came from more distant places, including Barrow-in-Furness; women there threw themselves into work that was highly reminiscent of some of the wartime efforts of the WVS. Nella's diary for the first half of February testifies to the aid organised in Barrow for the unfortunate victims elsewhere.

Tuesday, 3 February. I didn't feel so well and my face ached badly. The

---

* A succinct account of these floods is presented in David Kynaston, *Family Britain, 1951–57* (London: Bloomsbury, 2009), pp. 257–9. At Barrow's WVS Club meeting on 2 February 1953 'quite a number wondered if "H and atom bomb trials could possibly be the cause of the high tides"' that had inundated some coastal areas.

thought of all the homeless cold people in the flood areas haunted me. I packed a pair of shoes I can do without, some shirts Cliff once sent, two old but well mended vests of my own and two of my husband's, some underpants with worn knees – I cut and machined a hem and made them into shorts – and packed a little cretonne bag I made with a drawstring with a few sylkos,* cotton, darning wool and the necessary needles. I'd the good heart to pack up nine-tenths of my clothes, but they will have to do me much service yet, before I can part with them. I'll send 5s to the Mayor's Fund, and more if I can scrounge it out of my housekeeping. I can never interest my husband in giving anything away. He wouldn't have parted from his old underwear if I'd asked him ... [*Later*] Mrs Atkinson came in and said 'I've a big pile of things if you will pack and send them off for the flood victims'. I said I would, and stared at the two big armfuls she brought, costumes, coats, overcoats and suits that had belonged to a brother of Mr Atkinson's who died last year, and shoes of her own and Norah's.

Wednesday, 4 February. A ring brought me to the door, where a strange young woman stood smiling. She said 'Will you put these children's rubber boots and clothes in your parcel? Someone told me you would be sure to be sending something for the flood victims or would take them to the WVS office.' Then for the rest of the morning phone calls to ask if parcels could be brought or if I'd pack things and send them, and rings at the door with parcels, till before lunch my front sitting room looked like a second hand shop! I'd soup, and stewed rabbit enough, and cooked sprouts and potatoes, and we finished with a cup of tea. I planned to relax awhile when my husband went to lie down, but there was no rest for either of us – more knocks, rings and phone calls. I wondered wildly wherever I'd get paper and string to pack all, and thought of the sugar sacks I once bought off my grocer, and rang him to see if he would let me have some – they are doled out sparingly to people on a list usually, and he isn't a really pleasant man. I felt it just another part of my odd day when he *gushed* 'Certainly, Mrs Last. How many will you have? It will be a pleasure to send you as many as you want. Would you like some today?' I said 'Well, I think I could get them in four of those small sacks or three of the larger ones'. He said 'I'll send what I have and you must let me know later if you want more'. I went over all, and stitched all buttons on even if they were not a perfect match, and did little repairs.

My husband came down and when he saw what I was doing he offered to clean and polish all the shoes, and we will get some laces to replace worn ones. I asked everyone to spare odd bits of flannel and toilet soap, needles, cotton and mending wool, and packed them in little bags, if only paper ones. We were both tired by the time I made a late tea. There was a notice in the local *Mail* tonight saying the [*WVS*] office would be open every day this week for gifts, so perhaps people will send them there. Mrs Higham has a lot of oddments left at her house. There was toast and cream cheese, Turog† bread and butter and cake for tea, and it was nearly 7 o'clock before I rose to clear the table and wash up. I felt a bit tired, but unravelled two good home knitted sock legs and two big balls of darning wool. Mrs Higham said she had a huge pile of goodish socks if they were darned.

Thursday, 5 February. Another hectic day. I got four sacks packed neatly, folding and packing tightly all garments in an effort to avoid crumpling, if not creasing. I decided that any more things could go down to the WVS office, for big sacks have been provided from Regional. We went to Dalton for the meat. I left a note pinned on the curtain to say 'Back about 11 o'clock. Parcels of clothing for WVS can be left in garden or at no. 7.' ... We went into town when we returned from Dalton, the back of the car piled high with some quite good car rugs, a big old blanket that could be torn into babies' blankets, nappies tied up in a bundle, little woolly coats, little boys' clothes and some elderly women's clothes that had a note pinned on to say 'Call in later if these are suitable – have lots more of mother's clothes' and the name of a neighbour in the road behind whose mother died recently. The scene at the office was a surprise, even though I'd expected good response – looked as if there would be a van load when packed. We stayed. I'd have stayed over lunch time, but said Mrs Higham and I were coming down with a car load of things she had collected and took back an armful of pants, feeling really scornful of a woman's mentality who would send pants without buttons enough for decency, never mind use. I pictured a distraught man who felt hopeless and lost being handed pants with one button on the flies, and felt a 'Bad end to you' to the thoughtless person who sent them.

Friday, 6 February. We took parcels of clothes to the WVS. I longed to join the busy workers, sorting and packing. There's *such* a different atmosphere since merry capable little Mrs Woods took over, and she has nice helpers. Never was there so friendly a feeling. When old Mrs Manson and Mrs Howson were Clothing Officer and Deputy someone was always offending one or the other. Such good garments have been sent in, two quite wearable fur coats amongst the pile on the counter. Miss Willan asked if Mrs Higham and I could collect one night next week at the Odeon – most of the picture houses are having a Relief Fund collection. She asked in my husband's hearing and he said 'Of course you must go'. So I took him at his word! ...

I'd more buttons to sew on, and more clothes came in. They have had such a wonderful response at the [*WVS*] office they are keeping open till 8.30 each evening. It's such a small place to work in. The Railway van calls each day. Everyone is so eager to help. Collections at rugby and soccer matches tomorrow, dances, collections at others and efforts in every direction. The Round Table are canvassing for money if no clothes are available. In Barrow we won't have much coal for a few weeks. Householders are asked in an article in the *Mail* to 'use other available fuel, including nutty slack', as our supplies will be diverted to the East Coast. I scrambled eggs and made toast and there was Turog bread and butter and greengage jam and cake. I kept wishing I could have been at the WVS office helping. When I looked at them working so cheerily my mind went back to wartime, when, whatever our worries and anxiety, there was 'always tomorrow' ... I thought wistfully as I sat sewing I'd have liked to recapture, however slightly, that comradeship.

There was a ring and Mrs Higham's voice said 'I'm down at the office. Mrs Woods is off to London tomorrow to help with clothing. Will you lend her your [*WVS*] overcoat?' I couldn't refuse, and she is a very dainty person, but I *don't* like wearing anything of anyone else's, and that goes for my own that anyone else has worn. She will be away four days at least. I'll have it cleaned when she returns it, and wear my WVS suit for collecting at the Odeon. I felt mean to have that 'shrinking', but it's one of those things that, if you have it, it's as much a part of you as the colour of your hair. Mrs Woods came just after 9 o'clock. I'm only about 5 feet 1½ inches – in my shoes – and she is nearly half a head less!* Still, shoulders and sleeves were all right. She said 'Never mind it being too long. It will be warmer for travelling. Thank you *so* much, and I've already borrowed Miss Willan's dress. It's good of you both to lend them. I'm so fussy. You are the only two WVS I'd have liked to wear anything belonging to.' I felt I chuckled as I realised there were others as odd as myself! She is a merry little thing and laughed as she told of her rush to get ready. I said 'Your husband doesn't mind you going, then?' She said 'Dear me, why should he? I'm only going for a few days, and he knows enough to look after himself if all is in the house. He's not a child.' I didn't glance across at my husband, knowing darn well the fight I'd have had to put up, and if I'd insisted on going, the reproaches and recriminations, the feeling of guilt that spoiled enjoyment. I felt she didn't realise how lucky she was.

The next day she and Will drove to Spark Bridge to pick up some clothes that Aunt Sarah had collected. Her 'bundle was a bit old fashioned, but there was a good thick cape with a hood, and a grey homespun suit of Joe's I've remembered for years. All had a sweet musty smell. Wood smoke, lavender and smoke of tobacco struggled with the sweetish smell of stored apples, for Aunt Sarah has all her boxes and oddments in the attic. In two black bodices she had stitched white frills in the necks, crisp and freshly starched and ironed. I wondered if there were any old dear who *would* wear them – women like herself who had stayed still as regards fashions.'

---

* Will, for a man, was even slighter than Nella: he was 5 feet 3 inches in height and weighed 8 stone 8 pounds (8 June 1951).

Sunday, 8 February. A ring took my husband to the door as I was dressing. I heard an oddly pitched voice saying something about 'Looking for a little WVS lady who lives hereabouts', and felt a bit surprised to hear my husband asking him in. When I went into the living room a huge young fellow rose and said 'Good morning, ma'am. I'd like your advice about some clothes I have for the flood folks.' We began to talk. He is in one of the small flats made from several of the big houses on the main road into which our small road runs. I'd have said he was an American with his slow drawl, but he is a Canadian, working just now in the Yard. I said I'd gladly take charge of them, thinking 'I'll ring up Miss Willan and get her to send up for what I have if she wants all down before we get the car back'. He went and then I heard a car, and looking out saw a huge low slung grey car with two young men in. The boot was opened and a very large parcel lugged out. The one who had called said 'These are mostly boots, ma'am, but wrapped in a heavy coat to keep them together'. Before I could say 'Thank you – leave it in the hall there', his companion appeared from the open car door with his arms full of rugs, coats, suits and bright plaid hip-blouse[†] things Canadians wear. When they had finished I felt a bit dazed as I looked at the huge pile, women's clothes amongst them. I said 'How *generous* of you to spare all these marvellously warm garments', but the friend in a curious 'Hush your mouf' honied tones gave me to understand it was a relief to be rid of them. They had brought all as a matter of course and realised they 'would be a real "noosense" and expensive to store or tote round', and left me with the impression *I* was doing them a favour! ...

I had a rest on the settee after my husband went to lie down and then mended socks and put some elastic in two good pairs of corsets. I felt they would be better than with an ordinary lace, giving a wider fit. They are both made to measure corsets, only needing a bit of repair, but I wouldn't have insulted anyone by offering them before I soaked and scrubbed them. When I think of the giver I marvel – so beautifully turned out whatever she wears. I've heard her boast she can '*Never* use any other than Elizabeth Arden toilet requisites' and 'I *never* buy anything off the peg. I am so particular about fit and cut.'

Yet I lightly touched them as I poked the sleazy greasy things into hot
Tide suds!

The next day, 'Shoes and scarves and some good little pants and shirts came in a
parcel from my brother – none needed any attention – but I made some garters
from oddments of elastic in the parcel … When I was talking to Miss Willan over
the phone, she said 327 huge cigarette cartons and parcels nearly as large had
just gone. The Railway man had been "staggered" and had had to make several
trips.' (British Railways and the Post Office were delivering relief parcels free of
charge.) On Tuesday the 10th 'I packed the last of the oddments ready to go to
the WVS office, and then had a rest on the settee after taking a codeine.' By the
end of the week the rush was over for Nella and the other ladies of the WVS,
who had been kept uncommonly busy for nearly a fortnight, re-experiencing
some of the solidarities of wartime.

* * * * * *

In the mid-1950s passing scenes of daily life continued to attract Nella's notice,
and her diary was (as it had always been) sometimes an outlet for feelings that
otherwise she kept mostly to herself. Here are a few snapshots of life from her
sixty-sixth year, in 1955.

Monday, 14 February 1955. When my husband said he would like to
go down to the Bank, I hurriedly got ready, and shopped for flour and
yeast, and a packet of deep freeze cod fillets and one of boned kippers in
the serve-yourself Co-op. The yeast is at the counter where bacon and
fats, eggs and cheese are sold, and I was looking round, rather hoping
I'd see a small ham shank. Monday is a good day as a rule. The manager
– not been there so very long – a quiet, courteous type, was talking
to the four girls at the long counter and I heard 'Never "luv", or never,
never "ducks". Try and find out each customer's name and memorise
it. Avoid Christian names. In doubt, remember to say "madam".' I'd a
'came the dawn' feeling. Co-ops have always been a free and easy, often
slap-dash kind of shop. Brought up to the quiet easy courtesy of shops

in Ulverston, where generations served generations so of course knew all customers and still do, I always had a little distaste for the 'I'm as good as her anyway; who does she think she is complaining of so and so?' familiarity of the Co-ops – above all their impersonal manner. But to hear a little lecture on deportment made me think of the changes in policy the Co-ops are adopting. The girls in this shop are all extremely nice, eager to help if asked. No one could find fault and say the service was in any way off hand, though the shop where Mrs Higham deals – Co-op – has a very rude manner. I would never allow a trader, man or woman, to speak to me as Mrs Higham does. I'd quietly say 'Please don't bother. The dividend you pay doesn't make up for the discourtesy.' And I'd go elsewhere, *and* let them know at the Office why I was leaving.

Friday, 18 February. I felt so despondent all day. I use that word for want of a better to describe the cold dread in my heart and mind after reading we are going to make H-bombs in Britain. Common sense says it's imperative – we must 'keep up with the Joneses' – but I think of the article I once read in a 'Digest' before they were more than in the experimental stage. It alleged that while atom bombs *could* be 'broken down', H-bombs, once made, could never be used for anything but explosions. Where will they store the dreadful death-dealing things? They will never be buried deep enough in land or sea. While I've always maintained I thought the term 'when' rather than 'if' should be used about a third war, it's a shock to see one's own convictions becoming more plain in other people's views and articles.

Friday, 26 March. Cliff's letter came, with such good photos and articles about the open air Exhibition he is doing for a Melbourne newspaper. He seems to have got a nice looking group to help him, but oh dear, how we laughed at Cliff's beard! He told me he intended to grow one. He knows my opinion of beards – and those who grow them – but couldn't let well alone, and complained I'd not made any comment. When my next letter was written I put 'Remarks on growing a beard noted – I pass'! Still, I must confess he looked pretty good, and so very happy. The piece of sculpture he had in the Exhibition of his own was terribly, terribly Henry Mooreish. In an article to a reporter he explained the odd looking thing with one side of its (alleged) head scooped out, 'It's man in abstract, showing how little perception he really possesses'. And he expects to get £50. I often feel like the hen who hatched out a duckling. I utterly fail to understand any type of modern 'art'. Appreciation of it has been totally denied me, whether it's painting, sculpture, or some of the so peculiar noises made as music.

Monday, 23 May. I wonder who advises Royalty. I feel they were unwise when, if there is such a person, he or she agreed to Billy Graham preaching in the Royal Chapel. Democracy can go *too* far. Royalty should bend, not stoop, for there *is* a dividing line. Maybe it's my own reaction to any kind of hysteria or mob thinking. Perhaps it's an inborn horror of revivalist meetings – in my teens, with no films, youth centres, etc. we found interest in 'meetings'. Energetic ones easily the top attractions, cheap jack vendors in the open market a good second, but failing such, Kensitites, 'Gospel Tents', etc. were not to be scorned as words and more words poured from inspired mouths. Yet I could never follow friends to the 'mercy seat.' I felt, as I saw all reticence and reserve cast away, the same reaction as I would if clothes had been shed to show a stark, twisted body. My reaction to any type of nudity was relative to the grace and beauty of the undressing. What can be more revolting than the jelly bag type going in swimming? Private reactions or not, I do *not* approve of the Billy Graham, Danny Kaye 'get together' with the Queen. I often think her husband enjoys such little rebellious actions.

Tuesday, 24 May. We went to Spark Bridge ... Aunt Sarah had been hanging some tea towels on the line and had a light woollen scarf over her head as she came in the back door as we came in the front. She took it off as she greeted me – my husband took the dog for a walk straight from the car. I looked at Aunt Sarah – just couldn't believe my eyes. She has cut her hair – in a real Audrey Hepburn 'snaggle'*† – and looks astonishingly like Audrey too, with her wide dark eyes and small elfin face. I seized my writing pad and pencil and wrote 'You look like a film star. Whose idea was this?' She positively simpered as she said 'Ah, I cut it myself one day, and Ruth [*from next door*] tidied off the back. Makes a change.' I laughed and laughed – she took it all in good part. I think so many had admired her 'urchin cut' she was a bit conceited! It looked as if she had held a lock of hair and snipped it off about 1½ inches from her scalp. She looked a good *twenty* years younger from the prim Edwardian with upswept hair. I never remember her changing her hairstyle! ...

I was very interested in an article in tonight's local *Mail* of a marvellous piece of engineering by the Japanese – a bridge at Nagasaki. I recalled the first Japanese battleship to be built here, and the smiling, friendly, but so odd little men. I had an aunt whose son was threatened with T.B. – nowadays he would have been treated in a sanatorium but I don't think the seriousness of T.B. was recognised. He had to sleep with the window frames taken out, and a light muslin covered screen instead, to break the cold winds, and have milk, cream, eggs etc. beyond her means, and as she had a fairly large house she decided to take boarders. My father's people were Londoners and had a kind of inborn tolerance as regards people of other countries, so when she was told at the Yard bureau that only Japanese were on their list, especially when she heard the terms they would pay, she took three. That's about 50 years ago – or a little more perhaps – not long in a country's history. They had come to watch their ship being built and to learn all they could about engineering, and they stayed about two years. They addressed her always as 'honourable mother', were unbelievably good to the little invalid, gave no trouble of any kind, even keeping to their own custom of removing outdoor shoes and putting on straw slippers just inside the front door! When they went back, they and their families kept up correspondence and exchanged little gifts till World War One, when they seemed to lose touch.

Thursday, 14 July. Such a nightmare day, and I feel I dare not look forward to tomorrow. My husband was down first. He called '*Do* come quickly and look at Garry' and I ran down in my nightdress. As I took the little, limp, grey body with wide staring eyes, I knew if he wasn't dead, he hadn't much chance. I gave him a drop of whiskey in tea, got dressed, and rang up the vet at Ulverston, who said he would call as he had to come into this district. There's five of them altogether, but they have a wide 'beat'. He didn't come till after 11 o'clock, and the little dog had one convulsion after another till he couldn't stand. I nursed and soothed him, took him out and laid him on the cool lawn in the shade, helped him to the flower beds when he seemed to want the feel of earth under him – a bad sign when primitive people or animals want the feel of mother earth. I grew cold with dread as I saw my husband's ashen face and trembling hands, recalling the bad nerve storm he had when Shan We died. Somehow it was as if all the heartache I felt then rolled over me, and my terror grew as I remembered that my husband's health had worsened in the last three years. He had to go round to his mother's on business. The dog hadn't been so very bad till then, and I hurried upstairs to make the beds. I made them *very* sketchily, and didn't dust, so wasn't long out of the living room, but could hear a queer rattling sound and I feared the worst.

I was glad the vet came just then and saw him shaking and twitching. He gave him another good examination, saying again 'his heart and lungs are alright, his eyes don't show bloodshot and strain of infection. I'm frankly puzzled' – but he gave him an injection and left tablets. I said 'I've got both brandy and whiskey in the house', and I held up the little 'winter' bottle of my husband's of the latter, with about a tablespoonful in. He said 'I'll leave it to your discretion. I see you understand animals.' I said 'Not really, but I reared two delicate little boys and found the value of quiet, warmth – or coolness – lots of water, and above all a lot of petting.' He said he would come in tomorrow, and reflected as he went out that he was 'completely baffled'. It was rather curious as the day wore on how I kept remembering my old cairn's last days, though he was about fourteen and Garry is only three. I'd rung up Mrs Higham and explained we wouldn't be round. I said 'I *couldn't* leave Will. It would upset him beyond belief to cope with poor Garry.' My so often, almost frantic prayer rang through my heart and mind. I often find myself 'bargaining' – if I can only live the longer, I'll take *anything*. If the loss of a little cat and the threatened loss of his little dog could so distress my poor man, the mere thought of his helpless *abandonment* choked me.

We had had a sketchy meal at lunch time. Nerves often seem to settle in my throat and make me feel I cannot swallow if I chew food. My husband had soup and the bit of meat that was left and two sliced tomatoes, ground rice, and some fresh picked raspberries. I didn't take much of anything on my plate knowing I'd only pick at it. I made strong tea in the middle of the afternoon, and had a surprise call from a WVS friend, who wanted to borrow my WVS suit. She is taking some of the Darby and Joan club† to London. She is as clean as I am myself. I felt ungracious as I grudgingly lent it. I *don't* like wearing [*others' clothes*] or having others wear my clothes. She is the daughter of a nurse I had when I had my first baby and was brought up to all kinds of sickness, and is a St John's ambulance member. I could see she thought very little of poor Garry's chance to get better. He was very sick after taking his half tablet. After we had had bread and butter and several cups of tea – neither could eat – at tea time, I gave him a tablespoonful of warm water, and about half a teaspoonful of brandy in it, and crushed another of the sedative tablets in. Thank goodness for the peace that came over his little racked body. We took the piece of carpet and old coat from his basket and laid it on the mat in the garage. Poor little dog. He couldn't even climb in and out of his basket – and he slept peacefully. His convulsive jerkings and twitching stilled ...

12.30. The little dog was sleeping so peacefully when we came to bed. I've just been down – I found he had died quietly in his sleep. Dear God, how I dread morning.

Friday night, 15 July. Sleep fled altogether last night. At 2 o'clock I could tell if I lay thinking and thinking, it would only end in a blinding headache, and I knew well I'd need everything in the way of courage and energy later, so I gathered up my clothes and went downstairs. I didn't want my husband to find Garry lying dead, even if he *did* look peaceful and serene with an easy crossing. I still cannot believe that coaxing, restless little dog has gone out of our lives. I'd a little sadness. I'd never been able to return his love in full. I went out into the garden at dawn and walked on the lawn. Time *did* drag, for I could not read or sew, and I didn't want to waken my husband by any noise.

He seemed to know the worst without me telling him. The outburst I'd dreaded didn't come – but *so* much worse. A leaden bluish look came over not only his face but his hands. I'd made strong tea when I heard him stirring. He took it, spilled half, and looked blankly at the cup and saucer, as if seeing them for the first time. I began to be really frightened. I talked of the little dog, his cute ways, his cleverness, his love of a joke, talked myself to a standstill, powerless against the stunned, icy silence. He drank the remainder of his tea, and rose slowly to his feet, swayed slightly, and then went into the garage. I let him go alone. No one but me ever realised the deep and happy love they had for each other. I heard choking sobs and gentle coaxing talk. I went in, to see him stroking the little dog, but the dreadful blue look had gone from his face. I said 'I'm going to ask the vet when he calls if he knows where I can buy another – *today* if possible'. There followed passionate assertions he would never have another dog – another animal at all. I said flatly and firmly 'We *are* going to have another dog. Do you realise how very friendless and alone we are? Rarely have visitors. And the pitiful and tragic result is we are going to grow more narrow, and pity help us. We are getting too old to change.' He dug a little grave at the bottom of the garden. There was a lot of overblown roses needing cutting off. I saw two big buckets of fragrant, glowing roses, by the grave, and one was tipped into it, and I knew the other bucketful was to cover little Garry ...

My husband ate a good lunch, but I'd so nervy a throat I just could not swallow. Loss is a strange thing. I looked round for Garry, feeling with a sadness that 'never again' were perhaps the saddest words, and 'everything passes', if not happy sounding, carry vague comfort.

Saturday, 16 July. I packed sandwiches, tomatoes and bananas and we were out by 10.30. I felt like nothing on earth – and looked it too! My husband had the look of nervous energy and talked of the kennels where we were going, the prizes Mrs Drummond had won, how her dogs went all over the world – the Windsors have had three – and what an atmosphere of 'kindliness' there was amongst all the dogs – and the kennel maid. He showed no signs of fatigue! We rested after lunch under some shady trees on the roadside and called at 'Blencathra' at 1.30. We had a choice of two out of two slightly different litters. A really nice dog, fourteen months old. I kept out of the discussion, wouldn't give an opinion, though liked one plump little fellow with merry eyes and a vague resemblance to Garry at eight weeks – and he was the one my husband chose. He is a sandy blue. His undercoat is camel colour and the longer hair rather brindled.[†] I suggested his name could be Sandy. We paid eight guineas and the kennel maid's usual ten shillings and after a short rest we made for home ...

We have been very little on the Great North Road, even on the winding road to Levens Bridge to where all the Scot and Lakeland transport and cars throng ... Perhaps as I grow older I'm 'reverting', as I long for the peace and quiet of country ways of life and living, but at last I said 'I don't know if it's my fancy, but there seem at least four times the huge vehicles and large – unnecessary – wide cars', and my husband agreed. I said 'And never, *never* say to me again "I wish I could go off for long day trips and long holiday journeys" – it would be a penance rather than a pleasure'. Poor dear, just as so little upsets him now, even less uplifts. He glanced lovingly at me and said 'You *are* so wonderful, so kind, never complaining or finding fault with me'. Being tired and worn out – and I felt the strain and worry of the last few days beginning to creep over me – I said as tears pricked my eyes, 'Well, if you ever feel you would like me to start, just try bringing me along this hell fired road often'.

We stopped for tea, and discovered a little, really good trait of the pup. He had whined and squeaked on my knee. I put him in the box saying 'Now you are a nuisance already', but pitied the poor scrap, in the heat and his loneliness, and lifted him out on to the cool grass – where he passed a stream of water! Later we caught him in time several times ... If I'd needed confirmation that my husband was rapidly becoming more childlike I'd have got it, to see the way he mussed and played with the little trotting pup who, to his delight, retrieved a golf ball thrown for him and laid it at his feet. When, tired out so utterly, it crept between his feet and went to sleep, such a wave of gratefulness swept over me. I so want it to be my husband's own dog – it came easily when Garry was a pup – and I felt I mourned intensely for my Siamese. Beyond caring for and training Garry, he really *repelled* me. His ways and doggy smell, the touch of his coat after the soft fur my little cat kept so fragrantly clean, made me shudder. *Not* to make a fuss of little Sandy will be difficult, but until his affection has been firmly directed on my husband, I'll be very careful.

Garry does seem to have aroused conflicting feelings in Nella, for the following day she returned to praising him (although mainly because he had been a support to Will). 'I've realised this week how much I owed Garry, how odd his ways and worshipping love for my husband; and the feeling if I went to the hairdresser's or into shops, he wouldn't be waiting tense and irritable. Instead, he would have been strolling in the sunshine – if any – with Garry on his lead.'

Wednesday, 31 August. I rose in a poor way. My husband had a wild nightmare. I'm often puzzled at his real terror that he has lost me and cannot find or reach me. In some queer way that particular fear has been worse since Arthur came for his holiday [*earlier that month*]. I was putting water into the birds' bath when Mrs Atkinson called over to tell me a neighbour up the street had had to go to the Roose Hospital, where old or those really sick people are taken when nursing at home, for one reason or another, grows impossible. He has been a *very* hard drinker – a traveller for a local wine and spirit firm – and a very overbearing, dominating man since I've known him, about 20 years. We all feel torn for his second wife, a lot younger than he is, and they have a dreamy, gentle boy, thin as a lath, and like his mother, about worn out. That gave me a sadness, and added to my worry. I tidied, missing Mrs Salisbury, and made a cup of tea before we went down town. I needed shopping for myself and Mrs Atkinson before going to the chiropodist's at 11 o'clock ...

At 3.30 my husband began to wonder what we should do. I knew whatever I suggested would be wrong so I left him to make up his mind, and packed cheese sandwiches, flasks of tea and cake and agreed we should go to Lakeside and sit by the landing stages, watching the boats and Lake steamers. Only another fortnight and the steamers will cease to run. Two long special trains stood in the station. The last boats down were packed with hot, rather noisy people, who rushed to the waiting trains as if the guard had blown his whistle and they would be left. Such noise and bustle and hurry, and then the two packed trains drew out. The men on the steamer sluiced and scrubbed the decks, after the steamers had been manoeuvred into their place for the night. The row of parked cars, whose owners had been having tea in the hotel or cafes, thinned out till only four were left. Over the quiet, glass smooth Lake there seemed to be a wand waved. Slowly in the distance up the Lake, big sailed yachts appeared. From the near end, small ones glided, one with a scarlet sail, like a lovely flower as its image, mirrored in the still water. Looked like the other half of a wide petalled flower. Small youths from a YMCA came out in rowing boats, handling them surprisingly well. Fishermen appeared in skiffs and small boats and anchored, or at least stayed their oars, and began to fish. Peace and serenity ruled. The stress and bustle faded as if it had never been. We came home reluctantly, feeling we left little irritations behind. One of those still days that Walpole so loved about Keswick, and which he described so well.

While Nella's most vivid writing was largely over by the mid 1950s, she actually continued with her diary until 24 February 1966, a little over two years before her death (Will survived her by a year). In 1959 she turned 70, and age was catching up on her. There were, though, moments of buoyancy. Earlier that year she had written in a way that both hearkened backwards, partly with satisfaction, and took a degree of pleasure in the present (which she no longer found so readily attainable). That morning she was eager to get a letter from Cliff in Australia, for which forewarning was likely to come from the latest dog in the Last household.

Saturday, 3 January, 1959. Such a queer little dog, as if he knows how important the postman is to me. He softly growls in his throat when the postman is on the other side of the road! This morning I'd given up hope of a letter, when Sandy 'pointed' like an old gun dog, softly growling. I looked out of the front window and sure enough the postman was going up the other side of the road, and it was over five minutes before he was at our door. Cliff sent a snap of his car and the welcome news he had got his Terylene curtains. He has my love of 'luxury', of good things, and gives them a care to last. His joy in his nylon dressing gown, and even more these '*super* curtains, Dearie, perfect from either inside or out, so beautifully, perfectly made' etc ... He made us laugh when he went on 'I know you will be amused, but you are growing into someone between a fairy godmother and a clever craftsman'. As I said sadly to my husband, 'Umph, one who cannot kick herself into cutting and making a simple dress for herself'. I went out feeling like the Queen of Spain, so glad Cliff had got his curtains and Xmas parcels.

It was biting cold. I got celery and extra leeks and we went into the covered market. My husband said 'Do you see that odd looking couple over there? The woman looked hard at you as if going to speak. Do you know her?' I shook my head as I looked at the really grotesque little fashion plate, *far* too plump for the skin tight, too short skirt, lovely girlish little fur coat, only just below the waist, and a really comic 'wig' hat in fine feathers, as she tottered shakily on stiletto heels. But as I drew alongside and she turned I recognised a wartime colleague who helped for a while in Canteen. Quite a good worker. She never let us forget her husband was 'Admiralty'. She seized both my hands and gushed to the tall man at her side 'This is Mrs Last, you've heard me talk so much about and her love of the Canteen cats, Bodger and Tiny Tim, who went on to a minesweeper.' She lost her husband in the war, and married again, and her home for a while has been in Africa. Her husband had a slight accent, which I couldn't place, but he looked a very nice, kindly man – or did I think so when from our short conversation he showed himself a cat lover! I knew his wife had had a colourful life from childhood. Her father was an Army officer, and she was born and lived the first few years of her life in India. Granted, she tended to exaggerations.

I loved to hear her talk in Canteen. Her love of 'colouring' a narrative had extended to her war work in Canteen – well into a year, if my memory serves me right – but anyone could have been forgiven if they thought it was a round of gaiety. I reflected a little wistfully that we did laugh quite a lot at times.

EPILOGUE

Nella Last's diary can be read on many levels, and perhaps each of her readers is attracted to her writing for different reasons. What are some of the features of her diary that give it such vitality?

First, Nella was a sensitive and shrewd observer of her society, and she had a way with words that allowed her to present memorable portraits of life around her. Some of these portraits were of noteworthy events – the launch of a ship, gatherings of men in uniform, a wedding, holidays outside Barrow, a suicide – and her thinking about these events some-times sparked memories and ruminations. Nella had an eye for unusual happenings and unusual people, however 'unusual' might be construed, and she often allowed her reflections on these incidents and people to gallop off in unexpected and interesting directions. Her world was in many ways unremarkable, but she was able to bring zest to this everyday world – the squabbles in which she participated; conversations on the street or with a visitor in her sitting room or with Mrs Salisbury or at a wartime workplace; nagging frustrations and inconveniences; shared laughter; instances of personal tribulation or disappointment or tragedy. Hers was a small world, a world revolving around family, friends of her sons, neighbours and other women who like her worked as volunteers during the war, although we also see that she knew scores (perhaps hun-dreds) of Barrow's residents by name, some of them from schooldays, and was able readily to recall their families' circumstances from decades earlier. Strikingly, too, when Nella did remark on larger public affairs, her remarks were likely to be astute and clear-headed. While she was less prone than most people to comforting illusions about, for example, peace and prosperity, she did endorse very strongly measures for practi-cal reform, such as the Beveridge Plan for the foundation of a welfare state, and she struggled to empathise both with former enemies and with peoples traditionally seen by white Britons as inferior (notably black people). Through her writing we get vivid sightings of a domestic culture being in certain respects transformed, though on the whole fairly quietly, during the 1940s and early 1950s.

As well as observing the present, Nella also reflected on the past, and her memories – she owned to having a good memory – were usually precise and pointed, notably about everyday life in the early twentieth century. On 1 June 1953, the day before the coronation of Elizabeth II, she and Will 'looped round rather a poor quarter on our way to the Library, small terrace houses mostly tenanted by men who work at the Iron and Steel Works', and she compared the 'few draggled streamers of flags' on view, and the ugly 'pieces of coloured plastic pennants', with earlier celebrations she had observed. At 'other Coronations – even when minor royalties came from time to time to open a big bridge over the Walney Channel, open the Technical School, etc. – some of the short drab streets were turned into a fairyland, beautifully decorated, with wooden trellises over the fronts of the houses, and fresh boughs, fern and flowers covering all.' Her contrasts of past and present were sometimes nostalgic, at other times matter-of-fact. 'In my younger days the whole attitude of sex was toward that of something that had to be conquered,' she remarked in her reply to M-O's July 1939 Directive, 'something unnatural and unclean. I was married in ignorance and it was not until I'd had a baby that really the "full facts of life" were understood.' On New Year's Eve 1948 she recalled that 'The last day of the old year used to be a busy one, with people coming in to "get out of debt and start the New Year well". Now the superstition is dying or dead – few came today.' She more than once recalled having been an intense, bookish, inquisitive child, and some of her most vivid memories were of the weeks she had spent as a girl at her grandmother's farm. On 10 January 1956 she recalled her childhood role as a reader to others in this rural district. 'I was a welcome guest as I reeled off poems learned at school or outlined the plots of books I read. Country children used to be taught to "go and read a chapter for old so and so" for so many old people never learned to read. I can remember the delight when I took *David Copperfield* and read every darned word by a peat fire with the wind howling and making some tall old trees groan.'

Nella was also an observer of herself, and her diary was a key outlet for self-exploration – and also for self-revelations that were probably rarely if ever disclosed anywhere else. One of these revelations concerned the tension, or at least contrast, between her inner self and her social persona. Others tended to see her as vivacious, energetic and cheerful; she commonly saw herself as drained, worried and prone to melancholy. On 10 December 1939 she tackled this issue head-on. 'I wonder if there is such a thing as a really calm and serene person. People say to me that I'm "never rattled", "always gay", "don't look on the black side", etc. But I DO. Down inside me there is a black well in which such bogeys and demons of despair and depression live. I heap little stones on to the well-lid to keep them hidden. If I looked down into the well I'd see drowning men, harried starving women, and little children twisting in torturing gas, so I WILL NOT look. I would soon be having a nervous breakdown if I did not concentrate on something else, even if dollies or wax blossoms or collecting old clothes and newspapers or anything that I can think of that will either bring in money for wool or prevent waste. I feel such a hypocrite at times, though, when I realise what a pretence my "gaiety" really is, especially when Mrs Waite says "Little Last is a tonic". I think it was St Paul who said "Only the heart knoweth its own bitterness" and perhaps everyone we see and mix with are different inside.'

Nella Last's diary is testimony to the differences between life lived for and with others and life experienced only by the inner self. Up to the start of the war she had devoted herself to her sons and her husband and had not put herself centre-stage. She had paid a price for Will's and his family's lack of imagination and conventionality and their distaste for her 'oddness' – 'I've always had people poking sharp fingers into my dreams and hopes', she wrote on 2 May 1942. Still, she invariably took pains to be the model housewife, especially when it came to managing the household budget and preparing meals; and she worked hard not to fuel Will's anxieties and to do what she could to accommodate and reassure him, which often meant concealing her own fears. The war, as we have seen, enlarged her world. Its work gave her a chance to be upbeat and buoyant on a larger stage and, in a sense, to drown her worries in busyness. She also found new outlets for her creativity – previously these outlets had been severely constrained – and thus enjoyed the satisfaction of being productive and doing good things for others, whether the POWs who benefited from the money brought in at the Red Cross Shop or the youngsters who (she hoped) would be pleased with her dollies. Her efforts, too, she knew, were part of a larger national purpose. After 1945 she had to cast about for other worthwhile things to do.

As for her diary, she seemed to have mixed feelings. On one occasion, 16 February 1941, she wrote that 'It's impossible for me to grasp that diaries and what people – people like me, for instance – think about things are much use.' Still, she stuck to this daily writing with a degree of commitment – writing hundreds of hours every year, including her many letters – that is astounding. Despite frequently feeling worn out at bedtime, she could still toss off, as a rule, before turning off the lights, at least a thousand words of diary-writing. It is not clear exactly what this relentless composing meant to her. We might, perhaps, infer that she was fulfilling that 'craving' she had had in her youth to write books, an ideal that she always felt she was not clever enough to realise. Through this writing she did connect with others – she seemed to treat her diary as a sort of extended letter, with readers at MO as the recipients. She confessed in her diary to feelings that she could not reveal to the people in her life, and which were at times radically at odds with the self she showed to society. Thanks to Mass Observation's archiving of this private writing, later generations are able to enter into her world and become engaged with the mind of a woman whose life was both ordinary and extraordinary, both commonplace and uncommon, and certainly creative well beyond her own modest ambitions.

GLOSSARY

A-A	anti-aircraft
AFS	Auxiliary Fire Service
Arab	someone wandering, unsettled (meaning Cliff)
ARP	Air Raid Precautions
ATS	Auxiliary Territorial Service
bad hat	a mischief-maker, an incorrigible scamp (often used playfully)
bags	loosely fitting trousers
bank (verb)	to build up a fire with a tightly packed fuel so that it burns slowly
bass bag	flat plaited bag
Bemax	vitamin supplement
Brannigan	a brawler
brindled	a tawny or brownish colour, especially in streaks
C3 man	An Army medical category indicating that a man was only suitable for non-combatant work at home
Cassandra	prophet of gloom
char	cleaning woman
chara	charabanc – a large open bus, often used for sightseeing
clippies	women bus conductors
conchies	conscientious objectors
coolth	coolness
crock up	break down
Darby and Joan club	social club for old people
Disprin	painkiller, sedative
doll-eyed	foolish, tasteless
dollies	stuffed dolls made from scraps of fabric
DR	Directive Response to a questionnaire from Mass-Observation

ENSA   Entertainments' National Service Association
festa   festival, celebration
flapdoodle   nonsense, absurd person
Glastonburys   boots
gormless   slow-witted, lacking sense
haysel   haymaking season, hay
Herries   family in Hugh Walpole's historical fiction, set in the
                     Lakes
hip-blouse   shirt designed to hang out
houris   beautiful virgins of the Muslim paradise
inaffectedly   without artifice
ITMA   *It's That Man Again*, radio comedy programme, with
                     Tommy Handley
jankers   punished with confinement/imprisonment
job lot   miscellaneous group of items bought together
keen   to lament
lumber sale   rummage sale
machined   worked on a sewing machine
maffick   to rejoice extravagantly
Mail   *North-Western Daily Mail*
Marshall Aid   American financial assistance to Europe announced
(Plan)   in 1947, implemented from 1948
matric   qualified for admission to university, college or
                     polytechnic
M-O (or MO)   Mass-Observation
mules   a kind of slipper or light shoe
mulligrubs   ill temper, grumpiness
Newmarket   a gambling card game
ninon   a lightweight silk dress fabric
nowty   moody, sullen
offcomer   outsider, newcomer
parkin   a kind of gingerbread or cake made with oatmeal and
                     treacle
pied   mixed up, muddled

plovers	small, short-billed gregarious birds, typically feeding near water
points	credits used to buy controlled and rationed goods
polypodies	ferns
pontoon	a card game
posset	a drink of hot milk, curdled with alcohol (a delicacy)
pullet	a young hen
purdah	women screened from men by a veil or curtain
put on dog	put on airs, act pretentiously
rackety	noisy
Rawlinson	Nella's maternal family name (said to be a 'proud' people)
RCAF	Royal Canadian Air Force
RNVR	Royal Naval Volunteer Reserve
Sanatogen	restorative tonic wine
skit (verb)	to ridicule, attack
slack	inferior coal
sloes	fruit of the blackthorn
smudge fire	a smoky fire used to protect against insects or frost
snaggle	tangle
soul case	the body, especially under stress
suited	made agreeable
swale	shady place
Sylko	brand of sewing thread
tack	to stitch temporarily
tarbrush	having signs of black ancestry
tiddler	a small fish
topiary	plants/shrubs clipped to make ornamental shapes
Turog bread	whole meal bread ubiquitous in the north of England
WAAF	Women's Auxiliary Air Force
wee man	fairy, spirit
whims and whamseys	fanciful, capricious ideas
whin	gorse bush
WVS	Women's Voluntary Services
Yard	Vickers-Armstrongs shipyard in Barrow

MONEY AND ITS VALUE

During Nella Last's lifetime British currency was calculated in the following manner:

$$12 \text{ pence} = 1 \text{ shilling}$$
$$20 \text{ shillings} = £1$$

One shilling was written as 'is', a penny as 'id'. A farthing, by then little used, was a quarter of a penny. A guinea ('1 gn') was worth 21 shillings. A sum of, say, two pounds and four shillings was usually written at that time as £2-4-0 or £2/4/0; such an amount is presented in this book as £2 4s od.

Efforts to propose modern monetary equivalents are rarely helpful. Since the 1940s were years of widespread rationing, both during and after the war, the price of an item was sometimes less important than its availability (so while wages went up in wartime, finding suitable ways to spend money could be a challenge). Moreover, the household economy was for most people simpler and more spartan than it would be a couple of decades later. Material expectations were generally modest, some produce was home-generated, borrowing and bartering might be an alternative to buying, and recycling was normal. Nella was very price-conscious, and she is constantly reporting the prices of items in shops and elsewhere.

Among the reference points to keep in mind is the weekly wage: most full-time male wage-workers in Barrow in the 1940s were probably earning between £4 and £10 a week: the former for unskilled labourers, the latter for workmen with desired skills. Men were almost always paid considerably more than women. In 1947 Nella was paying her cleaning helper 1s 6d an hour, plus a hot lunch; and in 1948 an older man who was working for her as a gardener charged 'only' 2s an hour. During most of the 1940s Will supported his parents with £2 10s every week from his joinery business (one of the reasons Nella had to be frugal). It is useful to keep in mind that Nella's housekeeping budget in the early 1950s for one week was £4 10s 0d, and from this sum she had to pay for sundry items such as medications, periodicals and bus fares as well as make her purchases of meat, fish and fresh and processed food, not to mention the shilling a week that she bet on the football pools. Her husband seems to have been responsible for maintaining the car. The Lasts' household had little leeway for luxuries, especially after Will retired in 1950. They (for example) rarely ate out in the early 1950s, except on food they brought from home.

EDITING NELLA LAST'S DIARY

In her vast diary the four topics that Nella Last writes about most often are the weather, ill health, preparing meals and shopping. Together they probably comprise at least half of her output. These matters appear infrequently in this book for they rarely show her at her best as a writer. Writing about such mundane matters did, however, ensure that she was never out of practice, and that words always flowed readily from the tip of her pencil or pen. When she did have something interesting to say – stimulated, perhaps, by a Sunday outing in the car or an encounter in a shop or on Abbey Road, or an acquaintance arriving at 9 Ilkley Road, or some incident that brought back memories of childhood – she was well poised to put her thoughts into words. These are the occasions when she was most likely to tell a good story, or recount a lively conversation, or compose a vivid description of the countryside, or disclose some of her deeper feelings about the meaning of life. And these are the passages that we have chosen to highlight. Since they appear irregularly and often unexpectedly during the sixteen years covered in this book, some periods of her writing life are represented much more fully than others. For the editors of her writing it is as if they are viewing a collection of tens of thousands of snapshots, taken daily over many years, and choosing only the best to publish regardless of the date.

While the main task for editors of Nella Last's manuscript diary is to select what to publish and to shape these selections into chapters, there are several other ways in which we have exercised judgement and revised what she wrote. The following are the most important of these editorial interventions. (1) Since Nella did not use paragraphs, wherever they now exist they are our creations. (2) Her punctuation was casual, often whimsical. (Mispunctuation is a common feature of M-O diaries, indeed, of most diaries whose authors lacked the time or incentive to revisit what they had written.) We have routinely re-punctuated her writing to make it as clear and smooth-flowing as possible. (3) Obvious errors – she almost certainly wrote in haste, and usually at night – have been silently corrected. These include misspellings and phrases that lack a necessary word, such as a preposition, article or conjunction. (4) Very occasionally an additional word is needed to convey the meaning of a sentence. In these rare cases we have silently supplied a suitable candidate. (5) We have standardised the usage of particular words in order to ensure, for example, that a word is always spelt the same way, or that it is consistently capitalised or not capitalised, and that the prices of goods and services and other numerals are presented in a consistent form. (6) Nella was much given to underlining words for emphasis and to putting a great many words and phrases in inverted commas. We have eliminated these practices except in cases where they are helpful or even essential to grasping her full meaning, such as when she is reporting words actually spoken by others or when she had chosen language that was regarded as colloquial or not yet in common usage. (7) Three dots are used to indicate omissions in a day's entry *other than* those made before a selection starts and after it concludes. Omissions at the start and the end of what she wrote on a given day are more the norm than the exception, for her first and last sentences are generally less interesting than what comes in between. Many entire days of her writing – and she wrote almost every day – have been omitted altogether.

This may seem like a rather long list of editorial interventions. The need to make them stems in part from the fact that Nella had no reason to think that she should edit her own work, to polish or perhaps even to re-read what she had written. So her writing, while frequently rich and robust, tends to be raw. The photograph overleaf shows a page from her handwritten diary for Tuesday 26 March 1940 and gives a sense of the decisions that any editors would routinely have to make in converting her handwritten diary into pages suitable for a book.

...e had a while to wait. Planes droned or roared over head in the thick clouds which had gathered & air wardens pacing about made one have a sick feeling at the effect of a German bomber would have on the dense packed crowd. There were thousands by 1-30 & the last of the ten tugs had been manovered into place. Across Walney channel the open end of aircraft-carrier poked rather cautiously from stocks & we noticed men beginning to run about as if in answer to orders. A faint cheer which strengthened into a roar & she began to slide down to the boots of the tugs. Arthur & I were standing on car seats, our heads through sunshine roof so had a grandstand view. She gathered speed & smoothly slipped into waiting tide without a splash - like a smooth drawer being pushed out of table or chest. I'll never forget the cheer & 'God bless...

MASS OBSERVATION*

Mass Observation, which was set up in 1937, was created to meet a perceived need – to overcome Britons' ignorance about themselves in their everyday lives. MO aimed to lay the foundations for a social anthropology of contemporary Britain. Given that so many basic facts of social life were then unknown – opinion polling was in its infancy, social surveys and field studies had just begun (with a few exceptions, such as those of London by Charles Booth in the late nineteenth century) – how, it was asked, could the nation's citizens adequately understand themselves? This lack of knowledge was thought to be especially pronounced with regard to the beliefs and behaviour of the majority of Britons: that is, those without social prominence, and who had little political or intellectual influence.

It was vital, according to MO's founders, to focus on norms, customs, routines and commonalities. The goal was to help bring about a 'science of ourselves', rooted in closely observed facts, methodically and (sometimes) laboriously collected. And in order to pursue this science of society, MO recruited hundreds of volunteer 'Observers', who were asked to describe, to pose questions to others, to record sights and sounds, and sometimes to count. Their efforts at observing were likened to those of an anthropologist working in the field. One of the early publications that drew upon these findings was a Penguin Special from early 1939 written by MO's two leading lights, Charles Madge and Tom Harrisson, *Britain, by Mass-Observation*, which attracted lots of attention at the time.

Volunteers were crucial to MO. Without them it would not have been possible to acquire the facts on which a proper social science

---

* Mass-Observation dropped the hyphen from its name in 2006, thus becoming Mass Observation. We have chosen in this appendix consistently to adopt the current usage, except when the hyphen is used in titles.

would have to be based. And it came to be accepted by MO's leaders that these Observers would not only be data-collectors; they could also function as 'subjective cameras' that captured their own experiences, feelings and attitudes, and circumstances of living. This acceptance of the legitimacy of subjectivity in MO's enquiries was a major reason why diary-keeping came to be promoted as a promising vehicle of both social and self-observation. A diary was one way of recording; and it was a way that inevitably tapped into the individuality and inner life of one personality. MO's striving for a better social science, then, facilitated the production of a particularly personal form of writing; and from late August 1939, with another great war imminent, some people responded to MO's invitation to keep a diary and post their writing regularly (usually weekly, fortnightly or monthly) to MO's headquarters. Nella Last was one of the dozens – eventually hundreds – who responded to this initiative. She was, though, one of the few who wrote regularly during the war and continued to write regularly after 1945 – and her diary entries were unusually detailed.

These diaries – some 480 of them – have been held since the 1970s in the Mass Observation Archive at the University of Sussex. Numerous books have drawn upon these riches. Sandra Koa Wing (ed.), *Our Longest Days: A People's History of the Second World War, by the Writers of Mass Observation* (London: Profile Books, 2008), is an excellent anthology of extracts from MO's wartime diaries. Dorothy Sheridan's edited volume *Wartime Women: An Anthology of Women's Wartime Writing for Mass Observation* (London: Heinemann, 1990; later paperback editions) includes extracts from numerous diaries. Simon Garfield has edited three collections drawn from the MO Archive, all published by Ebury Press: *Our Hidden Lives: The Remarkable Diaries of Post-War Britain* (2004); *We Are at War: The Diaries of Five Ordinary People in Extraordinary Times* (2005); and *Private Battles: How the War Almost Defeated Us – Our Intimate Diaries* (2007).

Nella Last's wartime MO diary was the first to appear on its own as a book, in 1981, and others followed, including Dorothy Sheridan's edited *Among You Taking Notes ...: The Wartime Diary of Naomi Mitchison,*

1939–1945 (London: Victor Gollancz, 1985). Several other MO diarists have recently been published in volumes of their own. These include: two East Anglian diaries edited by Robert Malcolmson and Peter Searby, *Wartime Norfolk: The Diary of Rachel Dhonau, 1941–1942* (Norfolk Record Society, 2004), and *Wartime in West Suffolk: The Diary of Winifred Challis, 1942–1943* (Suffolk Records Society, 2012); *Love and War in London: A Woman's Diary, 1939–1942*, by Olivia Cockett, edited by Robert Malcolmson (Waterloo, Ontario: Wilfred Laurier University Press, 2005; 2nd edn, Stroud: The History Press, 2008); and four volumes edited by Patricia and Robert Malcolmson – *A Woman in Wartime London: The Diary of Kathleen Tipper, 1941–1945* (London Record Society, 2006); *A Soldier in Bedfordshire, 1941–1942: The Diary of Private Denis Argent, Royal Engineers* (Bedfordshire Historical Record Society, 2009); *Dorset in Wartime: The Diary of Phyllis Walther, 1941–1942* (Dorset Record Society, 2009); and *Warriors at Home, 1940–1942: Three Surrey Diarists* (Surrey Record Society, 2012; one of these three diarists, Leonard Adamson, wrote for MO). James Hinton, who is preparing a history of Mass Observation, has recently published a stimulating account of some of MO's most interesting diarists: *Nine Wartime Lives: Mass-Observation and the Making of the Modern Self* (Oxford: Oxford University Press, 2010).

The Mass Observation collection is open to the public and is visited by people from around the world. In 2005 it was given Designated Status as one of the UK's Outstanding Collections by the Museums, Libraries and Archives Council. Much helpful information, including details of the Friends scheme that helps to finance the Archive, which is a charitable trust, is available on its website: www.massobs.org.uk.

ACKNOWLEDGEMENTS

Working in the Mass Observation Archive, and with MO material, is always a pleasure, and we continue to be grateful to those at the University of Sussex who have supported our research. We wish in particular to thank Fiona Courage, Adam Harwood, Rose Lock, Jessica Scantlebury, and Karen Watson in Special Collections; and Owen Emmerson and Catrina Hey for doing a great deal of work on our behalf. Several people connected with Nella Last or persons mentioned in her diary have generously shared information with us, notably Kathleen (Holme) Emery and Margaret (Atkinson) Procter, both of whom also lent us family photographs, and Jerry Last and the late Peter Last, Nella's youngest and eldest grandsons. We have also appreciated the advice given us by the BBC Written Archives and the Cumbria Record Office and Local Studies Library in Barrow-in-Furness. Matthew Taylor, our copy editor, saved us from numerous errors and confusions, and our discussions with Gordon Wise at Curtis Brown have always been helpful and clarifying.

At Profile Books, we very much appreciate the keen interest of Daniel Crewe in Nella Last, her writing, and our work as editors. For this volume, we are especially indebted to Lisa Owens, who has been intimately involved in its production. She persuaded us to revise some of our editorial approaches, and this rethinking prompted us to produce a better and more wide-ranging book. She also made many detailed comments on the text, which gave us the opportunity to eliminate repetitions, tighten some passages, reconsider occasional statements, and anticipate possible questions and concerns of readers. We are glad to have been able to benefit from her sensitive editorial advice.

Nelson, British Columbia
June 2012

LIST OF ILLUSTRATIONS

1. Nella and Arthur, 1940 (Mass Observation)
2. Cliff Last in wartime (Photograph courtesy of Margaret Procter)
3. Barrow Bombed, 1941 (Photograph courtesy of *North West Evening Mail*)
4. Home from the Yard, 1950s (Photograph courtesy of *North West Evening Mail*)
5. Relaxing on the Coast Road, 1950s (Photograph courtesy of *North West Evening Mail*)
6. Jessie Holme with her daughter, Kathleen, late summer 1948
7. George Holme and Kathleen, 1949 (Photographs courtesy of Kathleen Emery)
8. The Poker Club at the Grammar School, 1950 (Photograph courtesy of Norman Raby)
9. Ilkey Road from the back, late 1940s. (Photograph courtesy of Kathleen Emery)
10. Cliff, in Australia in the 1950s (Photograph courtesy of Margaret Procter)
11. Nella, Will, and their dog, Garry, around 1953 (Photograph courtesy of Peter Last)

INDEX

Only substantial information or commentary concerning people, places, and subjects has normally been indexed, with an emphasis on subjects. Since references to shops, shopping, food or other provisions, rationing and radio programmes occur on dozens of pages, only the more detailed and informative of these passages have been indexed.